中国社会科学院语言研究所 主办
中国语言学会语音学分会 会刊
PAC Phonetic Association of China

第16辑

Chinese Journal of Phonetics

中国语音学报

中国社会科学出版社

图书在版编目（CIP）数据

中国语音学报．第16辑／中国社会科学院语言研究所主办．—北京：中国社会科学出版社，2021.12
ISBN 978－7－5203－9485－7

Ⅰ.①中…　Ⅱ.①中…　Ⅲ.①汉语—语音学—文集　Ⅳ.①H11－53

中国版本图书馆CIP数据核字(2021)第273831号

出版人　赵剑英
责任编辑　张　林
责任校对　王佳玉
责任印制　戴　宽

出　　版　中国社会科学出版社
社　　址　北京鼓楼西大街甲158号
邮　　编　100720
网　　址　http://www.csspw.cn
发行部　010－84083685
门市部　010－84029450
经　　销　新华书店及其他书店

印刷装订　北京君升印刷有限公司
版　　次　2021年12月第1版
印　　次　2021年12月第1次印刷

开　　本　787×1092　1/16
印　　张　10.5
插　　页　2
字　　数　281千字
定　　价　66.00元

《中国语音学报》编辑委员会

中国语言学会语音学分会委员会

目　录

AN ULTRASOUND AND EPG INVESTIGATION OF CORONAL FRICATIVES IN YANBIAN KOREAN

LI Yinghao, ZHANG Jinghua

Abstract This paper investigates the tongue gesture difference of the two-way coronal fricative contrast in Yanbian Korean through ultrasound imaging and electropalatography (EPG). Ultrasound imaging was applied to compare the mid-sagittal tongue contours of the fortis and non-fortis coronal fricatives. Results show that the two-way fricative contrast is distinguished by the positioning of tongue blade, anterior tongue body, and tongue root. The fortis fricative is characterized with higher tongue blade and anterior tongue body, and more fronted tongue root than the non-fortis fricative. However, this pattern is slightly blurred in the palatalized fricative contrast due to the inter-speaker variability. Part of the variability may be attributed to the supra-glottal cavity enlargement when the non-fortis fricative is realized as voiced. The acoustic examination shows that the frication duration and the spectral center of gravity are two defining acoustic properties that contrast the two fricatives. Whether the non-fortis fricative is realized as voiced fricative tends to be affected by vocalic context and gender. The EPG results show that the defining articulatory property for the contrast is the medial constriction degree at the alveolar region. The inter-speaker variability is solely found in the posterior region, which corresponds to the variability in the positioning of the anterior tongue body in the ultrasound investigation. The emergence of the inter-speaker variability in the production of the fortis/non-fortis fricative contrast calls for a more comprehensive model for the production of the Korean coronal fricatives which should entail aerodynamic and sociolinguistic factors.

Keywords Two-way fricative contrast, Yanbian Korean, Ultrasound, Electropalatography (EPG)

1. INTRODUCTION

The Korean language has two denti-alveolar coronal fricatives, which are mainly differentiated by articulation force in production. The one fricative produced with a prominent articulatory force is called the fortis fricative, usually transcribed as /s*/. ① The other fricative has relaxed articulatory configuration in the vocal tract, and is variously called the "non-fortis", "lenis", "aspirated", or "plain" fricative. In this paper we use the non-fortis fricative to term this fricative and transcribe it as /s/. Though the two coronal fricatives are fundamentally characterized by laryngeal distinctions [5, 10, 14, 16, 21], a more synergistic view has been proposed in a recent study in which the supra-laryngeal articulators are shown to be coordinated with the laryngeal articulation for encoding the articulatory difference between the two fricatives [17]. Given this, the current paper aims to further explore the fine-grained tongue gesture difference in both non-palatalized and palatalized realizations of the two fricatives.

Previous studies have shown that the supra-laryngeal articulations of the fortis and non-fortis coronal fricatives are different in both spatial and temporal domains [2, 3, 17, 18]. Compared with the non-fortis fricative,

① In the Korean phonetics literature, there has been no consensus for transcribing Korean fortis denti-alveolar fricative. It has been formerly transcribed as /s*/, /s'/ (for contrasting the voiceless non-fortis fricative /s/), or even /s/ (for contrasting the voiced non-fortis counterpart /z/). We followed [5] and transcribed the fortis fricative as /s*/.

the fortis fricative has narrower and longer apico-laminal alveolar constriction and more fronted tongue root either in the word-initial or word-medium position [17] . The electropalatographic (EPG) investigation provides much finer articulatory details of the shaping of the apico-laminal constriction for the coronal fricative contrast in Korean. For example, Baik [2, 3] found that the fortis fricative has a narrower coronal opening than the non-fortis fricative by measuring the groove width of constriction at the alveolar region, and the narrowed opening has more anterior positioning and is sustained longer for the fortis fricative. Moreover, less vocalic coarticulatory effect is found for the groove width of the fortis fricative compared to the non-fortis fricative. But a later palatographic study did not replicate the above EPG findings, particularly the groove width difference for the distinction [1] . The above studies indicate the elevation of the anterior portion of the tongue (tongue tip and blade) and the advancement of the tongue root are critical to the two-way fricative distinction. However, these studies based their findings either on the limited vocalic context (for example in [17] only low vowel context was considered) or non-word speech material (for example in [3] the sequences /iSi, aSa, uSu/ were used where /S/ was /s*/ or /s/). Given that the coronal fricatives are palatalized as palate-alveolar [ʃ*, ʃ] in high front vowel context, it is expected that the palatalized allophone of the fortis fricative would have more anterior tongue elevation and tongue body fronting than the palatalized lenis counterpart. Additionally, the above studies made use of the articulatory data from a rather small number of subjects (usually one or two speakers), which greatly undermines the generalizability of their results.

The majority of the articulatory and acoustic studies on the Korean fortis/non-fortis fricative contrast have focused on Seoul Korean, whereas that for Yanbian Korean is rather under-studied. From a general view, Yanbian Korean is the Korean vernacular spoken in Yanbian Korean Autonomous Prefecture. Based on the Korean dialect survey, Quan [27] proposed that Yanbian Korean is mainly comprised of two dialects: the Yukjin dialect (六镇方言), which is a dialect spoken by a small number of speakers in villages or cities along Tumen River, and the Hamkyungbukdo dialect (咸镜北道方言), which is the major Korean dialect widely spoken in the other areas in Yanbian Prefecture. In the recently-published minority language atlas in China [13], the Yukjin dialect is termed as the Northeastern Korean dialect, which is set apart from other major Korean dialects due to its unique phonetic and phonological features (see [32] for a review). The Korean dialect spoken outside the Yukjin dialect area in Yanbian Prefecture is termed as Mid-Northern dialect, which has been originated from Hamkyungdo (咸镜道) and Ryanggangdo (两江道) in the Korean Peninsula (excluding Yukjin dialect area), and is widely spoken in Yanji, Longjing, Dunhua, Helong, Wangqing and Antu. In this paper we focus on the Hamkyungbukdo dialect of Yanbian Korean based on our Korean language survey for old Korean speakers.

Yanbian Korean has the same denti-alveolar coronal fricative contrast as in most Korean dialects spoken in the Korean Peninsula. However, it has been observed that the palatalized allophones of the coronal fricatives have more anterior production in Yanbian Korean, which is argued to reserve the linguistic forms prior to Middle Korean [22] . Our previous phonetic investigation for the two-way fricative contrast in Yanbian Korean largely replicates the conclusions in Seoul Korean. The fortis fricative has more linguopalatal contact in the anterior area than the non-fortis fricative in disyllabic non-words, and the coronal constriction for the fortis fricative is less subject to the coarticulatory effect from the neighboring vowels [25] . Furthermore, both fricatives are proved to resist the boundary-induced coarticulatory effects, showing greater articulatory stability [24] . A recent acoustic investigation of Yanbian Korean showed that the non-fortis fricative has higher spectral center of gravity of frication noise than the fortis fricative, which suggests the possibility that the non-fortis fricative might have more anterior articulation and greater degree of constriction [26] . The current paper will test this possibility.

The likely voicing of the non-fortis fricative in intervocalic context complicates the supra-laryngeal gesture distinction. Though many studies have indicated that the non-fortis fricative in intervocalic context is rarely realized as voiced fricative, one study did find that a majority of the non-fortis fricative tokens were realized as voiced fricative, either fully or partially [5] . The glottal vibration in the production of stop or fricative consonants may give rise to the enlarged supra-glottal cavity to balance the aerodynamic requirements for simultaneous voicing at larynx and pressure build-up in the supra-laryngeal vocal tract [9, 19, 30] . For example, Fuchs et al. [9] found that the voiced post-alveolar fricative in German is produced with more fronted articulation compared with its voiceless counterpart. If the Korean non-fortis fricative is realized as voiced, then tongue fronting gesture will possibly attenuate the tongue gesture difference between the fortis and non-fortis fricatives. Such possibility will also be examined in the current paper.

Against the above, we carried out an ultrasound and EPG investigation of the two-way coronal fricatives in Yanbian Korean. The study is comprised of two instrumental investigations. The first concerns the comparison of the tongue contours of the coronal fricatives in connected speech through ultrasound imaging. Acoustic examination includes the temporal and spectral properties of the two-way fricative contrast, as well as the voicing status for the non-fortis fricative. The second is an EPG investigation on the linguopalatal contact patterns of the fricatives in monosyllable, word-initial, and word-medium conditions, which intends to supplement the findings of the mid-sagittal tongue contours for the fricative contrast.

2. ULTRASOUND INVESTIGATION

2.1 Materials and participants

The speech materials for the ultrasound investigation were part of a larger set of short sentences and phrases we designed for studying Korean consonant articulation. Three phrases and one sentence were used to acquire ultrasound images for the two fricatives. The target syllable CV (C stands for one of the denti-alveolar coronal fricatives and V for monophthongs /i/ or /a/) was placed between sonorant segments and in the medium position of a prosodic word (see Table 1). The vowel before the target syllable was /a/, /o/ or /e/. The tone for the target syllable was either high or low.

Ten old speakers of Yanbian Korean (6 females and 4 males) participated in the experiment. The age of the female speakers ranged from 65 to 77 with the mean age of 70.8. The age of the male speakers ranged between 67 and 80 with the mean age of 75. In what follows, UM and UF were used to refer to male and female participants, respectively. All speakers grew up in the rural areas in Yanji, Longjing or Wangqing. They were judged to speak the vernacular accent of Yanbian Korean through casual conversation with the second author in the screening interview and the familiarity check for the dialect word before recording. They reported using Korean as the dominant language in daily communication. All speakers but one were proficient in

Mandarin Chinese. All female speakers but one had working experiences in the Republic of Korea for more than five years, yet they reported only using Yanbian Korean even when working abroad. No articulation difficulty or voice pathology was reported by the speakers. All speakers were paid for their participation.

Table 1 Speech materials for the ultrasound investigation. The target syllable is underlined.

Target	Materials with the IPA transcription and English translation (Tone for the test syllable is in parentheses.)
사 [sa]	철저히 조<u>사</u>하다 [tsʰʌl. dzʌ. ɦi. tso. <u>sa</u>. ɦa. da] (High tone) A thorough investigation
싸 [s*a]	아이들의 떼<u>싸</u>움? [a. i. dɯ. ɾi. t*e. <u>s*a</u>. um] (Low tone) Juvenile's rumble
Target	Materials with the IPA transcription and English translation (Tone for the test syllable is in parentheses.)
시 [ʃi]	아름다운 사<u>시</u>절 [a. ɾɯm. da. un. sa. <u>ʃi</u>. dzʌl] (Low tone) Beautiful four seasons
씨 [ʃ*i]	이쁜 아가<u>씨</u>가 있다. [i. p*ɯn. a. ga. <u>ʃ*i</u>. ga. it. t*a] (High tone) There is a beautiful lady.

2.2 Recording and data processing

The recording was carried out either in a sound-attenuated lab or a quiet room. The MicroB ultrasound system was used for obtaining the ultrasonic images through the Articulate Assistant Advanced (AAA) software. The Ultrafit helmet was worn by the speakers, and the probe was stabilized to the helmet after adjusting the probe angle relative to the tongue contour. The depth of scanning was between 70 mm and 90 mm for clear imaging. The field view was set at 92°. The frame rate mostly fell around 81 frames per second. The speakers were given time to familiarize the materials, including the test materials for this paper, and then they were instructed to read the material list at a comfortable rate in recording. Each sentence or phrase was read five times in a row with an approximately one-second interval between consecutive tokens. For tokens with mispronunciation or unclear pronunciation, the speakers were asked to produce them for another 1–3 times.

The ultrasound videos and acoustic signals were separately exported from the AAA software and fed into a computer platform for obtaining key ultrasonic images. The speech signals were reviewed by the second author, and tokens with mispronunciation or unclear pronunciation were excluded. In total, 197 tokens were kept for analysis. The boundaries of frication interval were annotated in Praat [4]. For the fortis fricative, the boundaries of the frication interval were determined by the appearance of high-frequency noise. For the non-fortis fricative, the boundary between frication and aspiration intervals was first automatically determined following [31] and then manually adjusted. For tokens with unclear frication-aspiration boundary (particularly in the palatalized tokens), the vowel onset serves as the right boundary of the fricative interval. When the non-fortis fricative was realized with voicing, the boundaries were solely determined by the appearance of high-frequency noise.

The key ultrasound images were chosen at the midpoint of frication interval. The acquired key frames were submitted to the EdgeTrak [23] for manual tongue contours extraction. SS-ANOVA was conducted in R [28] for the coordinates of the tongue contours. The smoothing spline estimates and 95% Bayesian confidential intervals were obtained for the comparison of the mean tongue contours. The significant difference for the tongue curves of /s/ and /s*/, either in the

/a/ or /i/ context, was determined if the confidential intervals were not overlapped [6]. The individual palate shape was obtained by the upmost boundaries of tongue contours of Korean consonants /k*, ts*, ts, ts^h, t*, t, t^h, n, ɾ/ in the /a, i/ contexts produced by the speaker. We roughly divided the tongue contour into three parts relative to the highest point of palate (around the constriction location for /k*/ in the /i/ context) and alveolar ridge (the inflection point in the palate contour): tongue blade (prior to the inflection point), anterior tongue body (between the inflection point and the highest point), and posterior tongue body (posterior to the highest point). The tongue tip portion cannot be reliably obtained.

The acoustic measures include frication interval and three spectral moments, namely center of gravity (CoG), skewness, and kurtosis [8]. To measure the spectral moments, frequency components below 1000 Hz were excluded to diminish the voicing effect. The more fronted articulation and narrower constriction in the production of coronal fricative were expected to show higher CoG and kurtosis, and lower skewness [15]. Because the palatalized coronal fricatives have more posterior constriction in Korean, they were expected to have lower CoG [12, 20] and kurtosis, as well as higher skewness than the non-palatalized counterparts. The acoustic examinations were carried out in the /a/ and /i/ contexts, respectively.

2.3 Results

Before reporting the ultrasound data, we deem it necessary to have an overview of the voice status for the coronal fricatives, which will facilitate the interpretation of the tongue contours, in particular for the non-fortis fricative. Results show that all fortis fricative tokens were realized as voiceless fricatives, but the voicing of the non-fortis tokens depends on vowel context and gender. Nearly half of the tokens (40.9%) in the /i/ context were realized as voiced, and 28.6% of the tokens in the /a/ context as voiced. Male speakers predominantly realized the non-fortis fricative as voiced, particularly in the /i/ context. Two male speakers (UM1 and UM3) voiced all non-fortis tokens. For females, only five out of 115 tokens were realized as voiced.

Table 2 shows the smoothing spline estimates of the tongue contours of the two fricatives with 95% Bayesian confidential intervals. It can be observed that the fortis fricative generally has elevated anterior tongue body and more fronted tongue root than the non-fortis fricative. Secondly, the tongue contour difference between the two fricatives is more prominent in the /a/ than in the /i/ context. Thirdly, large inter-speaker variability can be observed in both vocalic contexts, particularly in the /i/ context.

In the /a/ context, five speakers (UF1, UF2, UF5, UM1, and UM2) whose tongue blade can be clearly defined have significantly higher tongue blade for /s*/ as compared with /s/. This indicates that the fortis fricative has more constricted narrowing at alveolar ridge. Eight speakers (excluding UF3 and UM3) show significantly higher anterior tongue body, and seven speakers (excluding UF3, UM2, and UM3) have significantly fronted tongue root for /s*/ as compared with /s/. These altogether indicate that tongue body elevation and tongue root advancement are two defining articulatory properties that distinguish the fortis/non-fortis fricatives in the /a/ context. The fortis fricative is characterized with more apico-laminal constriction, higher anterior tongue body and more fronted tongue root than the non-fortis fricative.

The tongue contours for the fricative contrast produced by one female (UF3) and one male speaker (UM3) deviate from those of other speakers. Speaker UF3 shows a reverse pattern in that the non-fortis fricative is produced with significantly higher anterior tongue body and more advanced tongue root than the fortis fricative. As this speaker did not voice the non-fortis fricative, the tongue root fronting is not necessarily motivated to enlarge the back cavity. Speaker UM3 has rather similar anterior tongue body gestures for the two fricatives; however, the fortis fricative has significantly higher posterior tongue body. The tongue root was not clearly captured by the ultrasound imaging, and the posterior portion of tongue contours for the two fricatives are overlapped. As speaker UM3 voiced all non-fortis fricative tokens, the small difference in the contours of the posterior tongue body is possibly indicative of the supra-glottal cavity enlargement. Speaker UM1 also voiced all non-fortis fricative tokens, but the supra-glottal cavity enlargement was not observed. Figure 1 shows the mean FFT spectra of the mid-portion frication noise for the non-fortis fricative produced by the two male speakers. It can be seen that both UM1 and UM3 have strong first harmonic (H1 in Figure 1), which is indicative of vocal fold vibration, but the magnitude for higher range of frequency (roughly between 3 – 8 kHz, see dotted area in Figure 1) is more peaked and compacted for UM1. It can be inferred that the emergence of supra-glottal cavity enlargement when producing the non-fortis fricative is related with the aerodynamic environment in the anterior vocal tract: the reduced power of high-frequency noise is more liable to incur supra-glottal cavity enlargement.

A series of independent t-tests were run to compare frication interval and three spectral moments of the fricatives produced by each speaker. In the following, we will only report the largest significance level for the significant results of each acoustic measure. Results show that speakers unanimously have longer frication duration for the fortis than the non-fortis fricative ($p < 0.001$). However, the three spectral moments show considerable inter-speaker variability. Only two females (UF1 and UF2) show significantly higher CoG and kurtosis, and lower skewness for the fortis ($p < 0.01$). The remaining females show a uniform pattern in that only kurtosis is significantly higher for the fortis ($p < 0.05$). Three males (except UM3) have significantly higher CoG for the fortis than the non-fortis fricative ($p < 0.05$), and only speaker UM2 has significantly lower skewness for the fortis ($p < 0.05$). UM3 shows no significant difference in the spectral moments between the fricatives, which matches the nearly indistinguishable tongue contours of the two fricatives.

The tongue contour difference for the palatalized allophones [ʃ] and [ʃ*] is characterized with more inter-speaker variability than their non-palatalized counterpart. Only three speakers (UF1, UF3, and UF6) show concomitant elevation of anterior tongue body and advancement of tongue root for the fortis as compared with the non-fortis fricative. Two speakers (UF5 and UM4) have significantly lower anterior tongue body and more posterior tongue root for the non-fortis fricative. Three speakers (UF2, UM2, and UM3) show significantly more fronted tongue root for the non-fortis fricative but the positioning of the anterior tongue body for the two fricatives differ across these speakers: UF2 shows no significant difference for the contours of the anterior tongue body; UM2 and UM3 show reverse patterns, with UM2 having significantly higher anterior tongue body for the non-fortis and UM3 for fortis. Speaker UF4 has significantly higher anterior tongue body for the fortis compared with the non-fortis fricative, but the tongue root gestures are virtually overlapped. For speaker UM1, the tongue body advancement tends to be the only articulatory correlate for the fortis fricative to contrast with the non-fortis fricative, with virtually no difference for the positioning of the anterior tongue body.

Table 2 Smoothing spline estimates of the tongue contours for /s/ and /s*/ in two vocalic contexts and 95% Bayesian confidential intervals for 10 speakers. UF means female speaker and UM male speaker. The curve above the tongue contours stands for individual palate shape. The arrowed line indicates the rough position of the inflection point at alveolar ridge. The tongue tip is on the right.

	[sa] *vs.* [s* a]	[ʃi] *vs.* [ʃ* i]		[sa] *vs.* [s* a]	[ʃi] *vs.* [ʃ* i]
UF1	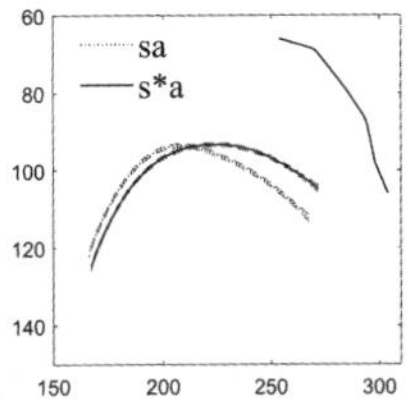	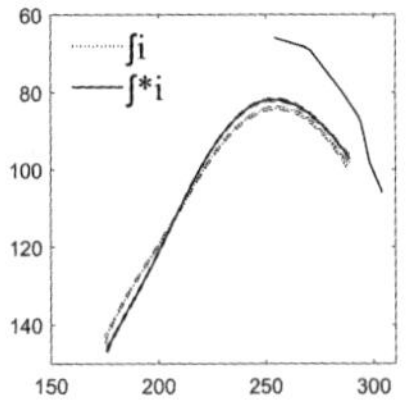	UF6	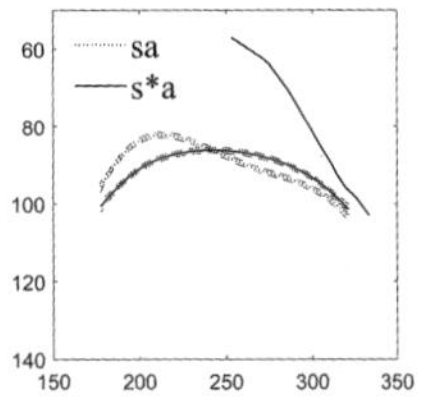	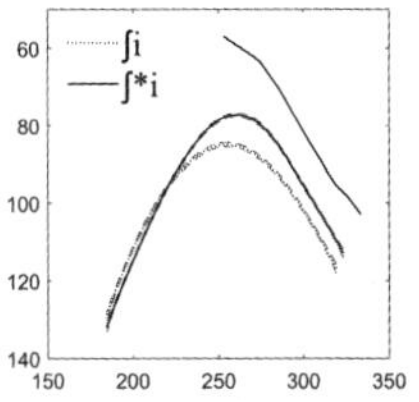
UF2	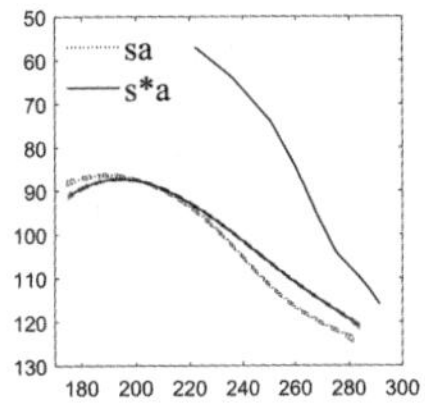	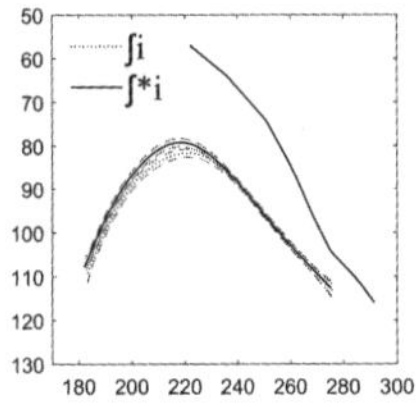	UM1	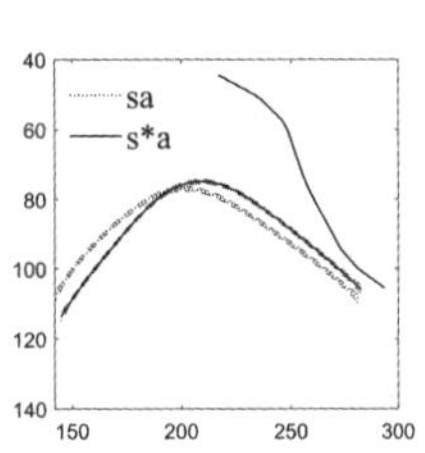	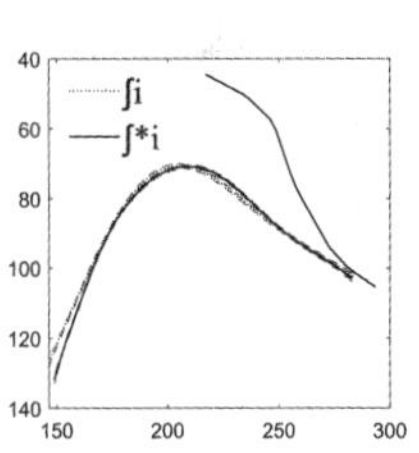
UF3	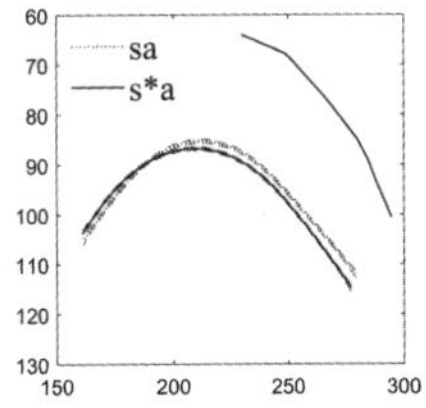	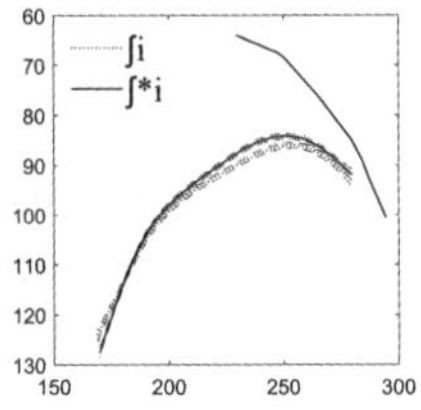	UM2	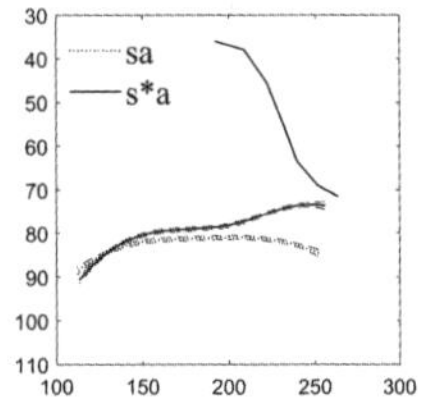	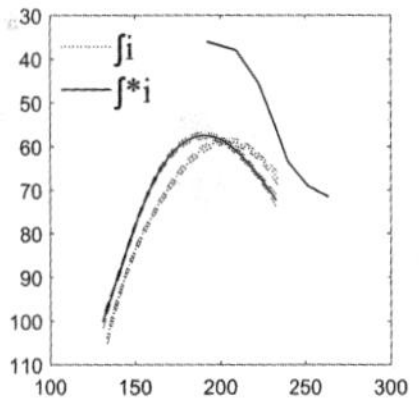
UF4	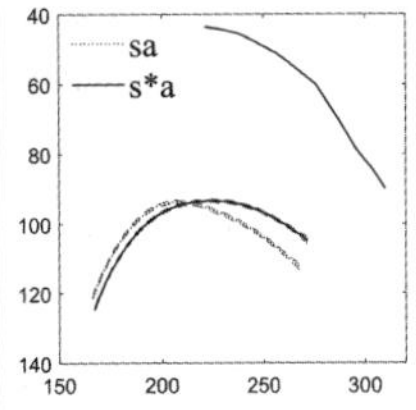	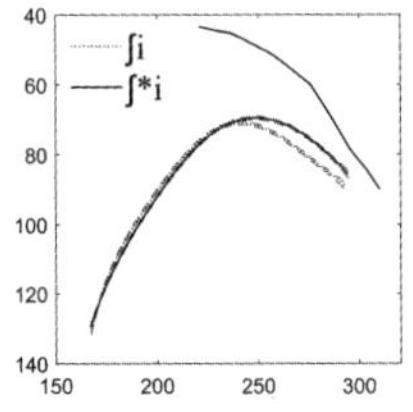	UM3	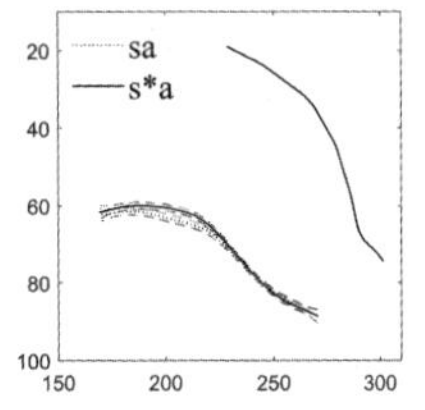	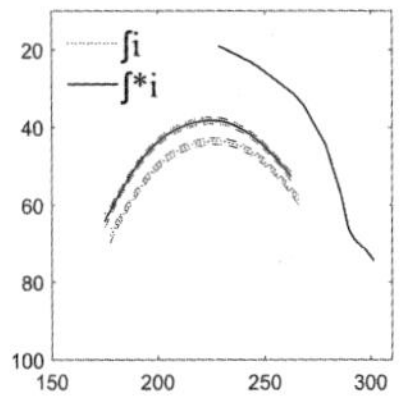
UF5	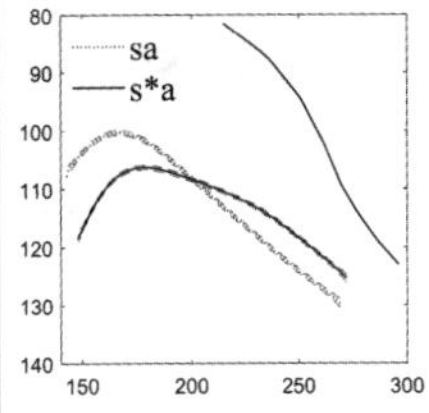	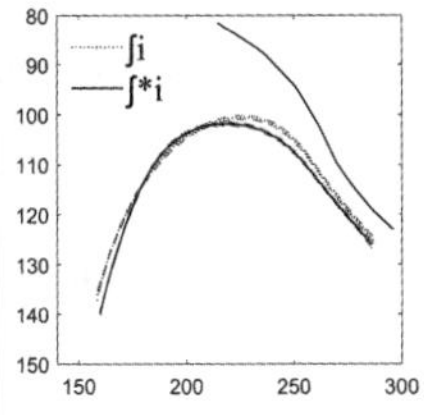	UM4	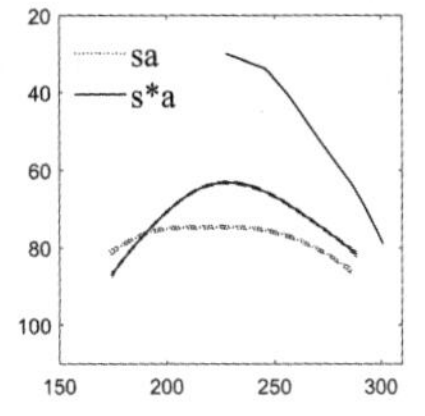	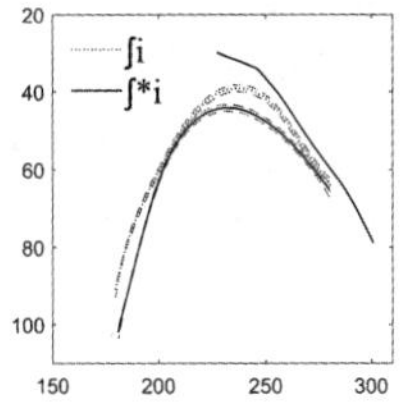

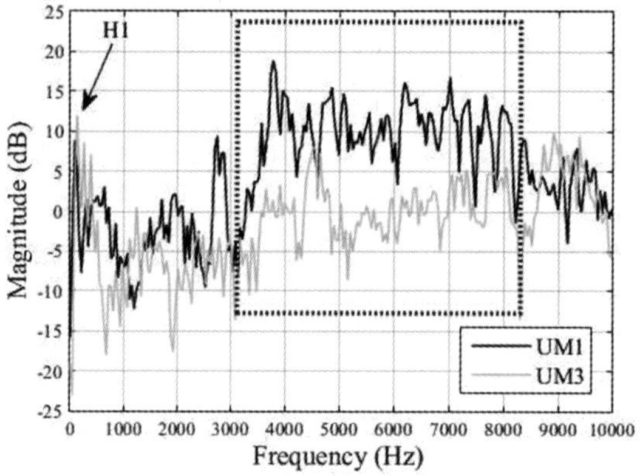

Figure 1 The mean FFT spectra of the mid-portion frication noise of two male speakers. H1 stands for the first harmonic. The dotted area shows the magnitude difference in the high-frequency range.

The acoustic examination shows that all speakers use frication duration to cue the fortis/non-fortis distinction. All males and two female speakers (UF4 and UF6) show significantly higher CoG for the fortis fricative. Four speaker (UF4, UM1, UM2, and UM4) show significantly lower skewness for the fortis as compared with the non-fortis fricative, and only one speaker (UF1) shows significantly higher kurtosis for the fortis fricative ($p < 0.05$). The spectral moments for UF5 go counter to the expected pattern with significantly higher CoG ($p = 0.07$) and kurtosis ($p < 0.05$), and lower skewness ($p < 0.05$) for the non-fortis fricative, which is in line with more constricted apico-laminal channel for the non-fortis fricative produced by this speaker.

2.4 Summary

Though considerable variability is observed, a general pattern shows that elevation of the anterior tongue body/tongue blade and fronted tongue root are two defining articulatory gestures to distinguish the fortis from the non-fortis fricative. The fortis fricative is characterized with substantial elevation of tongue blade and anterior tongue body, which results in more constricted apico-laminal narrowing. This is supported by the acoustic examination in that the fortis fricative has higher CoG and kurtosis, and lower skewness.

Large inter-speaker and even intra-speaker variability are also found. The inter-speaker variability tends to be contextually determined, with less articulatory variability found in the /a/ than in the /i/ context. This may be partly attributed to the palatalization effect in which the anterior tongue body is raised toward pre-palatal area and tongue root is concomitantly fronted, thus reducing the articulatory distinction between the two fricatives.

Intra-speaker variability emerges when reverse patterns for the tongue contour difference appear in two vocalic contexts produced by the same speaker. Speaker UF5, UM2, and UM4 show the expected difference of the position for the anterior tongue body in the /a/ context, but the reversed pattern is observed in the /i/ context.

The acoustic examination supports the general articulatory pattern. The fortis fricative has higher CoG than the non-fortis fricative, in particular for male speakers. Skewness and kurtosis differences are of decreasing importance in cueing the fricative contrast due to considerable inter-speaker variability. Finally, the occurrence of voiced non-fortis tokens tends to be conditioned by vowel contexts and genders. The advancement of the tongue root is found for some speakers who invariably voiced the non-fortis fricative, particularly in the /i/ context by male speakers. In addition, the emergence of the supra-glottal cavity enlargement might be related with the magnitude of the high-frequency noise when it is realized as voiced fricative.

3. ELECTROPALATOGRAPHIC INVESTIGATION

The difficulty of obtaining the tongue blade contour by ultrasound imaging can be compensated by EPG data, which shows detailed constriction shaping in the anterior vocal tract. In what follows we will examine the linguopalatal contact difference for the two-way fricative contrast.

3.1 Participants and materials

The EPG data was taken from a large EPG-phonetic corpus of Korean we had built. Three speakers (one male: EM1; two females: EF1 and EF2) aged between 40 and 50, and grew up in Yanbian Prefecture. They reported using Yanbian Korean as a major language in daily communication, and were proficient in Mandarin Chinese.

The speech materials consisted of 16 monosyllables and 313 Standard Korean words. In C1V (C2) monosyllables, C1 was one of the coronal fricatives which was followed by /a/ or /i/, and C2 was either zero coda or one of the seven codas /m, n, ŋ, p, t, k, l/. Each syllable was read at least twice with inter-stimulus interval of around one second. The test syllables C1V (C2) (C1 = /s/ or /s*/, V = /i/ or /a/) in Korean words were either in word-initial or word-medium position. These words were read once in citation form. Among the words, 201 words were read by all three speakers, 99 by two female speakers, and the rest 13 words by the male speaker.

Table 3 shows the sample numbers for monosyllable (S), word-initial (WI) and word – medium syllable (WM). As is seen, the frequency of the fortis fricative is far less than that of the non-fortis fricative in word-initial position (shaded cells in Table 3), thus the word-initial fricative is only used for calculating electrode contact frequency. The tones for the test syllables were not controlled.

Table 3 Sample numbers of the test syllables in monosyllable (M), word-initial (WI) and word-medium (WM) conditions. Shaded cells indicate small number of tokens.

Speaker	Condition	[sa]	[ʃi]	[s*a]	[ʃ*i]
EM1	M	27	28	25	25
	WI	50	45	7	2
	WM	34	35	33	37
EF1	M	17	20	21	21
	WI	81	69	10	5
	WM	46	44	49	43
EF2	M	30	32	30	29
	WI	84	76	16	5
	WM	45	44	53	44

3.2 Recording and data processing

Reading electropalatograph and ArticAsst software were used to obtain the linguopalatal contact data and speech signal. The recording was carried out in a sound-attenuated lab. The sampling rate for EPG data was 100 Hz, and the speech signal was sampled at 22050 Hz. The phonetic annotation criteria were similar to that in the ultrasound investigation. The key EPG frame was determined from the mode of contact ratio of the consecutive frames in frication interval, which was used for calculating electrode contact frequency and EPG indexes.

The articulatory zoning for the Reading electropalatograph is based on the anatomical landmarks. The first two rows of electrodes lie astride alveolar ridge, and thus the contact pattern in this area roughly corresponds to apico-laminal tongue gesture. The two rows immediately posterior to alveolar ridge is the pre-palatal area, and the linguopalatal contact in this area reflects the anterior tongue body involvement in making constriction. The first four rows are taken as the anterior region which registers the overall constriction shaping for fricatives. The rest four rows are taken as the posterior region with the lateral contact indicating tongue body elevation.

Five EPG indexes were measured. Total Contact (TA) was measured as the ratio of contacted electrodes against 62 electrodes. This measure roughly corresponds to the tongue body height, with larger TA indicating higher tongue position. The contact ratios for the anterior and posterior region (ANT and PST) were also measured. The ANT index reflects the gesture strength for tongue tip and blade, and the PST the anterior tongue body. Center of Gravity and Centrality Contact in the anterior four rows (CoGa and CCa) [7] were used to measure the constriction properties in the alveolar and pre-palatal area. The CoGa measured the concentration of the 'on' electrodes in the anterior four rows of electrodes. More anterior constriction usually has higher CoGa. CCa roughly correlates with the groove width at the alveolar region with a narrower groove width having higher CCa.

3.3 Results

Table 4 shows the contact frequency of the key EPG frames for the fricatives in monosyllable, word-initial and word-medium conditions produced by three speakers. It can be observed that a tapering constriction is formed in the anterior vocal tract with the narrowest point of constriction at alveolar ridge. Compared with the non-fortis fricative, the fortis fricative has shorter width of opening at the point of constriction. The palatalized allophones generally have the narrowest constriction at the alveolar area, supporting the anterior articulation for the palatalized fricatives [22]. Inter-speaker variability can be found in either non-palatalized or palatalized allophones. For example, speaker EF1 consistently have less linguopalatal contact in the anterior region in the /a/ context than the other two speakers.

Table 5 shows the results of the independent t-test results for the EPG indexes. The degree of freedom was Levene-adjusted if the homogeneity of variance was violated. Consistent difference is found for the tongue-palate contact patterns of the two

Table 4 Electrode contact frequency for the key frames of the fricatives in monosyllable (M), word-initial (WI) and word-medium (WM) conditions produced by three speakers. (In each cell, the order is EF1, EF2, and EM1. Cell in black indicates more than 80% contact, dark gray 60%—79%, light gray 40%—59%, and white 0—39%.)

Condition	[sa]	[s*a]	[ʃi]	[ʃ*i]
M				
WI	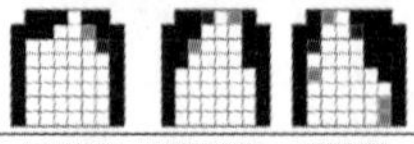	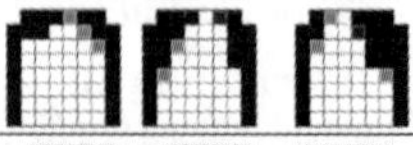		
WM				

fricatives in monosyllable condition. The fortis fricative, either non-palatalized or palatalized, has significantly higher TA (/a/: t (148) = −3.43, $p<0.001$; /i/: t (153) = −3.48, $p<0.001$) and ANT (/a/: t (148) = −4.42, $p<0.001$; /i/: t (143.23) = −8.45, $p<0.001$) than the non-fortis fricative. No significant difference is found for PST. The fortis fricative has significantly higher CoGa than the non-fortis fricative (/a/: t (148) = −4.95, $p<0.001$; /i/: t (138.28) = −7.24, $p<0.001$). The higher CCa for the fortis fricative in both vocalic contexts (/a/: t (102) = −5.45, $p<0.001$; /i/: t (121.72) = −11.02, $p<0.001$) indicates that it is produced with shorter groove of opening at the alveolar region than the non-fortis fricative.

The EPG measures for the word-initial fricatives were not analyzed due to the small sample number of the fortis fricative. In the following we only report the results for the WM condition. As is seen in Table 5, the fortis fricative, either non-palatalized or palatalized, has significantly higher ANT (/a/: t (258) = −3.14, $p=0.01$; /i/: t (245) = −4.05, $p<0.001$) and CCa (/a/: t (258) = −3.56, $p<0.001$; /i/: t (235.26) = −7.6, $p<0.001$) than the non-fortis fricative. Significant difference for CoGa is only found for the palatalized fricatives (t (245) = −6.68, $p<0.001$) with the fortis having higher CoGa. Different from the pattern found in monosyllable condition, the PST for the fortis fricative is consistently higher than that for the non-fortis fricative in either /a/ (t (243.57) = −2.53, $p<0.05$) or /i/ context (t (226.53) = 2.96, $p<0.01$). This appears to support the findings in ultrasound investigation, but the inter-speaker variability of the linguopalatal contact in the posterior area (see Table 4) indicates that the posterior contact difference may not be applied to all speakers. Finally, the differing tongue-palate contact frequency (TA) for the two fricatives only retains in the /a/ context (t (254.16) = −3.38, $p<0.001$).

Table 5 Independent t-test results for the EPG indexes in two vocalic contexts and in monosyllable (M) and word-medium (WM) conditions. ('F' stands for the fortis fricative and 'L' for the lenis fricative. '*n. s.*' indicates no significant difference. Significance levels: $^{*}p<0.05$, $^{**}p<0.01$, $^{***}p<0.001$.)

	M		WM	
	/a/	/i/	/a/	/i/
TA	L < F***	L < F***	L < F***	*n. s.*
ANT	L < F***	L < F***	L < F/**	L < F***
PST	*n. s.*	*n. s.*	L < F*	L < F**
CoGa	L < F***	L < F***	*n. s.*	L < F**
CCa	L < F***	L < F***	L < F***	L < F***

Taken together, these results indicate that the critical articulatory difference for the two-way fricative contrast lies in how the apico-laminal constriction is shaped. The fortis fricative involves extensive linguopalatal contact in the anterior region, which gives rise to the narrowed channel at alveolar ridge. Considering that the narrowest constriction lies at alveolar ridge and medial constriction degree (CCa) is consistently different between the two fricatives in all conditions, the significant difference found for CoGa is more related with the differing width of opening at alveolar ridge instead of constriction location.

Individual variability in the WM condition was also examined. Speaker EM1 chiefly encoded the fricative contrast through differing alveolar constriction degree (CCa) in both vocalic contexts (/a/: t (65) = −1.86, $p=0.067$; /i/: t (59.98) = −2.38, $p<0.05$) with the fortis having higher CCa than the non-fortis fricative. The fortis fricative also has significantly higher ANT than the non-fortis fricative (/a/: t (65) = −2.96,

$p < 0.01$; /i/: t (70) = −3.19, $p < 0.01$). Additionally, the fortis fricative incurs significantly more extensive linguopalatal contact than the non-fortis fricative in the /a/ context (TA: t (65) = −2.24, $p < 0.05$), which is the result of more constricted narrowing for the former. EF1 adopted the similar articulatory setting to distinguish the two fricatives, with significantly higher CCa for the fortis than the non-fortis fricative (/a/: t (93) = −2.98, $p < 0.01$; /i/: t (85) = −5.51, $p < 0.001$). More significant differences emerge in the palatalized allophones for this speaker. The fortis fricative has significantly higher CoGa (t (85) = −5.45, $p < 0.001$) than the non-fortis fricative. In Table 4, it can be observed that the fortis fricative produced by EF1 shows a clear trend of more fronted articulation and a narrower opening at alveolar ridge as compared with the non-fortis fricative. Finally, the linguopalatal contact in the whole palate and posterior region is significantly less for the palatalized fortis fricative as compared with its non-fortis counterpart (TA: t (85) = 3.71, $p < 0.001$; PST: t (85) = 4.64, $p < 0.001$). This finding matches the higher anterior tongue body gesture for the non-fortis fricative which is found for some speakers in the ultrasound investigation (see speakers UF5 and UM4 in Table 2). For EF2, all EPG indexes except TA in the /i/ context are significantly higher for the fortis fricative than the non-fortis fricative ($p < 0.001$), indicating a narrower constriction at the alveolar region and associated higher anterior tongue body in the production of the fortis fricative as compared with the non-fortis fricative. This is in line with the general pattern of the tongue contour difference for the two-way fricative contrast in the ultrasound investigation.

To sum up, the medial constriction at the alveolar area as measured by CCa is shown to be a consistent articulatory correlate for the two-way contrast of Korean fricatives for three speakers, which corresponds to the higher tongue blade and anterior tongue body in the ultrasound investigation. The tongue-palate contact in the first four rows of electrodes is shown to be positively correlated with the CCa. The overall tongue-palate contact is not shown to a reliable index for distinguishing the two-way fricatives, for significantly higher TA for the fortis fricative is only found for EF2 and EM1 in /i/ context, but EF1 shows a reverse pattern. The tongue-palate contact in the posterior four rows reflects inter-speaker articulatory variability for the palatalized allophones of the fricatives. Speaker EF1 shows more elevated anterior tongue body for the non-fortis than the fortis fricative.

3.4 Summary

The EPG results supplement the findings in the ultrasound investigation through probing into the tongue-palate contact characteristics of the two-way fricative contrast. The major findings basically confirm what is found in other Korean dialects [3, 18]. The defining articulatory feature distinguishing the two-way fricative contrast in Yanbian Korean lies in how the apico-laminal constriction is formed at the alveolar and pre-palatal region regardless of post-fricative vowel quality. With the point of constriction keeping relatively the same, greater constriction degree at alveolar ridge is found for the fortis than the non-fortis fricative. This is facilitated by extensive linguopalatal contact in the anterior region, which corresponds to more elevated tongue blade in the ultrasound investigation. However, the anterior tongue body gesture is liable to reflect inter-speaker articulatory variability.

4. DISCUSSION AND CONCLUSION

This paper investigates the supra-laryngeal gestural manifestation of the fortis/non-fortis fricative contrast in the vernacular of Yanbian Korean through ultrasound imaging and EPG. The findings in the ultrasound experiment largely replicate the results in [17]. In the /a/ context, the fortis/non-fortis fricative distinction is associated with the degree of the apico-laminal constriction and tongue body gesture. Compared with the non-fortis fricative, the fortis is characterized with more apico-laminal constriction, higher anterior tongue body, and prominent tongue root fronting. The voicing of the non-fortis fricative tends to be associated with the positioning of the tongue root, which is indicative of the supra-glottal cavity enlargement. However, the tongue root fronting in the case of the voiced non-fortis fricative tends to be constrained by the degree of the apico-laminal constriction. Narrower apico-laminal alveolar constriction, which results in more peaked and compacted energy in the high frequency range, possibly inhibits the tongue root fronting even when the non-fortis is realized as voiced.

We also examine the fortis/non-fortis distinction when they are palatalized. Despite the limitation of the ultrasound technology [29], a number of speakers do show the differing tongue blade gesture for the two fricatives, which resembles what is found in the /a/ context. Large inter-speaker variation is found for the positioning of anterior tongue body and tongue root. This may be attributed to the prominent tongue body elevation toward the pre-palatal area and fronting as a result of palatalization, which, in a way, attenuates the tongue contour distinction between the two fricatives. But the significant anterior tongue body elevation for the non-fortis fricative produced by some speakers (also found in the EPG data) tends to be motivated by the supra-glottal cavity enlargement in the case of voiced non-fortis fricative. The differing tongue contours of the two fricatives produced by speaker UM2 who voiced all palatalized non-fortis fricatives illustrate this aerodynamically-motivated articulatory maneuver. Differing magnitude of the tongue root fronting gesture may also emerge as required by the aerodynamic constraint for balancing the frication and voicing in the production of voiced non-fortis fricative. However, this possibility remains tentative because the active tongue body advancement as a result of palatalization might make the difference of the tongue contours for the two fricatives less prominent. More tongue imaging data with more speakers and varied speech tasks has to be built to test this possibility.

Inter-speaker variability is also found in the acoustic examination for the fricatives produced by old speakers. The frication noise duration is proved to be the only reliable acoustic measure which cues the two-way fricative contrast. Though the fricative contrast is generally cued by differing CoG, its functionality tends to be gender-specific. Male speakers more likely show differing CoG than female speakers when producing the two fricatives. One female speaker shows a reverse pattern that the non-fortis fricative has higher CoG, which was found in [26]. The voicing of the non-fortis fricative is also related with gender. Taken together, these findings show the gender-related articulatory variation in the production of the two fricatives in Korean, which has been codified as the "social-indexical marker" [11, 20]. However, how the articulation and acoustics of the two-way fricative contrast correlates with gender in Yanbian Korean remains to be explored.

The results in EPG investigation supplement the findings in the ultrasound investigation by providing the linguopalatal contact characteristics in the anterior vocal tract for the production of the two coronal fricatives. On the one hand, the EPG data show that the defining articulatory properties in distinguishing the two coronal fricatives lies in how the apico-laminal constriction is shaped in the alveolar region. Constriction degree with the associated magnitude of the tongue blade gesture turns out to be the most stable articulatory manifestation for the fortis/non-fortis fricative distinction. On the other hand, inter-speaker variability in terms of the linguopalatal contact in the posterior region matches the variability of the anterior tongue body gestures in the production of the palatalized non-fortis fricative.

To conclude, the majority of the findings are in accordance with what have been found in previous studies, but the inter-speaker variability in terms of articulation and acoustics of the two-way fricative contrast calls for a more comprehensive model which entails aerodynamic and sociolinguistic factors.

5. ACKNOWLEDG EMENTS

This work was supported by Korean Studies Grant (AKS-2019-R-74). The authors thank all speakers for their participation. We also thank two anonymous reviewers for the detailed suggestions.

REFERENCES

[1] Anderson, V., Ko, I., O'Grady, W. 2004. A palatographic investigation of place of articulation in korean coronal obstruents. *Korean Linguistics* 12, 1 - 24.

[2] Baik, W. 1994. *An Electropalatographic Study of Coarticulation in Korean VCV and CVC Sequences.* PhD dissertation, Georgetown University.

[3] Baik, W. 1998. On tensity of Korean fricatives (Electropalatographic study). *Speech Sciences* 4 (1), 135 - 145.

[4] Boersma, B., Weenink, D. 2020. Praat: Doing phonetics by computer (Version 6. 1. 15). https://www. fon. hum. uva. nl/praat/

[5] Cho, T., Jun, S. A., Ladefoged, P. 2002. Acoustic and aerodynamic correlates of Korean stops and fricatives. *Journal of Phonetics* 30 (2), 193 - 228.

[6] Davidson, L. 2006. Comparing tongue shapes from ultrasound imaging using smoothing spline analysis of variance. *Journal of the Acoustical Society of America* 120 (1), 407 - 415.

[7] Fontdevila, J., Pallarès, M. D., Recasens, D. 1994. The contact index method of electropalatographic data reduction. *Journal of Phonetics* 22 (2), 141 - 154.

[8] Forrest, K., Weismer, G., Milenkovic, P., Dougall, R. N. 1988. Statistical analysis of word-initial voiceless obstruents: Preliminary data. *Journal of the Acoustical Society of America* 84 (1), 115 - 123.

[9] Fuchs, S., Brunner, J., Busler, A. 2007. Temporal and spatial aspects concerning the realizations of the voicing contrast in German alveolar and postalveolar fricatives. *Advances in Speech Language Pathology* 9 (1), 90 - 100.

[10] Halle, M., Stevens, K. N. 1971. A note on laryngeal features. *Quarterly Progress Report* 101, 198 - 213.

[11] Han, K. -I. 2019. Effects on gender and age variations of Korean fricatives. *Studies in British and American Language and Literature* 132, 207 - 226.

[12] Hwang, H. K. 2004. Spectral characteristics of frication noise in Korean sibilants. *Malsori* 49, 31 - 50.

[13] Institute of Linguistics of Chinese Academy of Social Sciences, Institute of Ethnology and Anthroplogy of Chinese Academy of Social Sciences, Language Information Sciences Research Centre of City University of Hong Kong. 2012. *Language Atlas of China: Ethnic Minority Languages* (中国社会科学院语言研究所、中国社会科学院民族学与人类学研究所:《中国语言地图集(第2版):少数民族语言卷》,商务印书馆2012年版)。(Second Edition). Beijing: The Commercial Press.

[14] Iverson, G. K. 1983. Korean s. *Journal of Phonetics* 11 (2), 191 - 200.

[15] Jongman, A., Wayland, R., Wong, S. 2000. Acoustic characteristics of English fricatives. *Journal of the Acoustical Society of America* 108 (3), 1252 - 1263.

[16] Kagaya, R. 1974. A fiberscopic and acoustic study of the Korean stops, affricates and fricatives. *Journal of Phonetics* 2 (2), 161 - 180.

[17] Kim, H., Maeda, S., Honda, K. 2011. The laryngeal characterization of Korean fricatives: Stroboscopic cine-MRI data. *Journal of Phonetics* 39 (4), 626 - 641.

[18] Kim, S. 2001. *The Interaction between Prosodic Domain and Segmental Properties: Domain Initial Strengthening of Fricatives and Post Obstru-*

ent Tensing Rule in Korean. PhD dissertation, University of California, Los Angeles.

[19] Kohler, K. J. 1984. Phonetic explanation in phonology: The feature fortis/lenis. *Phonetica* 41 (3), 150 – 174.

[20] Kong, E. J., Kang, J. 2020. Gendered spectral patterns of sibilant fricatives in Seoul Korean. *Studies in Phonetics, Phonology and Morpholog* 26 (1), 1 – 19.

[21] Ladefoged, P., Maddieson, I. 1996. *The Sounds of the World's Languages.* Oxford: Blackwell.

[22] Lee, K.-M. 1998. *A Concise History of Korean Language (Revised Edition)* (*개정판 국어사개설*). Seoul: Thaehaksa.

[23] Li, M., Kambhamettu, C., Stone, M. 2005. Automatic contour tracking in ultrasound images. *Clinical Linguistics & Phonetics* 19 (6 – 7), 545 – 554.

[24] Li, Y., Zhang, J. 2014. An electropalatographic and electroglottographic study on domain-initial strengthening in Korean. Procecdings of the 9th International Symposium on Chinese Spoken Language Processing, Singapore, 406 – 410.

[25] Li, Y., Zhang, J. 2018. The electropalatographic and acoustic investigation of the coronal fricatives in Korean. *Chinese Journal of Phonetics* 9, 63 – 70. (李英浩、张京花:《朝鲜语舌叶齿龈擦者的 EPG 和声学分析》,《中国语音学报》2018年第9辑,第63—70页。)

[26] Oh, M., Hui, Y. 2015. An acoustic comparison of korean coronal fricatives in the Seoul and Yanbian Korean dialects. *Studies in Linguistics* 34 (1), 145 – 172.

[27] Quan, X. 1998. Yanbian Korean dialects (연변방언). *New Life with Korean* 8, 153 – 180.

[28] R Core Team. 2019. R: A language and environment for statistical computing. Vienna, Austria: R Foundation for Statistical Computing. http://www.R-project.org.

[29] Stone, M. 2005. A guide to analysing tongue motion from ultrasound images. *Clinical Linguistics & Phonetics* 19 (6 – 7), 455 – 501.

[30] Westbury, J. R. 1983. Enlargement of the supraglottal cavity and its relation to stop consonant voicing. *Journal of the Acoustical Society of America* 73 (4), 1322 – 1336.

[31] Yoon, K.-C. 2009. Identifying frication and aspiration noise in the frequency domain: The case of korean alveolar lax fricatives. *Phonetics and Speech Sciences* 1 (2), 105 – 110.

[32] Zhao, X., Xuan, D. 1986. Linguistic features in Liuzhen Korean dialect. *Minzu Yuwen* 5, 1 – 13. (赵习、宣德五:《朝鲜语六镇话的方言特点》,《民族语文》1986年第5期,第1—13页。)

LI Yinghao PhD He is a professor of College of Foreign Languages in Yanbian University. His research interest is experimental phonetics.
E-mail: leeyoungho@aliyun.com

Zhang Jinghua PhD She is an associate professor of College of Foreign Languages in Yanbian University. Her research interest is sociolinguistics.
E-mail: janggyunghwa@ybu.edu.cn

汉语方言中的基频微扰与振幅微扰

许　可　黄　玮　梁煜珠　冉启斌

摘　要　基频微扰（jitter）和振幅微扰（shimmer）分别体现声带振动的不规律性和不稳定性，是衡量嗓音特征的重要参数。本文通过提取 40 个汉语方言点常用词汇录音的 jitter 和 shimmer 数据，统计分析经纬度、地理方位的南北、湿度、性别、海拔等 6 个影响因素对其的影响，看到湿度、纬度对 jitter 和 shimmer 的影响较为重要，同时二者还受到性别的影响。就 40 个方言点而言，海拔不是影响 jitter 和 shimmer 的因素。湿度、纬度、性别等对正态化后的 jitter 和 shimmer 变异的预测分别可达 10.6% 和 8.4%。干燥、地理位置上更靠近北方的方言点，jitter 和 shimmer 都更高，声带振动越不规律、不稳定，同时，女性的嗓音表现更稳定、规律。

关键词　基频微扰，振幅微扰，汉语方言，嗓音声学表现

Jitter and Shimmer in Chinese Dialects

XU Ke　HUANG Wei　LIANG Yuzhu　RAN Qibin

Abstract Jitter and shimmer refer to the irregular small cycle-to-cycle variations in frequency and amplitude during voiced regions of speech. They are important measures of voice quality. In this study, these two parameters were extracted from recordings of common expressions in 40 Chinese dialects for statistical analysis. The paper is concerned with how jitter and shimmer are correlated with environmental factors such as longitude, latitude, altitude, geographical zones (North and South), and humidity. The finding shows that humidity and latitude have great effects on jitter and shimmer, and gender also affects the voice quality. Humidity, latitude and gender could indicate 10.8% of the variance in jitter and 8.4% of the variance in shimmer after normalizing the voice quality data. Results further show that jitter and shimmer are higher in dialectal zones in the North and drier climate, where people's vocal folds vibrate more irregularly and less precisely. And the voice quality of females is more stable and regular. Furthermore, altitude is not likely a factor showing significant impact on jitter and shimmer.

Key words Jitter, Shimmer, Chinese Dialects, Voice Quality

1. 引言

基频微扰（jitter）和振幅微扰（shimmer）是衡量嗓音特征的重要参数。jitter 指相邻周期间声波频率的变化率，反映声带振动周期间频率的差异，体现声带振动的不规律性；shimmer 是指相邻周期间振幅的变化率，反映声带振动周期间振幅的差异，体现声带振动的不稳定性。自 Lieberman［10］首次提出使用二者作为嗓音特征参数后，jitter 和 shimmer 被广泛应用于语音学和临床医学研究。

jitter 和 shimmer 代表的嗓音控制能力与语言演化，尤其是声调语言的产生有着密切的关系。声调音位需要发出相对精确的音高，对嗓音控制能力的要求较高，那么语言使用者的 jitter 和 shimmer 都应较低。基于环境对 jitter、shimmer 的影响以及 jitter、shimmer 与嗓音控制能力、声调语言产生的关系，［5］提出地理环境可能影响声调语言产生这一假设。他们以世界上 3756 种语言在地理上的分布对这一假设进行了验证，发现湿热的地理环境下，声调语言存在的概率更高，为人类语音系统受到环境影响提供了证据。［16］将这

一结论运用到汉语声调产生地域的研究中，通过中国境内8种语言/方言所在地域湿度、语言/方言 jitter 和 shimmer 等数据的统计分析，为汉语声调产生存在地域差异、南方声调产生先于北方的推测提供了数据支持。

以上对自然环境与声调产生进行的推测和论证，都以自然环境对 jitter、shimmer 的影响为基础观点之一，因此，探索何种因素、在何种程度上影响 jitter 和 shimmer 的表现对于语言演化与自然地理环境的关系就显得十分重要。

jitter、shimmer 影响因素的研究已有很多。嗓音表现由发声时声带的质量、紧张情况、内部摩擦力、声带表面黏液的浓度等生理机制及其振动模式等决定，而声带的生理机制又受到多方面因素的影响。

就环境因素而言，［12］指出，吸入干燥的空气会增加声带的紧张度以及控制声带发出合适声音的难度；［6］指出，声带表面黏度大小取决于声带组织中含水量的多少；［8］指出，声带对所吸入空气相对湿度的减少反应很灵敏；［5］指出，干燥寒冷的环境往往导致 jitter 和 shimmer 等声学参数的增大。这些研究都表明，湿度、温度等环境情况会影响声带的生理机制，进而影响到嗓音的表现。

此外，性别也是嗓音研究中备受关注的因素，对于性别是否对嗓音参数产生影响，学界存在争议。［11］指出 jitter 在成人之间具有显著的性别差异，成年女性的 jitter 绝对值大于男性；［20］对比分析了中国人的 jitter 和 shimmer 等参数在性别中的差异性，指出 jitter 和 shimmer 在性别之间无显著性差异；［9］指出，在普通话母语的儿童中，女性的 jitter 和 shimmer 都比男性要大；［1］指出，女性的 jitter 比男性要小。

另外，还有学者对影响嗓音的其他因素做了研究。［18］指出，性激素水平会对嗓音表现造成影响；［4］指出，由于嘎裂声、鼻音等发声习惯的不同，说不同方言的人之间可能会有不同的嗓音表现；此外，发不同的元音也会有不同的嗓音表现，［3］［13］等均有研究。

以上对嗓音表现影响因素的探索大多在控制较为严格的实验中进行，以实验组、对照组差异的显著性来判断因素是否对嗓音表现造成影响。一些可能影响声带生理机制、嗓音表现，进而影响人类语音系统的自然地理环境因素如海拔、经纬度（分别与气压、海陆位置等相关）等与嗓音表现的关系，目前还没有影响较大的探索性研究。也即，在以往的实验中，我们较为清楚地看到湿度等环境因素可能影响 jitter 和 shimmer，但湿度等因素对 jitter 和 shimmer 的影响有多大，还有多少因素可能对 jitter 和 shimmer 造成影响，仍是值得研究的问题。

汉语内部具有使用地域相异、声调数量不同的方言，是观察自然条件因素对嗓音表现、语音系统影响的重要材料。通过对 jitter、shimmer 的影响因素进行讨论，我们还可以进一步完善对汉语声调产生地域的推论［16］，将嗓音的南北差异细化为更小地域范围的比较。此外，目前对中国境内不同区域嗓音声学表现的研究并不多，尤其是对不同汉语方言的嗓音声学分析还很少见，本文可以为相关研究提供一些拓展。

本文以《现代汉语方言音库》40个方言点的录音材料为对象，以 jitter 和 shimmer 为参数系统性地考察汉语方言的微观嗓音声学表现，尤其着眼于从统计分析的角度考察性别、湿度、经纬度、海拔、地理位置的南北等因素对嗓音的影响。下面首先介绍实验情况。

2. 实验情况

2.1 实验材料

本研究中使用的《现代汉语方言音库》用有声的形式保存现代汉语方言，是中国社会科学院在20世纪90年代使用磁带进行录音的。［7］曾对磁带录音和数字信号录音的嗓音声学参数 jitter 和 shimmer 进行了对比，发现不论是绝对值 jitter（absolute jitter）还是百分比 jitter（percent jitter）在磁带录音中都要比在数字信号录音中高，并且在两种录音模式间的差异具有较高的一致性（r = 0.967，r = 0.954），百分比 shimmer（percent shimmer）在磁带录音信号中总体较高，但是两种录音模式之间的差异一致性较低（r = 0.481）。这就是说，磁带录音中的 jitter 比数字信号录音中的 jitter 要高，磁带录音中的 shimmer 比数字信号录音中的 shimmer 有的要高，有的要低。[7] 认为既然知晓了其中的关系，并且两种录音模式中参数数值的差异并不大，那么使用磁带录音来进行嗓音声学分析是可行的。我们赞同 [7] 的这一看法，尽管由于磁带录音的采样率较低，磁带录音的嗓音参数很可能与数字信号录音不同，但二者的差异在40个方言音档内部具有一致性，所以在本研究中使用了该批录音材料。

《现代汉语方言音库》共收录40个汉语方言点的录音资源。40个方言音档名称及其方言分区情况如表1所示。

表1　方言音档及其方言分区情况

方言音档	方言分区	音档数量（个）
上海 苏州 杭州 温州	吴语区	4
广州 南宁 香港	粤语区	3
厦门 福州 建瓯 汕头 海口 台北	闽语区	6
梅县 桃园	客家区	2
南昌	赣语区	1
长沙 湘潭	湘语区	2
歙县 屯溪	徽语区	2
太原 平遥 呼和浩特	晋语区	3
北京 天津 济南 青岛 南京 合肥 郑州 武汉 成都 贵阳 昆明 哈尔滨 西安 银川 兰州 西宁 乌鲁木齐	官话区	17

40个汉语方言音档中每个点均包含声韵调、常用词汇、构词法、语法例句、语篇等部分，本研究中使用的是“常用词汇”部分除“增补”部分（该部分是方言特色词语，不统一）外的182条词语。有的方言一个词语有多种说法也计算在列，如普通话中的“太阳”在北京方言中有“太阳、老爷儿、日头”三种说法。实际上，40个汉语方言音档共有常用词10443条，因此可以分别求得10443个jitter值和shimmer值。

2.2 数据提取

目前有多种实现嗓音声学参数提取的软件，诸如 VoiceSauce、Dr. Speech、Praat、USSA等，其中Praat是使用得比较广泛的软件。[19] 指出，Praat软件可以用于对声学参数进行分析，具有区分正常与病理性嗓音的能力。[14] 对Praat提取的jitter和shimmer准确度的调查也显示，Praat提取的jitter参数较为准确；虽然shimmer数据准确性缺乏适当标准，但Praat提取的shimmer值与 [14] 中算法提取结果相近。[1] [2] 等研究均使用Praat提取嗓音声学参数。我们也选择使用Praat进行数据提取。jitter和shimmer的算法也有很多，如jitter有jitter（local）、jitter（local，absolute）、jitter（rap）、jitter（ppq5）等；shimmer有shimmer（local）、shimmer（local，dB）、shimmer（apq3）、shimmer（apq5）等。jitter（local，absolute）和shimmer（local，dB）指某周期与下一周期声波时长差异绝对值的平均值、某周期与下一周期音强差异绝对值的平均值，分别以秒或毫秒、分贝为单位。jitter（local）则为jitter（local，absolute）与周期平均时长之比；shimmer（local）指shimmer（local，dB）与平均音强之比。jitter（rap）的算法与jitter（local）相似，但以相邻前后各一周期时长均值代替了jitter（local）中相邻下一周期时长。对应的shimmer算法是shimmer（apq3），以前后各一周期中音强的均值代替shimmer（local）中的相邻下一周期音强。jitter（ppq5）、shimmer（apq5）的计算方法与jitter（rap）、shimmer（apq3）的方法类似，但将相邻周期增加到了前后各两个（计算方法及其差异详见 [14]）。也即，除jitter（local，absolute）和shimmer（local, dB) 外，其他算法的区别仅在于对相邻周期个数的选择上。本文拟从自然环境条件对 jitter 和 shimmer 的影响方面［16］进行补充，因此采用［16］使用的两个参数，即 jitter（local）和 shimmer（local）。计算公式如下：

$$Jitt = \frac{\frac{1}{N-1}\sum_{i=1}^{N-1}|T_i - T_{i-1}|}{\frac{1}{N}\sum_{i=1}^{N}T_i} \quad (1)$$

$$Shim = \frac{\frac{1}{N-1}\sum_{i=1}^{N-1}|A_i - A_{i-1}|}{\frac{1}{N}\sum_{i=1}^{N}A_i} \quad (2)$$

公式（1）中 T_i 和 N 分别指提取的声门周期（glottal periods）时长和数量；公式（2）中 A_i 和 N 分别指提取的音强和数量。

过程上，本文首先使用 Praat 软件对录音材料进行标注，然后切分出所需的录音片段，随后使用脚本提取出录音的 jitter（local）和 shimmer（local）数据。

本研究拟考察的嗓音表现（即 jitter 值和 shimmer 值）的影响因素是性别、地理方位、经度、纬度、海拔、湿度等。其中只有性别不属于方言点的自然条件因素，但性别对嗓音表现的影响是不容忽视的，因此，我们将性别也纳入考量。40 个汉语方言音档中有 37 个音档仅有 1 位发音人，其中男性发音人 25 位，女性发音人 12 位；剩下 3 个音档中各有 2 位发音人，既有男性也有女性，我们记为混合性别。地理方位依据传统标准“秦岭—淮河”一线进行划分，“秦岭—淮河”以北为北方，有 14 个音档；“秦岭—淮河”以南为南方，有 26 个音档。经度、纬度和海拔数据来自网络公开资源。湿度使用各方言点相对湿度（Relative Humidity）数据，收集比较困难。鉴于音档中的一些区县并没有公开湿度的统计信息，我们通过《中国统计年鉴》、各地方统计年鉴等资料提取了近十年（2008—2017）音档所在地点的湿度数据，并分别取平均值以后作为本研究中各个方言点的湿度①。此外，建瓯、梅县、平遥、青岛、汕头、歙县、桃园、屯溪、温州、湘潭等 10 个方言点的湿度数据暂缺。利用湿度进行统计分析时，将这些方言点排除在外。

2.3 数据统计

本研究主要使用 SPSS 软件进行数据的统计与分析。为选择适合 jitter 和 shimmer 分析比较的方法，我们对所提取出的 jitter 和 shimmer 数据进行了总体分析，利用 GraphPad Prism 软件绘制了 jitter 和 shimmer 的小提琴图（Violin Plot），如图 1 所示。

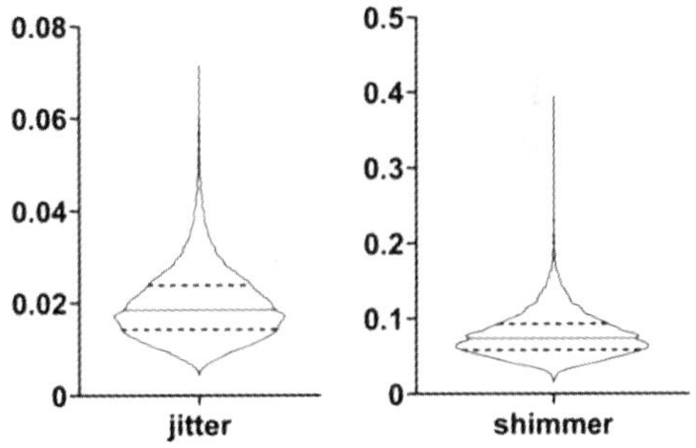

图1 jitter 和 shimmer 数值的小提琴

小提琴图的原理和箱线图相似，但能更好地反映数据分布的情况。图 1 中横实线代表中位数，下虚线表示第一四分位数，上虚线表示第三四分位数，上须和下须顶端分别代表最大值和最小值，“琴身”的胖瘦显示该数值出现的频率，数据越集中图形越胖。从图 1 可以看到，jitter 和 shimmer 的分布显然不是正态分布。接下来我们使用 SPSS 对 jitter 和 shimmer 进行了正态性检验，检验结果显示 jitter 和 shimmer 的数据均不符合正态分布（$ps < 0.001$）。

① 匿名审稿人指出，湿度数据与录音年代存在数据年份失配问题。一方面，对 20 世纪 90 年代相对湿度数据进行收集较为困难，不能完整收集到文中所需数据；另一方面，［17］对国内相对湿度 50 年的调查显示，各年份均值差异不超过 3%。［21］指出 1980—2018 年处于同一年代际（10—35 年）准周期波动中。因此我们认为使用相差 10—20 年的平均相对湿度数据仍然是可行的。

在各因素对嗓音表现的影响方面，尽管已有研究中对影响嗓音表现的因素进行了一些探索，但是大多都是基于一种或几种确定影响因素，设置对照组进行控制变量的实验研究。在本实验中，实验材料是确定的40个方言点的182个词录音的jitter和shimmer，在未知影响因素的情况下，观察湿度等6种影响因素是否影响嗓音表现以及怎样影响嗓音表现。因此，实验采用多元线性回归的方式，通过观察拟合模型和回归系数、显著性等参数，判断不同因素对jitter和shimmer的影响。由于多元线性回归要求数据残差具有正态性，我们使用对数函数log10对原始jitter和shimmer数据进行了正态化，将正态化后的jitter、shimmer分别称为transjitter、transshimmer。转换公式如公式（3）、公式（4）所示。

$$transjitter = lg(jitter) \quad (3)$$

$$transshimmer = lg(shimmer) \quad (4)$$

转换后，transjitter、transshimmer与jitter和shimmer的原始数据显著高相关（$r = 0.965$；$r = 0.967$；$ps < 0.01$），transjitter的范围在［-2.32，-1.14］，transshimmer在［-1.82，-0.40］。［8］也曾使用对数转换的方式对实验数据进行正态化处理。

3. 实验结果

由于本文对汉语方言中jitter、shimmer影响因素及其影响大小的探索，是基于jitter、shimmer与声调的关联。为了确认嗓音表现与声调的关联，我们首先使用SPSS以声调数量为分组依据，对40个方言点的jitter和shimmer数据进行了方差分析（ANOVA）。结果如表2所示，不同声调数量的方言jitter和shimmer差异显著［F_{jitter}（6，10436）$=55.707$，$F_{shimmer}$（6，10436）$=127.004$，$ps<0.01$］。由于不同声调的样本不均衡，语言演化与多种因素相关等原因，此次实验中不同声调数量方言的jitter和shimmer并没有呈现严格规律地随声调增多而下降的趋势（如声调数量为5个的方言jitter均值大于声调数量为3个的方言，小于声调数量为4个的方言）。但总体而言，声调数量与jitter和shimmer都存在显著的负相关关系（$\rho = -0.116$，$\rho = -0.089$；$ps<0.01$）。jitter和shimmer较大时，声调的数量更倾向于较少。扩展到声调产生（无声调即声调数量为0）地域嗓音的研究，本文认为［5］［16］对声调产生地域jitter和shimmer更低的推断是合理的；本文对jitter、shimmer影响因素的讨论也是对更有可能产生声调的环境进行讨论。

表2　不同声调数量对应的方言数量和嗓音表现基本情况

声调数量	方言数量	jitter均值±标准差	shimmer均值±标准差
3	3	0.0215±0.0073	0.0698±0.0239
4	13	0.0201±0.0080	0.0811±0.0266
5	5	0.0214±0.0082	0.0915±0.0353
6	8	0.0184±0.0063	0.0709±0.0200
7	6	0.0201±0.0080	0.0766±0.0318
8	2	0.0161±0.0051	0.0854±0.0301
9	3	0.0183±0.0070	0.0655±0.0247

3.1 transjitter与transshimmer的相关性分析及各影响因素数据分布

transjitter与transshimmer之间呈中度正相关关系（$r=0.503$，$p<0.01$），从图2中可以清晰地看到，transshimmer有随transjitter的增大而增大的趋势，即声带振动的规律性越差，稳定性也越差，与［9］的研究结果一致。

40个方言点的经度在东经87.63°（乌鲁木齐）至东经126.56°（哈尔滨），

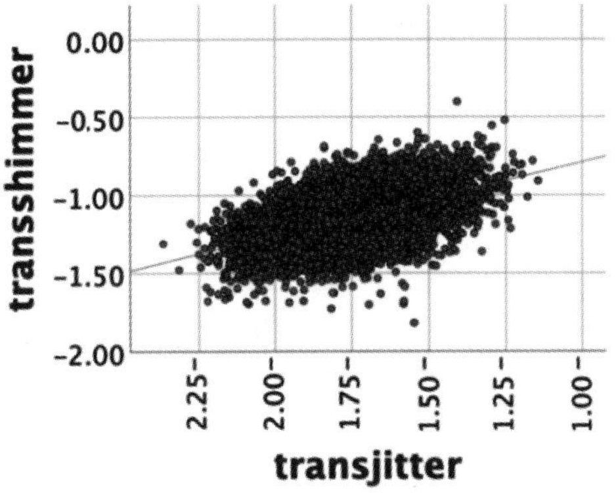

图 2　transjitter 与 transshimmer 包含趋势线的散点

纬度在北纬 20.07°（海口）至北纬 45.74°（哈尔滨），海拔在 3 米（杭州）至 2219 米（西宁），湿度在 46.5%（呼和浩特）至 81.4%（海口）。40 个方言点不同经度、纬度、地理方位、海拔、湿度、性别的录音数量情况如图 3 所示。图 3 中横轴为该影响因素的数值/类别，纵轴为该数值出现的频率（统计分析中使用了 40 个点 jitter、shimmer 的所有数据而不是平均值，40 个方言点的录音共计 10443 条，因此有数据的每个方言点 jitter 和 shimmer 的频数都超过 182 次）。其中，地理方位从左至右组 1 为南方，组 2 为北方；性别组 1 为男性，组 2 为女性，组 3 为混合性别。从图 3 中可以看到，40 个方言点的湿度、纬度、性别、经度、海拔等分布都不均衡。实验继续测量了各自变量的偏度。从表 3 中可以看到，经度、海拔的分布极不均衡。

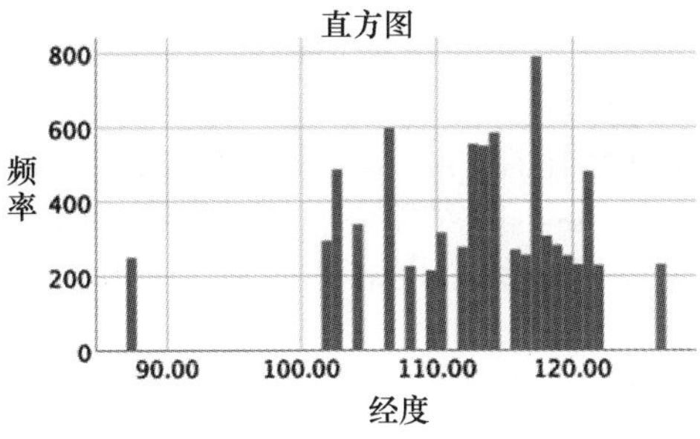

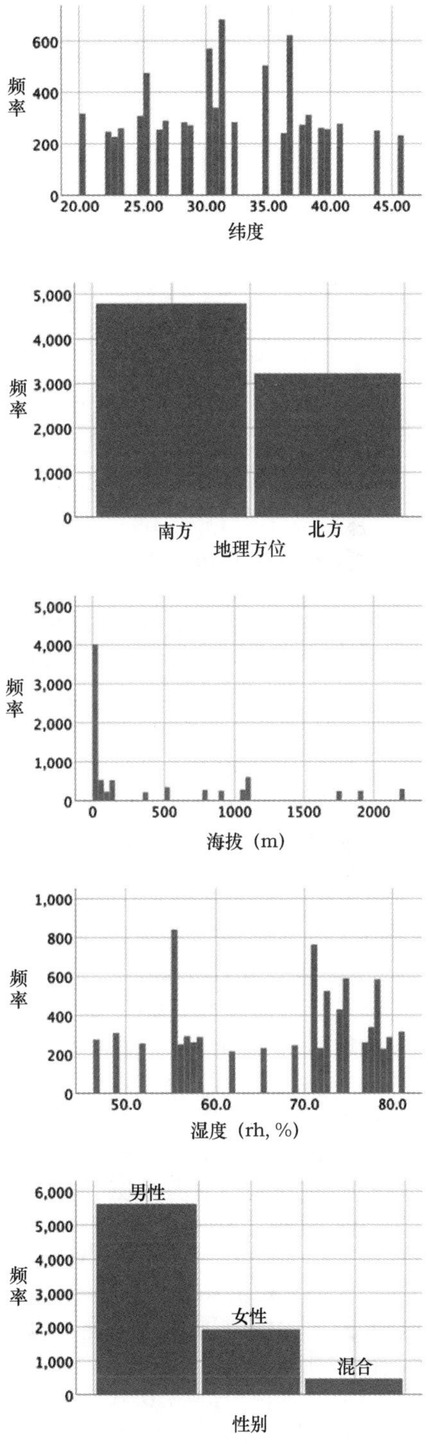

图 3　40 个方言点不同经度、纬度、地理方位、海拔、湿度、性别录音数量分布

表 3　各自变量偏度（偏度绝对值顺序）

自变量	偏度
纬度	0.323
湿度	-0.440
地理方位	0.600
性别	1.114
经度	-1.291
海拔	1.845

3.2 各因素对 jitter 的影响

实验首先检验了 jitter 与各影响因素之间的相关性。由于实验中各影响因素呈偏态分布，相关性检验使用 jitter 原始数据与连续变量因素（经度、纬度、湿度、海拔）进行斯皮尔曼秩相关（Spearman's correlation coefficient for ranked data）分析；由于变量类型和检验方式对样本数量的要求，检测分类变量（地理方位、性别）与 jitter 的相关性时，使用 40 点平均 jitter 与各变量的 Eta 平方系数（Eta - squared value，η^2）。表 4 显示了连续变量因素与 jitter 相关的大小和绝对值排序。

与 jitter 最为相关的是湿度，二者呈现负相关关系，湿度越大，jitter 越小，声带振动规律性越强，与［8］的研究结果一致。纬度与 jitter 的相关性其次，呈正相关关系。纬度越大，地理上越向北，jitter 越大，与［16］的研究结果相符。

jitter 为因变量，地理方位、性别为自变量时，η^2 分别为 0.410 和 0.348，地理方位、性别与 jitter 存在中度、中度偏弱的相关性，地理方位的相关性较性别更大。

偏度最大的两个因素，经度、海拔与 jitter 的相关性非常低，因此，实验首先排除了这两种因素。为进一步确定剩余 4 种因素对 jitter 的影响，实验继续以湿度、纬度、地理方位、性别为自变量，transjitter 为因变量进行了多元线性回归分析。

表 4　连续变量因素与 jitter 的相关性检验结果

	transjitter
湿度	-0.306**
纬度	0.247**
经度	0.140**
海拔	-0.076**

** 在 0.01 级别（双尾），相关性显著。

由于湿度、纬度为连续变量，地理方位、性别为分类变量（性别变量中，设置男、女、混合 3 个类别进行比较），实验采用步进与输入相结合的方法进行多元线性回归，并根据回归结果中各因素的共线性等参数对拟合模型进行调整，将较为相关的因素逐一排除，最终挑选出调整后 R^2 最高，也即拟合效果最好的一种模型进行详细报告。在对 transjitter 的拟合过程中，地理方位、纬度、湿度的共线性较高（3 种因素都被纳入模型时，湿度、地理方位 VIFs > 7；排除地理方位后，湿度、纬度 VIFs > 3），我们逐一排除了地理方位和纬度，将不同的拟合模型以数字顺序命名，表 4 显示了各拟合模型中不同因素的标准化系数及模型的拟合效果；标准化系数后的 * 表示 $p < 0.05$，** 表示 $p < 0.01$；“——”表示模型不包含这一因素。

由表 5 可见，所有的拟合模型都具有显著性，但模型 2，包含湿度、纬度、性别这 3 个影响因素的模型拟合效果最好，这 3 个因素可以解释 transjitter 变异的 10.6%。这一模型中，性别的影响力最大，女性的声带振动较男性更为规律。自然地理条件中湿度的影响力较纬度更大，湿度越高的地方，嗓音表现越好。同时，纬度与 transjitter 呈正相关关系，纬度越大，地理上越偏向北方的地方，transjitter 越大。自然地理环境对嗓音表现的影响显著存在。

表5　transjitter的多元线性回归分析模型

模型	湿度	纬度	地理方位（北方）	性别（女性）	性别（混合性别）	调整后 R^2
1	-0.172**	0.145**	-0.039	-0.143**	0.021	0.097
2	-0.156**	0.133**	——	-0.159**	0.028*	0.106
3	-0.257**	——	——	-0.152**	0.019	0.092

3.3　各因素对shimmer的影响

依据检验各因素对jitter影响的方法，实验对经度、纬度、海拔、湿度等影响因素与shimmer进行了斯皮尔曼秩相关检验，测算了地理方位、性别因素与40个方言点平均shimmer的 η^2 值。湿度的相关性检验仅使用有湿度数据的方言点的shimmer数据。表6按照相关性大小对连续变量因素进行了排序。纬度与shimmer相关性最强，纬度越高，更靠近北方，shimmer越大，声带振幅越不稳定。湿度与shimmer呈现负相关关系，湿度越大，shimmer越小。shimmer为因变量，地理方位、性别为自变量时，η^2 分别为0.221和0.325，性别与shimmer的相关性比地理方位高。

海拔、经度这两个偏态严重的因素与transshimmer的相关性也很低；同时，为与检验各因素对transjitter的影响的方法保持一致，实验排除经度、海拔因素，进一步以transshimmer为因变量，以纬度、湿度、性别、地理方位为自变量进行了多元线性回归。由于自变量中有连续变量和分类变量2种变量，回归仍以步进与输入相结合的方式进行。

表6　连续变量因素与shimmer的相关性检验结果

	shimmer（local）
纬度	0.201**
湿度	-0.186**

续表

	shimmer（local）
海拔	-0.112**
经度	0.025*

** 在0.01级别（双尾），相关性显著。

* 在0.05级别（双尾），相关性显著。

涵盖所有影响因素的模型1中，湿度的回归系数与相关性检验中符号相反，其标准化系数不具有显著性。由于模型1中地理方位（VIF>8）、湿度（VIF>7）共线性很高，我们去除了地理方位这一影响因素，并继续对transshimmer进行多元线性回归分析。第二次回归分析中，湿度、纬度的共线性较高（VIFs>3）。我们分别去除了纬度、湿度后对transshimmer再次拟合。表7显示了各回归模型中不同影响因素的影响大小及回归模型的效果、显著性。

模型2中，为以纬度、湿度、性别或以纬度、性别为自变量时，对transshimmer拟合的线性回归模型调整后的 R^2 较高，这3个因素能够解释transshimmer变异的8.4%。此时，影响最大的因素是性别，女性的transshimmer更低，声带振幅更稳定。此外，纬度对transshimmer的影响较湿度更大，纬度与transshimmer有显著的正相关关系，纬度越高，嗓音表现越差。湿度对transshimmer有显著的负影响，湿度越高，嗓音表现越好。

表7 transshimmer 的多元线性回归分析模型

模型	湿度	纬度	地理方位（北方）	性别（女性）	性别（混合性别）	调整后 R^2
1	0.027	0.060 **	0.133 **	-0.210 **	-0.135 **	0.086
2	-0.064 **	0.097 **	——	-0.198 **	-0.145 **	0.084
3	——	0.150 **	——	-0.197 **	-0.146 **	0.083
4	-0.144 **	——	——	-0.201 **	-0.149 **	0.081

4. 讨论

首先，本文40个方言点录音样本体现较高的自相关性。在多元线性回归分析前，我们对40个方言点的 transjitter 和 transshimmer 数据进行了 D-W 检验（Durbin Watson test），检验结果显示，DW（transjitter）< 0.2，DW（transshimmer）<1.1，40个方言点具有较高的自相关性。也即，由于方言点数量不足、分布不均，本次分析得出的结论对于40个方言点内部的解释力更强。要得出更为可靠的方言嗓音表现与影响因素结果，需要增加样本量，平衡方言点在各可能的影响因素中的分布情况。就目前的数据而言，纬度、湿度是对嗓音表现影响最大的两个地理环境因素，湿度越大，嗓音表现越好；纬度越低，嗓音表现越好。湿度对 jitter 的影响较湿度更大，纬度对 shimmer 的影响较湿度更大。

其次，实验结果部分，通过自变量偏度、与嗓音表现相关性2个参数，排除了经度、海拔因素进入回归分析。需要补充说明的是，由于关于地理环境因素与嗓音表现关系的研究较少，我们仍然探索性地以包含经度、海拔在内的6种因素为自变量，嗓音表现为因变量进行了多元线性回归分析。两个模型中，海拔都被排除在影响因素之外；经度的标准化系数则是所有影响因素中最高的。我们推测，这是由于地理方位、纬度、湿度这3个重要因素共线性较高，且40个方言点在东经100°至125°内较为集中，具有较高的自相关性。

我们认为，本文40个方言点嗓音表现的数据对汉语声调是否更可能产生于南方地区的讨论有重要意义。就实验结果而言，湿度较高、纬度较低的地方嗓音表现较好，与［16］的观察结果类似，且大致趋势是声调数量与 jitter 和 shimmer 都存在显著的负相关关系，基本符合［5］［16］关于声调语言与嗓音表现关系的推测。然而，必须承认的是，随着声调增多，不同方言的 jitter 和 shimmer 并非严格单调下降；回归模型的调整后 R^2 有限，说明备选因素的解释力不强。因此，要解释或预测具体某个地方声调产生与否或声调数量多少，目前我们所考虑的因素和模型尚不成熟。日后的研究需考虑结合其他可能的环境及各类影响因素。

最后，需要说明的是，由于方言传统上在特定区域内使用，本文并没有严格区分方言和方言所在地域。我们认为，地域自然环境及在此环境中形成、演化的方言都可能影响 jitter 和 shimmer 的表现，因此，可以直接以方言发音人在方言区的嗓音表现进行对比。本文分析使用的是由2000年前后的磁带语料转录的数字录音，但一方面同一批录音材料具有一定同质性，另一方面已有研究验证了录音材料与数字信号嗓音表现的相关性。实验通过多元线性回归的方法，以汉语方言为例探索了一种语言在不同地理区域上的嗓音声学表现的差异。具体地说，本文考察了可能影响嗓音表现的6种因素在40个汉语方言点中对 jitter 和 shimmer 的实际影响，发现湿度、纬度等方言点的自然特征对 jitter 和 shimmer 有显著影响，海拔等自然特征则没有显著影响。这为语言/方言的微观声学差异、自然环境与嗓音表现的内在关联等研究提供了一定依据。

5. 致谢

本文为国家社科基金重大项目“中国境内语言核心词汇声学数据库及计算研究”（19ZDA300）的成果之一。李爱军、贾媛、曾晓渝等老师为本文前期语料的获取提供了帮助；匿名审稿人对本文提出了细致中肯的修改意见，一并在此谨致谢忱。

参考文献

[1] Asiaee, M., Vahedian－Azimi, A., Atashi, S. S., et al. 2020. Voice quality evaluation in patients with COVID－19: An acoustic analysis. *Journal of Voice* in press.

[2] Brockmann, M., Drinnan, M. J., Storck, C., et al. 2011. Reliable jitter and shimmer measurements in voice clinics: the relevance of vowel, gender, vocal intensity, and fundamental frequency effects in a typical clinical task. *Journal of Voice* 25 (1), 44－53.

[3] Demirhan, E., Unsal, E. M., Yilmaz, C., et al. 2016. Acoustic voice analysis of young Turkish speakers. *Journal of Voice* 30 (3), 378. e21－378. e25.

[4] Esling, J. H. 2000. Crosslinguistic aspects of voice quality. In: Kent, R. D., Ball, M. J. (eds), *Voice Quality Measurement*. San Diego: Singular Publishing, 25－35.

[5] Everett, C., Blasi, D. E., Roberts, S. G. 2015. Climate, vocal folds, and tonal languages: Connecting the physiological and geographic dots. *Proceedings of the National Academy of Sciences* 112 (5), 1322－1327.

[6] Finkelhor, B. K., Titze, I. R., Durham, P. L. 1988. The effect of viscosity changes in the vocal folds on the range of oscillation. *Journal of Voice* 1 (4), 320－325.

[7] Gelfer, M. P., Fendel, D. M. 1995. Comparisons of jitter, shimmer, and signal－to－noise ratio from directly digitized versus taped voice samples. *Journal of Voice* 9 (4), 378－382.

[8] Hemler, R. J. B., Wieneke, G. H., Dejonckere, P. H. 1997. The effect of relative humidity of inhaled air on acoustic parameters of voice in normal subjects. *Journal of Voice* 11 (3), 295－300.

[9] Kong, J. 2008. A study on jitter, shimmer and f0 of mandarin infant voice by developing an applied method of voice signal processing. *Congress on Image and Signal Processing* 5, 314－318.

[10] Lieberman, P. 1961. Perturbations in vocal pitch. *The Journal of the Acoustical Society of America* 33 (5), 597－603.

[11] Sorensen, D., Horii, Y. 1983. Frequency and amplitude perturbation in the voices of female speakers. *Journal of Communication Disorders* 1, 57－61.

[12] Sundberg, J., Rossing, T, D. 1986. *The science of the singing voice*. De Kalb, Illinois: Northern Illinois University Press.

[13] Sussman, J. E., Sapienza, C. 1994. Articulatory, developmental, and gender effects on measures of fundamental frequency and jitter. *Journal of Voice* 2, 145－156.

[14] Teixeira, J. P., Gonçalves, A. 2014. Accuracy of jitter and shimmer measurements. *Procedia Technology* 16, 1190－1199.

[15] Teixeira, J. P., Oliveira, C., Lopes, C. 2013. Vocal acoustic analysis－jitter, shimmer and hnr parameters. *Procedia Technology* 9, 1112－1122.

[16] 冉启斌：《嗓音的南北差异与汉语声调产生的地域先后》，《语言研究》2020年第4期，第46—53页。

[17] 王遵娅、丁一汇、何金海、虞俊：《近50年来中国气候变化特征的再分析》，《气象学报》2004年第2期，第228—236页。

[18] 杨强、李焦兰、黄治物、陈辉霖、蔡韵琴、邓世和：《国人嗓音与性激素的关系》，《听力学及言语疾病杂志》1994年第1期，第1—4页。

[19] 叶志腾：《应用 Praat 软件分析成人嗓音声学参数》，硕士学位论文，福建医科大学，2009年。

[20] 于萍、韩冰、杨伟炎、韩东一：《不同性别嗓音客观检测参数的对比分析》，《听力学及言语疾病杂志》2004年第6期，第390—392、403页。

[21] 郑景云、方修琦、吴绍洪：《中国自然地理学中的气候变化研究前沿进展》，《地理科

学进展》2018年第1期，第16—27页。

许　可　南开大学汉语言文化学院，硕士在读，主要研究领域为实验语音学。
E-mail：xuke015@163.com

黄　玮　南开大学汉语言文化学院，硕士在读，主要研究领域为实验语音学。
E-mail：hwhw97@163.com

梁煜珠　南开大学文学院，博士在读，主要研究领域为实验语音学。
E-mail：minzu.ken@qq.com

冉启斌　南开大学文学院，博士，主要研究领域为实验语音学。为本文通讯作者。
E-mail：ranqibin@126.com

普通话单双音节声母唇形协同发音研究

梁昌维

摘　要　本文对汉语普通话单双音节声母起始位置的唇形在不同环境下的协同发音现象进行研究，结果发现：单音节中后接圆唇元音对声母产生的逆向协同发音影响是显著的，使唇高度、宽度、下颌高度等关键参数显著降低；u 做主元音时相比介音 u 能使前置辅音达到更圆唇的协同发音动作，i 和 ü 没有这样的效应；汉语普通话的卷舌声母唇形在协同发音中更倾向于保持自身较开的唇形，抵消下颌的闭合和后接圆唇元音的协同发音作用；卷舌韵母有类似的特性，并可以在协同发音中对后音节的声母产生增大唇开度、减小唇宽度的作用；协同发音中唇形与下颌的互动在不同环境下可能产生一致或不一致的运动；圆唇元音对后音节起始辅音的顺向协同发音作用使非唇音声母的唇宽度显著减小，并使唇高度分布更加聚集。

关键词　唇形，协同发音，汉语普通话，辅音，声母

Lip Coarticulation of Initials in Monosyllables and Disyllables in Mandarin Chinese

LIANG Changwei

Abstract This paper studied the coarticulation of the lip gesture in initials of Mandarin monosyllables and disyllables in different contexts. It was found that rounded vowels have significant regressive coarticulatory effect on preceding initials, leading to lower lip width, height and jaw opening. Also, /u/ in the syllable nucleus caused the preceding initials to have more round lip gestures than the prenuclear /u/, and such an effect was not found in the case of /i/ and /ü/ in both prenuclear and nuclear positions. Retroflex initials tended to keep their lip shapes more open, offsetting the lip rounding and jaw closing coarticulatory effect triggered by the following rounded vowels. Retroflex vowels showed similar effects, rendering the initials in the following syllables in an articulatory configuration with lips more open but narrower in width. Jaw and lips may be subject to consistent or inconsistent coarticulatory effects in different contexts. Rounded vowels may have significant progressive coarticulatory effect on the initials of the following syllables, decreasing the lip width and making the lip height in aggregated distribution.

Key words Lip, Coarticulation, Mandarin Chinese, Consonant, Initial

1. 引言

早期的语音学研究已经意识到唇形与语音之间存在联系，并将唇形作为描述一些元音的重要特征。20 世纪以来，随着声学技术手段的进步，唇形圆展与语音声学特征的联系逐渐得到研究；继而，言语感知研究的深入也使得包括视觉信息的可视语音成为语音学研究的重要部分。

协同发音，宽泛地讲，指的是这样的事实，即音系中的音段在所有环境中的实现并非完全相同，而是经常发生明显的变化，变得更接近相邻的或附近的音段[8]。其中后音段对前音段的影响则称为逆向协同发音，而前音段对后音段的影响称为顺向协同发音。

唇是发音器官中最容易观测的部分。早期对唇形及其协同发音的研究主要基于直接观测，总结出圆—展对立的区别特征。唇形在声学上主要表现为唇辐射的高

频提升作用，以及圆唇导致的第二、第三共振峰下降［6］。汉语普通话中的辅音都没有固定的目标唇形［18］，除唇辅音受到以唇为调音部位的限制以外，其他辅音受元音环境的影响都很明显。

内外唇宽度之和被认为是可以区别圆展唇的主要特征［19］，此外，唇开度、唇突度、唇面积、唇圆度也被作为区分圆展唇、作用大小各异的特征之一，唇开度也被认为在展唇和圆唇元音之间存在明显差异［20］。

已有的关于唇形协同发音的研究主要集中在元音，特别是VCnV序列的唇形时域转换，形成了几个主要模型，即前瞻模型［9］、锁时模型［1］等，前者认为非圆唇到圆唇的动作变化是平滑过渡，后者认为该过渡动作需要固定的时长，混合模型［13］则认为圆唇动作分为缓慢平滑变化的低速相，以及快速变化、需要固定时长的高速相。Löfqvist［11］提出了关于发音姿态的理论，认为每个语音单位的发音动作在时间上对其周围其他单位的影响呈现钟形分布，Cohen和Massaro［2］基于此实现了一个说话人头部模型。此类研究的主要关注点仍然在于构建适当的模型以模拟发音姿态参数的时域变化及其交互作用，而未及直接测量辅音在不同环境下协同发音的实际状态。

而关于辅音的唇形协同发音的研究比元音更少。大部分语言的辅音没有圆—展唇对立。法语的/ʃ，ʒ/被认为存在伴随的唇突动作，而/s，z/存在伴随的唇内收动作［3］，Faber［5］在其他语言上也有类似的发现。Farentani［7］认为，唇突动作延长前腔以降低擦音的中心频率，使龈后擦音/ʃ，ʒ/和龈擦音/s，z/的物理差异更大，更容易区分。McAllister［12］和Engstrand［4］指出，/uCu/条件下的辅音唇动作会在两个圆唇元音中间有所放松，以保证辅音的强度和动作。

随着技术的进步，利用多种形式的数据进行的语音多模态研究逐渐开展起来［16］，我们已可以对音节起始处的唇形进行直接的测量和研究。唇形协同发音的研究将作为面向语音合成、言语感知等方面的研究工作的一部分，加深我们对言语活动规律的认识。

2. 数据的采集与处理

2.1 录像的采集和面部标记点的标注

录像用的单音节表包括普通话1261个带调音节，双音节词表则依据“普通话水平测试用普通话词语表”［15］，除去多音节词和录像错误外，共计有11522个双音节词。

录像在北京大学中文系录音室进行。录像文件的像素为720×576，帧率为每秒25帧，录音采样率为48000Hz，单声道。发音人为一位在北京电视台工作的播音主持专业人员，女性，普通话一级甲等。

我们使用Dlib库［10］中的功能进行图像处理和人脸关键点检测。我们使用其中的人脸检测器，对所录视频的每一帧进行人脸检测，并对识别到的人脸范围使用Dlib库中提供的已经训练好的机器学习人脸关键点检测模型，进行68个人脸标记点的自动检测（见图1）。该工作由复旦大学潘晓声实施。

图1 68个面部标记点的定义［14］

2.2 数据的提取和处理

为获取声母唇形的协同发音特性，我们选取单音节字的声学起点所对应的视频帧和双音节词第二个音节的声学起点对应的视频帧用于数据提取。我们采用Matlab2016b软件，基于能量和短时过零率曲线的语音端点检测技术，获取每个单音节语音开始处和双音节第二音节开始处的视频帧。

我们使用下列参数表现唇形特征：外唇垂直高度（人中到外唇最下端的垂直距离，52号点与58号点纵坐标的垂直距离）、内唇垂直高度（内唇最高点到内唇最低点的垂直距离，63号点与67号点纵坐标的垂直距离）、外唇水平宽度（外唇最左端到外唇最右端的水平距离，49号点与55号点横坐标的水平距离）、内唇水平宽度（内唇最左端到内唇最右端的水平距离，61号点与65号点横坐标的水平距离）、下颌高度（使用下颌最低处的9号点到鼻下端的34号点纵坐标的垂直距离）。提取上述参数后，我们将视频每帧中的所有参数除以该帧的头部宽度（1号点与17号点的水平距离）进行归一化处理，以消除摄像机远近差异的影响。在后面的数据分析中，我们将内外唇宽度相加，作为一个“唇宽度”参数；将内外唇高度相加，作为一个“唇高度”参数。

数据的统计分析使用SPSS20软件进行，统计时对样本的5个参数进行统计特征计算和统计检验。画图时则使用内外唇高度之和、内外唇宽度之和、下颌高度，每张图选取其中两个参数做二维图。未经说明时，画图的每个数据点是该标签条件下各样本的平均值。

3. 单音节声母唇形的协同发音

3.1 圆唇环境声母的协同发音

圆唇环境是最有特点的声母协同发音环境。圆唇条件下双唇内撮，唇展开的程度和开口的程度都因此减小，因而可以推测在圆唇条件下前置声母的唇高度、宽度、下颌高度、唇面积等参数都可能会减小，而唇突度、唇圆度等参数可能会有所上升。下文将对圆唇环境下的前置声母的唇高度、宽度、下颌高度等参数的分布进行分析。由于本文采用的样本是不同的音节，5个参数的分布不一定满足正态性，因此需要使用非参数检验方法对样本均值差异是否显著进行统计检验。本文使用Mann－Whitney U检验进行统计检验，判断两组样本均值差异是否显著。

本节将所有单音节按四呼分类，即以i、u、ü为主元音或介音的三类各为一类，其余为一类，对i类—ü类和u类—开口类这两组中圆唇是否使前置声母的5个参数产生显著差异进行检验。

3.1.1 i类—ü类

i类—ü类的唇宽度—唇高度分布如下。其中，＊号黑色为ü类，＋号灰色为i类。

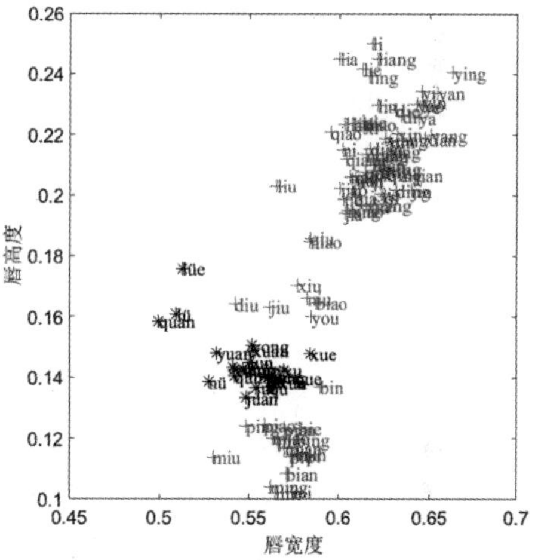

图2 i类—ü类的唇宽度—唇高度分布

图2中，除唇音声母明显处于唇高度最小的范围以外，ü类的唇高度和唇宽度分布整体上小于i类。ü类的5个参数均相对i类有所下降，其中唇高度参数的下降最为明显。

对5个参数做Mann－Whitney U检验，5个参数均为显著（$p < 0.001$），可以认为ü类的内外唇宽度、高度和下颌高度均显著低于i类。也即，ü元音的圆唇在声母开始位置已经使整个唇的宽度和高度显著减小了。

3.1.2 u类—开口类

u类—开口类的唇宽度—唇高度分布如图3所示。其中，＊号黑色为u类，＋号灰色为开口类。

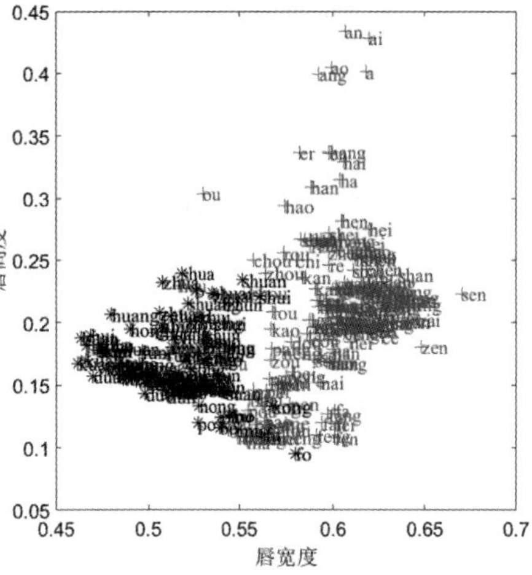

图3 u类—开口类的唇宽度—唇高度分布

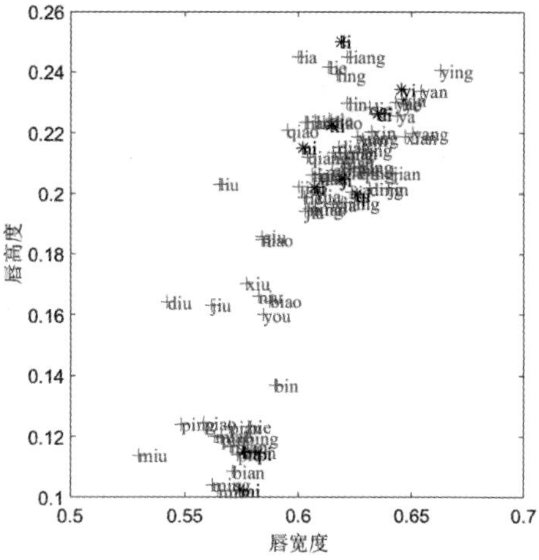

图4 i元音类和i介音类的唇宽度—唇高度分布

图3中，u类的唇宽度分布整体上明显小于开口类。u类的5个参数均值相对开口类有所下降，其中唇高度参数的下降更为明显。对5个参数做Mann－Whitney U检验，5个参数均为显著（$p<0.001$），可以认为u类的内外唇宽度、高度和下颌高度均显著低于开口类。也即，u元音的圆唇在声母开始位置已经使整个唇的宽度和高度显著减小了。

综上所述，后接圆唇元音对声母产生的逆向协同发音影响是显著的，在声母开始的位置，整个唇的高度和宽度以及下颌高度均在后接圆唇元音条件下显著低于非圆唇条件，以上参数均是圆唇协同发音特征的表现。

3.2 高元音作介音与主元音时的差异

汉语普通话中，高元音i、u、ü既可以作介音又可以作主元音。它们作为主元音和介音时是否对辅音协同发音产生不同的影响，这是值得关注的问题。我们对此进行了分析，并发现了有趣的情况。

3.2.1 i主元音与i介音

i元音类和i介音类的唇宽度—唇高度分布如图4所示。其中，＊号黑色为i元音类，＋号灰色为i介音类。

可以看出，i元音条件下与i介音条件下前置声母唇宽度、唇高度的分布以及5个参数的均值差异都不大。对5个参数做Mann－Whitney U检验，差异均不显著（$p>0.05$）。可以认为，i元音条件下与i介音条件下前置声母的唇形协同发音动作的差异不显著。

3.2.2 u主元音与u介音

u元音类和u介音类的唇宽度—唇高度分布如下。其中，＊号黑色为u元音类，＋号灰色为u介音类。

图5中u元音类的分布范围似乎比u介音类的唇高度略低，其均值也有一定的差异。对5个参数做Mann－Whitney U检验可以看到与i类明显不同的状况。u为主元音和介音的情况下，除外唇宽度外的四个参数的差异均为显著（$p<0.001$）。也即，u元音条件下，前置声母的协同发音存在比u介音条件下更显著的圆唇动作，达到更小的唇高度和宽度；前置声母的唇形受到u元音和u介音明显不同的逆向协同发音作用。

3.2.3 ü主元音与ü介音

ü元音类和ü介音类的唇宽度—唇高度分布如图6所示。其中，＊号黑色为ü元音类，＋号灰色为ü介音类。

可以看出，ü元音条件下与ü介音条件

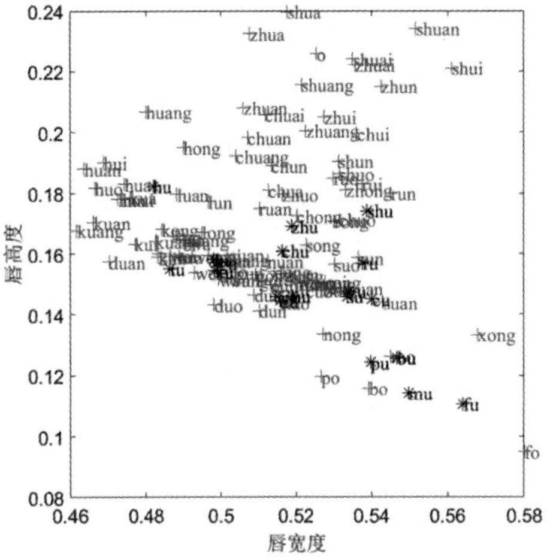

图5 u元音类和u介音类的唇宽度—唇高度分布

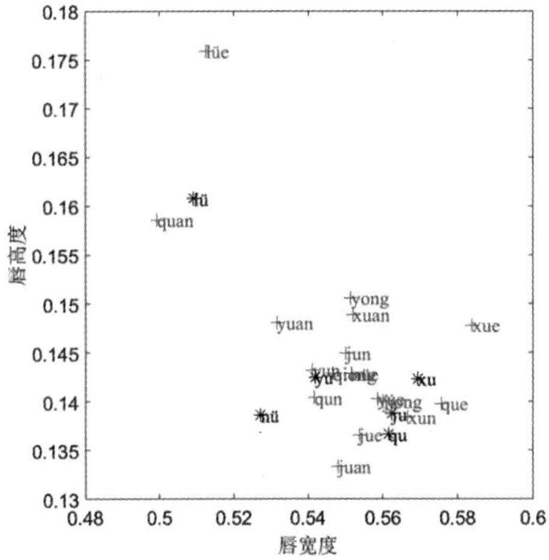

图6 ü元音类和ü介音类的唇宽度—唇高度分布

件下前置声母唇宽度、唇高度的分布差异不大，5个参数的均值差异也不大。对5个参数做Mann - Whitney U检验，5个参数均不显著（$p > 0.05$）。可以认为，ü元音与ü介音条件下前置声母的唇形协同发音差异不显著。

综上所述，我们可以发现，在做介音和元音时对前置辅音唇形协同发音影响的一致性上，u与i、ü有着不同的表现。两个前高元音在介音和主元音位置上对前置辅音产生了一致的唇形协同发音作用，而u做主元音时会比做介音时对前置辅音的圆唇程度产生更强的影响，使前置辅音达到更圆唇的动作。

我们可以从语音动作的控制上推测这一差异的原因。/u/做介音时，其发音动作可能受到时长限制而被截短，因而不能到达标准/u/元音的圆唇程度和舌位。动作控制不同，元音/u/和介音/u/对前置辅音的协同发音作用因而不同。相比来说，前高元音/i/和/y/较少地受到这种作用的影响，在介音位置上其发音动作也通常是比较到位的。因此，它们在主元音和介音位置上对前置辅音的协同发音作用的程度体现出相对一致的状况。

3.3 卷舌声母的特殊性

从前面图5中已经可以注意到，后接u元音条件下不同前置声母的协同发音动作分布在较大的范围，其中卷舌声母分布在有一定差异的空间范围内，如图7所示。其中，＊号黑色为卷舌声母类，＋号灰色为其他声母类。

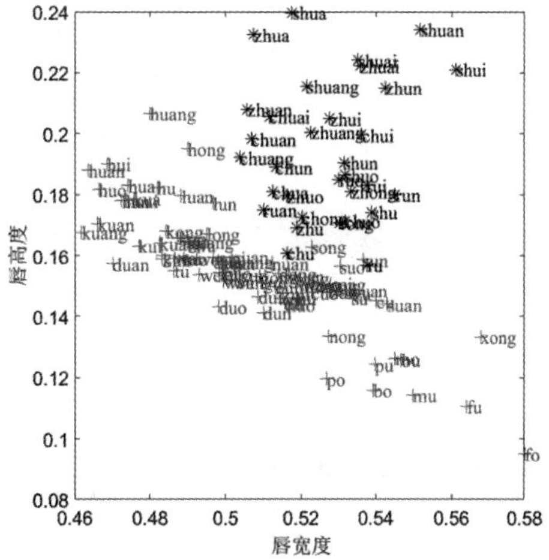

图7 u元音条件下的唇宽度—唇高度分布

我们可以明显地看到，卷舌声母后接

u 的情况下，其声母起始位置的唇高度分布明显要大于其他声母。在唇高度方向上，卷舌声母更大程度保持其唇部特有的发音动作。相比于很多没有唇部目标动作的声母，卷舌声母在后接 u 环境下有更大的唇高度。从均值上看也可以得出相似的判断。Mann – Whitney U 检验结果符合预期，除下颌高度外的四个参数均为显著（$p < 0.05$）。可见，卷舌声母会在一定程度上抵抗 u 的圆唇协同发音影响，保持略大的唇开度和唇宽度。这与前人“/ʃ，ʒ/存在唇突动作”的论断可能是相似的状况。汉语卷舌声母与法语龈后擦音/ʃ，ʒ/具有比较相似的发音部位和声学性质，在各自的音系中也与声学上相近的齿龈塞擦音、擦音占据类似的对立位置，其唇形动作的特殊性可能与/ʃ，ʒ/有类似的感知的动机。

从另一个角度观察参数也能发现卷舌声母的特殊性。图 8 每个点为一个音节，黑色文字标注的为卷舌声母，斜直线为拟合曲线。

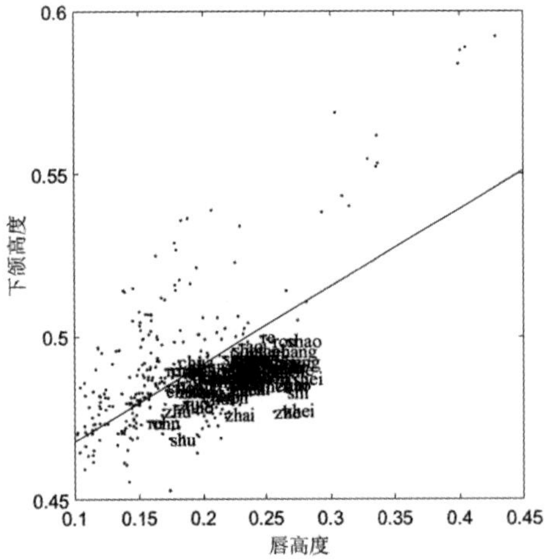

图 8　所有音节的下颌高度—唇高度

将各音节的下颌高度—唇高度画在图 8 中，可以看到数据点主要分布在左下—右上的对角线周围，其拟合曲线是 $y = 0.2381x + 0.4439$。如果不受唇的调音动作影响，唇高度与下颌高度应该是接近正相关的状态，而特殊的调音动作会使其偏离直线。可以看到，卷舌声母的数据点几乎全部处在拟合直线下方，相当一部分点处在拟合直线下方较远的位置。也即，卷舌声母的唇高度倾向于达到比下颌开度所对应的正常唇高度更大的位置。虽然由于卷舌动作的需要，下颌达到了更闭的位置，但唇形仍然保持较开的状态。

综合上述分析，可以认为，汉语普通话的卷舌声母唇形在协同发音中相比其他声母更倾向于保持自身较开的唇形，对于下颌的闭合和后接圆唇元音的协同发音作用有一定程度的抵消。这可能是为了保持卷舌声母区别于其他声母的声学、视觉或感知特征。

3.4　介音—主元音配合与唇—颌运动的互动

前文提到，下颌高度—唇高度图中偏离拟合曲线较远的音节声母可能有特殊的协同发音作用或下颌、唇形动作。偏离于曲线下方的主要是前文所述的卷舌声母。图 9 将所有音节画在了同一张图上，每个点为一个音节，观察图 9 中偏离拟合曲线上方的点也可以发现一些有趣的现象。

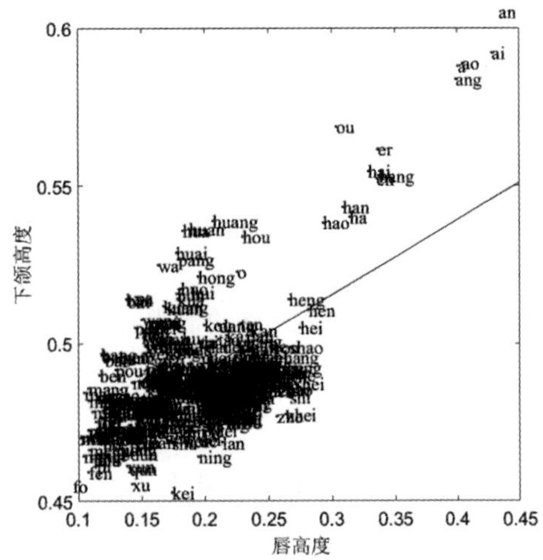

图 9　所有音节的下颌高度—唇高度

我们可以看到，图 9 右上方偏离拟合曲线的点主要是以 a 和 ha 开头的音节。汉语的h/x/声母虽然被认为是软腭擦音，但其实际调音情况是很不稳定的，在协同发音中h可以比g、k更容易地被后接元音同化，成为与后接元音调音动作接近的擦音。而a类元音需要的较大开口度，在不受辅音影响的零声母音节和受辅音影响很小的h声母音节中，则很容易达到很大的开口度；而唇形并没有对应地产生下颌那么大幅度的运动。

在拟合曲线的左上方较远处，我们还可以看到“零声母/h声母+u介音+中低元音”和“唇音声母+中低元音”的组合出现在这些位置上，如huang、pa等音节。这些音节的起始唇形在u介音和唇音声母的双重限制下达到很闭的、唇高度很小的程度，但后接的中低元音使得下颌已经预先打开，致使这些数据点偏离了拟合曲线。也即，下颌的协同发音运动显然也存在前瞻模型的过程，在唇形尚保持在很闭的状态的时候已经预判了下一个调音动作，并在较少地影响前面的闭口音段调音的情况下预先实行了这一预判。

综上所述，协同发音中下颌的运动和唇的运动在不同环境下存在复杂的互动，二者通常保持一致的开合变化，但在特定条件下呈现出不一致的互动。声母本身或介音的协同发音要求圆唇、唇高度宽度缩小时，后接主元音的协同发音作用可能同时使下颌下降到与唇高度变化相背离的位置；声母本身的唇形要求也可能抵抗后接元音的协同发音作用，使唇形高度的减小程度远小于后接元音协同发音通常所能造成的影响，也使唇形高度的减小未能达到与下颌抬升程度相配合的程度。唇形与下颌受到协同发音的影响可能使其运动一致性减小。

4. 双音节词第二音节声母唇形的协同发音

双音节词为第二音节声母唇形提供了前后两个环境，因此双音节的声母唇形协同发音将比单音节更复杂。前音节开头的声母距离第二音节太远，因此研究的主要目标是第二音节的开头声母，探讨这些声母在受到第二音节元音协同发音影响的同时如何受到第一音节末音段的圆唇动作的影响。

4.1 对典型圆唇元音的顺向协同发音的检验：uCi、wCi、üCi

我们在第一音节的结尾选择典型的圆唇元音：u韵母、u韵尾（画图时记作w以示区别）和ü韵母，在第二音节的首元音为典型的展唇元音i的情况下，研究中间的第二音节首辅音唇形受到第一音节末元音的影响。

4.1.1 uCi

图10展示了前元音u对后接音节声母唇形参数的影响。其中，灰色*为uCi条件下数据点的分布，黑色+为单音节Ci条件下的数据点。

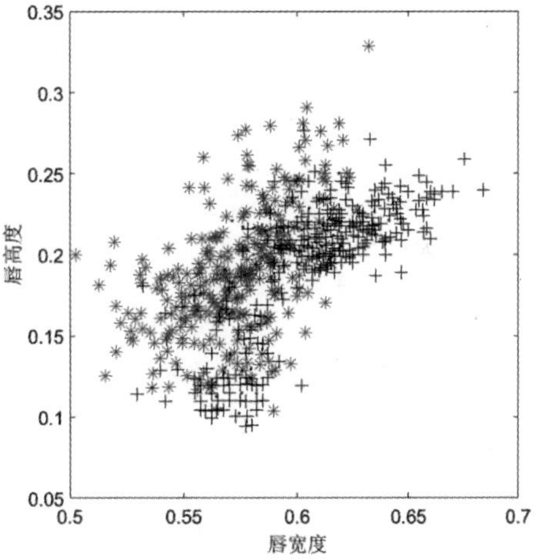

图10 前元音u对后音节声母的唇形影响

可以发现，在前音节u情况下，Ci的唇宽度分布小于单音节的情况，标准差也显示唇高度分布更聚集。对5个参数做Mann-Whitney U检验，除外唇高度外均属显著（$p<0.05$），可以认为位于Ci前的前音节u主元音对后音节辅音的唇形产生了显著的协同发音效应，其效应主要使内外唇宽度明显降低，但对高度的影响较小；前音节的u抑制了后音节在i影响下的展唇色彩。

4.1.2　wCi

图11展示了前韵尾u对后接音节声母的唇形参数的影响。其中,灰色*为wCi条件下数据点的分布,黑色+为Ci条件下的数据点。

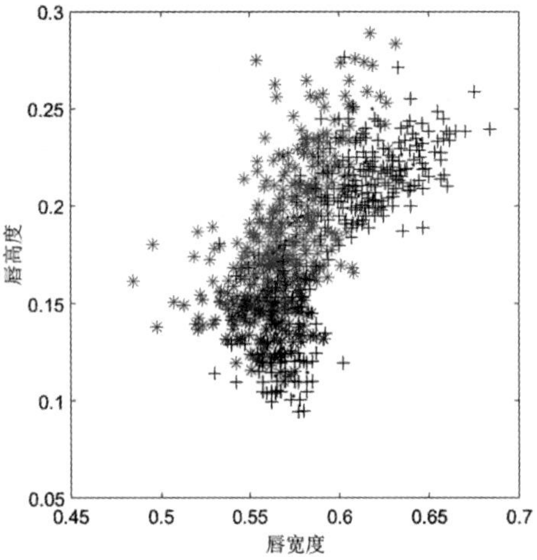

图11　前韵尾u对后音节声母的唇形影响

本类的词例较多,数据点更密集。在前音节u韵尾的情况下,Ci的唇宽度和唇宽度的分布均小于单音节的情况,同时分布的分散程度更低。对5个参数做Mann-Whitney U检验,各参数均为显著($p<0.001$),据此认为位于Ci前的前音节u韵尾对后音节辅音的唇形的高度、宽度和下颌高度均产生了显著的协同发音效应,使上述唇形参数均出现了显著的减小,辅音起始处唇形比无前置u韵尾的情况下更圆。

4.1.3　üCi

图12展示了前元音ü对后接音节声母唇形参数的影响。其中,灰色*为üCi条件下数据点的分布,黑色+为单音节Ci条件下的数据点。

与uCi的情况类似,前音节ü情况下Ci的唇宽度分布同样小于单音节的情况,基于标准差可以认为唇高度分布更聚集。对5个参数做Mann-Whitney U检验,本类也呈现与uCi类接近的特征,除内外唇高度外各参数差异显著($p<0.001$),可

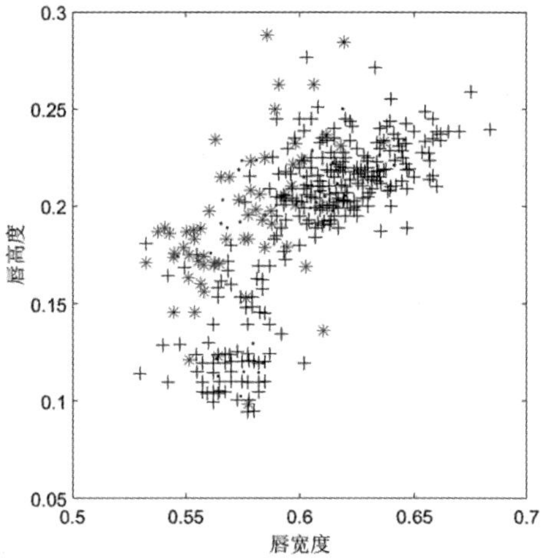

图12　前元音ü对后音节声母的唇形影响

以认为,位于Ci前的ü对后音节辅音的唇形产生了显著的协同发音影响,内外唇宽度受此影响明显降低,但唇高度受到的影响不明显。

以上3类典型圆唇元音对后音节起始辅音的顺向协同发音呈现相似的分布特征:非唇音声母的唇宽度显著减小,而唇高度也分布更聚集。可见,前音节圆唇的限制对后音节起始辅音的唇形的协同发音作用使唇形的变异程度减小,并将前音节圆唇的唇宽度特征加在了后音节起始辅音上。

4.2　唇形的限制:ʅCi

前文提出普通话卷舌辅音呈现出与其他辅音不同的唇形协同发音特性,这些辅音有自身的唇形特征,其唇形受到协同发音的影响相对其他辅音更小。与这些辅音完全同部位的元音/ʅ/是否也可以将其唇形特征通过协同发音影响后接的辅音?下面将对此进行分析。

图13展示了前元音/ʅ/对后接音节声母的唇形参数的影响。其中,灰色*为ʅCi条件下数据点的分布,黑色+为Ci条件下的数据点。

观察数据点的分布和均值可以判断在前置/ʅ/条件下唇宽度有一定程度的下降,

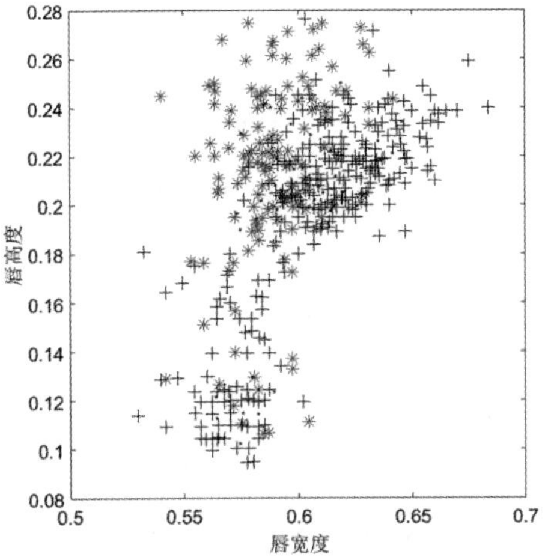

图13 前置元音/ʅ/对后音节声母的唇形影响

而唇高度存在较明显的上升，这可能是/ʅ/元音自身接近圆唇的动作对后接辅音的协同发音影响。对5个参数做Mann - Whitney U检验，5个参数的差异均为显著（$p<0.05$）。也即，前置/ʅ/元音的条件确实像前置圆唇元音的条件一样，显著地降低了唇宽度；同时，与卷舌辅音在协同发音中倾向于保持其唇高度的特征类似，前置/ʅ/元音也显著地提高了后置辅音的唇高度，呈现出独特的协同发音模式。

5. 结论和讨论

经过本文的分析，可以得出以下结论。

在单音节中，后接圆唇元音对声母产生的逆向协同发音影响是显著的，在声母开始的位置整个唇的高度和宽度以及下颌高度均在后接圆唇元音条件下显著低于非圆唇条件，唇高度、宽度和下颌高度参数均是圆唇协同发音特征的表现。

高元音u与i、ü在做介音和主元音时对前置辅音唇形协同发音影响的一致性上有不同的表现。两个前高元音在介音和主元音位置上对前置辅音产生比较一致的唇形协同发音影响，而u做主元音时会比做介音时对前置辅音的圆唇程度产生更显著的影响，使前置辅音达到更圆唇的协同发音动作，这可能是其发音动作机制所导致的。

汉语普通话的卷舌声母唇形在协同发音中，相比其他声母，特别是相比没有唇部目标动作的声母，更倾向于保持自身特有的唇部动作，对于下颌的闭合和后接圆唇元音的协同发音作用有显著的抵消。卷舌韵母同样有类似的特性，并可以在协同发音中对后音节的声母产生相应的作用，使唇高度增大、宽度减小。此后的研究可以对卷舌辅音和元音此种生理特性的形成原因进行研究，从声学上和感知上验证这些特征的意义。

协同发音中下颌的运动和唇的运动在不同环境下存在复杂的互动，二者通常保持一致的开合变化，但在声母本身的唇形动作要求或前后环境的协同发音动作限制下可能呈现出不一致的互动。

圆唇元音对后音节起始辅音的顺向协同发音作用使非唇音声母的唇宽度显著减小，并使唇高度分布更聚集。前音节圆唇的协同发音作用使后音节起始辅音唇形的变异程度减小，并将前音节圆唇的唇宽度特征加在了后音节起始辅音上。

本文仍有很多未尽之处，同样的材料也有条件从更多切入点进行研究。例如，如果可以进行基于时域变化的唇形参数提取，对双音节唇形来说可能获得更清晰、更容易解释的协同发音规律。

进一步的研究也需要将协同发音的具体特征实现在发音人模型上，建立由有生理和物理意义的规则参数驱动的发音人面部模型，为语音合成与其他研究和应用提供更优的言语视觉信息。

6. 致谢

本研究受到教育部基地重大项目“基于语音多模态的语音本体研究”（17JJD740001）资助。本文受到北京大学孔江平教授指导，文中视频面部参数提取由复旦大学潘晓声博士实现，在此谨致感谢。

参考文献

[1] Bell – Berti, F. , Harris, K. S. 1981. A temporal model of speech production. *Phonetica* 38 (1 –3), 9 –20.

[2] Cohen, M. M. , Massaro, D. W. 1993. Modeling coarticulation in synthetic visual speech. *In: Magnenat – Thalmann, N. , Thalmann, D. (eds), Models and Techniques in Compnter Animation. Japar.* Springer, 139 – 156.

[3] Descout, R. , Boë, L. J. , Abry, C. 1980. Labialité vocalique et labialité consonantique, Labialité et Phonétique, *Publications de l' Université des Langues et Lettres de Grenoble*, 111 –26.

[4] Engstrand, O. 1981. Acoustic constraints or invariant input representation? An experimental study of selected articulatory movements and targets, *Reports from Uppsala University Department of Linguistics*7, 67 –95.

[5] Faber, A. 1989. Lip protrusion in sibilants. *The Journal of the Acoustical Society of America* 86, S1, TT4.

[6] Fant, G. 1973. *Speech Sounds and Features*. Cambridge, MA, US: The MIT Press.

[7] Farnetani, E. 2006. Labial coarticulation. In: Hardcastle, W. J. , Hewlett, N. (eds), *Coarticulation: Theory, Data and Techniques*. Cambridge: Cambridge University Press: 144 – 163.

[8] Hardcastle, W. J. , Hewlett N. 2006. Introduction. In: Harolcastle, W. J. , Hewlett, N. (eds) *Coarticulation: Theory, Data and Techniques.* Cambridge: Cambridge University Press: 1 –4.

[9] Keating, P. A. 1988. The window model of coarticulation: articulatory evidence. *Papers in Laboratory Phonology I*26, 451 –470.

[10] King, D. E. 2009. Dlib – ml: A Machine Learning Toolkit. *Journal of Machine Learning Research*, 10, 1755 – 1758.

[11] Löfqvist A. 1990. Speech as audible gestures. In: Teager, H. M. , Teager, S. M. (eds) *Speech Production and Speech Modelling*. Dordrecht: Springer, Dordrecht: 289 – 322.

[12] McAllister, R. 1978. Temporal asymmetry in labial co – articulation, *Papers from the Institute of Linguistics, University of Stockholm* 35, 1 –29.

[13] Perkel, J. S. 1986. Preliminary support for a hybrid model of anticipatory coarticulation. *Proceedings of the 12th International Conference of Acoustics.*

[14] Sagonas, C. , et al. 2013. 300 faces in – the – wild challenge: The first facial landmark localization challenge. *Proceedings of the IEEE International Conference on Computer Vision Workshops.*

[15] 国家语言文字工作委员会:《普通话水平测试实施纲要》,商务印书馆 2004 年版。

[16] 孔江平:《语音多模态研究和多元化语音学研究》,《中国语音学报》2008 年第 1 辑。

[17] 李英浩:《基于动态腭位的汉语普通话协同发音研究》,《中国语音学报》2017 年第 7 辑。

[18] 潘晓声:《汉语普通话唇形协同发音及可视语音感知研究》,博士学位论文,北京大学,2011 年。

[19] 潘晓声、孔江平:《普通话圆唇研究》,《语言学论丛》2014 年第 2 期,第 96—108 页。

[20] 吴宗济、林茂灿、鲍怀翘:《实验语音学概要》(增订本),北京大学出版社 2014 年版。

梁昌维 北京大学中国语言文学系语言学实验室,博士研究生,主要研究领域为实验语音学、言语产生。
E-mail: s. l. c. m. t@ 163. com

附录 统计数据

3.1.1 单音节声母唇形：i 类—ü 类

附表1　i类—ü类的5个参数的统计特征

类型		外唇宽度	内唇宽度	外唇高度	内唇高度	下颌高度
i	均值	0.3181	0.2895	0.1516	0.0406	0.4817
	N	279	279	279	279	279
	标准差	0.01144	0.01971	0.02060	0.02369	0.00902
ü	均值	0.3031	0.2459	0.1367	0.0076	0.4724
	N	68	68	68	68	68
	标准差	0.00824	0.01683	0.00813	0.00416	0.00910

附表2　i类—ü类的Mann-Whitney U检验

	外唇宽度	内唇宽度	外唇高度	内唇高度	下颌高度
Mann-Whitney U	2603.500	876.000	4170.000	3421.500	4199.000
Wilcoxon W	4949.500	3222.000	6516.000	5767.500	6545.000
Z	-9.282	-11.609	-7.168	-8.180	-7.132
渐近显著性（双侧）	0.000	0.000	0.000	0.000	0.000

3.1.2 单音节声母唇形：u 类—开口类

附表3　u类—开口类的5个参数的统计特征

类型		外唇宽度	内唇宽度	外唇高度	内唇高度	下颌高度
u	均值	0.2907	0.2203	0.1488	0.0158	0.4892
	N	353	353	353	353	353
	标准差	0.01051	0.01827	0.01584	0.01370	0.01711
开口	均值	0.3155	0.2805	0.1613	0.0480	0.4956
	N	557	557	557	557	557
	标准差	0.01109	0.01889	0.03387	0.03221	0.02601

附表4　u类—开口类的Mann-Whitney U检验

	外唇宽度	内唇宽度	外唇高度	内唇高度	下颌高度
Mann-Whitney U	10537.500	3318.500	67454.500	40122.000	83778.000
Wilcoxon W	73018.500	65799.500	129935.500	102603.000	146259.000
Z	-22.723	-24.588	-7.988	-15.065	-3.763
渐近显著性（双侧）	0.000	0.000	0.000	0.000	0.000

3.2.1 单音节声母唇形：i 主元音与 i 介音

附表5　i 元音类—i 介音类的5个参数的统计特征

类型		外唇宽度	内唇宽度	外唇高度	内唇高度	下颌高度
i 元音	均值	0.3172	0.2919	0.1498	0.0399	0.4803
	N	44	44	44	44	44
	标准差	0.00995	0.01679	0.02599	0.02651	0.01127
i 介音	均值	0.3183	0.2891	0.1520	0.0408	0.4819
	N	235	235	235	235	235
	标准差	0.01171	0.02021	0.01948	0.02319	0.00854

附表6　i 介音类—i 元音类的 Mann-Whitney U 检验

	外唇宽度	内唇宽度	外唇高度	内唇高度	下颌高度
Mann-Whitney U	4888.000	4715.000	5020.000	5167.000	4905.000
Wilcoxon W	5878.000	32445.000	32750.000	32897.000	5895.000
Z	-.574	-.926	-.305	-.006	-.540
渐近显著性（双侧）	0.566	0.354	0.760	0.995	0.589

3.2.2 单音节声母唇形：u 主元音与 u 介音

附表7　u 元音类—u 介音类的5个参数的统计特征

类型		外唇宽度	内唇宽度	外唇高度	内唇高度	下颌高度
u 元音	均值	0.2926	0.2297	0.1394	0.0092	0.4770
	N	68	68	68	68	68
	标准差	0.01053	0.01843	0.01481	0.00720	0.01004
u 介音	均值	0.2902	0.2180	0.1511	0.0173	0.4922
	N	285	285	285	285	285
	标准差	0.01047	0.01753	0.01526	0.01440	0.01715

附表8　u 介音类—u 元音类的 Mann-Whitney U 检验

	外唇宽度	内唇宽度	外唇高度	内唇高度	下颌高度
Mann-Whitney U	8337.000	6307.500	5733.000	5811.500	3771.000
Wilcoxon W	49092.000	47062.500	8079.000	8157.500	6117.000
Z	-1.790	-4.474	-5.235	-5.134	-7.831
渐近显著性（双侧）	0.073	0.000	0.000	0.000	0.000

3.2.3 单音节声母唇形：ü主元音与ü介音

附表9　ü元音类—ü介音类的5个参数的统计特征

类型		外唇宽度	内唇宽度	外唇高度	内唇高度	下颌高度
ü元音	均值	0.3031	0.2457	0.1362	0.0067	0.4719
	N	21	21	21	21	21
	标准差	0.00795	0.01762	0.00879	0.00455	0.01112
ü介音	均值	0.3031	0.2461	0.1369	0.0081	0.4726
	N	47	47	47	47	47
	标准差	0.00844	0.01665	0.00792	0.00395	0.00818

附表10　ü介音类—ü元音类的Mann-Whitney U检验

	外唇宽度	内唇宽度	外唇高度	内唇高度	下颌高度
Mann-Whitney U	480.500	492.500	449.500	363.000	467.000
Wilcoxon W	1608.500	1620.500	680.500	594.000	698.000
Z	-.173	-.013	-.584	-1.736	-.352
渐近显著性（双侧）	0.863	0.989	0.559	0.083	0.725

3.3 单音节声母唇形：卷舌声母的特殊性

附表11　后接u类的卷舌声母与非卷舌声母的5个参数的统计特征

类型		外唇宽度	内唇宽度	外唇高度	内唇高度	下颌高度
非卷舌	均值	0.2883	0.2180	0.1449	0.0102	0.4903
	N	268	268	268	268	268
	标准差	0.01008	0.01905	0.01466	0.00657	0.01869
卷舌	均值	0.2980	0.2274	0.1606	0.0332	0.4849
	N	83	83	83	83	83
	标准差	0.00813	0.01336	0.01212	0.01558	0.00822

附表12　后接u类的卷舌声母与非卷舌声母的Mann-Whitney U检验

	外唇宽度	内唇宽度	外唇高度	内唇高度	下颌高度
Mann-Whitney U	5064.000	7494.500	4249.000	1483.000	10023.500
Wilcoxon W	41110.000	43540.500	40295.000	37529.000	13509.500
Z	-7.503	-4.492	-8.511	-11.943	-1.360
渐近显著性（双侧）	0.000	0.000	0.000	0.000	0.174

4.1.1 双音节词第二音节声母唇形：uCi

附表13　uCi条件与单音节Ci条件下的5个参数的统计特征

类型		外唇宽度	内唇宽度	外唇高度	内唇高度	下颌高度
Ci	均值	0.3181	0.2895	0.1516	0.0406	0.4817
	N	279	279	279	279	279
	标准差	0.01144	0.01971	0.02060	0.02369	0.00902
uCi	均值	0.3086	0.2647	0.1528	0.0365	0.4765
	N	304	304	304	304	304
	标准差	0.01164	0.01514	0.01856	0.02115	0.01252

附表14　uCi条件与单音节Ci条件下两类的Mann-Whitney U检验

	外唇宽度	内唇宽度	外唇高度	内唇高度	下颌高度
Mann-Whitney U	23814.000	14353.000	39562.500	35482.000	29501.000
Wilcoxon W	70174.000	60713.000	85922.500	81842.000	75861.000
Z	−9.153	−13.809	−1.401	−3.409	−6.354
渐近显著性（双侧）	0.000	0.000	0.161	0.001	0.000

4.1.2 双音节词第二音节声母唇形：wCi

附表15　wCi条件与单音节Ci条件下的5个参数的统计特征

类型		外唇宽度	内唇宽度	外唇高度	内唇高度	下颌高度
Ci	均值	0.3181	0.2895	0.1516	0.0406	0.4817
	N	279	279	279	279	279
	标准差	0.01144	0.01971	0.02060	0.02369	0.00902
wCi	均值	0.3060	0.2628	0.1468	0.0306	0.4761
	N	449	449	449	449	449
	标准差	0.01132	0.01414	0.01727	0.02063	0.01242

附表16　uCi条件与单音节Ci条件下两类的Mann-Whitney U检验

	外唇宽度	内唇宽度	外唇高度	内唇高度	下颌高度
Mann-Whitney U	27919.000	18177.500	47330.000	45614.000	42080.000
Wilcoxon W	128944.000	119202.500	148355.000	146639.000	143105.000
Z	−12.585	−16.116	−5.548	−6.171	−7.452
渐近显著性（双侧）	0.000	0.000	0.000	0.000	0.000

4.1.3 双音节词第二音节声母唇形：üCi

附表17　üCi条件与单音节Ci条件下的5个参数的统计特征

类型		外唇宽度	内唇宽度	外唇高度	内唇高度	下颌高度
Ci	均值	0.3181	0.2895	0.1516	0.0406	0.4817
	N	279	279	279	279	279
	标准差	0.01144	0.01971	0.02060	0.02369	0.00902
üCi	均值	0.3081	0.2673	0.1539	0.0391	0.4679
	N	64	64	64	64	64
	标准差	0.01015	0.01671	0.01724	0.02067	0.01247

附表18　üCi条件与单音节Ci条件下两类的Mann-Whitney U检验

	外唇宽度	内唇宽度	外唇高度	内唇高度	下颌高度
Mann-Whitney U	4449.000	3611.500	8528.500	7842.500	2813.500
Wilcoxon W	6529.000	5691.500	10608.500	9922.500	4893.500
Z	-6.262	-7.432	-.558	-1.518	-8.550
渐近显著性（双侧）	0.000	0.000	0.577	0.129	0.000

4.2 双音节词第二音节声母唇形：ʅCi

附表19　ʅCi条件与单音节Ci条件下的5个参数的统计特征

类型		外唇宽度	内唇宽度	外唇高度	内唇高度	下颌高度
Ci	均值	0.3181	0.2895	0.1516	0.0406	0.4817
	N	279	279	279	279	279
	标准差	0.01144	0.01971	0.02060	0.02369	0.00902
ʅCi	均值	0.3125	0.2769	0.1573	0.0565	0.4707
	N	140	140	140	140	140
	标准差	0.00875	0.01303	0.01711	0.02216	0.01000

附表20　ʅCi条件与单音节Ci条件下两类的Mann-Whitney U检验

	外唇宽度	内唇宽度	外唇高度	内唇高度	下颌高度
Mann-Whitney U	13491.500	11726.000	17109.500	11546.500	7702.500
Wilcoxon W	23361.500	21596.000	56169.500	50606.500	17572.500
Z	-5.165	-6.675	-2.070	-6.830	-10.118
渐近显著性（双侧）	0.000	0.000	0.038	0.000	0.000

昆剧净和老生行当情感念白发声研究

黄慧怡　董　理

摘　要　本文以昆剧净和老生行当的念白为研究对象，通过对喉头仪信号特征的分析，考察了四种情感（中性、悲伤、愤怒和高兴）下两个行当念白的发声特点。通过对音高、接触商的分布特征及二者的共变关系的探讨，得出结论：不同行当不同情感的音高和接触商分布具有显著差异；相同情感下不同行当的音高和接触商分布具有显著差异；在高、中、低三个音高区域内，各情感的嗓音选择策略不同；老生和净在念白中都使用了正常嗓音和紧嗓音等发声类型；相较于中性念白，悲伤和高兴念白会部分使用较松的嗓音，愤怒则更多地使用较紧的嗓音；老生比净使用了更多比例的较松嗓音且嗓音类型更丰富。本研究的结果显示，情感和行当特征对念白的嗓音特征都有影响，且行当特征影响情感的表达策略。

关键词　净，老生，情感念白，喉头仪

A Study on the Emotional Stage Speech of Colorful Face Role and Old Man Role in Kunqu Opera

HUANG Huiyi　DONG Li

Abstract The voice characteristics of the stage speech with four emotions (neutral, sad, angry and happy) were investigated for two Kunqu Opera male roles, the Colorful Face Role and the Old Man Role. Two parameters, pitch and contact quotient, were extracted from the electroglottographic signals. The distribution characteristics of the pitch and the contact quotient and the correlativity between these two parameters showed that: 1) the distribution of pitch and contact quotient both showed significant differences between emotions and between roles; 2) the phonation strategies differed between emotions in each of three pitch ranges; 3) both the Colorful Face Role and the Old Man Role adopted the modal voice and the pressed voice in their stage speech; 4) compared to the neutral stage speech, the sad and the happy stage speeches were observed to have more voices with low vocal fold adduction degree, while the angry stage speech showed more voices with high adduction degree; 5) the Old Man Role used more voices with low vocal fold adduction degree than the Colorful Face Role, and showed richer phonation variations. This study indicated that both emotions and features of a role affected the voice characteristics, and the features of the role also influenced the emotional expression strategies.

Key words Colorful Face Role, Old Man Role, Emotional stage speech, Electroglottography

1. 引言

昆剧是我国传统戏曲中最古老的剧种之一，其语音表现形式主要包括演唱和念白两大类。正如民间谚语“千金话白四两唱”所云，念白的难度和重要性更甚于演唱。昆剧的角色可以按照性别、年龄、性格等特征由不同的演员来呈现，演员的基本分类被称为行当，行当下又分为不同的家门。各行当均具有自身独特的发音特点[11]。

净和老生是昆剧中两种主要的男性行当，其饰演的角色类型导致两个行当的发声共性与差异兼具。老生通常扮演正直刚毅有地位的中年或老年男子，表演大多庄重、沉着和老练，其嗓音要求高亢宽亮。净行角色的脸谱颜色与其性格特征一致，如红面通常扮演威武刚毅、忠义赤诚、富有正义感的人物，以忠臣、帝王、神灵为

多；黑面通常扮演勇猛刚烈、粗鲁豪爽的大将军或英雄好汉。净的嗓音浑厚洪亮，表演以威武沉毅、粗豪雄浑为基调［11］。按照传统演唱理论，这两个行当都使用大嗓来演唱和念白，因此其嗓音存在很多相似之处。但是由于角色特点的差异，二者在用嗓上会做出调整，使其更符合角色的年龄与性格，如净会使用比老生更紧的嗓音来演唱［4］。

前人研究表明，在表达不同情感时，发声类型会随之变化［1］，且发音人的性别、年龄等特征也会影响情感表达的策略，进而影响语音的声学特征［6，7］。净和老生的音高、音强和长时平均功率（LTAS，Long－Term－Average Spectra）分析结果显示，行当间参数特征不同，且可能受到情感色彩的影响［3，5］。在语音形式更为灵活的念白中，这两个行当也可能表现出发音策略上的异同。这些特征一方面诠释了昆剧中老年男性语音审美的特点；另一方面展示了不同角色特征带来的情感表现策略的差异，对进一步认知此类源于生活而高于生活的语音情感表达方式及其复杂性有积极贡献。因此，本文尝试从发声的角度对净和老生行当的情感诠释策略加以探索。

发声信息通常可以使用声学信号或喉头仪（EGG）信号来获取。前者需要通过逆滤波手段来获取声源信号，此种方法在基频高、音色转换迅速的艺术嗓音中会受到较大的影响，导致声源信号提取不理想。与之相对，后者可以直接用于发声类型的判断，尤其适用于正常嗓音和紧嗓音等声门完全闭合的发声类型。前人研究表明，从EGG信号中获取的基频、开商、速度商和音调抖动可以用来区分不同的嗓音类型［10］。在艺术嗓音中，与开商相对应的接触商能够较稳定地反映出声带接触面积的变化［4］。当接触商变大时，声带接触面积增大，声音更紧；反之亦然。接触商也会受到基频的影响。在正常嗓音中，基频与接触商成正比［10］，在较高的基频范围内，基频上升带来的声带拉长会导致接触商随基频的上升而下降［4］。

在前人研究的基础上，本文将从嗓音特征入手，对昆剧净和老生行当的情感念白进行分析，并尝试回答以下问题：（1）净及老生行当不同情感念白中嗓音参数的分布特征是否存在差异；（2）在表达相同情感时，两个行当运用嗓音的策略是否一致；（3）角色特征如何影响嗓音策略。

2. 方法

本文邀请了四位国家级昆剧演员作为发音人，净和老生各两位。其中两位净（净1和净2）和一位老生（老生1）来自江苏省演艺集团，另一位老生（老生2）主要就职于上海昆剧团。录音时演员根据要求自行选择了四种感情色彩（中性、悲伤、高兴和愤怒）的念白段落，每种感情色彩4段，同行当的两位演员选择段落不完全一致。两位净演员选择了剧目《钟馗嫁妹》《宝剑记》《单刀会》《牡丹亭》里的段落，两位老生演员都选择了剧目《烂柯山》《琵琶记》《长生殿》《浣溪沙》里的段落，此外，老生1还选择了《荆钗记》《寻亲记》《一捧雪》《千忠戮》的段落，老生2还选择了《牡丹亭》《桃花扇》《连环计》《奇双会》的段落。演员先按照舞台形式演绎念白段落，再用普通话说出念白词。后者使用了最平常的发音方式，作为正常嗓音的信号来源与艺术嗓音形成对照。

录音在安静的房间完成，同时采集了语音和EGG两路信号，采样频率为40kHz，量化精度为16bit。录音材料先以句子为单位进行切分，邀请5位非戏剧背景的普通听众对其进行情感判断，如一半以上听众认定该句念白带有某种情感，就把这句念白认定为情感鲜明的语音素材，作为本研究的分析对象。最后的分析对象中，净1共129句、净2共102句、老生1共125句、老生2共215句。

参数提取使用了基于Matlab平台的VoiceLab 1.0，该程序对喉头仪信号先用二阶小波变换的方法去除了低频抖动和高频噪声，随后计算出基频和接触商，其中接触商的计算使用了35%的尺度算法（如

图1所示)，即以EGG振幅的35%的位置作为声带接触段的起止点，并用接触段时长除以周期计算出接触商。每周期对应一个基频数据和一个接触商数据，作为分析的原始数据。

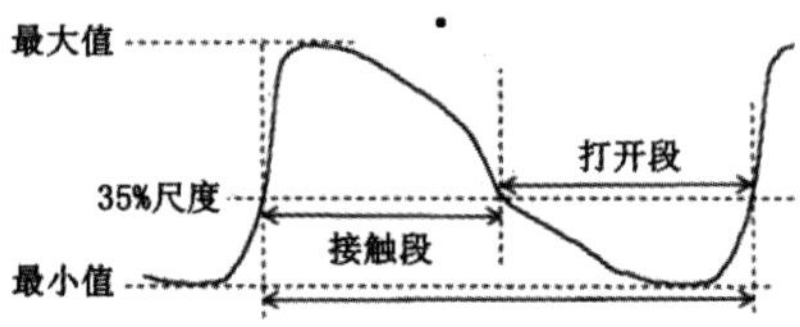

图1　EGG接触商35%算法示意图

先手动剔除原始数据前0.5%和后0.5%的数值（置信区间99%），后导入SPSS中进行统计分析，其中基频被转换为半音形式，见公式1。

$$P_i = 39.86 \times \lg \frac{F0_i}{F0_{ref}}, i = 1,2,3,\ldots,n \quad (1)$$

其中，P_i为i帧的音高，n为帧数，$F0_i$为i帧的基频测量值，$F0_{ref}$为基频参考值，本文设为55Hz，220Hz对应24半音。

所有的均值和标准差都是通过SPSS的描述统计功能计算得出的。在下文3.3部分分析接触商随音高的变化规律时，通过SPSS的描述统计功能得出四种情感每个半音取整后接触商对应的均值和标准差。由于音高和接触商数据都不满足正态分布，所以后文3.1和3.2节使用塔姆黑尼T2（Tamhane's T2）检验对音高和接触商数据四种情感两两进行了差异显著性检验，具体使用SPSS的比较平均值的单因素分析中的事后多重比较功能完成。此外，通过SPSS一般线性模型单变量中的功效估计功能计算得出。偏η^2，作为效应量估算值的参考指标，则通过SPSS一般线性模型的单变量中的功效估计功能完成用于净和老生接触商的效应量估算。做图皆通过Origin软件完成。

3. 结果

3.1　净和老生的音高分布特征

表1显示了净和老生演员音高的均值和标准差。从均值上看，净和老生四种情感念白的音高要明显高于普通话的音高，悲伤、愤怒和高兴的音高均值都略大于中性。从标准差上看，两位净演员和老生1四种情感念白的音高变化要明显比普通话的丰富，老生2的和普通话的比较接近。净和老生愤怒和高兴的音高变化幅度都小于中性，两位净演员和老生2悲伤的音高都比中性的变化略丰富，老生1则相反。两位净演员愤怒、高兴的音高变化都小于中性，其中净2更明显。两位老生演员愤怒和高兴的音色变化都小于中性，且两者的四种情感的音高变化差异都较小，其中老生2的尤其小。塔姆黑尼T2检验结果显示，各行当不同情感间的音高差异均显著，且与普通话的音高也具有显著差异（$p<0.05$）。

表1　净和老生的音高均值（半音）与标准差（半音）

情感	参数 \ 发音人	净1	净2	老生1	老生2
悲伤	均值	29.2	29.9	29.7	28.2
	标准差	6.1	6.3	5.9	5.8
愤怒	均值	30.1	32.2	30.3	31.1
	标准差	6.0	5.1	5.3	4.9
高兴	均值	28.3	30.9	29.7	28.2
	标准差	6.2	5.1	5.2	5.1
中性	均值	27.1	29.7	25.6	27.3
	标准差	6.7	6.1	6.5	5.4
普通话	均值	15.9	15.9	16.9	18.6
	标准差	3.2	3.3	4.2	5.8

行当间相比，均值上，净的普通话的均值小于老生，但净四种情感的音高均值整体上却大于老生，这说明净行演员在念白中使用了更高的基频，且与自身发音条

件无关。两个行当在表达情感时存在诸多共性：二者愤怒、悲伤和高兴的音高均值都大于中性；二者愤怒的音高均值都最大。标准差上，净的普通话标准差小于老生，但净四种情感的音高标准差大于老生，这说明净在表达念白情感时音高变化比老生更丰富。净与老生愤怒和高兴的音高变化都小于中性。老生1的某些特征与老生2不一致，而与净一致：净和老生1悲伤的音高变化小于中性，老生2则相反；净和老生1中性的音高变化都相对最丰富，老生2悲伤的音高变化最丰富。塔姆黑尼T2检验结果显示，相同情感下两行当间的音高差异均显著（$p<0.05$）。

图2和图3显示了净和老生的音高参数的分布细节。箱线图中间的横线代表中位数，箱线图两端代表1/4和3/4位点，线的两端代表5%和95%位点，下文箱线图亦同。四分位距反映了核心数据的分散程度，线的长度反映了数据多样化的程度。

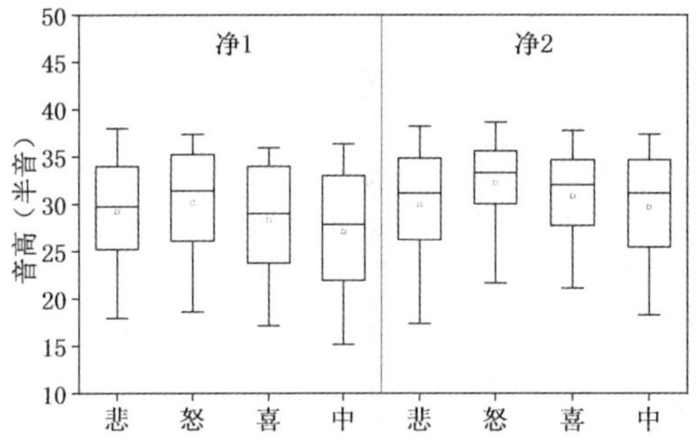

图2 净的音高分布箱线图

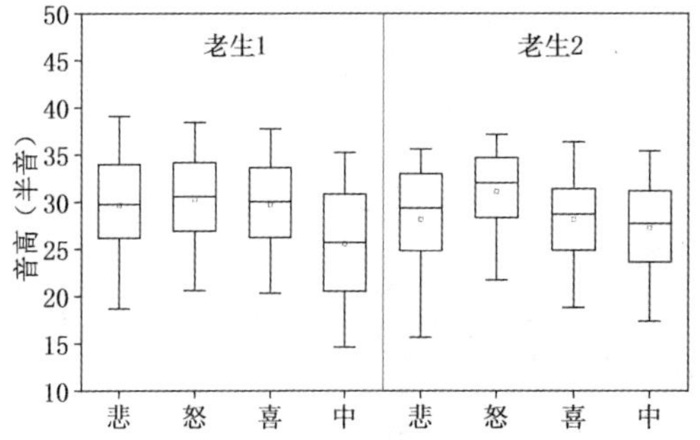

图3 老生的音高分布箱线图

从四分位距来看，两位净演员悲伤的音高分散程度相似，其他情感音高分布从分散到集中依次为中性、高兴和愤怒。老生愤怒和高兴的音高分散程度相似，且都比中性和悲伤的分散程度明显要低，即数据分布更为集中。行当间相比，两个行当都表现为中性音高数据最分散，在悲伤和中性的关系上，行当间表现出交叉相似现象，即净1与老生1相似，而净2与老生2相似。

从箱线图两端线的长度来看，净表现为悲伤音高多样性最强，高兴最弱，两位演员愤怒的多样性差异较大。老生也表现为悲伤音高多样性最强，其与愤怒和中性多样性差异较大，两位演员高兴的多样性差异较大。行当间相比，两个行当数据多样性相似，且都表现为悲伤的多样性最强。净行内部一致性较高，老生1表现与净行相似，老生2则不同。

从中位数和各位点的位置关系来看，两个行当的数据均表现为中位数以上数据集中、中位数以下数据分散，这种不对称现象在净行当中更为明显，暗示着净比老生更倾向于通过降低音高去丰富念白的音高变化。

3.2 净和老生的接触商参数

表2显示了净和老生的接触商均值与标准差。从均值上看，净和老生的全部念白均使用了比正常说话更紧的嗓音；净的悲伤、愤怒和高兴念白在发声时声带都比中性念白更紧，其中悲伤与中性较为接近，愤怒和高兴在演员间表现不一致。老生愤怒的念白在演员间表现相似，且都比其他情感嗓音更紧，悲伤、高兴和中性的差异相对较小。从标准差上看，两个行当念白的嗓音松紧变化都比正常说话丰富，悲伤的音色变化都最为丰富；净高兴的音色变化丰富性弱于中性，老生则相反；愤怒在行当间表现出交叉相似的情况，即净1与老生2相似，净2与老生1相似。塔姆黑尼T2检验结果显示，各行当不同情感间的接触商差异均显著，且与普通话的接触商也具有显著差异（$p<0.05$）。

表2　净和老生的接触商均值与标准差（%）

情感＼参数＼发音人		净1	净2	老生1	老生2
悲伤	均值	61.3	65.5	61.7	57.3
	标准差	9.0	7.3	10.0	10.6
愤怒	均值	64.6	65.6	64.6	65.5
	标准差	6.9	5.8	8.5	7.4
高兴	均值	61.9	67.9	64.3	56.0
	标准差	7.9	4.8	7.1	8.8
中性	均值	60.3	64.6	63.0	57.7
	标准差	8.3	5.6	6.7	8.3
普通话	均值	52.6	56.8	52.1	49.8
	标准差	5.6	4.5	5.6	6.0

行当间相比，根据塔姆黑尼T2检验结果，相同情感下两行当间的接触商差异均显著（$p<0.05$）。从均值上看，净的接触商大于老生，尤其在愤怒情感下二者最为接近，在悲伤和高兴情感下二者差异较大。从标准差上看，老生的标准差都大于净，暗示着净的嗓音相对老生更为集中。

图4和图5显示了净和老生的接触商的分布细节。从图中可以发现，各行当两位演员接触商的分散程度差异较大。两位净演员均表现为中性的接触商数据最分散，悲伤的数据次之，高兴和愤怒的接触商在演员间表现不一致。老生演员均表现为悲伤的接触商数据最分散，中性和高兴的分散程度一致，愤怒的接触商在演员间表现不一致。与标准差所示一致，愤怒念白特征在行当间表现出交叉相似。

结合箱线图两端线的长度，相同情感下同行当两位演员的数据分布范围更为接近。从线的长度来看，两位净演员均表现为悲伤多样性最强、中性多样性最弱，愤怒和高兴与中性相似。老生演员念白的多样性均表现为悲伤比中性和愤怒更多样，高兴比中性更多样，演员间高兴和愤怒的差异略大。

从中位线和各位点的分布位置来看，净和老生演员中位线以上的数值都相对集中，中位线以下的数值相对分散，其中净的数据不对称性略大于老生。从箱线图下端线和上端线的长度来看，净和老生的四种情感都表现为下端线比上端线长，这意味着净和老生都倾向于用放松程度不同的嗓音去丰富念白的音色。不对称性最大的情感在行当间也存在交叉相似的情况，净2和老生1是悲伤念白最不对称，而另两位演员是愤怒最不对称。值得注意的是，部分情感中下端线的位置低于普通话的接触商均值，暗示着其可能使用了部分正常嗓音。

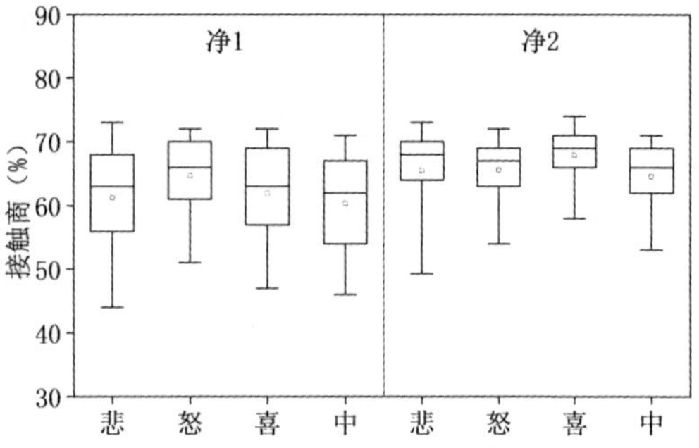

图4　净的接触商分布箱线图

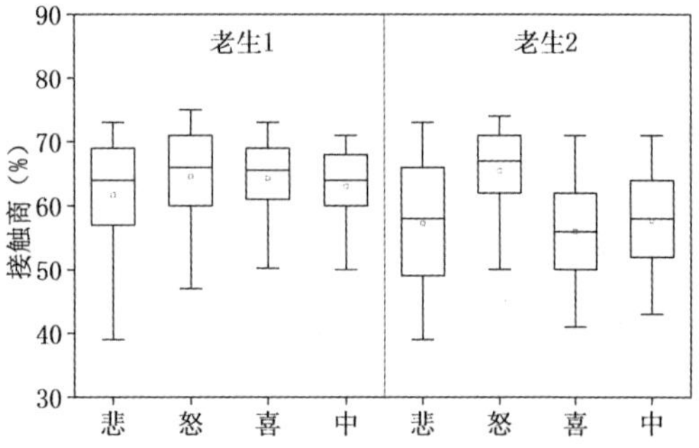

图5　老生的接触商分布箱线图

3.3　净和老生的接触商随音高的变化规律

基频和接触商数据并不独立，二者存在一定的共变关系，因此有必要分析各音高范围内接触商的分布情况，以反映各数据间产生显著差异的具体原因。

图6和图7分别呈现了两位净演员悲伤和中性情感在各半音范围内（基频转换

为半音时进行了四舍五入取整，每一半音对应多个原始基频）接触商的均值和正标准差。从变化趋势上看，接触商与音高的关系不是线性的，在不同的音高范围内，其共变方向不一致。与中性相比，同一发音人悲伤和中性的接触商随音高变化趋势相似，但情感间的差异在发音人间不完全一致。

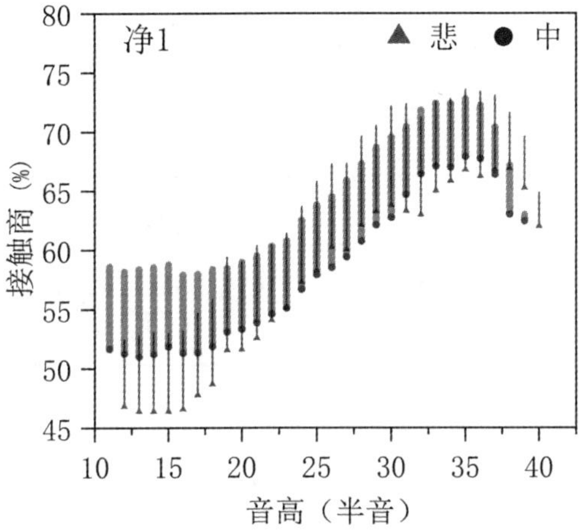

图6 净1悲伤和中性接触商随音高的变化

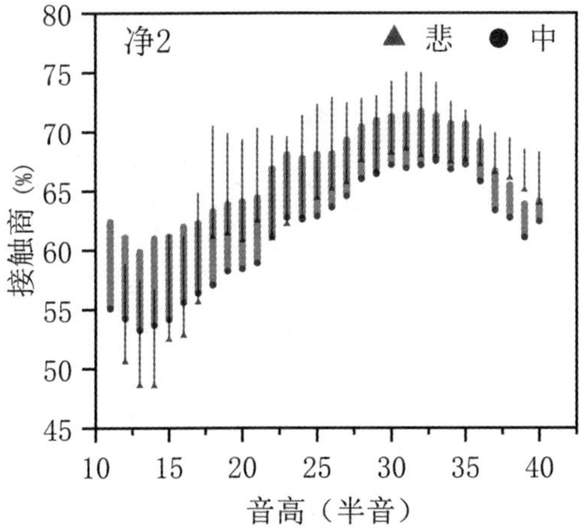

图7 净2悲伤和中性接触商随音高的变化

悲伤和中性念白的接触商随基频的变化规律在演员间略有不同，净1表现为“平、升、降”三个阶段，净2表现为“降、升、降”。在低音区域内（低于18/17半音的音高区域内，“/”前对应净1，“/”后对应净2，下同），净在中性念白中使用了与正常说话一致的正常嗓音，在悲伤中则使用了接触商更低，即更松的嗓音。在中音区域内（19—30/18—31半音），悲伤和中性接触商重叠比例较高，悲伤的接触商或递增速率大于中性，或整体高于中性。在高音区域内（31/32半音以上），悲伤的接触商随音高上升而下降的速率小于中性，二者接触商差异随之变大。以中性念白为参照，净行用在低音区域更松、高音区域更紧的嗓音来呈现悲伤情感，中音区域的发声策略在演员间不同。

标准差显示了各音高上嗓音的丰富程度。两位演员的悲伤念白在全部音域内都显示出比中性更大的接触商标准差，暗示着其包含更为丰富的嗓音变化。从标准差随音高的变化趋势上看，各演员不同情感间表现一致，演员间表现不同：净1表现为标准差先缓慢增加后减小，而净2则表现为标准差持续减小。这意味高音区域的嗓音变化比中低音区域更有局限性。从发声类型上看，从中音区域开始，净的发声类型随音高变化逐渐从正常嗓音过渡到紧嗓音。

图8显示了两位老生演员悲伤和中性接触商随音高变化的情况。从均值和标准差的变化特征可以发现，老生也可以按接触商特征将音高分为三段。在低音和中音区域，老生通过更松和更为丰富的嗓音变化来诠释悲伤情感，在高音区域，悲伤情感的嗓音变化仍比中性丰富，但在发声类型选择上演员间策略不同，老生1使用更紧的嗓音，老生2使用更松的嗓音。两位演员在低音区域使用的发声类型也不同。老生1在中性念白中几乎未使用正常嗓音，在悲伤念白中其声带振动模式比正常嗓音略紧。老生2在其中性和悲伤念白中均使用了正常嗓音。从以上特征可以发现，净和老生在诠释悲伤情感时，嗓音策略相似，仅在音域范围、松紧程度上略有差异。

图9显示了两位净演员愤怒和中性接触商随音高的变化情况。从图中可以发

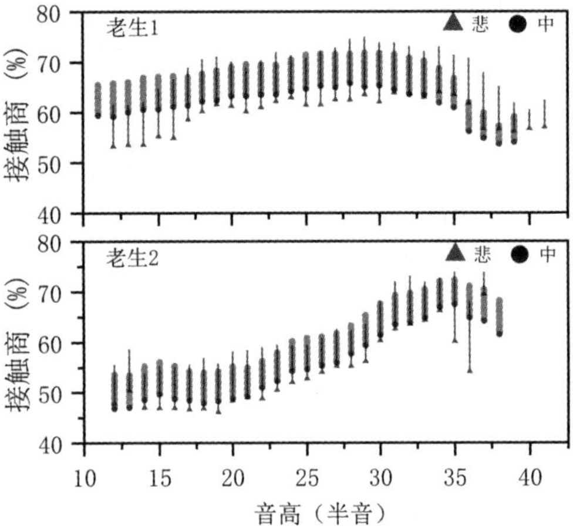

图8　老生悲伤和中性接触商随音高的变化

现，两位演员表现愤怒的嗓音策略既有共性，又有差异。其共性表现为在全部音域都通过更紧的嗓音表达愤怒情感。二者的差异表现在以下两个方面：一是在哪个音域范围内与中性情感下接触商存在较大差异，净1在中音区域愤怒与中性念白差异最明显，而净2在低音区域表现最明显；二是嗓音的多样化程度，净2通过更丰富的嗓音松紧变化来区分愤怒和中性的情感，但净1愤怒和中性的嗓音松紧变化程度相似。

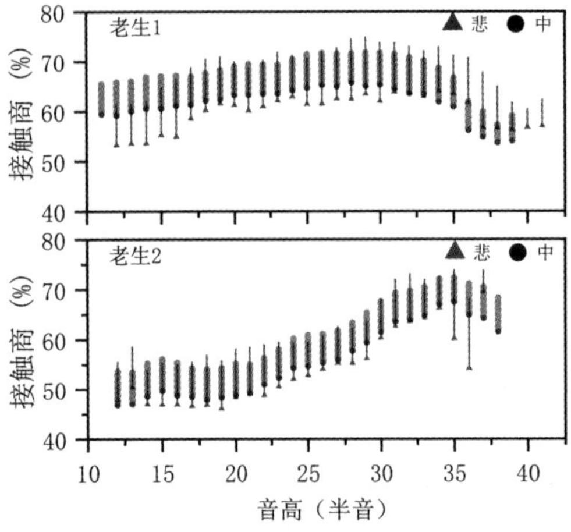

图9　净愤怒和中性接触商随音高的变化

两位老生演员表现愤怒的策略存在一定的差异，见图10。老生1通过更丰富的音色变化呈现愤怒情感，而老生2愤怒和中性的音色变化十分相似。在低音区域，老生1通过更松的嗓音区分愤怒与中性的情感，老生2则通过更紧的嗓音；中音区域，老生1嗓音松紧十分相似，难以区分情感，老生2则通过更紧的嗓音区分愤怒与中性的情感；高音区域，两位老生演员都通过更紧的嗓音区分愤怒与中性的情感，其中老生1愤怒和中性的嗓音松紧差异比老生2更大。

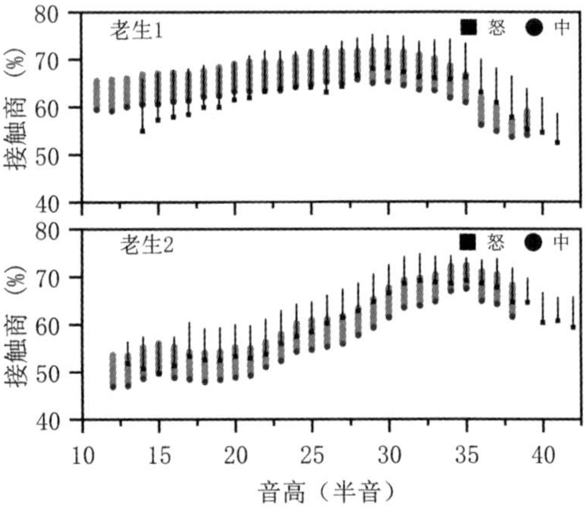

图10　老生愤怒和中性接触商随音高的变化

行当间相比，在呈现愤怒情感时，两个行当都用到了更紧的嗓音，但老生1在低音区域还通过更松的嗓音区别于中性情感。在使用更紧的嗓音表达愤怒情感时，各演员应用的音高区域不同，行当内和行当间均有差异。在音色变化的丰富程度上，行当间表现出交叉相似的情况，净2和老生1都通过更丰富的嗓音松紧变化来表现愤怒情感，而净1和老生2则与中性变化程度相似。

从图11可以发现，两位净演员在表现高兴情感时使用的策略差异较大。净1在低音区域通过更松的发声状态呈现高兴情感，而净2则在全音域范围内通过更紧的发声状态去呈现；净1在低音区域使用了比正常嗓音更松的嗓音，而净2则几乎未使用正常嗓音。二者的高兴和中性的音色变化程度十分接近，无法通过嗓音丰富程度加以区别。

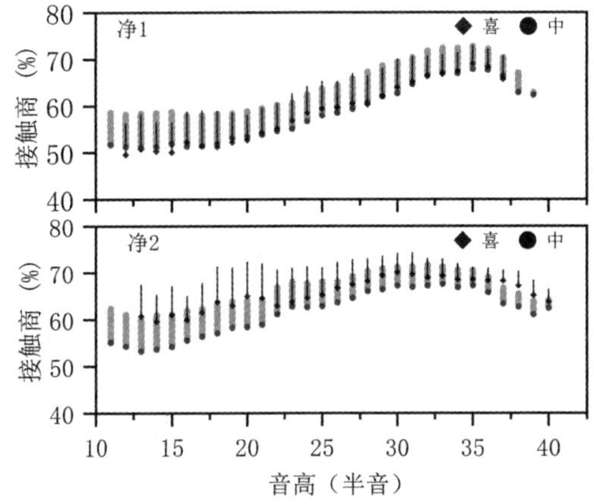

图11　净高兴和中性接触商随音高的变化

从图12可以发现，老生表现高兴情感策略与净差异较大。两位老生演员都是通过比中性更松的嗓音状态和更丰富的嗓音松紧变化程度表达高兴的情感。该策略应用的音高区域在演员间略有差异。老生1主要表现在低音和高音区域，而老生2则贯穿其整个音域。

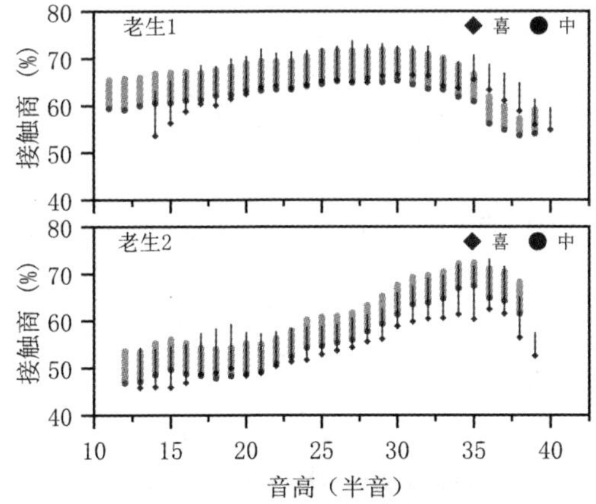

图12　老生高兴和中性接触商随音高的变化

行当间相比，在嗓音松紧程度上，净的策略不一致，净1和老生都通过比中性更松的发音状态来呈现高兴的情感，净2则通过更紧的发音状态来呈现。在嗓音松紧变化程度上，净的高兴和中性的音色变化程度十分接近，老生则通过更丰富的嗓音松紧变化表达高兴情感。

4. 讨论

当前的研究每个行当只有两位发音人，个案因素对总变异的解释比例可以通过偏 η^2 来反映。该检验需要数据满足正态分布。本文的数据不符合正态分布，在进行正态得分转换后，音高数据不符合正态分布，接触商数据符合。接触商数据偏 η^2 值见表3。当用 η^2 作方差分析效果大小的指标时，$\eta^2=0.01$ 时属于小的效果，在 $\eta^2=0.06$ 时属于中等效果，在 $\eta^2=0.14$ 时属于大的效果［9］。表3结果显示，净和老生愤怒的偏 η^2 处于小的效应量，悲伤和高兴处于大的效应量，中性处于中等和大的效应量之间，所有情感汇总处于中等和大的效应量之间。这说明两位净演员和两位老生演员的接触商参数对行当总体变异的解释程度在中等水平以上。

表3　净和老生接触商的偏 η^2 的值

情感＼发音人	净	老生
悲伤	0.145	0.158
愤怒	0.007	0.010
高兴	0.279	0.450
中性	0.071	0.134
汇总	0.096	0.134

从图6—图12中我们可以发现，净和老生两个行当均在低音区域使用了接触商比普通话低的发声类型。此类发音在中性和悲伤中较常见，在高兴情感中只出现在一半演员的念白中，在愤怒情感中较少见。结合四位演员普通话的接触商分布范围可以发现，除老生1的悲伤外，其他念白的接触商下限均在其正常嗓音范围内。而老生1则可能使用了少量的气嗓音，来增强其悲伤的表现力。因此，绝大部分情况下，这两个行当在念白中均使用了正常

嗓音和比正常嗓音更紧的高内收正常嗓音［2］和紧嗓音。

从分析结果我们可以发现，情感表达策略与行当的关系非常复杂。第一种情况是行当内策略一致或基本一致，如都使用更紧、更松或更多样的嗓音来表现某种情感，演员间差异在于应用该策略的音高区域。第二种情况是在表现同一情感时存在行当间交叉相似的情况，即每个行当均表现出两种策略类型，且行当间策略一致。第三种情况是同行当演员使用策略完全相反，如在表现同一情感时一位使用更松的嗓音，一位使用更紧的嗓音。第一种情况的策略我们可以推断其为该行当表现情感的策略。第二种情况的策略我们可以认为是昆剧中老年男性行当表现情感的策略。第三种情况则可能受到诸多因素的影响。首先，可能受到念白所含情感类型是否单一的影响。如在表达愤怒情感的语句中，部分语句的听辨结果同时包括愤怒和悲伤，因愤怒的比例更大而归入愤怒类。这源于情感表达中存在“悲愤”这一类别，即既悲伤又愤怒。演员在表现愤怒情感时，如果使用“悲愤”的模式，则发声类型与单纯愤怒的发声类型不同。其次，可能受到情感子类型间差异大小的影响。如高兴的表达既可以使用音高和音强等级均较高的形式，也可以使用音高高而音强弱的形式。前者对应了较紧的发声类型，后者则对应较松的发声类型。在表现高兴时，演员可以根据自己的理解来选择不同的子类型进行表现，进而反映出不同的发声特征。因此，在后续研究中应该循序渐进，逐层展开。

我们以中性念白为参照，即认为其他情感念白是在中性念白特征的基础上变化而成。通过比较发现，有些情感的发声变化体现在整个音域，有些则体现在个别音域，有些甚至只体现在某一两个半音上，有时这些半音并不相邻。不同的策略应用的场景不同，达到的效果也不同。如愤怒情感通常选择第一种策略，全音域范围内都使用更紧的嗓音。在这种情况下，不管音高处于何种范围内，愤怒的情感表达都非常明确。悲伤较多选择第二种策略，悲伤在低音区域内使用更松的嗓音，因为在不使用假声的情况下漏气程度更强的声音在低频区域出现更自然，与悲伤情感在语言或非语言中表达的一致性更强。第三种策略见于多种情感表达，其特征与相邻音高嗓音特征差异较大，使得每次使用该类声音都会引起特别注意，进而加强情感信息的获取。因此，情感的表达策略不仅仅是参数整体分布差异的问题，还需要考虑诸多细节变化。

净和老生行当的情感念白表现出诸多共性，但也存在部分差异，这些差异是由角色特性不同导致的。净要通过音色塑造角色威武刚毅的特点，而老生则需要呈现沉着庄重的人物形象，因此在表现情感时，对嗓音的选择存在差异，因为嗓音越紧，高频能量越高［11］，声音听起来更有力。因此，在表现悲伤时，净在中音区域使用了比老生更紧的嗓音；在表现愤怒时，老生在低音区使用了更松的嗓音，而在净的嗓音中未观察到此种策略；在表现高兴时，净使用更紧的嗓音且音质较为集中，而老生在中音区域使用了更松且更富于变化的嗓音。以上特征均体现了角色特征对嗓音选择策略的影响。

5. 结论

本研究分析了中性、悲伤、愤怒和高兴四种情感下昆剧净和老生两个行当念白使用的嗓音策略。结果发现，情感类型和行当特点均影响嗓音特征，且同一情感可以使用不同的嗓音类型来诠释。净和老生在念白中主要使用正常嗓音及比正常嗓音更紧的发声类型，但各发声类型在不同情感念白中的使用比例不同。以中性念白为参照，悲伤和高兴念白会部分使用较松的嗓音，而愤怒念白则多以更紧的嗓音来表现。相较于威武粗犷的净，沉着稳重的老生通常表现为更多地使用较松的嗓音，且嗓音变化更为丰富。这意味着情感语音识别和合成应将人物性格差异考虑在内。此外，角色的共性带来发声类型和情感表达策略的相似性，但即使相同行当演员仍会存在嗓音使用策略的差异，暗示着情感表达的复杂性及可能存在多种情感子类型，未来需要更细化的情感分类来充分展示情感与嗓音的对应关系。

6. 致谢

本研究得到国家社会科学基金项目“昆剧多行当念白的情感发声研究”（16CYY047）的经费支持。

参考文献

[1] Birkholz, P., Martin, L., Willmes, K., Kröger, B., Neuschaefer – Rube, C. 2015. The contribution of phonation type to the perception of vocal emotions in German: an articulatory synthesis study. *The Journal of the Acoustical Society of America* 137, 1503 – 1512.

[2] Dong, L., Kong, J. 2021. Electroglottographic analysis of the voice in Young Male Role of Kunqu Opera. *Applied Science – Basel* 11, 3930.

[3] Dong, L., Kong, J., Sundberg J. 2014. Long – term – average spectrum characteristics of Kunqu Opera singers' speaking, singing and stage speech. *Logopedics, phoniatrics, vocology*, 39, 72 – 80.

[4] Dong, L., Sundberg, J., Kong, J. 2014. Formant and voice source properties in two male Kunqu Opera roles: A pilot study. *Folia Phoniatrica et Logopaedica* 65, 294 – 302.

[5] Dong, L., Sundberg, J., Kong, J. 2014. Loudness and Pitch of Kunqu Opera. *Journal of Voice* 28, 14 – 19.

[6] Hanson, H., Chuang, E. 1999. Glottal characteristics of male speakers: acoustic correlates and comparison with female data. *The Journal of the Acoustical Society of America* 106, 1064 – 1077.

[7] Linville, S., Fisher, H. 1985. Acoustic characteristics of perceived versus actual vocal age in controlled phonation by adult females. *The Journal of the Acoustical Society of America* 78, 40 – 48.

[8] Zhang, Z. 2015. Vibrational and acoustic consequences of changes in subglottal pressure, vocal fold stiffness, vocal fold approximation, and vocal fold thickness. *The Journal of the Acoustical Society of America* 138, 1809 – 1809.

[9] 胡竹菁、戴海琦：《方差分析的统计检验力和效果大小的常用方法比较》，《心理学探新》2011年第3期。

[10] 孔江平：《论语言发声》，中央民族大学出版社2002年版。

[11] 吴新雷：《中国昆剧大辞典》，南京大学出版社2002年版。

黄慧怡 深圳大学人文学院，硕士研究生，主要研究领域为语音声学与生理分析，情感语音。
E-mail：1900072009@email.szu.edu.cn

董 理 深圳大学人文学院，博士，研究领域包括声学语音学、生理语音学、声乐语音学等。
E-mail：dongli@szu.edu.cn

昆剧小生行当情感念白声学研究

董 理 谈 笑

摘 要 昆剧被誉为中国戏曲的“百戏之祖”，涵括了个人特征迥异的多个行当，其中，扮演青少年男子的小生行是一个情感特征十分鲜明的行当。本文从声学角度对小生行当两位演员中性、高兴、悲伤、愤怒四种情感的音高、音强、音长三个语音要素特征进行了分析。结果发现，情感间存在多维度的差异。中性和高兴区分度相对较低；高兴和愤怒的音高平均水平高于中性和悲伤；中性、愤怒的音高变化幅度最大，而悲伤的音高变化最小；中性和高兴的音强平均水平和变化幅度大于愤怒和悲伤；悲伤的时长平均水平最长，而愤怒最短。音高和音长参数对情感类别划分有显著贡献。三种情感念白感知度间参数差异较小，悲伤程度主要受时长特征影响，高兴和愤怒程度与音高特征有关。昆剧小生行念白的情感表现伴随语音的声学特征变化，情感的表现是多维度声学特征共同作用的结果。

关键词 昆剧，念白，小生，情感语音

An Acoustic Study on Young Man Role's Emotional Stage Speech in Kunqu Opera

DONG Li TAN Xiao

Abstract Kunqu Opera is regarded as the ancestor of Chinese opera, in which there are several roles with different personal characteristics. The Young Man Role is a male role with distinctive emotional features and acts as a young or middle-aged male personage. This study focused on the pitch, loudness and duration characteristics of four emotional stage speeches: neutral, happy, sad and angry, from the perspective of acoustics. The results showed that the acoustical parameters varied between emotions. Neutral and happy stage speeches share a lot of similarities. Happy and angry stage speeches have higher mean fundamental frequency than neutral and sad ones. Neutral and angry stage speeches demonstrate the largest fundamental frequency variations while the sad stage speech the smallest. Neutral and happy stage speeches show higher means and standard deviations of sound pressure level than sad and angry ones. For duration, the sad stage speech has the longest mean word length while the angry one has the shortest. The pitch and duration parameters contribute significantly to the classification of emotional categories. The differences between stage speeches with diverse affective intensity are small. The affective intensity of the sad stage speech is mainly influenced by the duration feature and that of happy and angry stage speeches is concerned with the pitch characteristics. In conclusion, the stage speeches of the Young Man Role exhibit different acoustic al features in different emotions.

Key words Kunqu Opera, Stage speech, Young Man Role, Emotional speech

1. 引言

昆剧作为“我国现存最古老的剧种之一”[1]，有“词海曲山”之称[2]，也被称作中国古典“剧诗”，是“戏剧与诗的高度统一，表现出强烈的抒情性”[3]，是中国第一个也是世界首批被列入“人类口头和非物质遗产代表作”的项目。

昆剧的表演可以分为“唱、念、做、打”四种形式，其中与语音相关的是演唱和念白两部分。念白是一种舞台语言形式，简单说就是“用歌唱发声方式来‘说’”[4]，又称“宾白”。“宾白”的出处有两种说法，一是出自明代徐渭《南词叙录》的“唱为主，白为宾，故曰宾白”

[5]；二是“两人对说曰宾，一人自说曰白”[6]。念白在昆剧表演中占有十分重要的地位，按唱念的相对难度有“一白、二引、三曲子”的说法。关于念白的特性，前人从不同的角度进行了探讨。一是戏曲艺术家从自身演艺经验总结而出的唱论。如俞振飞认为念白的要领可以概括为“音乐性”和“语气化”[7]。程从荣从声调、语调、节奏三个方面总结了念白区别于其他说话方式的特点：“字音声调的升降起伏幅度很大”；“调域被扩宽，声调的高低升降变化被夸大”；“字音分布的音区变化”；“节奏形式丰富多彩”；“念白音流中的节奏单元具有较强的相对独立性”；节奏单元“整齐具体又富于变化”；“速率对比及其多层次性”[4]。二是运用现代语音学手段对念白进行的较为客观的呈现。如韩启超[8，9]采用声学实验的方法，从时长、音高、调值方面对比了念白与用中州韵说话之间的差异，其实验结果与经验式的叙述存在一定的出入。

昆剧行当总的可以分为“生、旦、净、末、丑”五个大类[10]。“行当”是“传统戏曲演员专业分工的类别”[11]，是根据戏剧中不同脚色的“自然属性”（年龄、性别等）、“社会属性”（身份、职业等）、“表演风格”（庄或谐）、“艺术家的美学判断”（颂善惩恶的美学倾向）、“表演技术专长”（唱功、武功等）几个要素划分形成的[12]。行当对戏剧的表演有着积极的作用，一是使脚色形象鲜明，帮助观众直观了解人物；二是为表演提供了一种“独特的造型语言”，成为“戏曲演员进行形象创造的造型手段”；三是为演员根据专业分工提供了行当归属，术业有专攻[8]。

“小生”是“生行的一支，主要扮演青少年男子”[11]。早期的南戏并没有老生和小生之分，明代“出现了小生的名目，但仍是生的副角”，到了清中叶，“小生与老生已从生行中分化出来并有了分工”[12]。相较于老生，小生“少了一些对历史价值的担当，多了一些对现实情感的执着”[13]。小生的表演追求“雅、洒、发”，这三个字分别指儒雅、潇洒、柔而有刚[14]。另外，小生最重要的一个特点是“唱念用真假嗓”[15]，真嗓即“阳调、低宽音”，假嗓即“阴调、高光音”[16]。小生行的用嗓方式及脚色特点使得其情感表现尤为丰富。

前人对昆剧小生行的实验研究较少，主要出现在多行当声学特征的比较当中。Dong 等人[17，18]进行的多行当分析中涉及小生演唱和念白的音高、音强和频谱特征。与其他行当相比，小生的声学特征与闺门旦和小花旦较为相似，与老生和净差异较大。不同发音模式相比，小生念白比演唱的音强更强，音高更高，音强和音高的变化更丰富。韩启超[19]对昆剧小生念白的时长、音高和音强做了较为细致的分析，发现昆剧念白一方面延续了昆剧语音审美表现的一般手段，另一方面会根据曲情来调整念白的特征。可见，情感是影响念白声学特征的一个重要因素。

在情感语音的研究中，愤怒、快乐和悲伤是目前认可度比较高的三种基本情感[20]。各情感均对应独特的声学特征。Murray 和 Arnott[21]就合成语音中情感模拟的问题对人类声音的情感发声特点进行了总结：在愤怒情感下，语速轻微变快、平均音高变得非常高、音高区间大、音强更大、音质带呼吸声、音调突然升高、咬字紧张；在高兴情感下，语速变快或变慢、平均音高变高、音高区间变大、音强更大、音质带呼吸声且刺耳、音高变化平稳且音调向上、咬字正常；在悲伤情感下，语速轻微变慢、平均音高轻微变低、音高区间变小、音强变小、音质洪亮、音调向下、咬字含糊。此外，瞬时能量、瞬时过零率等语音特征[22]对识别正常、喜悦、愤怒、悲伤等情感也有贡献。

在情感的表达中，语音特征会受到发音人性别和个人特征[23—25]等因素的影响。即使同在戏曲环境下，不同行当在诠释情感时也会采取不同的策略[26，27]。前人研究[19]发现曲情影响念白的特征，但各种情感对念白声学特征的具体影响还未有明确结论，小生行不同于其他行当的情感诠释模式也亟待探究。因此，本文将从情感语音的角度进行声学实验，通过参数差异显著性分析、参数描述性分析，对比得出小生行当不同情感间、同一情感不同感知程度间的念白表现差异。

2. 方法

本文选取了两名江苏省昆剧院的国家级小生行当演员。两名演员分别自行选择中性、高兴、悲伤、愤怒四种情感各四段念白。演员在录制中按照舞台上表演的状态展示各自选用的念白。录音在安静的起居室完成，将索尼电容式麦克风悬挂在演员唇部下方15厘米处，使用PowerLab系统采集语音信号，采样频率为40kHz，分辨率为16bit。录音后使用声级计记录相应的1000Hz校准音的声级，用于绝对声级的计算。录音结束后，按句子对语音材料进行切分。每段念白的整体情感特征鲜明，但各句子的情感强度存在差异。为了能够筛选出具有代表性的语句，本研究增设了听辨实验。

听辨实验通过某网络平台发布，为防止疲劳，将语音材料编入四份问卷进行听辨。每一份问卷包含两位演员四种情感的念白各一段，共计八段念白。将不同情感的念白交叉排列，且每份问卷排列顺序各不相同。听辨实验以选择题的形式进行，每一题展示一句念白音频，下设“中性、高兴、悲伤、愤怒、其他”五个选项。四份问卷选择题数量为50—66题不等。共收集到34名被试的实验问卷，根据作答完整程度以及所用时长，筛选出了20份质量较高的听辨结果，用于后续的统计分析。根据20名被试情感判定的比例，将各句念白在演员情感分类的基础上进行了二次筛选和分类。在演员认定为某一情感的基础上，如果16—20人也认同为该情感的念白，则被标记为情感极明确型；11—15人认同为该情感的念白，则被标记为情感较明确型；6—10人认同为该情感的念白，则被界定为情感可感知型；0—5人认同为该情感的念白，则被划入情感隐晦型。前三类被作为情感语音的代表语料。此外，哭声、笑声等直白表现情感的语句也被剔除，最终保留的句子数量见表1。

表1　应用于实验的句子数量统计表

情感	感知分类	演员1	演员2	合计
中性	极明确	5	8	13
	较明确	8	10	18
	可感知	5	6	11
	合计	18	24	42
高兴	极明确	7	7	14
	较明确	4	5	9
	可感知	6	6	12
	合计	17	18	35
悲伤	极明确	16	8	24
	较明确	6	7	13
	可感知	8	3	11
	合计	30	18	48
愤怒	极明确	10	7	17
	较明确	6	6	12
	可感知	3	4	7
	合计	19	17	36

选定分析素材后，使用WaveSurfer软件对各句念白的音高、音强和音长数据进行了提取，其中，基频数据经人工二次校正，声压级数据按照声级计数值进行了校准。不同情感的念白参数被导入Excel表中，并通过单因素方差分析确定在0.05水平上具备显著性差异的参数对，得到影响小生念白情感表达和感知的因素。此外，在情感类别分析中以情感类型为因变量、各参数为自变量进行了多元线性回归分析，以确定各参数对情感判断的贡献。在情感强度分析中，为了避免人为分组对连续听辨结果数据分析的影响，本文还使用SPSS软件以听辨实验被试认同数量为因变量对数据进行了多元线性回归分析。

3. 结果

下文将从音高、音强、音长几方面分

析小生情感念白的语音特征。首先对本研究涉及的参数做如下定义。音高方面，基频均值（F0_M）和基频标准差（F0_SD）是每句念白基频的平均值和标准差，单位为半音（基于55Hz，36半音对应440Hz)，分别反映每句话音高的平均水平和变化程度。音强方面，声压级均值（SPL_M）和声压级标准差（SPL_SD）是每句念白声压级的平均值和标准差，单位为分贝，分别反映每句话音强的平均水平和变化程度。音长方面，时长均值（Time_M）是每句念白中每个字时长的平均值，单位为秒，反映每句话中单字音长的平均水平；时长标准差（Time_SD）是每句念白中每个字时长的标准差，单位为秒，反映每句话中单字音长的变化程度。本文选用每项参数的均值进行参数间差异比较。

3.1 情感间比较

从F0_M和F0_SD在情感间的单因素方差分析的检验结果（见表2）可知，F0_M可以区分除中性和悲伤、高兴和愤怒两组情感外的其他情感，而中性和愤怒之外的其他情感都可以通过F0_SD进行区分。由此可知，各情感间至少可以通过一项音高参数加以区分。

表2 音高各参数之间显著性差异检验结果

参数	情感	高兴	悲伤	愤怒
F0_M	中性	0.000*	0.483	0.008*
	高兴		0.000*	0.215
	悲伤			0.005*
F0_SD	中性	0.000*	0.000*	0.158
	高兴		0.000*	0.040*
	悲伤			0.000*

*：在0.05水平上具备显著性差异

图1和图2显示了各情感F0_M和F0_SD的数据分布情况，柱形图展示了各参数的均值，误差线显示了各参数的标准差。综合表2的显著性差异检验结果，可得到如下结论：在F0_M上，高兴和愤怒的参数值明显大于中性和悲伤。即小生行当高兴和愤怒情感念白的音高平均水平显著高于中性和悲伤。在F0_SD上，中性和愤怒的参数值明显大于高兴和悲伤，句子间高兴的参数变异最小，悲伤的参数变异最大。即小生行当中性和愤怒情感念白的音高变化幅度较大，二者明显大于句间表现统一的高兴念白，而悲伤情感念白音高的变化幅度最小且句间变异程度高。

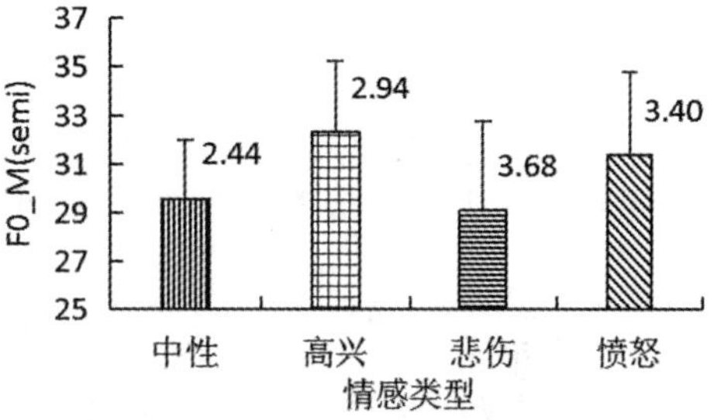

图1 基频均值柱形图（数据标签为标准差）

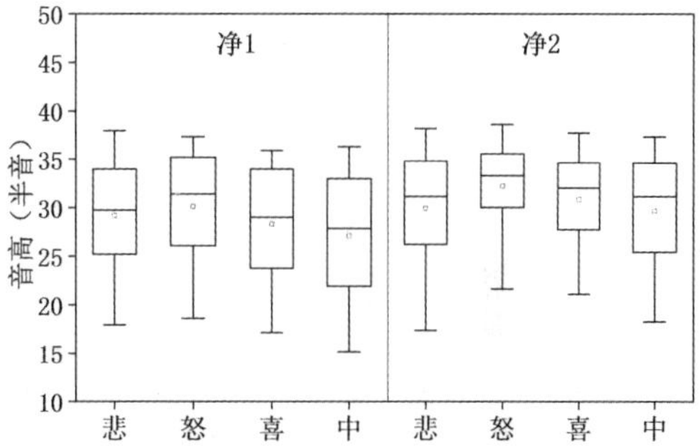

图2 基频标准差柱形图（数据标签为标准差）

音强方面，从表3可以发现，中性和高兴无法通过音强的任一参数进行区分，悲伤和愤怒仅能通过SPL_M区分、中性和愤怒仅能通过SPL_SD区分，其他情感间都可以通过声压级的两个参数辨别。

表3 音强各参数之间显著性差异检验结果

参数	情感	高兴	悲伤	愤怒
SPL_M	中性	0.491	0.000*	0.079
	高兴		0.000*	0.020*
	悲伤			0.000*

续表

参数	情感	高兴	悲伤	愤怒
SPL_SD	中性	0.06	0.000*	0.000*
	高兴		0.000*	0.004*
	悲伤			0.192

*：在0.05水平上具备显著性差异

图3和图4显示了各情感SPL_M和SPL_SD的分布情况，综合表3的显著性差异检验结果，可得到如下结论：在SPL_M上，四种情感中，中性和高兴的参数较大且句间变异小，悲伤的参数最小且句间变异大。在SPL_SD上，中性和高兴的参数明显大于愤怒和悲伤，句间变异前者小于后者。由此可知，小生行当中性和高兴情感念白的整体音强明显强于愤怒和悲伤，前一组与悲伤念白的整体音强差异更大，伴随更大幅度的音强变化，且各句整体音强特征一致性更高。

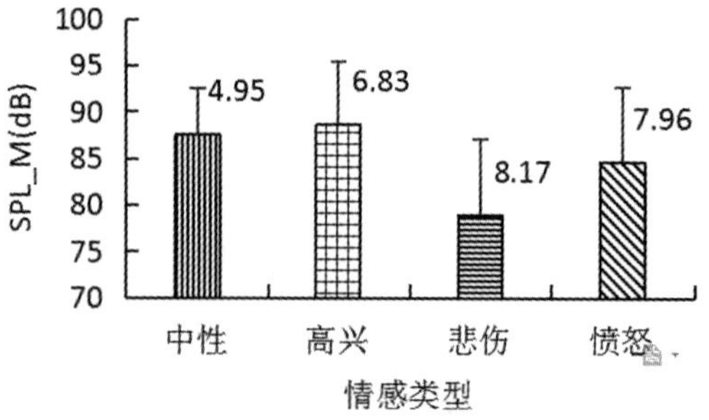

图3　声压级均值柱形图（数据标签为标准差）

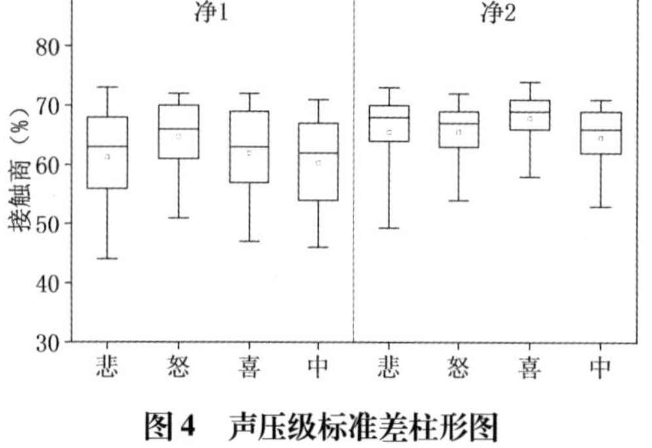

图4　声压级标准差柱形图（数据标签为标准差）

单字时长结果（表4）显示，中性和高兴无法通过时长的两个参数进行区分，除此之外，Time_SD不能区分中性和悲伤、高兴和愤怒，而Time_M则可以反映除中性和高兴一组外所有其他情感间差异。

表4　音长各参数之间显著性差异检验结果

参数	情感	高兴	悲伤	愤怒
Time_M	中性	0.294	0.012*	0.000*
	高兴		0.003*	0.007*
	悲伤			0.000*
Time_SD	中性	0.328	0.075	0.029*
	高兴		0.026*	0.190
	悲伤			0.003*

*：在0.05水平上具备显著性差异

图5和图6是不同情感Time_M和Time_SD的柱形图，综合表4的显著性差异检验结果，可得到如下结论：在Time_M上，悲伤情感的时长明显长于中性和高兴，其句间时长变异最大，而愤怒情感的时长最短。在Time_SD上，悲伤情感显著大于高兴和愤怒情感，且句间变异明显大于其他情感；中性情感明显大于愤怒情感。小生行当悲伤情感念白中字的时长普遍较长，字长变化较为丰富，句间时长特征差异较大；而愤怒情感念白中字的时长普遍较短，且字长变化较小，高兴和中性情感的特征居于二者之间。

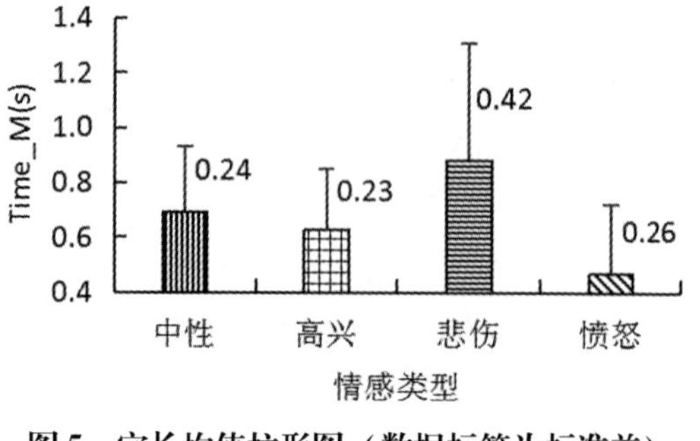

图5　字长均值柱形图（数据标签为标准差）

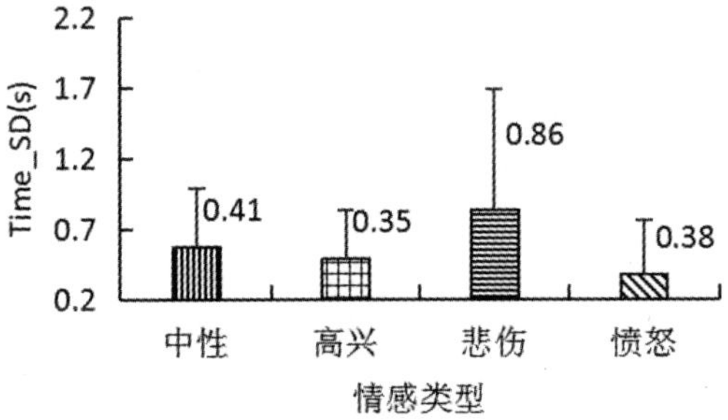

图6 字长标准差柱形图
(数据标签为标准差)

为考察各参数对情感判断的贡献，根据以上结果，将悲伤、中性、高兴和愤怒分别赋值为1、2、3、4，以各参数为自变量进行多元线性回归分析，结果发现，使用逐步回归的方法，模型成立（$p<0.05$），Time_M、F0_M、F0_SD、Time_SD依次进入方程（$p<0.05$），SPL_M和SPL_SD被排除在外。由此可知，在本文涉及的四种情感类型中，音长和音高参数对情感类别的判定有显著贡献，音强参数贡献不显著。

3.2 同一情感不同感知程度间比较

中性情感念白在三种不同感知水平下，音高、音强和音长的六项参数均值均没有显著差异（显著水平为0.05）。由此可见，中性念白不同组别内部一致性较高。

表5为高兴情感在不同感知水平下六项参数的均值数据。根据单因素方差分析结果，以下组别的参数存在显著差异（$p<0.05$）：情感较明确比情感可感知的念白F0_M更大，情感极明确比情感可感知的F0_SD更小。可见，不同组别的高兴念白间的差异主要体现在音高上，平均音高更高、音高变化更小的句子高兴情感更鲜明。以听辨实验被试认同数量为因变量，以各参数为自变量进行多元线性回归，结果发现，采取步进的方式，只有F0_SD进入回归方程（$p<0.05$），标准化系数为-1.893。

表5 高兴情感不同感知程度参数均值

参数 \ 情感	极明确	较明确	可感知
F0_M（半音）	32.8	33.7	30.8
F0_SD（半音）	6.8	7.0	8.0
SPL_M（分贝）	86.4	91.8	88.9
SPL_SD（分贝）	20.2	20.2	18.4
Time_M（秒）	0.62	0.75	0.58
Time_SD（秒）	0.54	0.54	0.39

表6为不同感知情况下小生行当悲伤情感念白的六项参数的均值数据。在小生行当悲伤情感念白中，情感极明确比情感可感知F0_SD更小、Time_M更大；情感较明确比情感可感知Time_M更大、Time_SD更大（$p<0.05$）。在影响悲伤感知程度的参数中，时长参数贡献比其他参数更大。除时长外，悲伤情感明确的念白句子还伴随音高变化小的特征。多元线性回归分析发现，采取步进的方式，只有F0_SD进入回归方程（$p<0.05$），标准化系数为-1.165。

表6 悲伤情感不同感知程度参数均值

参数 \ 情感	极明确	较明确	可感知
F0_M（半音）	29.7	29.1	27.8
F0_SD（半音）	5.4	6.2	7.0
SPL_M（分贝）	78.5	80.9	77.8
SPL_SD（分贝）	16.4	17.8	15.6
Time_M（秒）	0.99	0.89	0.63
Time_SD（秒）	1.06	0.79	0.41

表7为不同感知情况下小生行当愤怒情感念白的六项参数均值数据。全部参数中只有一组存在显著差异（$p<0.05$），即情感极明确的愤怒念白F0_M明显大于情感可感知的愤怒念白。多元线性回归结果显示，采取步进的方式，只有F0_M进入回归方程（$p<0.05$），标准化系数为0.39。

表7 愤怒情感不同感知程度参数均值

情感 / 参数	极明确	较明确	可感知
F0_M（半音）	32.0	32.5	28.0
F0_SD（半音）	8.2	7.8	7.7
SPL_M（分贝）	86.3	85.0	80.1
SPL_SD（分贝）	17.8	18.2	15.7
Time_M（秒）	0.45	0.56	0.35
Time_SD（秒）	0.36	0.51	0.17

由此可见，小生行当四种情感念白不同感知程度间参数差异并不大。同一情感不同感知程度之间最多有两个参数有显著差异。另外，情感极明确的念白和情感较明确的念白在四种情感下六项参数均无显著差异。不同情感用于区分情感强度的语音要素不同，高兴和愤怒主要依赖音高参数，而悲伤主要依赖时长参数。音强在任何情感中都未发挥区别情感强度的作用。

4. 讨论

在对小生行当两位演员念白情感的研究中，发现如下问题值得进一步讨论。

第一，情感念白段落中并非所有的句子都带有鲜明的目标情感。在全部的235句念白中，情感隐晦型所占比重最高，为30%，情感可感知型所占比重最低，为18%。由此可知，念白中的情感表达是有层次的，在表现情感时，有接近一半的句子情感特征不够鲜明，为其他句子情感的表达做了铺垫。各情感的感知效率不同，结果如图7所示。四种情感中，悲伤情感的念白最容易被辨识，其次是愤怒，二者分别有40%和34%的句子被绝大部分被试明确判定。高兴情感的念白最不容易被识别，有将近一半的句子属于情感隐晦型。中性情感念白的不明确性则最低。明显表现高兴的句子数量最少可能是由多方面的原因造成的。一是与昆曲儒雅、内敛的审美特征有关；二是与小生行较高的音域有关，音域较高使得听众很难判断较高的语音是源于高兴情感的表达还是艺术语音的需要。这点从中性念白的听辨结果中也可见一斑。听众在判断中性情感时，情感极明确型的数量反而比情感较明确的比例少，这与其他情感的结果正相反。这暗示着，观众对带有音乐性的语音材料是否带有某种情感是存疑的，较强的旋律感使得念白听起来总似带有某种情感色彩。此外，对演员1和演员2的中性念白被判定为高兴的句子进行统计（见表8），结果显示，有相当数量的中性句子被判断为带有高兴色彩，再次印证了这一假设。

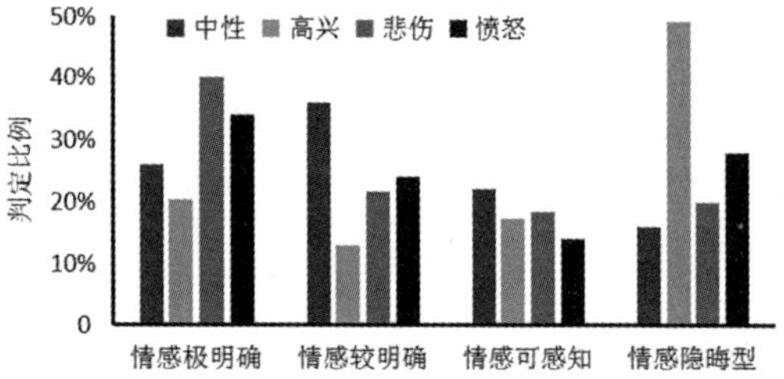

图7 小生念白各情感判定人数比例

表8 小生行当两位演员中性情感念白误判率

	判定为高兴多于中性的句子占比	判定为高兴的人数大于5的句子占比
演员1	13.04%	39.13%
演员2	7.41%	29.63%

第二，中性情感与高兴情感的相似性在参数中有所体现。在小生行当不同情感念白的比较中发现，中性和高兴情感只有音高参数存在差异，高兴情感F0_M更大但F0_SD更小。可能是因为高兴情感念白普遍使用最高的音高进行表演，变化幅度受到限制，而念白不论什么情感都是在表演，需要积极的状态，所以中性情感在F0_SD和SPL_SD两个参数上都是四种情感中最大的。由于中性情感念白表演的积极性以及与高兴情感的相似性，中性情感与高兴情感的混淆度较高。

第三，各参数区分情感的效力不同。本文进行小生行当念白情感分析时，应用到的音高、音长、音强的六个参数中，F0_SD的区别能力最强。此外，在不同感知程度的比较中，情感鲜明的念白 F0_SD 更小。因此，认为 F0_SD 是一项比较稳定的参数，不同情感具有被广泛认可的音高变化幅度。

第四，参数的局部特征可能影响情感的表达。本文的数据分析主要以句子为单位，即假定情感的表达负载在整个句子上。在结合听辨实验的基础上，这一方法优于以语段为单位进行分析。但此种方法仍存在一定的不足，因为情感的表达可能依托比句子更小的语言单位，如短语或词。此种情况下，以句子为单位进行参数计算可能使得部分鲜明的特征因平均而无法凸显。句内的参数标准差大小可在一定程度上反映句子内部数据的变化幅度，从当前结果看，悲伤情感下情感较明确比情感可感知 Time_SD 更大，高兴和悲伤中情感鲜明的念白 F0_SD 反而更小。因此可以猜测时长的局部特征对情感的表达可能产生一定的影响。此外，本研究发现音强在句子层面不影响情感的外显程度，但音强在区分情感时是有作用的，二者的不一致也可能与分析单位为句子有关。后续研究中需进一步以更小的语言单位为分析对象，尤其是对当前研究中呈现的无显著差异的参数，需要再次验证其在更小的语言单位中的作用。

第五，对情感程度的分组需要更多听辨结果支持。前文多元线性回归分析中将被试认同数量设为因变量，认同数量的变化单位为 1，即认为认同数量每增加 1 都意味着情感的强烈程度有所增强。但实际上，这种增加可能受到听辨误差的影响，或多参数的交互作用影响，使得研究难以发现各参数对听辨结果的影响程度。因此，有必要对数据进行分组，使组间的情感差异得以累积，进而找到影响情感感知的参数。当前研究尝试性地将语料分为四组，分组后发现的影响情感感知结果的参数数量多于多元线性回归结果，实现了分组的目的，但分组的标准仍值得商榷。在同一情感不同感知程度的对比中发现，有显著性差异的参数较少，且情感极明确与情感较明确的念白之间普遍不存在显著性差异。一方面，可能是因为不同感知程度的念白样本较少，无法展示出参数的聚集效应，之后的研究中可以通过增大样本量来增强数据分布的稳定性和可靠性；另一方面，可能是各感知程度的念白之间一致性较强，听众判断结果差异是由随机因素造成的，之后的研究中可以通过增加听众数量，增多听辨次数，以保证听辨结果的稳定性。本文对情感极明确和情感较明确的分类是否必要，需要进一步的数据验证，如仍无显著区别，在后续的分析中，应将两组结果合为一组。

第六，听辨实验的设计需要考虑多重因素的影响。听众在听辨过程中，可能会受到上一句的情感影响，出现延续上一句听辨结果的现象。另外，是否在实验中为听众提供文本信息，还有待讨论。一方面听众基本上都没有接触过昆剧，一时无法脱离文本而接受信息；另一方面，若提供文本信息，则听众在判断情感时会受到句意影响。被试选择上，本次研究调查的被试差异较大，年龄从 20 岁到 55 岁不等，学历也涵盖本科、研究生，性别也不一致。一方面数据来源多样，反映的情况更加广泛；另一方面，由于人群分散，文化背景等因素不同，数据相对分散，反映情况不够集中。因此，听辨实验对象也有待讨论。未来研究中可以考虑根据昆剧观众画像进行特定人群的听辨实验。

5. 结论

本文通过对小生行当中性、高兴、悲伤、愤怒四种情感的音高、音强和音长三个维度的研究分析，发现不同情感在多维度上表现出差异，同一情感不同感知程度上差异较小。小生行中，中性和高兴区分度相对较低。高兴和愤怒的音高平均水平高于中性和悲伤。中性和愤怒的音高变化幅度最大，而悲伤的音高变化较小。中性和高兴的音强平均水平最高，悲伤最低，且中性和高兴的音强变化幅度大于愤怒和悲伤。悲伤的时长平均水平最长，而愤怒最短。各类参数对情感类别划分的贡献不同，音高和音长参数对其有显著贡献，音强参数贡献不显著。不同情感用于区分情感强度的语音要素不同，高兴和愤怒主要依赖音高参数，而悲伤主要依赖时长参数。本文运用声学的方法客观地展示了昆剧小生行情感念白的特征，在戏剧嗓音情感表现方面做出了多方面的探索，对艺术嗓音和情感语音研究有一定的推动作用。

6. 致谢

本研究得到了国家社科基金项目“昆剧多行当念白的情感发声研究”（16CYY047）的经费支持。

参考文献

[1] Dong, L., Kong, J., Sundberg, J. 2014. Long-term-average spectrum characteristics of Kunqu Opera singers' speaking, singing and stage speech. *Logoped. Phoniatr. Vocol.* 39, 72-80.

[2] Dong, L., Sundberg, J., Kong, J. 2014. Loudness and pitch of kunqu opera. *Journal of Voice* 28, 14-19.

[3] Ortony, A., Turner, T. J. 1990. What's basic about basic emotions? *Psychological Review* 97, 315-331.

[4] Murray, I. R., Arnott, J. L. 1993. Toward the simulation of emotion in synthetic speech: A review of the literature on human vocal emotion. *The Journal of the Acoustical Society of America* 93, 1097-1108.

[5] Ververidis, D., Kotropoulos C. 2006. Emotional speech recognition: Resources, features, and methods, *Speech Communication* 48, 1162-1181.

[6] Han, Q., Sundberg, J. 2016. Duration, Pitch, and Loudness in Kunqu Opera Stage Speech. *Journal of Voice* 31, 255. e1-255. e7.

[7] 白云生:《生旦净末丑的表演艺术》，中国戏剧出版社 1959 年版。

[8] 蔡正仁:《丰富多彩的昆曲小生艺术》,《戏剧》1985 年第 7 期，第 39—41 页。

[9] 程从荣:《戏曲念白的艺术特点》,《戏剧》1997 年第 1 期，第 95—98 页。

[10]（明）单宇：《菊坡丛话》，明成化年间刻本。

[11] 董理、陈奕瑜:《昆剧老生和小丑情感念白声学特征比较研究》,《澳门语言学刊》2021 年第 57 期，第 24—32 页。

[12] 董理、林扬:《昆曲小花旦情感念白声学特征分析》,《南方语言学》2021 年第 17 辑，第 88—96 页。

[13] 顾兆琳:《昆剧曲学探究》，中西书局 2015 年版。

[14] 韩启超:《南昆念白声学实验分析》（一），《中国音乐学》2014 年第 4 期，第 102—114 页。

[15] 韩启超:《声学视域下昆曲小生念白的字声规律探赜》,《戏曲艺术》2020 年第 41 期，第 102—112 页。

[16] 何时希:《关于小生的念白——兼及姜妙香先生》,《上海戏剧》1983 年第 6 期，第 38 页。

[17] 黄克保:《论“行当”（续)》,《艺术百家》1989 年第 4 期，第 104—116 页。

[18] 冷鑫:《戏曲行当审美研究》，中国艺术研究院，2015 年。

[19] 李强、刘晓峰、贺静:《基于语音特征的情感分类》,《小型微型计算机系统》2016 年第 37 期，第 85—388 页。

[20] 刘明澜:《论昆曲唱腔的艺术美》，《中国音乐学》1993 年第 3 期，第 27—38 页。

[21] 上海艺术研究所、中国戏剧家协会上海分会:《中国戏曲曲艺词典》，上海辞书出版社 1985 年版。

[22] 吴新雷:《二十世纪前期昆曲研究》，春风文艺出版社 2005 年版。

[23] 吴新雷:《中国昆剧大辞典》，南京大学出版社 2002 年版。

[24] 谢波:《普通话语音情感识别关键技术研究》，浙江大学，2006 年。

[25] 俞振飞:《振飞曲谱》，上海文艺出版社 1982 年版。

[26] 张立华、杨莹春:《情感语音变化规律的特征分析》,《清华大学学报》（自然科学版）2008 年第 48 期，第 42—47 页。

[27] 中国戏曲研究院:《中国古典戏曲论著集成》（三），中国戏剧出版社 1959 年版。

董　理　深圳大学人文学院，博士，主要研究领域为声学语音学和生理语音学。
E-mail: dongli@ szu. edu. cn

谈　笑　深圳市宝安区松岗第一小学，学士，主要从事声学语音学研究。
E-mail: tanxiao_1998@ sina. com

山东快书语音声学分析

王　璐　马睿启

摘　要　本文通过对山东快书专业演员的快书语音进行声学分析，探讨了快书的语音声学特征。研究结果表明：(1) 时长与语速上，快书语速明显快于朗读形式，时长缩短 20%—30%；句子越长语速越快。(2) 基频分布上，快书总体上比朗读的音高更高，基频分布曲线也更分散。(3) LTAS 分析结果表明，快书语音在 3000—5000Hz 频段信号强度高于朗读；所有发音人快书语音中均未出现歌手共振峰，部分发音人的快书语音中出现了演讲者共振峰。

关键词　山东快书，语速，基频，长时平均谱

An Acoustic Analysis of Shandong Clapper Ballads

WANG Lu　MA Ruiqi

Abstract This paper discusses the acoustic characteristics of Shandong Clapper Ballads. The results show that (1) the speaking rate of Shandong Clapper Ballads is faster than the normal reading, and the duration is shortened by 20% –30%. The more the number of words, the faster the speaking rate of clauses. (2) The overall F0 range of the Clapper Ballads is higher, and the F0 distribution is more dispersed than the normal speaking. (3) The spectral energy of the ballads in the high frequency band of 3000 – 5000Hz is significantly stronger than the normal reading. No singer's formant was observed in the average spectrum, but the speaker's formant appeared in the ballads performed by three speakers.

Key words Shandong Clapper Ballads, Speaking rate, LTAS

1. 引言

山东快书是一种以说唱形式叙述故事的传统曲艺形式［17］，其语速较快的特点决定了其语音性质的特殊性，是探究语速影响语音声学特征的良好素材。

语速即说话人的发音速度（speaking rate），可以用每秒的音节数进行计量，也可以用音节的平均时长来计量。一般认为，剔除停顿后的话语才能反映不同说话者真实的说话速度差异［8，10］，因此本研究用剔除停顿后的话语计算单位时间内的音节数来测算语速。

语速的改变是通过压缩或者延长音节的时长来实现的。不同语言具体的语速改变方式可能不同。对于正常朗读风格且无局部窄焦点的语句，音节—节奏型语言的音节具有等时性的趋势，语速变化均匀分布在整个语句，可以认为其语速变化为线性方式；而重音—节奏型语言，其语速改变主要影响句中非重读音节时长，也就是说语速变化并不均匀分布于整个语句，可以认为语速变化为非线性方式［8，10，19］。但有研究表明，受篇章中韵律结构的影响，汉语语速变化也可能呈现非线性方式，即语速变化并非均匀分布［8，15］。还有研究者基于韵律层级模型，详细分析了汉语不同韵律单位的语速变化规律，可总结为“启动—高速—降速”［20］。

语速的变化还会导致音高和音域的变化。有研究者对快、中、慢三种语速的话语总体音高进行分析，发现语速加快会使语句总体音高升高、总体音域增大［8］。还有研究者发现，不同语速对不同声调的

影响不同，总体上语速加快使得音高升高，调域变窄［14］。可见，研究一般认为语速和总体音高为正相关关系，但语速对音域的具体影响结论则不一致。此外，其他语言的研究结论也不相同。对比三种语速的英语语句的韵律特征，整句话音域大小呈现中速 > 快速 > 慢速的趋势，即语速的加快和减慢均使音域减小［16］。对法语的研究发现，快速语篇与中速语篇相比整体基频下降，且音域变小。语速加快也会引起语调的变化，但会受发音人个体差异和音节在篇章中位置的影响［3］。

长时平均功率谱（Long Term Average Spectrum，LTAS）是对语音短时频谱的长时平均，可以呈现一个声音的全部频谱特征，被广泛应用在多种传统曲艺形式的分析上［4—7，9，11—13，18，21—23］。西方美声唱法歌手在3000Hz附近出现一个显著的峰，称为“歌手共振峰”（singer's formant）［5］；专业演讲者在3500Hz左右出现一个显著的峰，称为“演讲者共振峰”（speaker's formant）［2］。研究者对京剧老生和花脸的语音分析结果显示没有出现歌手共振峰［4，6］，对京剧花净的分析则发现存在歌手共振峰［11］。关于昆曲的研究认为，昆曲各行当均不存在歌手共振峰，净行存在演讲者共振峰［9，13］。也有研究者认为，优秀的京剧和昆曲演员具备歌手共振峰［21，22］。对含灯大鼓的研究表明，“含灯”说话或演唱会导致LTAS在高频段的部分低于正常说话/演唱的谱曲线［23］。对学院派民歌的分析显示，男声2900Hz附近存在歌手共振峰，而女声高频区的包络峰是否为歌手共振峰还需要进一步确定［12］。对维吾尔十二木卡姆的LTAS分析结果显示，存在演讲者共振峰但不存在歌手共振峰［7］。

以往还没有研究对山东快书语音特点进行专门分析，快书的时长变化规律是怎样的？快书的基频分布情况如何？快书是否存在演讲者共振峰或歌手共振峰？本文将围绕以上问题，采用实验语音学的方法，分析比较快书与朗读语音的时长、基频、长时平均功率谱等数据，以初步揭示快书的语音特点。

2. 研究方法

2.1 发音人及录音情况

发音人为四位山东快书演员，男女各两位，年龄为24—29岁，均为曲艺社专业演员，有10年以上的山东快书学习经历。录音在安静室内进行，录音设备包括领夹式麦克风（Sony ECM-44B）、调音台（Behringer xenyx 302）、外置声卡及笔记本电脑。使用Adobe Audition软件对信号进行录制，采样频率为44100Hz，量化精度16比特。

2.2 发音材料

我们选取的山东快书选段包括《矬大嫂》《怕》《打针》，发音人用快书表演和朗读两种形式进行文本录制，快书表演和朗读各读两遍。

2.3 分析方法

为分析快书语音的时长分布规律，我们使用Adobe Audition软件对快书的小句进行切分，计算时长和小句字数。使用Excel统计各种长度的小句出现的频数，计算发音人在快书表演和朗读两种形式下快书选段每个小句字数以及各小句的时长与字数之比情况。

为考察快书语音的基频分布情况，我们将语音导入Praat软件，Analyse Periodicity - To Pitch以及Convert - Down to Pitchtier得到音频各个时间点的基频值并进行人工修正。使用Excel的数据分析—直方图功能，得到不同基频区间内点的分布比例和基频分布图，并对快书表演和朗读两种形式的基频分布差异进行比较。

LTAS分析能反映一段语流中说话人的全部频率分量以及各频率分量与强度之间的关系。我们选取时长为30—40s的文本相同的快书和朗读语音，去除空白段和辅音，将音频导入Wavesurfer软件，参数设置为语音采样频率20kHz，分析带宽为303Hz，FFT点数为128个，分析频率范围为0—5000Hz，利用LTAS分析功能获得长时平均谱［9］。进一步观察快书表演和朗读两种形式下长时平均功率谱的差异，判断是否存在歌手共振峰、演讲者共振峰。

3. 研究结果

3.1 语速分析

3.1.1 时长分析

山东快书在听感上较之日常话语语速较快。我们统计了四位发音人快书表演形式和普通朗读形式下三个选段的时长（如图1所示），以确认快书表演是否存在语速加快的现象。

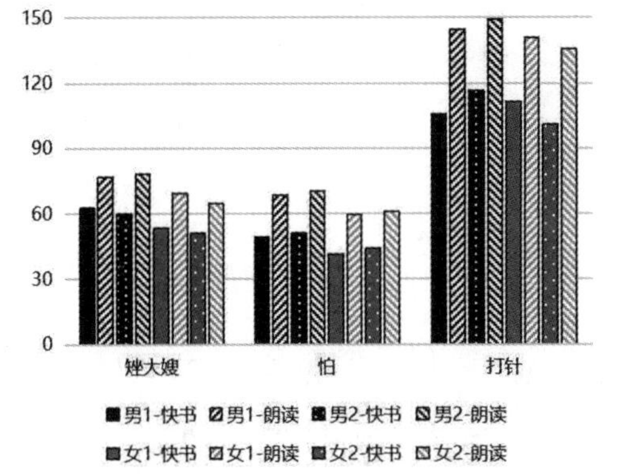

图1 四位发音人快书与朗读各选段时长（s）

我们进一步计算了不同选段的快书表演与普通朗读的时长之比（如表1所示）以及平均值M和标准差σ，以分析语速具体改变的程度。

表1 四位发音人快书与朗读各选段时长比（%）

选段	男1	男2	女1	女2	M	σ
矬大嫂	81.3	76.7	77.0	79.2	78.5	1.9
怕	71.9	72.6	69.8	72.2	71.6	1.1
打针	73.0	78.1	79.1	74.4	76.2	2.5

由图1、表1可知，所有发音人使用快书表演三种选段时所用的时长，较之朗读该选段文本的时长均有明显的减小，这说明山东快书确实存在语速提升的现象。比较三个选段时长，《打针》的时长最长，快书表演时长均值M＝108.8s，标准差最大（σ＝5.9%），说明其快书时长变化幅度最大，朗读时长M＝142.7s，快书与朗读平均时长比为76.2%，时长比标准差也是最大的（σ＝2.5%）；《矬大嫂》的时长次之，快书表演时长均值M＝56.8s，标准差σ＝4.7%，朗读时长M＝72.3s，快书与朗读时长比均值M＝78.5%，标准差σ＝1.9%；《怕》的时长最短，快书表演时长均值M＝46.5s，标准差最小（σ＝3.8%），说明其快书时长变化幅度最小，朗读时长M＝64.9s，快书与朗读平均时长比为71.6%，时长比标准差也是最小的（σ＝1.1%）。

选段的时长与篇幅有关。《打针》转写文本约60个小句，篇幅最长，时长最长，快书表演和普通朗读的时长均超过了100秒，《怕》转写文本约24个小句，《矬大嫂》转写文本约29个小句，三者篇幅《打针》＞《矬大嫂》＞《怕》，因此，篇幅越长，时长越长。

快书表演的时长标准差的序列与时长序列一致，时长越长的选段，时长标准差越大。除了与选段时长有关，还可能与选段本身内容和表演形式有关。《打针》选段的时长变化最大，该选段讲述了一个老人去医院打针的故事，62个小句中约40个小句为人物对话内容，另外还有丰富的拟声词，比如模仿扎针声音的“扑哧”，表演者在表现这部分时没有固定的板式要求，更多的是通过动作、表情和对话模拟场景进行表演，所以表演该选段所用时长会受到发音人对动作、对话等科白①的处理方式有所不同的影响。而时长变化最小的选段《怕》的24个小句均为陈述句，罗列了诸多人、事物害怕的对象，内容相对简单。选段《矬大嫂》讲述了一个大嫂的故事，29个小句中有8个小句为对话内容，内容较之《打针》相对简单，较之《怕》则相对复杂，其快书表演时长的变化范围也介于二者之间，也就得到了

① 科白，指戏曲中的动作与道白。

解释。

不同选段的时长改变程度也存在差异。由于时长比值均小于1，比值越小，快书较之朗读的时长压缩程度越大。由表1可知，三个选段的快书时长压缩程度为《怕》>《打针》>《矬大嫂》。其中，选段《怕》的变化程度最大，快书时长较普通朗读压缩近30%，明显高于另外两个选段。这可能是由于该选段为单人陈述，缺乏对话表演，因此表演者得以自始至终用较快的语速进行表演。同样因为选段内容形式相对简单，快书表演与朗读时长比也相对比较稳定。而选段《矬大嫂》和选段《打针》包括人物对话、拟声词等相对形式灵活的内容，其时长比变化范围也相应就比较大。

进一步比较四位发音人各选段的时长可以发现，除了第一位男发音人表演《打针》的时长稍短于第一位女发音人，如前所述，《打针》选段时长变化范围大与表演者处理科白的方式相对自由有关，其余的快书表演抑或普通朗读，男发音人的时长都要长于女发音人相应形式相应选段的时长，即女发音人的语速总体上要快于男发音人。

综上可知，快书表演较之朗读形式语速有明显加快，女发音人较之男发音人语速更快，三个不同选段的时长及其时长改变比例存在一定差异，造成差异性的原因可能与快书选段的长度、内容形式有关。

3.1.2　小句字数与时长的关系

山东快书的基本句式是“二、二、三”的七字句形式，但是，通过对快书选段进行转写和分析，我们发现，不同小句的字数实际上存在着一定的差距。这一方面是因为快书演员在实际表演过程中，会出现“衬字”的情况，进而导致每个小句的字数可能存在变化，比如句中插说“那个”“这”等，使句子长度超过七个字。另一方面，还存在一些字数较少的短语（如“这一天”），即使在有衬字的情况下也不可能达到七个字，因此还存在字数不足七个的句子。

本节对快书选段中小句的字数、时长及两者之间的关系进行分析。统计各小句字数，由于存在“那”“这”“了”等衬字，不同发音人的小句字数存在细微差别，我们统计了四位发音人各个字数的小句对应的平均频数，如表2所示。

表2　快书选段小句字数及对应频数

小句字数	男1	男2	女1	女2	平均频数
3	3	5	4	5	4.3
4	10	8	6	8	8.0
5	5	4	6	4	4.8
6	2	2	1	1	1.5
7	22	23	24	22	22.8
8	25	25	26	27	25.8
9	21	22	22	24	22.3
10	13	11	9	8	10.3
11	7	8	10	9	8.5
12	4	3	2	4	3.3
13	1	2	3	1	1.8

从表2中的平均频数来看，四位发音人的快书选段出现频率最高的是7—9字的小句，并且与3—6字、10—13字的频数相比差距明显。为了方便统计与归类，我们将小句按照字数分成三组，分别为“短句”（3—6字）、“中句”（7—9字）和“长句”（10—13字），来进一步研究不同长度的小句中时长与字数间的关系。分组的主要依据是表2中的快书选段小句字数频数分布，同时结合了对选段文本录音内容的比较。判断“短句”与“中句”的边界时，我们主要考虑的是6字与7—9字的小句相比频数相差很大。判断“中句”与“长句”的交界时，除了因为7—9字与10字的小句相比频数差距较大之外，我们还考虑到发音人对10字及以上的小句进行处理时存在差异，有的发音人倾向于将其分成两个甚至三个小句，有的发音人则处理成一个长的小句，但不同的

发音人对7—9字长度的小句的处理则比较一致。

令各种字数小句的时长为Ts，计算小句中每个字的平均时长为Tw。按照上述分组方式，我们统计了不同发音人每组小句的Ts与Tw最小值的平均值Ts-min、Tw-min，最大值的平均值Ts-max、Tw-min，以及组中所有小句的平均时长Ts-mean、每个字的平均时长Tw-mean，计算结果如图2所示。

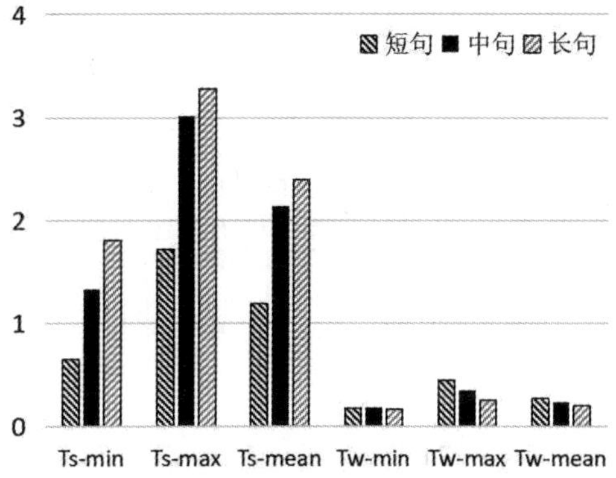

图2　三种长度的快书小句Ts、Tw各项数据平均值统计（s）

通过对比图2中“短句”“中句”“长句”三组小句的各项时长数据，我们可以发现，三组数据存在显著差异。随着句子由短到长，即小句的字数由少到多，小句时长Ts的最大值Ts-min、最小值Ts-max、平均值Ts-mean均呈现不断增加的趋势。但是需要注意的是，这种时长随字数增多的增加并不是线性的，“长句”的小句时长Ts各项平均数值较之“中句”数值的提升量，相对“中句”较之“短句”而言，提升的幅度是比较小的。可见，小句的时长与字数长短并没有严格的对应关系。比如，“短句”组Ts的最大值出现在四字句中，而并非组内最长的六字句；“中句”组Ts的最小值出现在八字句中，而非组内最短的七字句。

比较每个字的平均时长Tw，我们可以发现，Tw-min稳定在0.15—0.18秒，Tw-max随着句子长度的增长而不断减小，变化范围为0.26—0.45秒，相应地，Tw-mean也随着小句字数的增加逐渐减小。这一现象提示我们，快书小句中Tw-min基本不受句子长度的影响，在短句、中句、长句三组中时长变化不大，而Tw-max会随着句子字数增加，时长明显缩短，语速加快，进而使得较长的小句时长的增速变缓。这与Ts各项数据随着小句字数的增加，呈非线性增长的结果是一致的。

进一步分析各类小句的时长分布呈现上述结果的原因，我们认为可能是由于山东快书的起源受山东大鼓的影响，它具有明显的板式。传统戏曲中的板式是板眼（节拍）形式的简称，指的是每一小节中拍子强弱、时长的模式。而为了适应这种板式，快书中每个小句的字数虽然有所不同，但是节拍要求每个小句需要做出相应的调整，因而快书表演者会根据字数的多少自发地调节语速，从而改变小句的总时长，使得不同字数的句子节拍形式趋于一致，以符合板式的要求。这种调整的外在表现，就是我们观察到的小句长度的增加会伴随语速加快、总时长的增长减缓的现象。

3.2　基频分布分析

计算不同发音人分别用快书表演和朗读两种形式进行文本录制的基频F0的分布，得到基频分布曲线如图3所示。

图3中实线是发音人的朗读形式基频分布情况，虚线是快书表演形式的基频分

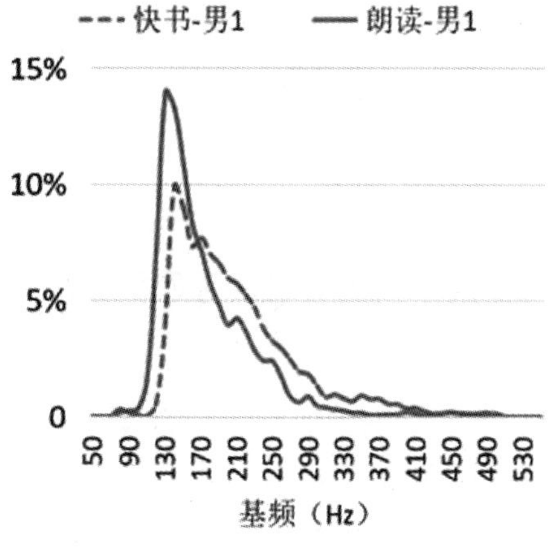

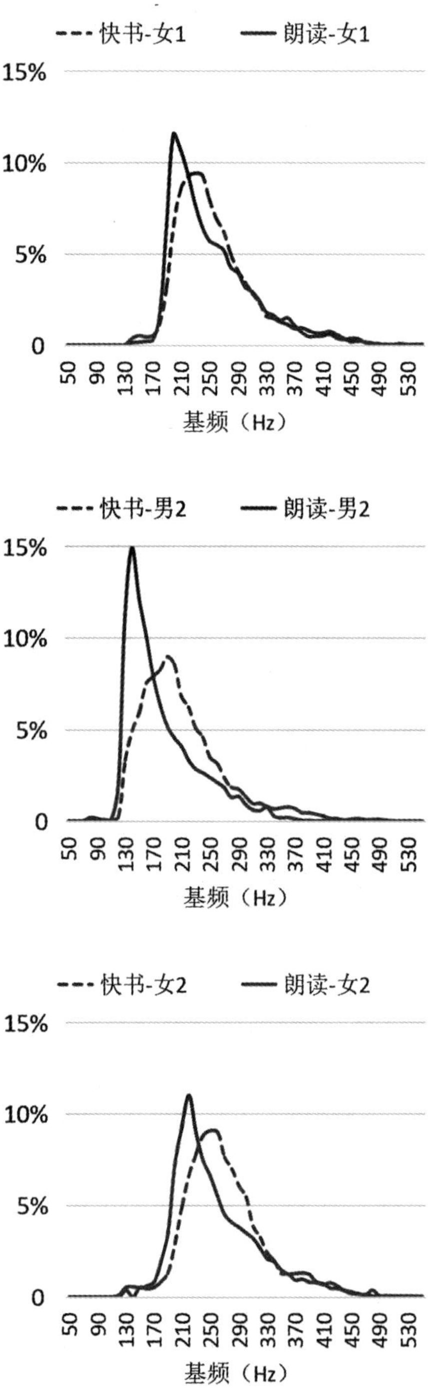

图3　三种语速下四位发音人快书表演和朗读两种形式下的基频分布

布情况。对比男女发音人的曲线，我们可以发现，女发音人基频分布在男发音人右侧，即女发音人基频明显高于男发音人，这与女性的音高比男性高的生理事实一致。对比同一发音人快书表演和朗读两种曲线的基频分布，可以发现快书表演曲线较之朗读曲线呈现出沿横轴右移的趋势，说明快书表演形式的音高要高于朗读形式。

我们进一步对男性发音人和女性发音人分别在快书表演和朗读两种形式下的基频的中位数和平均值进行了计算，结果如表3所示。

表3　男性发音人和女性发音人在快书表演和朗读两种形式下的基频分布（Hz）

	快书－男性	朗读－男性	快书－女性	朗读－女性
中位数	189.3	165.2	248.7	223.5
平均值	211.3	179.9	267.6	235.9

由表3可知，不论是男性发音人，还是女性发音人，快书表演形式下基频的中位数与平均值均要比朗读形式的相应数值高出20Hz以上。该结果与观察到的快书曲线更靠右的趋势相符，快书表演基频整体上高于朗读形式下的基频。

为进一步考察语音基频分布情况，我们对图3中的快书和朗读曲线进行了半高宽的计算。半高宽又叫半峰宽，指的是曲线的峰值高度为一半时的峰宽度。以第一位女发音人的快书曲线数据为例，其快书曲线的峰值为9.4%，位于230Hz处，峰值的一半约为4.7%，计算百分比在4.7%以上的横坐标区间，得到200—280Hz的区间，即半高宽区间，半高宽为80Hz；其朗读曲线的峰值均明显高于快书曲线，峰值为11.6%，位于200Hz处，峰值的一半约为5.8%，计算百分比在5.8%以上的横坐标区间，得到190—240Hz的区间，得到半高宽为50Hz。同样的方法，我们计算得到快书语音的平均半高宽为 87.5Hz，朗读语音的平均半高宽为 50.0Hz，可以发现，朗读曲线的峰的宽度明显小于快书曲线。由此可知，朗读曲线比快书曲线的峰值更高，且峰的宽度更窄，说明整体数据分布要更加集中。据此我们可以得出结论：表演者在进行快书表演时音高的分布趋向于更加分散，这可能是由于对比普通朗读，快书表演要求发音人用更加抑扬顿挫的语调进行表演，导致音高的范围增大、变化程度增强，表现在数据上就不如朗读形式的分布集中。

3.3 长时平均功率谱（LTAS）分析

四位发音人快书表演和朗读两种形式下的语音的长时平均功率谱如图 4 所示。

图 4 中的实线和虚线分别代表快书表演和普通朗读两种形式。从图 4 可以看

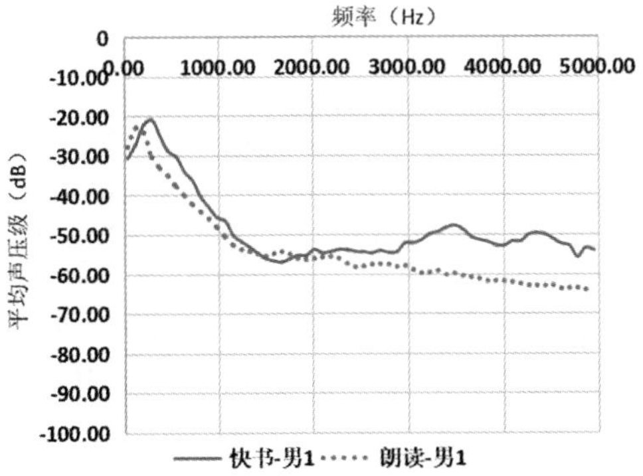

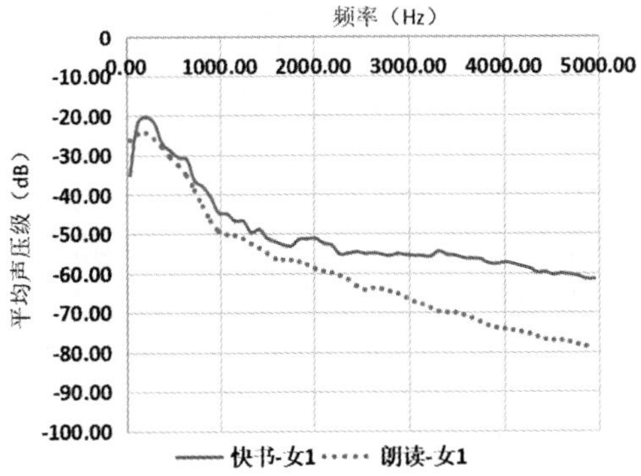

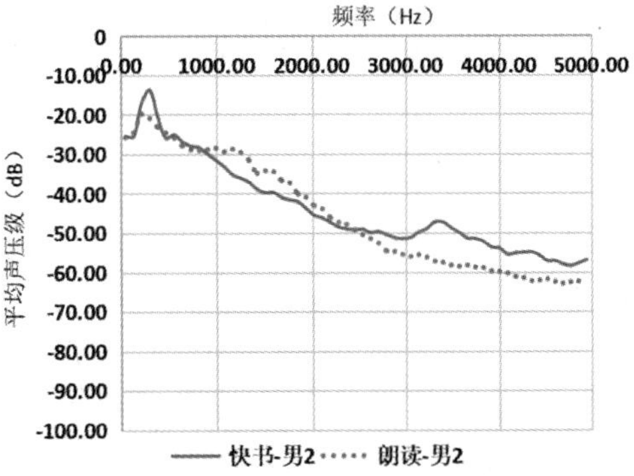

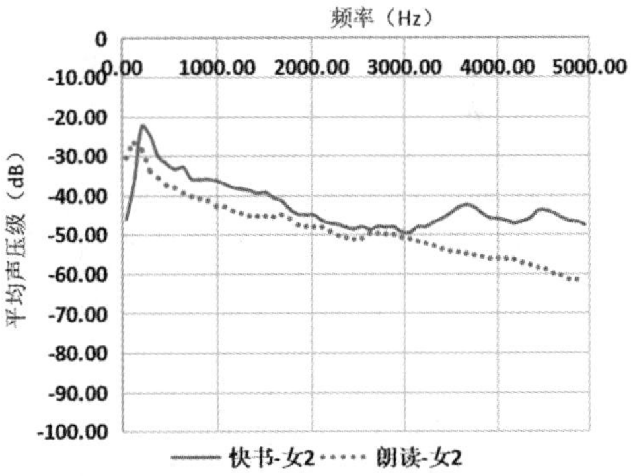

图 4　四位发音人快书表演和朗读两种形式下的长时平均功率谱

出，朗读曲线与快书曲线在 0—2000Hz 时频谱走势大致相同，在较低频段的 200—400Hz 出现能量最高点，之后持续下降。朗读曲线与快书曲线在 2000Hz 处开始产生较大区别。其中，朗读曲线在 2000Hz 之后继续下降，但下降速度逐渐放缓；快书曲线在 2000Hz 附近停止下降，开始小幅度的回升，快书语音的声压级持续高于朗读语音。在 3000—5000Hz 的频段，快书曲线最多高出朗读曲线约 10dB 以上，说明快书语音在高频段的信号强度要更大。

不同表演者语音的长时平均功率谱存在一定差异，较之快书语音的谱曲线，与之对应的朗读形式的谱曲线走势差别较小。这显示出不同的快书表演者表演同样的快书选段时会表现出各自风格的独特

性。四位发音人的快书曲线的差异主要体现在3000Hz以上的高频段：一位女发音人在该频段的谱曲线保持缓慢下降，没有出现波峰；其余三位发音人在3500Hz附近出现波峰；还有两位发音人在4500Hz附近出现了较小的波峰。下面就快书语音是否存在歌手共振峰或演讲者共振峰的问题进行讨论。

由图4可知，全部四位发音人的快书表演与普通朗读两种形式下的语音在歌手共振峰的频率范围内均没有出现明显的波峰，因此均不存在歌手共振峰。要对这一现象的原因进行分析，我们首先可以从歌手共振峰的意义出发：歌手共振峰是歌剧表演者为了让歌声能够穿透嘈杂的伴奏的管弦乐队交响乐的低频能量，演唱者调整声道，增强3000Hz附近的高频能量，从而歌声能够顺利地被观众听到［5，9］。然而，山东快书的表演伴奏并不存在这样声强很强的乐器，演员完全可以无伴奏清唱表演或者仅用快板进行伴奏，因此这一表演形式决定了并不需要表演者具有歌手共振峰。不仅如此，快书表演对吐字清晰、发音准确的要求较高，而歌手共振峰的存在会导致元音音质之间的界限模糊，进而可能导致听众对字词的理解产生误会，影响故事表达的效果，因此快书表演不仅没有必要存在歌手共振峰，反而需要尽量避免其出现。

演讲者共振峰是LTAS的3000—4000Hz频段出现的波峰，一般认为是男性发音人喉头降低，导致咽腔宽度增大，进而导致第四共振峰F4降低，与第三共振峰F3聚集而形成的能量较大的峰。演讲者共振峰通常让人有良好音质（better normal voice quality）的感知，受过专业声音训练的演员更容易出现明显的演讲者共振峰［2］。本研究中，由图4频谱所反映出的波峰频率和强度，我们可以将两位男发音人和一位女发音人的频谱上3500Hz附近出现的波峰判断为演讲者共振峰。可见，演讲者共振峰不局限于男性发音人，女性发音人也可能出现演讲者共振峰，这与［7］的研究结果也是一致的。另外，虽然另一位发音人的快书曲线没有表现出明显的演讲者共振峰，但是在相应频段也显示出了强于朗读语音的高频能量。

4. 研究结论与展望

通过对发音人在快书表演和朗读两种形式下的时长、基频分布以及长时平均功率谱进行考察，本研究较为全面地初步探讨了快书的语音声学特点。

时长分析结果表明，山东快书表演形式对比朗读形式，语速发生了较为明显的加快，时长减少的幅度在20%—30%。时长变化幅度的差异可能受选段本身长度，文本中动作、对话等科白因素的影响。另外，快书选段存在句子越长（字数越多）则语速越快的现象。值得注意的是，小句时长随字数增多的增加并非是线性的，字数越多的句子语速越快，以保证不同字数的句子节拍形式趋于一致，符合快书板式的要求。

通过对发音人在快书表演、朗读两种形式下语音的基频中位数、平均值进行分析，我们发现，表演者在快书表演形式，较之朗读形式，总体音高明显增高，女性发音人基频高于男性发音人。基频分布曲线的峰值与半高宽的分析结果表明，快书语音的基频分布比朗读语音的更加分散。这可能是由于快书表演需要发音人用更加抑扬顿挫的语调，导致音高变化相对丰富，因而基频分布趋于分散。

LTAS分析结果显示，发音人的朗读曲线与快书曲线在2000Hz处开始产生较大区别，在2000—5000Hz的较高频段，快书表演形式下的语音信号强度持续高于朗读形式，差距最大时声压级能够高出10dB以上。所有发音人的快书语音均不存在歌手共振峰，有三位发音人的快书语音出现了演讲者共振峰。

最后，本研究存在一定的不足和进一步研究的方向。首先，由于条件所限，目前发音人为两男两女，未来可以进一步扩大样本对本实验结果进行验证；其次，本研究得出了快书中不同长度的小句语速变化规律不同，但受篇幅所限，对于小句内部不同层级单位的节奏特性没有作更进一步的具体分析。此外，有关英语说唱音乐的频谱分析研究表明，押韵词和非押韵词、节拍上的词和非节拍上的词其频谱特征都会有所不同［1］。山东快书作为“汉语的说唱艺术”，其节奏特性和频谱特征还有待今后更多的研究继续深入挖掘。

5. 致谢

感谢孔江平教授对本研究的悉心指导。感谢审稿专家提出的宝贵的修改意见。

本研究得到教育部基地重大项目“基于语言多模态的语言本体研究”（17JJD740001）的资助。

参考文献

［1］Ammirante P, Copelli F. 2019. Vowel formant structure predicts metric position in hip－hop Lyrics. *Music Perception*, 26（5）, 480.

［2］Bele, I. V. 2006. The speaker's formant. *Journal of Voice* 20（4）, 555－578.

［3］Hsin－Huei Chiou, Watson, P. 2005. The effect of speaking rate on supersegmentals: An acoustic and perceptual analysis. *Journal of the Acoustical Society of America* 118（3）, 2024.

［4］Sundberg, J., Gu, L., Huang, Q., et al., 2012. Acoustical study of classical peking Opera Singing. *Journal of Voice* 26（2）, 137－143.

［5］Sundberg J. 1974. Articulatory interpretation of the “singing formant”. *Journal of the Acoustical Society of America* 55（4）, 838－844.

［6］Sundberg, J. 2003. Research on the singing voice in retrospect. *TMH Quarterly Progress & Status Report* 45, 11－22.

［7］艾则孜·阿不力米提、孔江平：《维吾尔十二木卡姆的语音和嗓音声学初探》，《信息通信》2019年第8期，第1—4页。

［8］曹剑芬：《语速特征及其变化》，载《第六届全国现代语音学学术会议论文集》，2003年，第151—156页。

［9］董理：《昆曲的调音和发声研究》，博士学位论文，北京大学，2015年。

［10］［英］哈特曼：《语言与语言学词典》，上海辞书出版社1981年版。

［11］韩宝强、项阳、林秀娣：《中西歌唱发声体系声音形态的比较研究》，《文艺研究》1996年第2期，第80—91页。

［12］黄强、黄平、顾立德：《学院派民歌唱法唱声的长时平均谱特征》，《中国音乐》2013年第1期，第162—167页。

［13］黄强、黄平、顾立德：《昆曲唱声的长时平均谱特征探究》，《中国音乐》2014年第3期，第106—112页。

［14］江海燕：《语速对语句内部音高变化的影响》，《首都师范大学学报》（社会科学版）2015年第3期，第103—107页。

［15］李爱军、祖漪清、李洋等：《汉语普通话篇章语速变化模式初探》，《声学技术》2007年第4期，第242—247页。

［16］李洋：《语音合成中的语速研究》，硕士学位论文，天津大学，2007年。

［17］王力：《山东快书的艺术特色》，《戏剧丛刊》2010年第4期，第126—128页。

［18］王士谦：《嗓音机制和歌手的共振峰——兼答Sundberg》，《音乐艺术》1993年第1期，第66—73页。

［19］殷治纲：《基于节拍概念的语言节奏时长描述系统》，载《第十二届全国人机语音通讯学术会议（NCMMSC2013）论文集》，2013年。

［20］殷治纲：《基于韵律层级模型的汉语朗读语篇语速研究》，《中国语音学报》2019年第2期，第63—74页。

［21］于善英、池万刚：《京昆艺术嗓音声音形态分析与研究》，《音乐探索》2009年第2期，第19—22页。

［22］于善英：《不同歌唱类型歌手共振峰特征及音色形成的机理研究》，《音乐研究》2010年第2期，第74—80页。

［23］张春连：《含灯大鼓的声学研究》，硕士学位论文，北京大学，2015年。

王　璐　北京大学对外汉语教育学院，在读博士生，研究方向为语音学、二语语音习得与教学。
E-mail：wanglulj@pku.edu.cn

马睿启　北京大学中国语言文学系，硕士（已毕业），研究方向为语音学。
E-mail：mrq@pku.edu.cn

脱口秀演员、非演员和 AI 对喜剧脚本语音呈现的差异

冯雅心　汪高武

摘　要　同样的喜剧脚本，脱口秀演员说出来会比未接受过训练的非演员幽默效果更好，这说明幽默效果除依赖文本外，还借助于语音表达的韵律节奏。人工智能合成出同样文本的语音，其幽默效果则更比不上真人说话。为了验证和研究这三种语音呈现的差异，本文比较了相同文本下脱口秀演员、非演员和某 AI（人工智能）所呈现的语音（3 组共 12 段语音）的声学韵律特征。结果表明：专业脱口秀演员的语气词、插入语的语速变化较为灵活；词团语流速度和单位时间内音高变化幅度最大；在强调手段上，脱口秀演员将强调词时长拉得最长，反常停顿的时长最长。以上几个方面非演员的表现均次于脱口秀演员，但好于 AI。

关键词　情感语音，幽默语音，韵律特征，脱口秀表演，智能语音

The Phonetic Differences in the Voice of Stand-up Comedians, Non-comedians and AI When Performing Comedy Scripts

FENG Yaxin　WANG Gaowu

Abstract For the same comedy script, stand-up comedians can provide a more humorous speech performance than non-comedians, which shows that humor does not only rely on words, but also on speech rhythm and prosody. Furthermore, the synthesized speech by AI is less humorous than non-comedians. In order to verify and study the differences of these three kinds of speech, this paper compares the prosodic features (12 audio segments divided in 3 groups) presented by stand-up comedians, non-comedians and synthesized speech, when the same script is used. The results show that professional comedians use the most flexible speech speed in modal particles and word groups, and has the largest pitch ranges per unit time. They increase word durations the most when they emphasize, and they also have the longest “abnormal pause” durations. The performance of non-comedians is not as good as that of the comedians in the above areas, but still better than AI.

Key words Expressive speech, Emotional speech, Humor speech, Prosodic features, Stand-up comedy, Artificial Intelligence

1. 引言

脱口秀（此处指 stand-up comedy，又译为单口喜剧、脱口秀喜剧，而非指访谈节目 talk show）以单人表演为主，通过语言内容及其呈现达到让观众笑的效果［8］。优质的脱口秀喜剧表演，即使忽略演员在视觉上的呈现，仅仅凭声音，也会令人捧腹。但非演员根据同一语言脚本表演的语音的幽默感则会减弱。而 AI 根据同一段文本进行语音合成，产生的幽默感又比非演员更弱。

由此可见，在文本相同的情况下，喜剧语音的幽默感取决于语音表演。能产生幽默效果的语音表演又可以分为特殊的语音构成形式（双声、叠韵、重复等）和韵律特征的变化［12］。由特殊的语音构成造成幽默效果实质上仍然是由文本决定（给定具有双声、重复等固定语音形式的文本，任何人来表演都会产生类似的效果），而韵律特征的变化则并非来自文本。即使是同一文本，不同个体的发音韵律特征不同，达成的幽默效果也不同。目前学

界对言语幽默的研究主要集中在幽默的文本表达、幽默的自然语言处理上，与语音相结合的研究集中在情感语音领域特别是情绪和态度方面，将语音韵律与幽默相结合的研究还并不深入。基于此，本文结合幽默文本，借鉴情感语音研究的方法开展研究。在情感语音的分析中，韵律特征分析主要包括基频特性、语速特性、能量特性［11］。又可以细分为时长、能量、最大基频、基频范围、基频特征等参数（情感语音转换实验）［13］。本文结合前人研究，并根据具体表演情况，选择适当的韵律参数。

本文选取综艺节目《脱口秀大会》和《吐槽大会》演员4位（排除肢体表演型脱口秀演员和明星嘉宾），2男2女，每人5分钟左右表演音频。根据其表演记录下文字脚本/台词（约为4000字），然后选取与表演该段脱口秀演员性别、年龄相对应的、普通话水平测试在一级以上的非演员，根据同样的文字脚本进行语音表演并录音。录音设备为戴尔笔记本电脑，内置麦克风，采样率为22050Hz。同时将脚本文字输入开放性语音合成平台，根据表演者性别和年龄找到对应的AI发音人（AI发音人选自微软云开放语音合成平台的TTS功能模块［1］，该平台使用深度神经网络进行语音合成，有9位不同性别和年龄的发音人以供选择。另外还可以设置各种情感、场景的发音风格，本文均选用“默认”发音风格，然后由平台输出合成语音）。最后得到3组共12段语音，均转换为WAV文件，单声道，采样率22050Hz。运用Praat（Ver. 6. 1. 26）软件对这12段语音通过听辨和观察波形图、频谱图，分别测量其基频、时长、停顿等韵律特征，并利用Microsoft Excel 2016、IBM SPSS Statistics 26对数据进行统计处理。

2. 语气词、插入语的语速

脱口秀表演中，演员往往会加入一些插入语，比如“啊”“对吧”“哈”“哦”“哇”“哇哦”等，使得语言更加灵活。演员和非演员在说这些插入语时会比较自由，体现在相同的插入语往往会根据上下文语境而调整其韵律特征，使其能更加协调地融入整个句子的韵律或者达到夸张的效果，进而增强表演效果。与插入语相近的是语气词，比如表疑问、感叹和惊讶语气的“啊”“哎”等。AI合成语音对这些语气词的识别与合成已经比较成熟，会根据具体语境来调整音强、音高和时长，比如对于“啊”的合成，AI已经能比较成熟地将它作为一个音强较轻、时长较短、音调较低的语气词放在句尾或者句中，但仍不能将作为插入语的“啊”与作为语气词的“啊”区分开（韵律均合成为语气词“啊”）。虽然AI会根据语境来调整语气词的韵律，但调整的幅度非常小，比较单一。此外，AI目前仍不能根据文本合成疑问语气的语气词，而是一律识别并合成为轻声的语气词。本文根据四位演员的用语习惯选取4个反复出现的具有代表性的插入语，分别是思文：哇；周奇墨：啊（记为啊$_1$）；池子：啊（记为啊$_2$）；杨笠：你知道吧。每个插入语选择20个样本，共80个样本。由图1可见，随着合成字数的增加，AI发音时长大幅度增加，而演员和非演员的增加幅度则较小。说明AI在合成语音时还是以字为单位的音节之间的简单叠加，而真人则会根据语境对插入语音节之间的关系进行调整，这就导致了虽然插入语“你知道吧”有4个字，但演员说起来很快，将插入语融入语流之中，而AI合成的则占时较长，听起来较为突兀。

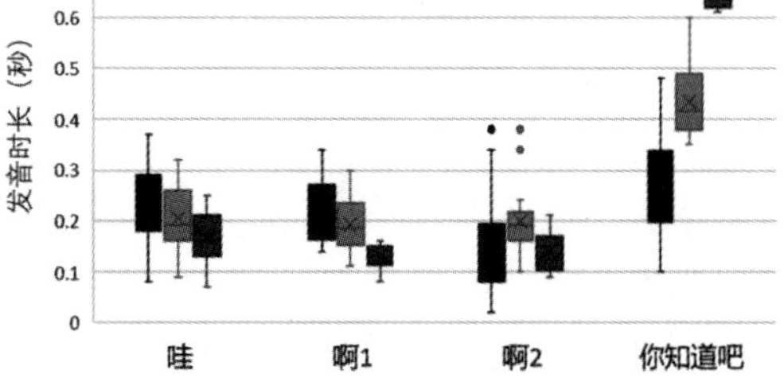

图1　插入语发音时长箱形图

由图1可见，演员的插入语发音时长（绝对时长，插入语“啊”“哇”只有一个音节，虽然受语境、语气影响较多，但个体差异的影响较小）标准差大于非演员，更大于AI，说明演员的插入语发音在韵律上更加灵活，不同语境下的发音时长差别较大，非演员次之，AI最为单一。进一步观察可见演员与非演员的标准差之间的差要小于非演员与AI之间的差，说明真人之间的差异小于真人与AI之间的差异，AI对出现在不同位置的相同音节组合的韵律的合成和调整还距真人有一定距离。

表1中的主体间单因素方差分析显示，演员、非演员和AI的4个插入语的发音时长均有显著差异，具体体现在：“哇”，演员与AI发音时长存在显著差异（$p=0.03$）；“啊$_1$”，AI与演员和非演员发音时长存在显著差异（$p<0.01$）；“啊$_2$”，AI和非演员发音时长存在显著差异（$p=0.03$）；“你知道吧”三者之间均存在显著差异（$p<0.01$）。插入语“啊$_1$”和“哇”，人类发音人内部存在显著差异；以上4个插入语，AI均与人类发音人存在显著差异，说明在插入语语速上，AI与人类发音人的差异要大于人类发音人内部的差异。

表1　插入语时长各发音组间显著性
（$p<0.05$ 为显著，+表示显著，-表示不显著）

	哇	啊$_1$	啊$_2$	你知道吧
演员与非演员	-	-	-	+
演员与AI	+	+	-	+
非演员与AI	-	+	+	+

3. 词团内部语流

“词语的聚合成分在进行语言表达的过程中需要看做被独立运用的、不可分割的一个语义体，在自然语音处理环节应当使这些单音节字的关系聚合起来……将汉语自然语言中的语义集合体命名为‘词团’。”[5]例如“我觉得快递车上应该贴一个易燃易爆的标识”这句话中“我觉得”和“易燃易爆的标识”就是两个词团，均由多个词组成，在韵律上不可分割。词团与停延段和韵律短语相似但有区别，词团不需要以停顿或延宕来与前后韵律单位区分，词团的单位要小于韵律短语，但又可以大于韵律词（可以由几个韵律词组成），介于二者之间，选取词团是为了更加灵活地观测语音流中各韵律单位之间的组合情况和节奏。本文在每段语音中随机提取20个词团，4位表演者共80个词团，并在对应的非演员表演者、AI表演者的语音中选取对应的词团，计算词团内语速（词团内不存在停顿），按频次分布得出图2。由图可见，脱口秀演员的词团内部语流速度分布较散（标准差2.28），非演员的分布较为集中（标准差1.40），AI则更为集中（标准差1.28）。分布越集中，则速度较为恒定，听觉上让人感到较为单调。单一的语速难以起到突出重点、区分、设置特定情境的功能，这些都影响了AI的表演效果。

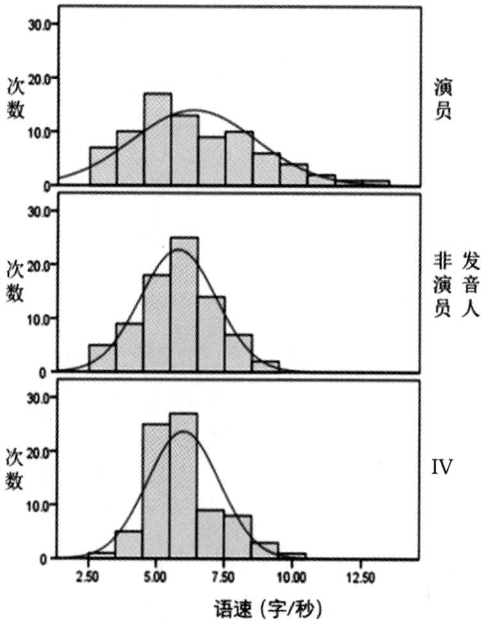

图2　词团内部语速分布

4. 音高变化幅度与特殊情景语境的音高变化特点

为探求演员、非演员和AI在整体上

的音高变化程度，将4位表演者对应的4组语音（每组包含演员、非演员和AI的表演语音）导入Praat，提取整段语音的基频数值（每隔0.025秒提取一个基频值，删除基频值连续为0的部分），并对基频进行归一化处理，见公式（1）：

$$a = \frac{p - p_{min}}{p_{max} - p_{min}} \quad (1)$$

其中p为任意取值点原始基频值，a为归一化后该点的基频值，$0 \leqslant a \leqslant 1$，$p_{min}$、$p_{max}$分别为该段语音中最小、最大基频值。为了衡量基频变化的程度，将归一化后的基频数据错项相减（类似于微分运算），求和并除以总时长，最后得到单位时间内音高变化幅度F，如公式（2）所示：

$$F = \frac{|a_1 - a_0| + |a_2 - a_1| + \cdots + |a_n - a_{n-1}|}{t} \quad (2)$$

其中t为整段语音时长，单位为秒。

四段语音各表演者单位时间内音高变化幅度F的值如表2所示。

表2　单位时间内音高变化幅度值F

发音人 / 原创表演者	演员	非演员	AI
思文	1.33	1.04	2.26
周奇墨	1.46	0.86	0.85
池子	1.22	0.78	0.99
杨笠	1.44	1.16	0.96

可见演员的F值要普遍高于非演员和AI，说明其表演语音的音高变化幅度更大。“思文”的AI表演者音高变化幅度高于演员和非演员是由于这里所选的AI表演者全程音高起伏过大，听感上表现为全程情绪过于饱满，AI语音合成会通过适当增强音高起伏来达到使语音情感饱满的效果，但为思文所选择的这位AI表演者把这种方法不加选择地运用在所有语境中，导致F值高于演员和非演员，但幽默效果并未增加（经过3人听辨，对AI合成语音与演员、非演员语音进行对比）。这说明，幽默效果固然跟丰富的音高变化相关，但也要看变化的具体分布模式。其可能原因见下文的一些分析。

脱口秀表演中涉及用语言手段进行情景再现、情景设置的环节。表演者在讲述一个故事的时候，往往会通过变化丰富的语言来再现这个情景，比如会通过改变语音情感来表达惊讶、兴奋、难过等心理状态，让表演更加生动从而达到一定的反差效果，进而达到幽默效果。在情景重现的过程中，会以陈述语音为基础，改变多种语音特征来生动地再现情景中人的状态，例如通过调节音高等方式。脱口秀演员的表演往往更加生动甚至夸张，而普通人和AI则不容易将叙述状态和情景设置状态生动地、明显地区别开。

值得注意的一点是，音高的变化起伏能够使AI语音情感更加饱满，但如果不区分语境而对所有语句都合成为大幅度的音高变化，那么就失去了某些语境中特殊的音高变化起到的区分情景等特殊功能，也使得整段语音显得单调。思文原创喜剧语音的AI发音人合成的语音从头至尾呈现出一致的大幅度音高变化，这导致其F值很高，但听起来仍然不生动、不幽默。选取思文语音中一段典型的情景再现语音：“哇你还要装作很生气的样子，（说）哼，我就知道你现在的眼光这么差，哼!”前半句是陈述状态，后半句是撒娇情景再现状态，整句的意思是，“你”装作很生气的样子，撒娇地说“哼，我就知道你现在的眼光这么差，哼!”由图3可见，演员思文撒娇情景下的音高以陈述音高的平均线为基准，大幅度上下运动变化。整体音高提升、音高变化快而灵活，体现了撒娇情境下语音的典型特征，其生动的表演也博得了观众的笑声。非演员撒娇状态下的整体音高也高于陈述状态，但上扬幅度没有演员大，变化速度没有演员快，生动效果不如专业演员。AI的撒娇情境下的音高变化幅度也很大，但与其陈述状态的音高变化幅度相似，因此没有起到区别的作用，听感上比较单调。

情景语境下的音高变化与叙述语境相比不一定呈现出与上述撒娇语境相同的情

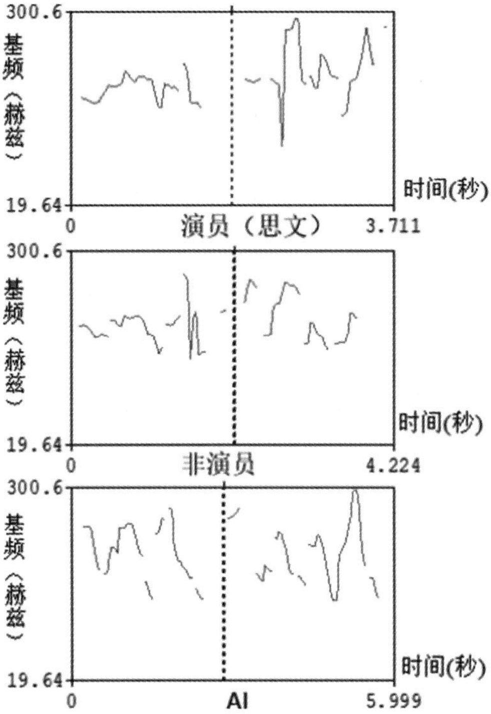

图3 叙述—撒娇音高对比

况，不同的语境其音高变化有不同风格，不同语境也可以通过时长、音强甚至可以通过改变音质来表达。本文所选的语音中包含撒娇、威胁和调侃三种情景语境，如表3所示，生动的撒娇情景语音音高的变化幅度较叙述态大，而生动的威胁、调侃情景语音音高变化幅度较叙述态小，通过最高基频与最低基频的差值可见，各位演员的音高变化对比最为明显，非演员和AI则并不明显，甚至并没有体现出情景的变化。

表3 常态与情景下最高与最低基频差值（赫兹）

情景＼发音人	演员		非演员		AI	
	叙述	情景	叙述	情景	叙述	情景
撒娇	57	136	100	102	126	114
威胁	131	79	80	67	118	122
调侃	131	30	110	147	93	54

5. 强调手段

脱口秀演员通常会通过一些韵律手段如延长和停顿，来达到强调或反差的幽默效果。

5.1 延长时长

句重音是语言交流的重点，知觉上，听者对重音作用成分感到突出感和醒目感（conspicuousness），这种知觉效果的声学基础是音高模式的突变和时长的增加［2］。Eefting发现通过语音合成实验提出时长的增加为听者提供加工强调信息的时间［4］，而强调可以导致音节时长增加25%左右［3］。仲晓波等人发现当句子重音强调词或词中的某个音节时，时长均会增加且时长的增加集中在这个词的重读音节或强调音节上［14］。

通过延长时长可以强调关键词，可以夸大该词所表达的意义。亚里士多德关于幽默的乖讹论认为期望与实际之间的差异是幽默的来源，“并且这种不协调程度越大，越出其不意，幽默效果就越强烈。因此‘一致性’与‘冲突’是幽默产生的两个基本特征。”［7］比如例句：你就会觉得特别凄凉。“凄凉”两个字的延长让人感受到了被夸张渲染过的事件场景和氛围，而事件本身并非一个严肃的悲剧事件，这种反差让人感到惊讶，进而产生幽默效果。本文选取脱口秀脚本中60处引发观众笑声、掌声的强调词（这些词的妙用在语言层面上可以产生幽默效果，演员的强调进一步放大了这种效果），计算强调词时长占所在句子时长的百分比，并取平均值，得到演员、非演员和AI的值分别为34%、29%、25%。可见，专业演员在强调词的时长占句子时长的比例最高、强调力度最大，非专业演员次之，AI最差。

主体间单因素方差分析显示（见表4），各个发音人之间的强调词时长占比存在显著差异（$p = 0.03$），AI和非演员之间不存在显著差异，而二者与演员之间存在显著差异。说明在运用强调手段达成幽默效果上，只有专业的喜剧演员才能对这些特殊的词汇进行强调，非演员虽然在发音上自然，但对能造成幽默效果的词并无特殊处理，说明造成差异的主要原因是对幽默进行表达的能力，而不是简单的机器类人的能力，机器即使做到人类发音的自然，仍无法甄选并对某些词做特殊的语音合成（如延长时长表达强调）以表达幽默效果。

5.2 反常停顿

“停顿前后的话语（概念或命题）多是违反逻辑的同一律的。”［9］当人们听完停顿前的话语，对这一部分有了心理期待，形成一种心理定式，当后面的话语语义偏离已经形成的心理期待，会使人产生惊讶、错愕感。停顿可以加强心理定式的沉淀，使得前后语义对比更加强烈，进而增加幽默效果。这种停顿不是韵律单位之间的节奏性停顿，远长于韵律词、韵律短语之间的停顿且常常出人意料，因此称之为反常停顿。比如本文所选的一个例句，背景为父亲对儿子的工作不满，抱怨说以后不用也用不上儿子赡养。儿子先说“爸你真别说了”，并在这里停顿。听到这里，观众形成心理定式：儿子对父亲的抱怨不满，想让父亲停下来别说了，之后的停顿加强了心理定式。随后语义偏转：“你写下来。”儿子并不是对父亲的这句话不满，而是想趁机让父亲写下来，作为将来不用尽赡养义务的证据。到这里，听众的心理定式受到很大的冲击，观众产生惊讶之余感受到事件由一个严肃的家庭话题变成了一个晚辈的小聪明闹出的笑话，产生幽默效果。

本文选取20处与上文所举的例子类似的反常停顿，计算停顿时长占所在句子时长的百分比［百分比 = 停顿时长/（停顿时长 + 发音时长）］。这里的句子是指由停顿前后的2个小句和停顿组成的语义完整的单位。例如：“爸你真别说了——你写下来”。句子时长 = 两个小句的时长 + 停顿时长，并取平均值，得到演员、非演员、AI的时长百分比分别为26%、8%、15%。专业演员停顿的时长占整句时长的比例要高于非演员和AI。AI的反常停顿时长比高于非演员，这是由于目前AI合成的语音不论在语义上是否形成反常停顿都存在0.3秒左右停顿。表4主体间单因素方差分析显示，各发音人之间的词团内部语速存在显著差异（Brown-Forsythe检验 $p = 0.002$），具体体现在演员与非演员之间存在显著差异，演员与AI之间不存在显著差异，这是由于AI合成语音的停顿实际上是无差别的停顿，与演员所展现的反常停顿有根本性的差别。

表4 强调词及反常停顿占整句时长比显著性
（$p < 0.05$ 为显著，+表示显著，-表示不显著）

	强调词	反常停顿
演员与非演员	+	+
演员与AI	+	-
非演员与AI	-	-

6. 结论

声音四要素构成的轻重、停连、快慢等是能产生幽默效果的语音修辞［10］。本文的研究表明，在一段语流中，专业脱口秀演员的插入语的语速变化较为灵活，词团语流速度和音高的变化域最大、变化速度最快、变化最为灵活；在强调手段上，脱口秀演员将强调词时长拉得最长，具有最长的反常停顿。整体上看，脱口秀演员最为灵活，AI最为单一。

目前AI合成语音在情感的自然度和类人程度上已经取得了很大进步，如AI表演者会对语气词进行轻声化的处理，让它听起来更加自然；同一个语气词“啊”在不同的文本位置（甚至是相同的语流环境下）合成为不同的时长；在词与词之间添加呼吸音等都让人感到很自然。但为了保证语音合成的稳定可靠，有些与人类类似的特征是被弱化了的，比如AI在不同位置发出的同一个语气词和插入语的时长是参差不齐的，但这种参差不齐是有上下限的，而这个变化域无法囊括人类在表达，特别是表达幽默（再现情景、夸张）

时会用到的极限。还有为了追求情感的饱满而被过度强化的特征，如音高不分语境、语义而进行大幅度的起伏变化。此外，还有受限于语音合成手段而造成的机械性韵律特征，如词与词之间的普遍停顿。被过度强化的机械性韵律特征造成了图4中“F值平均值”和“反常停顿时长占比平均值”这两个参数AI的表现偏高却并没有取得更好的幽默效果。

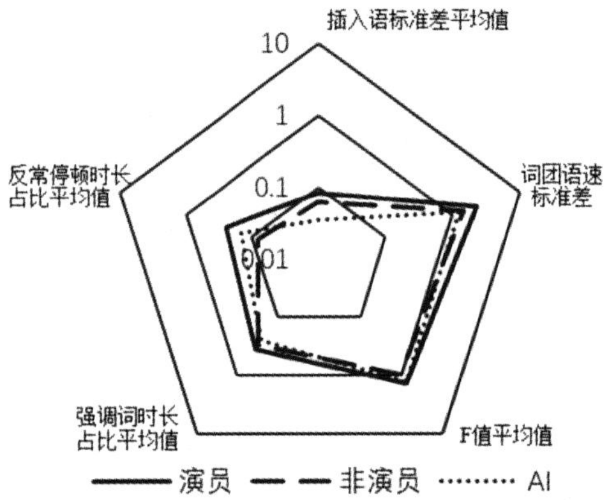

图4 各参数总结（对数刻度图）

幽默的不一致原理要求幽默的产生伴随出人意料的情绪转折，其中伴随逻辑的转折，这要求人在说话时做出违反常规的行为，如反常的停顿、夸张的音高等。幽默能力是一种有目的性的违反常规的能力，而目前的AI语音合成是遵循统计规律来运行和不断优化的，这是对AI幽默语音韵律发展的挑战，也是一个很好的关于人机差异的重要议题。本文试图通过对比演员、非演员和AI的语音来找出典型的幽默语音所普遍具有的韵律特征。实际上脱口秀表演产生语音幽默的原因要复杂得多，比如幽默也是一种互动的产物。脱口秀演员在与观众的互动中、在观众的影响下创造节奏，每场表演的节奏都不尽相同［6］。幽默韵律也不是靠各因素的简单组合和提前计划而产生的，但除了互动中临时的、不可控制的因素外，幽默韵律一定有其内在的规律。艺术是可以用科学解释的，人的经验和智慧是可以用显性语言表达的。虽然目前的科技水平离解释、再现、生成艺术还很遥远，但这也正需要我们一步步去探索。

目前本文主要描述了一些韵律特征的不同，但要判断这些特征是伴随的，还是真正的影响因子，需要控制变量做对照听辨实验。我们也计划下一步调节各种韵律特征，并衡量其幽默效果，从而找到真正有影响作用的韵律特征因子。例如，恰当的停顿，是演员把握节奏达到幽默效果的诀窍之一，在统计分析找到规律之后，还要选择一定数量的表演语音，调节停顿时长，打乱后让听众对听到的语音幽默效果打分，这样就可能找出最佳的停顿设置规律和影响效果。这个实验控制变量的难度较大，我们计划在下一步的工作中进行。

7. 致谢

本研究得到国家自然科学基金“基于X光和MRI磁共振成像的汉语普通话发音生理模型研究”（11974054）的支持。

参考文献

［1］Speech Studio，https：//speech. microsoft. com/.

［2］Eady，S. J.，Cooper，W. E. 1985. Speech intonation and focus location in matched statements and questions. *The Jornal of the Acoustical society of America* 80，402－413.

［3］Eefting，W. 1991. The effect of “information value” and “accentuation” on the duration of Dutch words，syllables，and segments. *The Jornal of the Acoustical society of America* 89，412－424.

［4］Eefting，W. 1992. The effect of accentuation and word duration on the naturalness of speech. *The Jornal of the Acoustical society of America* 91，411－420.

［5］樊强：《人工智能（AI）播音语链内生成结构研究》，《电视研究》2009年第2期。

［6］［美］格雷格·迪安：《手把手教你玩脱口秀》，梁海源、程璐译，浙江人民出版社2018年版。

［7］林飞鸿、张冬瑜、杨亮、徐博：《幽默计算及其应用研究》，《山东大学学报》（理学版）2016年第7期，第1—10页。

［8］宋启瑜：《脱口秀初探》，《曲艺》2014年第7期。

［9］王世凯:《口语停顿的修辞功能》,《修辞学习》2000年第4期。
［10］吴土良:《语音要素与幽默言语》,《语言与翻译（汉文）》2000年第4期。
［11］谢波、韦璇、陈根才、陈纯:《普通话情感语音数据库及其韵律特征的统计分析》,载《第一届中国情感计算及智能交互学术会议论文集》,北京,2003年。
［12］谢伦浩:《论幽默的语音修辞构成》,《云梦学刊》2002年第2期。
［13］熊文婷、崔丹丹、孟凡博、蔡莲红:《情感语音的韵律特征分析与转换》,载《第八届中国语音学学术会议暨庆贺吴宗济先生百岁华诞语音科学前沿问题国际研讨会（PCC2008/ISPF2008）论文集》,北京,2008年。
［14］仲晓波、杨玉芳:《汉语普通话句子重音在时长方面的声学表现》,《心理学报》2003年第35期。

冯雅心 北京师范大学文学院,硕士研究生,主要研究领域为语音学,情感语音。
E-mail: fyx98@ bnu. edu. cn

汪高武 北京师范大学文学院副教授,主要研究领域为实验语音学 。
E-mail: wgw@ bnu. edu. cn

相声贯口声学实验研究

李晓媛　刘　文

摘　要　贯口是相声演员的基本功，表演时依靠其特殊的语言节奏给听众以美感。本文以《报菜名》《夸住宅》《莽撞人》三段经典相声中的名词罗列片段为研究对象，按贯口字数划分为单字、双字、三字和四字不同字组，运用声学分析提取时长、基频、共振峰、谐波振幅差值、倒谱峰值凸显和谐噪比等参数，将贯口表演与正常诵读进行对照。研究发现：时长方面，贯口明显小于正常诵读，节奏更紧凑；音高方面，贯口普遍高于正常诵读，且音域变化范围更为宽广；共振峰模式上，二者基本一致，表明贯口发音时与正常诵读的音色一致；信噪比方面，贯口低于正常诵读，说明前者除普通换气外还存在“偷气”现象；频谱特征上，贯口与正常诵读在低频处未呈现出显著性差异，但在高频处贯口有着更强的高频能量，使其音色更为明亮。本文通过对贯口表演的发声进行声学量化，寻找出了其发声特性并阐释了背后的声学原理，这不仅可以为相声表演者提供一定的指导参考，还有利于相声艺术的科学化保护与传承。

关键词　相声贯口，声学分析，时长，音高，共振峰，频谱能量，信噪比

An Acoustic Study on the Guankou in Crosstalks

LI Xiaoyuan　LIU Wen

Abstract Guankou is the basic skill of crosstalk actors, who take advantage of its special rhythm to make the audience enjoy it. In this study, the segments containing long sequences of nouns from the three classic crosstalk sections of “Baocaiming”, “Kuazhuzhai” and “Mangzhuangren” are taken as the research object. According to the number of syllables, these nouns are further divided into monosyllabic, bisyllabic, trisyllabic and quadrisyllabic sequences. The duration, F0, formants, harmonic amplitude differences, cepstrum peak prominence and harmonic-to-noise ratio were used to compare Guankou with normal readings. Results have shown that the duration of Guankou is significantly shorter than that of the normal reading, and its rhythm is more compact. Generally, the pitch range of Guankou is higher, and the vocal register is wider than the normal reading. The formant patterns between Guankou and the normal reading are not significant different, indicating that the timbre in the two styles is similar. The harmonic-to-noise ratio of Guankou is lower than that of the normal reading, which indicates that Guankou is more breathy in speech. In addition, there is no significant difference in the low-frequency spectrum between Guankou and the normal reading, but the high frequency energy of Guankou is stronger, meaning that the timbre of Guankou is brighter. This study described the vocal characteristics of Guankou and explained the acoustic principles behind them. These results not only provide some guidance and reference for crosstalk performers, but also contribute to the scientific protection and inheritance of crosstalk art.

Key words Crosstalk Guankou, Acoustic Analysis, Duration, Pitch, Formant, Spectrum, SNR

1. 引言

相声贯口作为传统曲艺形式，在新时期重焕生机，涌现了一批相声新秀，同时也引起了学界对于这门口传文化传承与发展的关注。贯口，又叫“趟子”“贯活”，指相声演员通过大段的、一气呵成的独白展现口齿基本功和语言韵律美的表演［15］。按照内容的不同，相声贯口可以分为名词罗列类、故事类与赞赋类［8］，其中名词罗列类作品数量最多、演出最常使

用，因而也最具代表性。

贯口发音时，要求表演者做到“变、稳、清、顺”［16］。从听者角度来讲，词不能说得太快，以免使得观众心里紧张，或者印象模糊。另外，说的时候不能像背书，要有一定的腔调。一般应根据剧中的情绪，像日常说话一样地叙述出来［7］。相声贯口的前人研究主要来自相声从业者对自身表演经验的总结，不论是从表演者自身还是从听众听感的角度，这种传统的相声贯口研究均停留在主观描述的层面上，未能对其背后的声学特性及对应的生理机制做出科学阐释。而对传统说唱、戏曲念白等其他以“说”为主的曲艺形式亦有前人进行了一些相关研究。其中，音高、时长和音强是研究者们的普遍关注点。罗常培［12］基于前人的方言类比法对京剧韵白的四声调值进行了转写。林焘［11］使用音高仪绘制了老生行当中常用的16个双音词的基频曲线，归纳了四声在京剧韵白中的具体调值与连续变调情况，指出京剧韵白的四声可以分为高调（T55、T35）与低调（T12、T31）两类，而正是高低调的分别对变调规律起着重要作用。索朗德吉等［13］在对藏族说唱艺术《格萨尔》的研究中指出演员的情感表达主要依靠其音高、音强的变化，在表现忧伤情感时，其基频变化舒缓、能量较弱；表现高昂的情绪时，基频起伏较大、能量较强。韩启超［6］以昆曲小生行当为研究对象探究了昆曲念白的时长与音高特征，文章指出在昆曲念白中尾字普遍长于首字，音高则呈现出“低开—中高—低收”的基本形态。董理［5］通过提取等效声级、声压级和基频对比分析了昆曲中演唱、念白与读曲词三种发音模式的音强与音高，实验指出所有行当中念白的音高最高、音强最大且分布与细节变化较演唱更集中，而在行当内部基频与等效声级呈正相关，即演员提高音高的同时会增大音强。

综合前人研究，相声贯口已具有一定的理论研究基础，但实验研究相对匮乏。声学研究理论与技术的进步为我们对其进行科学解读、量化描写提供了新路径。基于上述相关研究及相声发展现状，本文的研究问题主要集中于以下两个方面：第一，贯口表演背后是怎样的声学特性；第二，基于声学研究结果，我们可以为相声贯口学习者提供怎样的借鉴与参考。

2. 实验方法

实验发音人为山东大学相声协会专业青年相声演员，师从河北相声名师刘志和，学艺十载，以“说”见长。

本实验选取《报菜名》《夸住宅》《莽撞人》三段经典相声中的贯口片段作为研究对象，按贯口中不同韵律单元（含词、短语及小句）的音节数量划分为单字、双字、三字和四字不同字组。录音内容共计202个音节，其中包括单字组16个、双字组48个、三字组90个以及四字组48个。录音包括同一发音人的两种发音模式：第一，按照舞台表演方式诵读贯口选段；第二，按照普通话字音诵读贯口选段。贯口表演为实验组，普通话正常诵读作为其声学分析时的对照组。两种发音模式各录制一遍。

录音在山东大学语音实验室中进行。录音使用SONY ECM－44B电容式麦克风，通过XENYX调音台、SBX外置声卡与联想S405笔记本电脑连接，录音软件选用Cool Edit Pro 2.1，采样率44100Hz，采样精度为16bit。

语音信号的分析首先使用Cool Edit Pro 2.1软件对不同字组进行切音，之后在Praat中对每个音节的元音段进行逐一标注，使用VoiceSauce分析软件分别提取不同字组贯口表演与正常诵读的时长、基频（F0）、共振峰（F1、F2和F3）、谐波振幅差值（H1* － H2*、H1* － A1*、H1* － A2*和H1* － A3*）、倒谱峰值凸显（CPP）和谐噪比（HNR）等参数。

3. 实验结果

通过对两种模式的语音信号进行提取与处理，我们得到了一个小型的声学参数数据库。根据得到的数据，本节将从（1）

音高与时长；（2）共振峰与频谱参数；（3）信噪比三个方面来阐释本文的实验结果。

3.1 音高与时长

作为一种强调语言节奏的艺术表现形式，相声贯口在表演时有其独特的艺术发声方式。本小节主要从音高和时长两个方面来对比分析贯口表演与正常诵读两种发声模式的声学特性。音高是人们对声音高低的感知，是一个心理学概念，基频（F0）是其在客观物理层面的反映［10］。因此参数上我们选择用基频对音高进行量化描写。

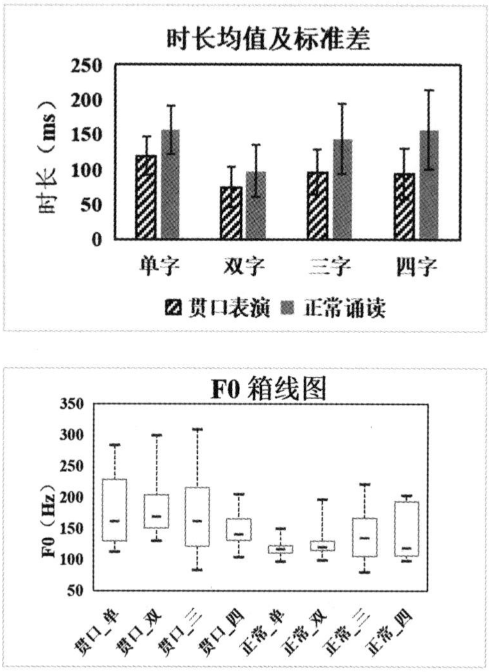

图1　贯口表演与正常诵读时长（上）与F0（下）

图1呈现了贯口表演与正常诵读时长及F0的整体情况。时长方面，各字组呈现出一致的特点：贯口表演的时长总体小于正常诵读，平均单个音节缩短44.68ms。这表明贯口表演具有更为紧凑的节奏。

音高方面，贯口表演的音高总体高于正常诵读，音高分布范围为83.11—308.75Hz（225.64 Hz，标准差为52.28Hz），较正常诵读的79.63—221.12 Hz（141.49 Hz，标准差为36.94Hz）更为宽广。但与时长不同，随着单个词字数的增加，贯口表演与正常诵读的音高差异在各字组间逐渐缩小，至四字组中二者的音高已不存在显著性差异（$p = 0.41$）。

除整体差异外，贯口表演的艺术发声特点也体现在音节间时长与音高的变化趋势上。各字组变化趋势总体一致，以下以单字组为例进行说明。图2呈现了单字组贯口表演与正常诵读的F0及时长信息。其中，时长以直方图体现，对应右侧纵坐标；F0走势以折线图体现，对应左侧纵坐标。横坐标表示不同音节，数字1—8分别对应单字组的“轮、螺、伞、盖、花、罐、鱼、长”八个音节。

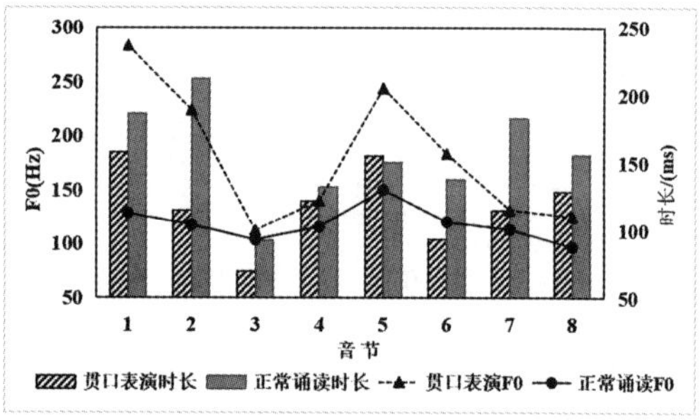

图2　贯口表演与正常诵读单字组F0与时长统计

贯口表演时长虽总体较短，但部分重读音节的时长非常接近甚至略大于正常诵读。这表明贯口表演随着内容与情感的变化存在着明显的急缓之变，而非一味求快。具体来看，贯口表演在时长上的这种急缓之变与正常诵读时有着相似的趋势，二者的相关系数为0.77。

在音高变化趋势上，各字组贯口表演与正常诵读均呈正相关。在语音中韵律单元间的边界位置常发生音高重置现象，即音高从开始说话时的初始值开始下降，有时会达到说话者音高范围的下限，如果发音人要继续发音，音高必须重置到一个较高的水平。这一现象在贯口表演与正常诵读中保持一致，二者在相同的音节位置上存在着明显的音高重置，即如图2中的音节5。但同时贯口表演与正常诵读的这种相关性存在着明显的字组间差异：三字、四字组的相关性（r = 0.70）要强于单字、双字组（r = 0.53）。这说明单个词字数的多少是影响贯口表演者整体音高变化的一个重要因素，字数越多贯口表演就越接近正常诵读时的音高模式。

3.2 共振峰与频谱参数

表1 贯口表演与正常诵读共振峰均值（Hz）

		F1	F2	F3
单字	贯口表演	563.15	1342.47	2762.03
	正常诵读	554.37	1299.45	2544.59
双字	贯口表演	462.15	1241.38	2630.10
	正常诵读	439.70	1238.69	2576.03
三字	贯口表演	527.57	1423.00	2696.02
	正常诵读	474.71	1388.16	2659.67
四字	贯口表演	476.44	1336.09	2716.38
	正常诵读	453.38	1461.03	2761.95

表1显示了贯口表演与正常诵读的共振峰均值。统计分析表明各字组贯口表演与正常诵读的F1、F2和F3之间均不存在显著性差异（$ps > 0.05$）。这表明贯口表演发音时调音模式与正常诵读一致，在节奏较快、抑扬起伏较大的状态下也没有产生额外的弱化、脱落等音变现象。

不同频段的谐波振幅差值显示了发音时的能量变化情况［1］。谐波振幅差值越大说明能量衰减越快，音色越暗淡；反之，能量衰减缓慢，高频能量强，音色则更加明亮。

图3显示了贯口表演与正常诵读在不同频段上的能量变化情况。在H1*—H2*这个参数上二者非常接近，未呈现出显著性差异（$ps > 0.05$），在各个字组之间亦没有表现出规律性差异。

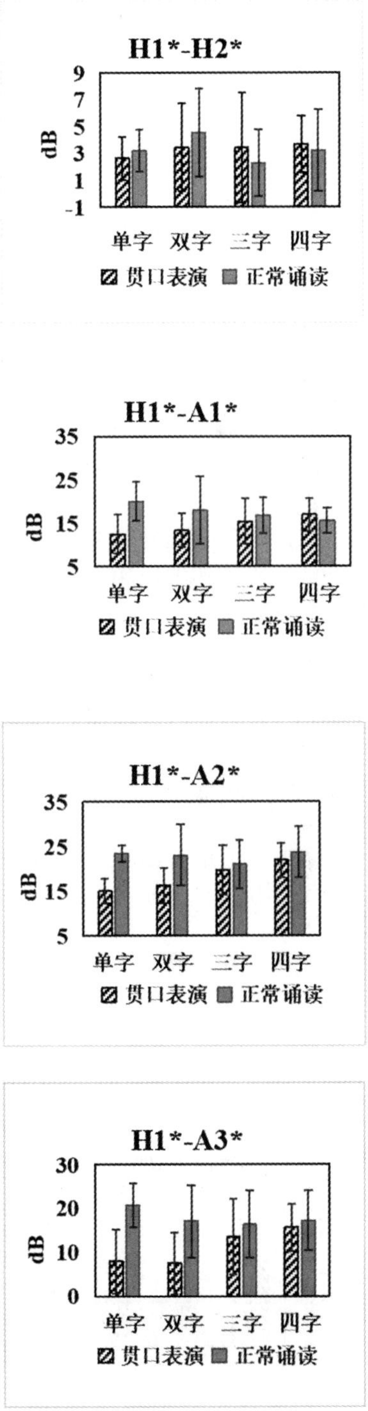

图3 贯口表演与正常诵读谐波振幅差均值及标准差

在 H1*—A1* 上，除四字组外，贯口表演均小于正常诵读，其中单字与双字组呈现极显著差异（$p = 0.0001$，$p = 0.0031$）；至于 H1*—A2* 四个字组的贯口表演均小于正常诵读，但三字组、四字组的差异尚不显著；最终在 H1*—A3* 所显示的高频段内，二者的差异进一步增大，除四字组外均呈现出了显著性差异（$ps < 0.05$）。

此外，我们也可以观察到谐波振幅差值在贯口表演内部亦存在着明显的差异，大致呈现出单字组 < 双字组 < 三字组 < 四字组的等级序列，且单字、双字组同三字、四字组差异明显，前者远小于后者。这表明，相比于正常诵读，贯口表演在发音时其声带闭合程度更高、能量衰减更缓慢，拥有更为强劲的高频能量，从而形成更加明亮的音色，其中以单字组与双字组的表现最为突出。

3.3 信噪比

信噪比测量的是信号能量与噪音能量之间的比值。信号中噪音成分越多，信噪比就越低，反之则越高。在环境噪音恒定的情况下，信噪比反映的是发声效率问题，即声带振动时是否出现声门漏气现象从而影响语音信号的质量［4］。一般使用谐噪比（HNR）和倒谱峰值凸显（CPP）进行量化分析，本小节将通过这两个参数来考察贯口表演的发声呼吸情况。

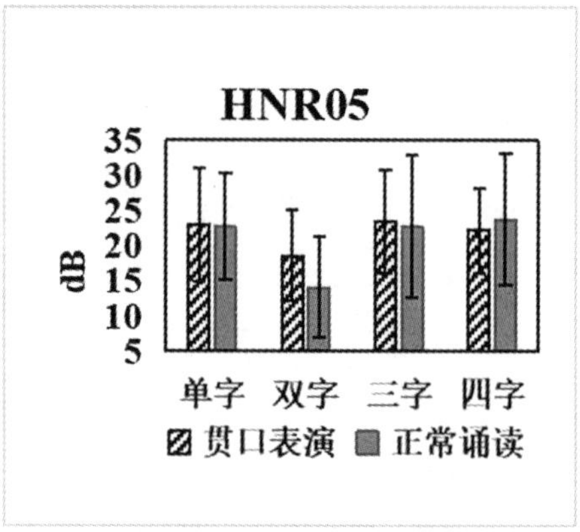

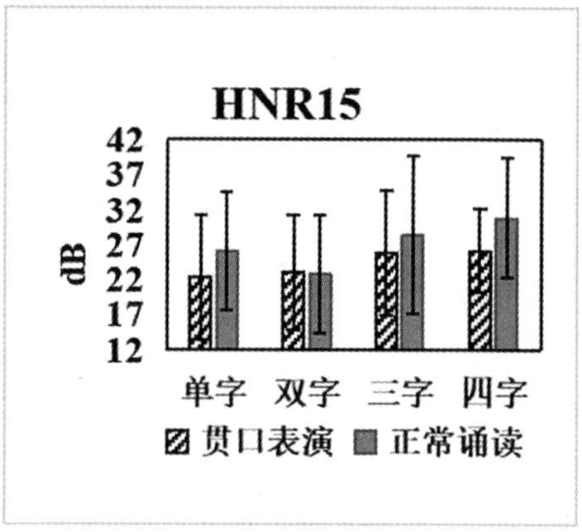

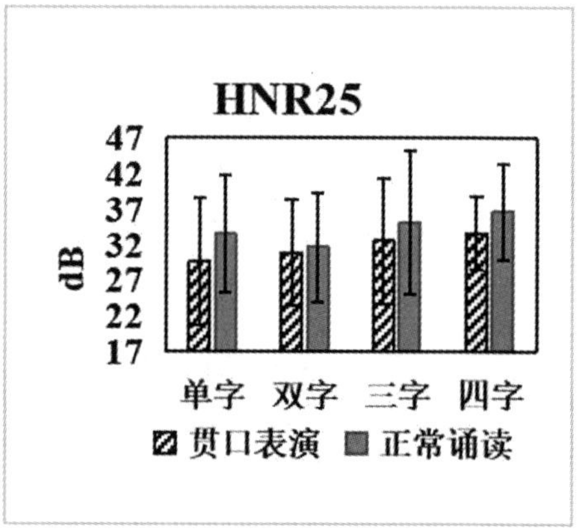

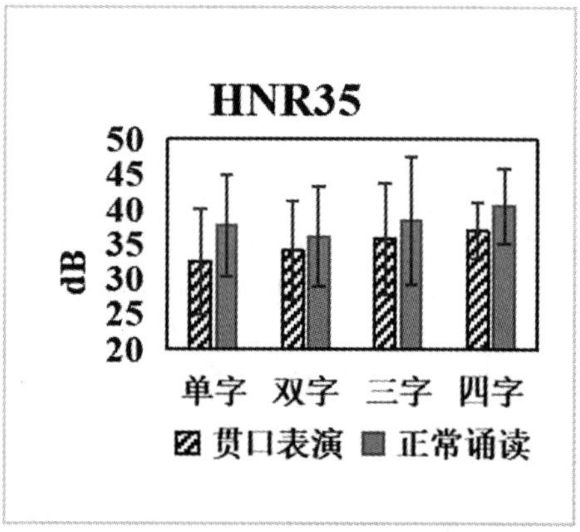

图 4 贯口表演与正常诵读 HNR 均值与标准差

图 4 显示了不同频段上贯口表演与正常诵读的 HNR 均值。HNR05 指的是 0—500 Hz 的谐噪比，HNR15 是 0—1500 Hz 的谐噪比，HNR25 是 0—2500 Hz 的谐噪

比，HNR35 是 0—3500 Hz 的谐噪比。从图中可以看到，在低频区域两种语音模式的 HNR 并没有呈现出规律性的差异，而随着频率范围的扩大与升高逐渐呈现出贯口表演小于正常诵读的趋势，至于 0—3500 Hz 的频段（HNR35），二者在四个字组上都表现出了显著性差异（$ps<0.05$）。

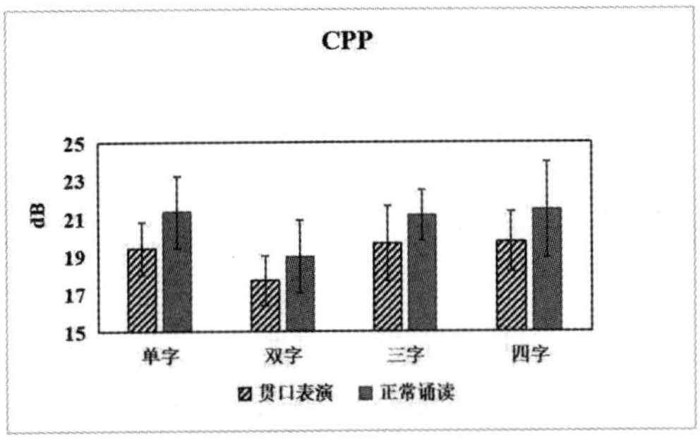

图5　贯口表演与正常诵读 CPP 均值与标准差

倒谱峰值凸显（CPP）可以对言语产生中的呼吸度等级提供准确的预测［2］［3］，CPP 值越低，表明语音信号中的呼吸成分越多，反之则呼吸成分越少。图5显示了二者的 CPP 均值与标准差。从图5中我们可以看到，在 CPP 方面二者的差异更为明显，贯口表演平均比正常诵读低 2 dB，四个字组全部存在着显著性差异（$ps<0.05$）。

综合 HNR 和 CPP 两个参数，可以说明贯口表演发音时较正常诵读含有更多的呼吸成分。结合谐波振幅差值的结果来看，相声贯口在高频范围内信噪比较正常诵读更低，但同时其高频能量却更为强劲，因此本文认为这并非是发音时由声带闭合不严而导致的漏气，而是为了保证长时间持续发音时的平稳、顺畅，贯口表演较正常诵读有着更多的呼吸次数，即除与正常诵读相同停顿处的普通换气外，贯口表演发音过程中还同时伴随有“偷气”的现象。

4. 讨论与结论

本文对相声贯口表演与正常诵读的语音信号进行了对比分析，基于音高、时长、共振峰、谐波振幅差值及信噪比等声学参数对贯口表演背后的声学特性进行了量化描写。

本项研究的结果主要包括以下几点：第一，贯口表演发音时音节时长较短，节奏紧凑，但时长变化模式与正常诵读相似；第二，贯口表演的音域较正常诵读更高、更广，以单字组与双字组最为突出，随着字数的增多其音高模式逐渐近乎正常诵读，完整的贯口作品中并非单一字组一贯到底，往往是不同字组交叉出现，正是这种字组间的音高差异使得贯口表演具有了艺术发声的特点；第三，在节奏更快、抑扬起伏更大的状态下，贯口表演保持了与正常诵读相同的调音模式，从而保证了发音的清晰、准确；第四，贯口表演较正常诵读保持了更为强劲的高频能量，音色明亮，同时在贯口内部呈现出随单个词字数增多高频能量递减的等级序列，即结构越简单其能量衰减越缓慢；第五，在信噪比方面，贯口表演显示出更多的呼吸成分，存在更多的呼吸次数。

基于本文声学研究的结果，贯口表演者在训练时应重视对调音器官的控制、强化对声带的调节，从而在更短的时间内完成与正常诵读同样精准的调音活动。同时还应加强换气、偷气等呼吸技巧的训练，为持续发音提供充足的动力。另外，根据贯口表演在音高、谐波振幅差值等参数上呈现出的字组间差异，表演者在训练时还应针对不同字组采取不同的学习策略，如单字组与双字组表演更注重节奏鲜明、抑扬有致，且发音时声带紧张程度较高；而三字组与四字组则更强调平稳顺畅，发音时更接近于正常诵读。

5. 致谢

本研究得到山东大学基本科研业务费资助项目“平调范畴化感知的物理心理基础及其神经机制”（2019GN08）资助。文章初稿曾在 PCC2021 宣读。

参考文献

[1] Bickley, C. 1982. Acoustic analysis and perception of breathy vowels. *Speech Communication Group Working Papers I*, MIT, Cambridge MA 73 –93.

[2] Fraile, R., Godino – Llorente, J. I. 2014. Cepstral peak prominence: a comprehensive analysis. *Biomedical Signal Processing & Control*, 14 (1), 42 –54.

[3] Hillenbrand, J., Cleveland, R. A., Erickson R. L. 1994. Acoustic correlates of breathy vocal quality. *Journal of Speech Language and Hearing Research* 37 (4), 769 –778.

[4] Klingholz, F. 1987. The measurement of the signal – to – noise ratio (SNR) in continuous speech. *Speech Communication* 6 (1), 15 –26.

[5] 董理:《昆曲的调音和发声研究》,博士学位论文,北京大学,2015年。

[6] 韩启超:《南昆念白声学实验分析》,《中国音乐学》2014年第4期,第102—114页。

[7] 侯宝林:《侯宝林谈相声》,黑龙江人民出版社1983年版。

[8] 侯宝林、汪景寿、薛宝琨:《曲艺概论》,北京大学出版社1980年版。

[9] 姜昆、贾德臣:《中国传统相声大全》,作家出版社2017年版。

[10] 孔江平:《实验语音学基础教程》,北京大学出版社2015年版。

[11] 林焘:《京剧韵白声调初析》,载《王力先生纪念论文集》,商务印书馆1990年版,第74—90页。

[12] 罗常培:《京剧中的几个音韵问题》,载《罗常培语言学论文集》,商务印书馆2004年版,第424—450页。

[13] 索朗德吉、孙婷、达哇彭措:《〈格萨尔〉说唱的声学分析》,《西北民族大学学报》(自然科学版)2014年第95期,第29—34页。

[14] 吴宗济、林茂灿:《实验语音学概要》,高等教育出版社1989年版。

[15] 薛宝琨:《相声大词典》,百花文艺出版社2012年版。

[16] 赵兵:《台词贯口训练》,《戏剧艺术》1992年第3期,第77—85页。

附录

附录1　相声贯口录音语料

字组	语　料
单字组	轮 螺 伞 盖 花 罐 鱼 长
双字组	或攻 或战 或进 或退 或争 或斗 不攻 不战 不进 不退 不争 不斗
三字组	欧美伽 艾尔金 麦格纳 金壳套 银壳套 铜壳套 铁壳套 金三针儿 银三针儿 乌利文 亨得利 人头狗 把上弦儿 双卡子 单卡子
四字组	南煎丸子 苜蓿丸子 三鲜丸子 四喜丸子 鲜虾丸子 鱼脯丸子 饹炸丸子 豆腐丸子

李晓媛　山东大学文学院,硕士,研究兴趣包括实验语音学、口传文化。
E – mail: 1524399159@ qq. com

刘　文　(通讯作者)山东大学文学院,副研究员,博士,硕士研究生导师,主要研究领域为语言记录、嗓音发声类型和言语感知。
E-mail: liuwen3214@ 163. com

白语儿童焦点韵律的习得和发展

刘增慧　梁淑芬

摘　要　研究探索白语儿童焦点韵律习得的发展路径。实验在半自然的语境下，引导5岁至7岁的白语儿童产出处于不同焦点条件下的“主语—动词—宾语”（SVO）句子。本研究考察了白语儿童在其母语的不同声调中将韵律参数（包括时长和音高）用于焦点编码方式。结果发现，白语儿童在5岁时，试图在个别声调中通过变化平均音高来区分窄焦点和焦点后。6岁，白语儿童开始探索通过使用韵律参数来编码焦点，这样的探索既涉及对时长的变化也涉及对音高的变化。7岁是一个重要的发展阶段，白语儿童已经完全展现出和白语成人完全一致的通过变化时长来编码焦点的能力。因而，研究结果显示，白语儿童对其母语白语焦点韵律编码的习得与发展受到母语背景和语言普遍性的双重影响，呈现阶段性并最终向白语成人靠拢。

关键词　白语，儿童语言习得，韵律焦点

The Development of Prosodic Focus-Marking in Bai-Speaking Children

LIU Zenghui　LIANG Shufen

Abstract This study examines the developmental trajectory of prosodic focus-marking in Bai-speaking children. Sentences in the “subject-verb-object”(SVO) structure were elicited from the age group of five to seven in varied focus conditions in a semi-spontaneous setting. The use of prosodic cues, including duration and pitch for encoding focus, was examined in different lexical tones. We have found that Bai children at the age of five distinguished tones in the narrow focus and post-focus positions by varying the mean pitch. They started to explore the use of prosody for encoding focus at the age of six. Additionally, the seven-year-old is a critical age for Bai children’s prosodic development in terms of using prosody for encoding focus in a fully adult-like fashion. These results thus showed that the acquisition of prosodic focus-marking in Bai children proceeds in stages before ultimately reaching the adult-like proficiency.

Key words Bai, Child language development, Prosodic focus-marking

1. 引言

语音习得是儿童语言发展的一个重要方面［26，30］，而韵律发展是语音发展中的一个重要板块。对儿童语言中的韵律习得和发展进行描写、分析和解释是儿童语音发展研究的重要任务之一。然而，与较为成熟的元音、辅音和声调发展研究相比［22，23，28］，韵律发展的研究仍有待深入。本研究关注白语儿童焦点韵律编码的习得情况。焦点韵律编码指的是通过韵律手段来凸显或者标记句子中的新信息［9，10］。

学界对于儿童语音发展的研究主要侧重于对语音发展总体态势、语音系统习得顺序以及习得过程中音位产出错误类型的描写，并讨论了影响儿童语音习得进程的因素［26］。我国的儿童语音研究主要是针对普通话儿童的语音习得发展，代表性的研究有李嵬等［22］、李宇明［23］、许政援［27］、刘兆吉等［25］、朱智贤［31］。

近年来，对单语儿童焦点韵律编码的习得顺序研究成为学界的研究热点之一［1，4，5，7，15，17，19，21］。已有研

究发现，韵律系统的跨语言差异塑造了不同母语背景儿童焦点韵律习得的发展路径［1，5，7，8，17，20，21］。［20］和［21］分别考察了汉语和韩语单语儿童焦点韵律编码的发展路径。这些研究发现，汉语儿童在7岁或8岁时已经能够既使用时长又使用音高来区分窄焦点和焦点前的内容，而韩语儿童却只掌握了使用时长而非音高来区分窄焦点和焦点后的内容。Yang［21］认为这样的差异主要归因于汉语和韩语中音系线索和语音线索在焦点韵律编码使用上的不同。具体说来，在韩语中，插入不同层级的韵律短语划分（prosodic phrasing）被认为是焦点编码的主要手段，而韵律边界的语音实现则是次要手段。但在汉语中，通过变化音高和时长的语音实现手段是焦点编码的主要手段。然而，已有研究多关注韵律手段较为丰富的语言（比如汉语、英语、荷兰语等），对使用韵律手段较为局限的语言（比如白语等）关注较少。白语，主要为生活在中国云南省大理白族自治州的白族所使用，是汉藏语系中的一种声调语言。已有研究发现，在白语中，只有时长用于焦点编码，即在白语中，焦点成分与其作为焦点后成分相比，只有时长延长了［12，13，24］。

本研究考察以白语作为第一语言的儿童焦点韵律编码的习得及发展情况，考察年龄范围从5岁至7岁，旨在探明白语韵律系统如何塑造以白语为母语的儿童韵律焦点的习得和发展路径，探讨白语儿童韵律发展的阶段和规律。

2. 研究方法

2.1 图片配对游戏

本研究采用了［5］所使用的图片配对游戏来引导白语儿童在半自然语境中产出SVO句。选择此方法主要因为：第一，实验对象是学龄前儿童，还并无文字识读的能力，尤其是对白语文字体系；第二，这一方法也曾应用于对汉语单语儿童焦点韵律编码发展的考察，采用同一方法便于对不同母语背景的习得研究进行更为合理的比较。

在图片配对游戏中，一共使用了三组图片。实验员为白语南部方言的母语者（23岁，女）。在实验过程中，实验员和发音儿童各手持一组事先排好顺序的图片，第三组图片散落在实验操作的桌子上。在实验员的图片中（第一组），总有一些信息是缺失的，比如，主语、动作、宾语，或者三者都缺失。发音儿童的图片（第二组）包含某个完整的事件。发音儿童的任务是帮助实验员将第一组（实验员的图片）和第三组（散落在桌子上的图片）挑选出来并配成一对（如图1所示）。

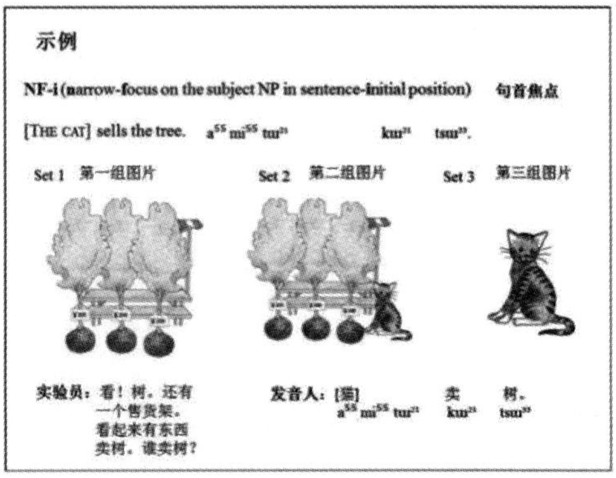

图1 引导“［猫］卖树”的实验流程示例

以图1中位于句首位置的主语成分为窄焦点（NF-i）的句子“［猫］卖树”为例。第一步，实验员从她手里的图片（第一组图片）中拿出一张，通过说——/nɔ^{33} xa^{33}！tsɯ^{33} . tse^{55} tsɯ^{35} kɯ^{21} xuo^{44} ŋv^{33} lɯ^{44} tɕa^{55} tɕa^{55} le^{21} . sa^{42} ʐy^{35} a^{55} tɯ^{21} tsɯ^{33} lɯ^{33} ui^{33} kɯ^{21}tsɯ^{33}/.（“看！树，还有一个售货架。看起来有小动物卖树。”）——这一句子将发音儿童的注意力集中到图片上，并同时描绘图片上的内容。在提出引导问题之前进行这样的操作，是为了保证图片上的实体对于发音儿童来说是已知（given）信息。第二步，实验员针对这张图片提问：/a^{55}tɯ^{21}kɯ^{21}tsɯ^{33}/（“谁卖树?”）第三步，发音儿童从他/她的图片（第二组）中翻开一张来，并仔细进行观察。第四步，实验员重复问题，发音儿童根据其图片回答问题：/a^{55} mi^{55} tɯ^{21} kɯ^{21} tsɯ^{33}/

（“［猫］卖树。”）最后，实验员从第三组图片中找出带有缺失信息的图片来，并将图片配对。游戏的规则要求发音儿童产出完整的句子，并且不能将其手里的图片展示给实验员。

但句中的动词为对比焦点（CF-m）时，实验员提出的问题是：/ŋɔ^{33} tsɔ^{42} k^{h}ua^{33}tɯ^{21} kɯ^{21}tsɯ^{33}/（“我猜，狗卖树。”）随后，发音儿童从他/她的图片（第二组）中翻开图片并对前述信息进行更正。

2.2 实验材料

在图片游戏中，共有五组不同焦点条件下的SVO句，包括：位于句首的名词性主语为窄焦点（NF-i）、位于句中的动词为窄焦点（NF-m）、位于句末的名词性宾语为窄焦点（NF-f）、位于句中的动词为对比焦点（CF-m）以及宽焦点（BF）。

白语有三种声调类型：平调（/55/、/44/、/33/）、降调（/42/、/31/、/32/、/21/）、升调（/35/）。为了保证实验时长适中，本研究在三个声调类型中各选取一个声调作为类型代表并将其纳入实验设计中：/55/为平调的代表，/21/为降调的代表，/35/为升调的代表。

在白语南部方言中，当名词充当句子主语时，其后需伴随一个量词来组成名词短语。但是当名词充当句子宾语时，名词短语的量词可以被省略［29］。本研究选择了四个名词主语，在所有的目标句中这些名词主语后都跟着同一个低降调的量词/tɯ^{21}/（只）。白语中的三个调类中所选取的每个声调（即高平调/55/、低降调/21/、中升调/35/）在动词位置都出现两次。六个单音节动词和四个单音节名词性宾语组成24个动词短语，每个动词短语都出现在5种焦点条件中。这样的设计能够引导出120个动词短语。4个名词性短语依次与120个动词短语组合，从而最终构成120个唯一的目标句。这120个目标句被分为两个列表，每个列表包含实现在不同句子中的5个焦点条件和所有的6个声调代表，但是动词短语被一分为二，分别在两个列表中。如此编排，就可以实现每一位发音儿童参与的是一个含有60个目标句的列表。表1展示了构成SVO句子的选词。

表1　SVO目标句选词一览
（每个词均采用IPA和汉译标示）

<table>
<tr><th>主语</th><th>动词</th><th>宾语</th></tr>
<tr><td>a^{55}mi^{55}tɯ^{21}
猫（只）</td><td rowspan="4">ts^{h}u^{55}
闻
pɔ^{35}
包
kɯ^{21}
卖
xua^{55}
画
ma^{35}
抹
pa^{21}
搬</td><td>ɕui^{55}li^{55}
梨</td></tr>
<tr><td>ɕo^{42}tɯ^{21}
熊（只）</td><td>ts^{h}u^{33}
草</td></tr>
<tr><td>k^{h}ua^{33}tɯ^{21}
狗（只）</td><td>tsɯ^{33}
树</td></tr>
<tr><td>thɔ^{55}lɔ^{55}tɯ^{21}
兔（只）</td><td>fv^{44}
笔</td></tr>
</table>

2.3 实验对象和实验过程

9位来自3个年龄组的白语儿童参与了本实验，其中3位5岁（1个女孩和2个男孩）、3位6岁（1个女孩和2个男孩）、3位7岁（3个女孩）。本研究进行时，所有的儿童均为学龄前儿童，均未开始接受正式标准汉语教育，但可以进行极简单的汉语沟通。所有参与本研究的发音儿童都在中国云南省大理白族自治州喜洲镇的村庄里长大。发音儿童在家里习得白语——第一语言，在7岁之前主要是通过大众媒体接触到汉语。

实验员对发音儿童单独进行测试，在测试中和测试外均只使用白语与发音儿童沟通。每个实验分为两个部分，每个部分包括30个实验测试项。为了避免发音儿童疲劳或是注意力涣散，每个部分的实验结束后会暂停，并让发音儿童适当休息。一位发音儿童完成一个部分的实验大约需20至25分钟。所有的实验都在喜洲镇金圭寺村某村民家中一个安静的房间中完成。实验采用便携式录音设备ZOOM H1进行录制工作，采样率为44.1kHz，16比特。为了将来的训练工作，实验全程进行了影像记录。在正式实验结束之后，一份语言背景和家庭语言使用问卷会发放给儿童的抚养人并请其完成。

2.4 语音标注

首先，采用音标和字符对实验所收集的语料进行转写和标注。如果发音儿童回答的句子符合下列筛选条件之一就将被排除在分析之外：(1) 并不是对目标问题的答案；(2) 包含自我纠正；(3) 回答显示出犹豫（即在发音儿童作出回答之前发出的长“嗯”声）；(4) 在回答句中，发音儿童就词或者语序的选择偏离目标句。在所有获取的语料中，56% 的回答句（有效数据项 = 607，被试人数 = 9）纳入下一步的语音分析中。

动词是本研究的韵律分析目标。本研究采用 Praat 语音分析软件［3］进行分析，根据声波图、宽带频谱图、音高线和听觉印象［18］来对动词进行声学标注。本研究采用自编写的 Praat 脚本对音高相关取值点的音高值（单位：赫兹 Hz）和音段相关取值点的时间值（单位：毫秒 ms）进行自动抽取。每一个动词的五个声学参数被抽取和计算出来：音高最大值、音高最小值、音高变化（在当前实验设计中，目标动词是单音节，因而在对目标词进行声学参数提取时，音高变化即为单音节内音高最大值和音高最小值的差值）、平均音高、时长。在所有符合筛选条件的回答句中，无法从 101 个句子（占所筛选回答句的 16.7%）中获取可靠的音高信息。因而，这些回答句被排除在和音高相关的测量和分析之外。

3. 统计分析和结果

3.1 统计分析

为了探究焦点的作用，笔者比较了动词在焦点和非焦点条件下的测量数据。也就是，NF-m 条件（动词是焦点）和 NF-i 条件（动词在焦点后）以及 NF-m 条件（动词是焦点）和 NF-f 条件（动词在焦点前）；为了考察焦点域存在差异的不同焦点类型，笔者比较了动词在窄焦点条件（NF-m）和宽焦点条件（BF）下的测量数据；为了考察不同焦点类型的差异，笔者比较了动词在对比焦点条件（CF-m）和非对比焦点条件（即窄焦点条件 NF-m）下的测量数据。

笔者采用了 R 软件［16］中的“lme4”［2］和“lmerTest”程序包［11］来运行线性混合效应模型。在所有搭建的统计模型中，都将“声调”和“焦点条件”作为固定变量（fixed factors），“说话人（即发音人）”作为随机变量（random factors）。在上述列出的四组对比当中，“焦点条件”有两个层级（即研究问题中涉及的两种焦点条件），“声调”指的是目标动词的不同声调，包括三个层级（即平调、升调、降调）。结果变量/因变量是动词的时长、音高变化（除平调外）和平均音高。参考［6］和［14］，本研究采用逐步构建和检验的多层级建模方式，模型搭建的具体步骤见表 2。进行模型搭建时，只有在统计学意义上能显著提高模型拟合度的变量和交互效应才会被保留，直到达到拟合度最高的最佳模型。当拟合度最高的最佳模型建立后，本研究只归纳和理解最佳模型。

表 2　模型搭建步骤一览

模型	新增变量
模型 0	仅纳入“说话人”作为随机截距
模型 1	+ 声调
模型 2	+ 焦点条件
模型 3	+ 声调：焦点条件

3.2 年龄：5 岁

3.2.1 时长

测试焦点（焦点和焦点后、焦点和焦点前）在 5 岁组中时长表现的模型拟合度比较表明，拟合度最高的最佳模型只包括声调的主效应［χ^2（2）= 33.788，$p<0.001$；χ^2（2）= 21.111，$p<0.001$］。

测试焦点域（窄焦点和宽焦点）在 5 岁组中时长表现的模型拟合度比较表明，拟合度最高的最佳模型只包括声调的主效应（χ^2（2）= 15.063，$p<0.001$）。

测试对比度（窄焦点和对比焦点）在 5 岁组中时长表现的模型拟合度比较表明，

拟合度最高的最佳模型只包括声调的主效应（χ^2（2）=11.402，$p<0.01$）。

因而，没有证据表明此年龄组的白语儿童在其白语的任一声调中通过变化时长来区分窄焦点（232.3ms，SD=62.2）和焦点后（228.6ms，SD=59.2）、焦点前（232.1ms，SD=48.7）、宽焦点（263.4ms，SD=57.7）、对比焦点（248.7ms，SD=62.8）。

3.2.2 音高变化（除平调外）

测试焦点（焦点和焦点后、焦点和焦点前）在5岁组中音高变化表现的模型拟合度比较表明，拟合度最高的最佳模型只包括声调的主效应（χ^2（1）=10.838，$p<0.001$；χ^2（1）=6.954，$p<0.01$）。

测试焦点域（窄焦点和宽焦点）在5岁组中音高变化表现的模型拟合度比较表明，拟合度最高的最佳模型只包括声调的主效应（χ^2（1）=4.892，$p<0.05$）。

测试对比度（窄焦点和对比焦点）在5岁组中音域表现的模型拟合度比较表明，所有固定变量均未能提高模型拟合度。

因而，没有证据表明此年龄组的白语儿童在其白语的升调和降调中通过变化音高来区分窄焦点（60.4Hz，SD=29）和焦点后（44.3Hz，SD=23.3）、焦点前（54.9Hz，SD=28）、宽焦点（65.3Hz，SD=35.9）、对比焦点（66.6Hz，SD=26.7）。

3.2.3 平均音高

测试焦点（焦点和焦点后）在5岁组中平均音高表现的模型拟合度比较表明，拟合度最高的最佳模型包括声调和焦点的交互主效应（χ^2（2）=8.79，$p<0.05$）。笔者通过在每一个声调中检验焦点条件的作用来探索交互效应的细节。然而，进一步的分析表明，这一年龄组的儿童在/55/调（estimate=−10.513，df=15.691，t=−0.607，p=0.553）和/35/调（estimate=1.293，df=28，t=0.125，p=0.901）中并未通过变化焦点成分的平均音高来区分窄焦点和焦点后。但在/21/调（estimate=60.58，df=20，t=2.965，$p<0.01$）中通过变化焦点成分的平均音高来区分窄焦点（278.6Hz，SD=73.6）和焦点后（218Hz，SD=21.3），如图2所示。

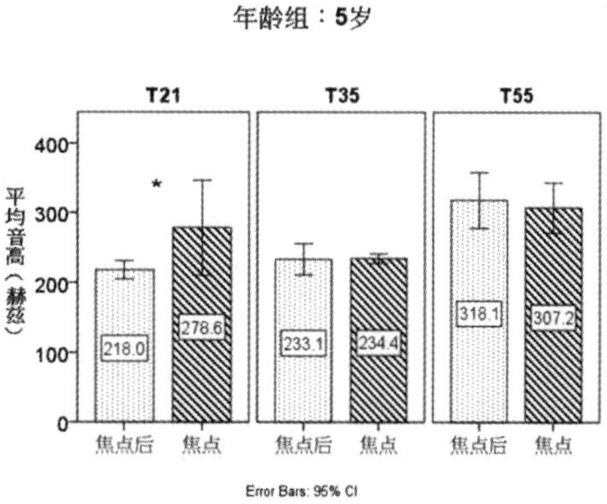

图2　5岁组中焦点后的平均音高（赫兹）和焦点的平均音高（赫兹），显著性差异用星号*标示

测试焦点（焦点和焦点前）在5岁组中平均音高表现的模型拟合度比较表明，拟合度最高的最佳模型只包括声调的主效应（χ^2（2）=19.003，$p<0.001$）。因而，没有证据表明此年龄组的白语儿童在其白语的任一声调中通过变化平均音高来区分焦点（263.7Hz，SD=51）和焦点前（265Hz，SD=70.5）。

测试焦点域（窄焦点和宽焦点）在5岁组中平均音高表现的模型拟合度比较表明，拟合度最高的最佳模型包括声调和焦点的交互主效应（χ^2（2）=6.792，$p<0.05$）。笔者通过在每一个声调中检验焦点条件的作用来探索交互效应的细节。然而，进一步地分析表明，这一年龄组的儿童在/55/调（estimate=−7.945，df=16.418，t=−0.448，p=0.66）、/35/调（estimate=7.195，df=20，t=1.479，p=0.155）和/21/调（estimate=61.04，df=14，t=2.004，p=0.065）中均未通过变化焦点成分的平均音高来区分窄焦点和宽焦点。

测试对比度（窄焦点和对比焦点）在5岁组中平均音高表现的模型拟合度比较表明，拟合度最高的最佳模型只包括声调的主效应（χ^2（2）=37.44，$p<0.001$）。因而，没有证据表明此年龄组的白语儿童

在其白语的任一声调中通过变化平均音高来区分窄焦点和对比焦点（256.1Hz, SD = 52.9）。

3.3 年龄：6岁

3.3.1 时长

测试焦点（焦点和焦点后、焦点和焦点前）在6岁组中时长表现的模型拟合度比较表明，拟合度最高的最佳模型只包括声调的主效应（χ^2（2）= 27.029, $p <$ 0.001; χ^2（2）= 26.42, $p < 0.001$）。因而，没有证据表明此年龄组的白语儿童在其白语的任一声调中通过变化时长来区分窄焦点（209.3ms, SD = 77.1）和焦点后（208.3ms, SD = 85.3），或焦点前（208.4ms, SD = 70.5）。

测试焦点域（窄焦点和宽焦点）在6岁组中时长表现的模型拟合度比较表明，拟合度最高的最佳模型包括声调的主效应（χ^2（2）= 11.303, $p < 0.01$）以及焦点条件的主效应（χ^2（1）= 8.232, $p < 0.01$）。这说明，这一年龄组的儿童在所有声调中均通过缩短焦点成分的时长来区分窄焦点（209.3ms, SD = 77.1）和宽焦点（246.1ms, SD = 102.5），如图3所示。

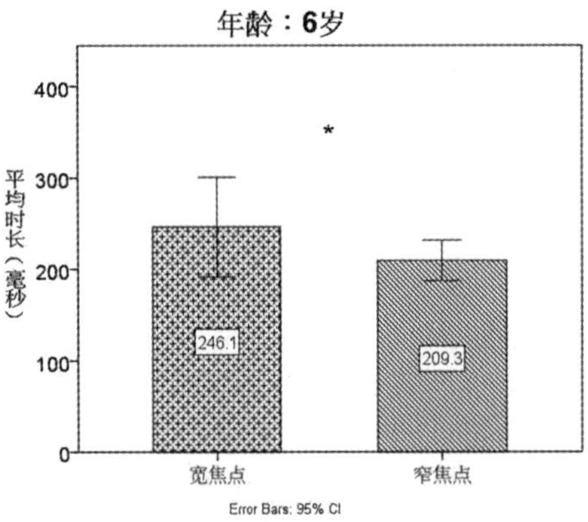

图3 6岁组中宽焦点的平均时长（毫秒）和窄焦点的平均时长（毫秒），显著性差异用星号*标示

测试对比度（窄焦点和对比焦点）在6岁组中时长表现的模型拟合度比较表明，拟合度最高的最佳模型包括声调的主效应（χ^2（2）= 30.732, $p < 0.001$）；焦点条件的主效应（χ^2（1）= 4.889 $p < 0.05$）。这说明，这一年龄组的白语儿童在所有声调中均通过缩短非对比焦点成分的时长来区分窄焦点/非对比焦点和对比焦点（229.7ms, SD = 61.7），如图4所示。

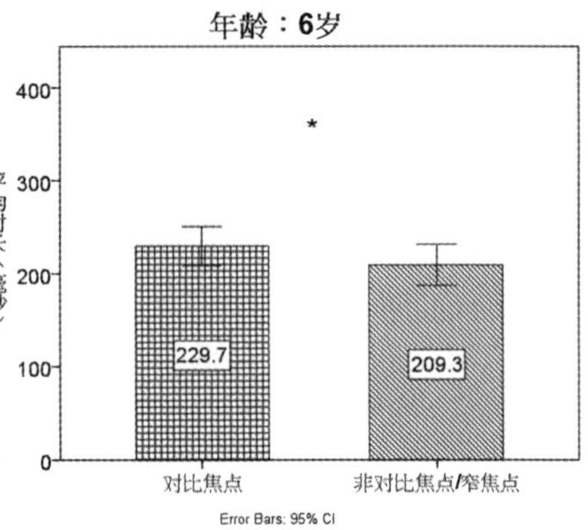

图4 6岁组中对比焦点的平均时长（毫秒）和非对比焦点/窄焦点的平均时长（毫秒），显著性差异用星号*标示

3.3.2 音高变化

测试焦点（焦点和焦点后）在6岁组中音高变化表现的模型拟合度比较表明，拟合度最高的最佳模型只包括声调的主效应（χ^2（1）= 13.032, $p < 0.001$）。因而，没有证据表明此年龄组的白语儿童在其白语的升调和降调中通过变化音高来区分窄焦点（44.4Hz, SD = 18）和焦点后（40.4Hz, SD = 16.3）。

测试焦点（焦点和焦点前）在6岁组中音高变化表现的模型拟合度比较表明，拟合度最高的最佳模型包括声调和焦点的交互主效应（χ^2（1）= 6.732, $p < 0.01$）。笔者通过在每一个声调中检验焦点条件的作用来探索交互效应的细节。进一步分析表明，这一年龄组的儿童并未在/21/调（estimate = −11.314, df = 11.338, t = −1.356, $p = 0.202$）中通过变化焦点成分的音高最大值与最小值之间的差值来区分窄焦点和焦点前。然而，在/35/调中，进一步分析揭示出焦点条件的主效应（χ^2（1）= 5.977, $p < 0.05$）。这说明，这一年龄组

的儿童在/35/调中通过扩展焦点成分的音高最大值与最小值之间的差值来区分窄焦点和焦点前（37.3Hz，SD = 13.9），如图5所示。

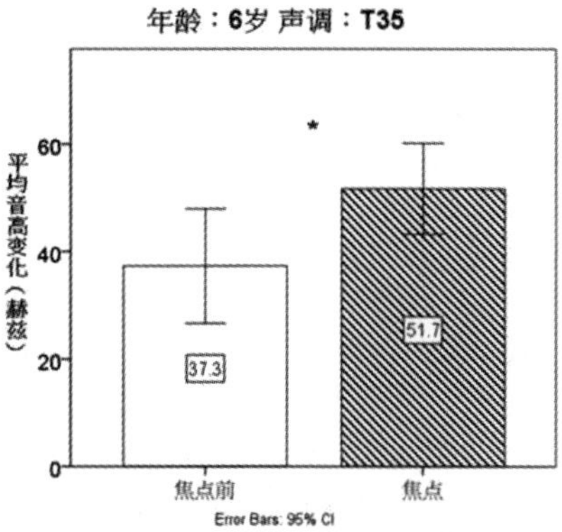

图5　6岁组中/35/调焦点前成分的平均音高变化（赫兹）和焦点成分的平均音高变化（赫兹），显著性差异用星号＊标示

测试焦点域（窄焦点和宽焦点）在6岁组中音高变化表现的模型拟合度比较表明，拟合度最高的最佳模型包括声调和焦点的交互主效应（χ^2（1）= 4.075，$p < 0.05$）。笔者通过在每一个声调中检验焦点条件的作用来探索交互效应的细节。然而，进一步地分析表明，这一年龄组的儿童并未在/35/调（estimate = 12.410，df = 12.719，t = 1.384，$p = 0.190$）和/21/调（estimate = −16.604，df = 9.243，t = −9.243，$p = 0.075$）中通过变化焦点成分的音高最大值与最小值之间的差值来区分窄焦点和宽焦点。

测试对比度（窄焦点和对比焦点）在6岁组中音高变化表现的模型拟合度比较表明，拟合度最高的最佳模型只包括声调的主效应（χ^2（1）= 8.403，$p < 0.01$）。因而，没有证据表明此年龄组的白语儿童在其白语的升调和降调中通过变化音高来区分窄焦点和对比焦点（47.1Hz，SD = 23.2）。

3.3.3　平均音高

测试焦点（焦点和焦点后、焦点和焦点前）在6岁组中平均音高表现的模型拟合度比较表明，拟合度最高的最佳模型只包括声调的主效应（χ^2（2）= 31.47，$p < 0.001$；χ^2（2）= 29.851，$p < 0.001$）。

测试焦点域（窄焦点和宽焦点）在6岁组中平均音高表现的模型拟合度比较表明，拟合度最高的最佳模型包括声调和焦点的交互主效应（χ^2（2）= 6.392，$p < 0.05$）。笔者通过在每一个声调中检验焦点条件的作用来探索交互效应的细节。然而，进一步地分析表明，这一年龄组的儿童并未在/55/调（estimate = 10.89，df = 25，t = 0.657，$p = 0.517$）、/35/调（estimate = 44.93，df = 27，t = 1.888，$p = 0.070$）和/21/调（estimate = −34.04，df = 21，t = −1.423，$p = 0.169$）中通过变化焦点成分的平均音高来区分窄焦点和宽焦点。

测试对比度（窄焦点和对比焦点）在6岁组中平均音高表现的模型拟合度比较表明，拟合度最高的最佳模型只包括声调的主效应（χ^2（2）= 45.534，$p < .001$）。

因而，没有证据表明此年龄组的白语儿童在其白语的任一声调中通过变化平均音高来区分窄焦点（251.5Hz，SD = 57.5）和焦点后（244.5Hz，SD = 51.6）、焦点前（249Hz，SD = 58.1）、对比焦点（245.8Hz，SD = 50.2）。

3.4　年龄：7岁

3.4.1　时长

测试焦点（焦点和焦点后）在7岁组中时长表现的模型拟合度比较表明，拟合度最高的最佳模型包括声调的主效应（χ^2（2）= 36.97，$p < 0.001$）和焦点条件的主效应（χ^2（2）= 5.836，$p < 0.05$）。这说明，这一年龄组的儿童在所有声调中均通过延长焦点成分的时长来区分窄焦点（218.5ms，SD = 68.8）和焦点后（195.3ms，SD = 59.6），如图6所示。

测试焦点（焦点和焦点前）在7岁组中时长表现的模型拟合度比较表明，拟合度最高的最佳模型只包括声调的主效应（χ^2（2）= 26.292，$p < 0.001$）。

测试焦点域（窄焦点和宽焦点）在7岁组中时长表现的模型拟合度比较表明，

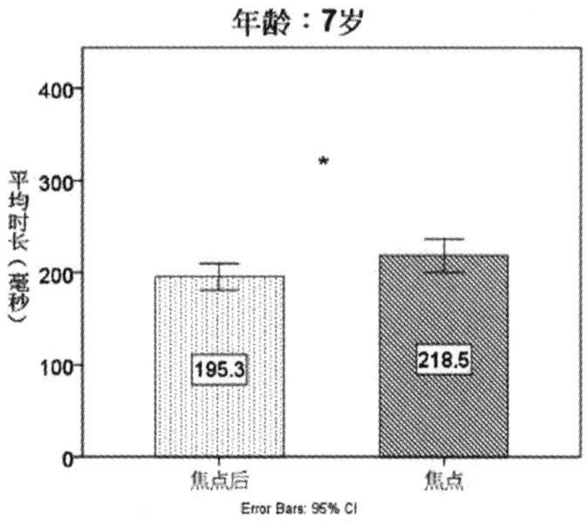

图6　7岁组中焦点后成分的平均时长（毫秒）和焦点成分的平均时长（毫秒），显著性差异用星号＊标示

拟合度最高的最佳模型只包括声调的主效应（χ^2（2）=23.927，$p<0.001$）。

测试对比度（窄焦点和对比焦点）在7岁组中时长表现的模型拟合度比较表明，拟合度最高的最佳模型只包括声调的主效应（χ^2（2）=28.499，$p<0.001$）。

因而，没有证据表明此年龄组的白语儿童在其白语的任一声调中通过变化时长来区分窄焦点和焦点前（227.7ms，SD=71.5）、宽焦点（224.8ms，SD=61.2）、对比焦点（219ms，SD=65.5）。

3.4.2 音高变化

测试焦点（焦点和焦点后）在7岁组中音高变化表现的模型拟合度比较表明，拟合度最高的最佳模型只包括声调的主效应（χ^2（1）=6.842，$p<0.01$）。

测试焦点（焦点和焦点前）在7岁组中音高变化表现的模型拟合度比较表明，所有固定变量均未能提高模型拟合度。

测试焦点域（窄焦点和宽焦点）在7岁组中音高变化表现的模型拟合度比较表明，所有固定变量均未能提高模型拟合度。

测试对比度（窄焦点和对比焦点）在7岁组中音高变化表现的模型拟合度比较表明，拟合度最高的最佳模型只包括声调的主效应（χ^2（1）=4.686，$p<0.05$）。

因而，没有证据表明此年龄组的白语儿童在其白语的升调和降调中通过变化音高来区分窄焦点（43.1Hz，SD=26.6）和焦点后（32.8Hz，SD=24.3）、焦点前（40Hz，SD=29）、宽焦点（50.2Hz，SD=23.6）、对比焦点（44.4Hz，SD=26）。

3.4.3　平均音高

测试焦点（焦点和焦点后、焦点和焦点前）在7岁组中平均音高表现的模型拟合度比较表明，拟合度最高的最佳模型只包括声调的主效应（χ^2（2）=47.21，$p<.001$；χ^2（2）=28.281，$p<0.001$）。

测试焦点域（窄焦点和宽焦点）在7岁组中平均音高表现的模型拟合度比较表明，拟合度最高的最佳模型只包括声调的主效应（χ^2（2）=29.666，$p<0.001$）。

测试对比度（窄焦点和对比焦点）在7岁组中平均音高表现的模型拟合度比较表明，拟合度最高的最佳模型只包括声调的主效应（χ^2（2）=42.157，$p<0.001$）。

因而，没有证据表明此年龄组的白语儿童在其白语的任一声调中通过变化平均音高来区分窄焦点（257.5Hz，SD=61.9）和焦点后（250.9Hz，SD=55.4）、焦点前（248.8Hz，SD=62）、宽焦点（266.6Hz，SD=62.7）、对比焦点（253.1Hz，SD=57.6）。

3.5　小结

本实验结果表明，白语儿童在5岁时通过提高/21/调焦点成分的平均音高来区分焦点和焦点后；6岁时，白语儿童在白语的/35/调中通过扩展焦点成分的音高最大值和音高最小值之间的差值来区分焦点和焦点前，且在所有白语声调中通过缩短焦点成分的时长来区分窄焦点和宽焦点、窄焦点/非对比焦点和对比焦点；7岁时，白语儿童通过延长焦点成分的时长来区分焦点和焦点后，但既不通过变化时长也不通过变化音高来区分焦点和焦点前以及不同的焦点类型。白语儿童焦点韵律编码发展阶段如表3所示。

表3　白语儿童焦点韵律编码发展一览

年龄	焦点 vs. 焦点后	焦点 vs. 焦点前	窄焦点 vs. 宽焦点	窄焦点 vs. 对比焦点
5岁	/21/调平均音高 >	—	—	—
6岁	—	/35/调音高 >	时长 <	时长 <
7岁	时长 >	—	—	—

4. 结论与讨论

本研究采用实验法，探索了母语为白语儿童焦点韵律编码的习得和发展。研究结果表明，白语儿童对其母语白语焦点韵律编码的习得呈阶段性发展，且发展过程呈现曲折并最终向白语成人靠拢的趋势。具体来说，白语儿童在5岁时，试图在个别声调中通过变化平均音高来区分窄焦点和焦点后。6岁，白语儿童显然开始探索使用韵律参数来编码焦点，这样的探索既涉及对时长的变化，也涉及对音高的变化。不过，这一阶段的探索和白语成人的表现仍有差异。7岁是一个重要的发展阶段，白语儿童已经完全展现出其通过变化时长来编码焦点、和白语成人完全一致的能力［12，13］。

与已有针对汉语、芬兰语、英语、荷兰语、瑞典语、韩语、德语等儿童研究结论一致的是［1，5，7，8，17，19，20］，本研究发现，韵律系统的跨语言差异塑造了不同母语背景儿童韵律焦点习得的发展路径。有趣的地方在于，本研究在考察使用韵律手段编码焦点方面较为局限的白语后发现，儿童语音的习得与发展不仅受到母语背景的影响，还表现出语言普遍性的效应。这一语言普遍性影响表现为：白语儿童存在探索通过变化音高相关韵律参数编码韵律焦点的习得阶段，尽管在其母语的输入中并无任何与韵律编码相关的音高变化。

5. 致谢

本研究得到了云南省哲学社会科学规划项目“白汉双语儿童语言发展实验研究”（编号：QN202039）的经费支持。衷心感谢云南大学民俗学专业学生杨识余及其家人在本研究的田野调查工作中给予的大力支持。研究过程中还得到了 Aoju Chen、Hans van de Velde 等先生的指导。

参考文献

［1］Arnhold, A. 2016. Complex prosodic focus marking in Finnish: Expanding the data landscape. *Journal of Phonetics* 56, 85 – 109.

［2］Bates, D., Mächler, M., Bolker, B., Walker, S. 2015. *lme4: Linear mixed-effects models using Eigen and S4*. http://CRAN.R-project.org/package = lme4

［3］Boersma, P., Weenink, D. 2006. *Praat: Doing phonetics by computer* (Version 5.4.01). http://www.praat.org/

［4］Chen, A. 2009. The phonetics of sentence-initial topic and focus in adult and child Dutch. In Vigário, M. C., Frota, S., Freitas, M. J. (eds), *Phonetics and Phonology: Interactions and Interrelations*. Amsterdam: John Benjamins Publishing, 91 – 106.

［5］Chen, A. 2011. Tuning information packaging: Intonational realization of topic and focus in child Dutch. *Journal of Child Language* 38, 1055 – 1083.

［6］Field, A., Miles, J., Field, Z. 2012. *Discovering Statistics Using R*. Los Angeles: SAGE.

［7］Grigos, M. I., Patel, R. 2010. Acquisition of articulatory control for sentential focus in children. *Journal of Phonetics* 38, 706 – 715.

［8］Grünloh, T., Lieven, E., Tomasello, M. 2015. Young children's intonational marking of new, given and contrastive referents. *Language Learning and Development* 11 (2), 95 – 127.

［9］Gundel, J. K. 1999. On different kinds of focus. In: Bosch, P., Van de Sandt, R. (eds), *Focus: Linguistic, Cognitive, and Computational Perspectives*. Cambridge: Cambridge University Press, 293 – 305.

［10］Gussenhoven, C. 2007. Notions and subnotions in information structure. *Acta Linguistica Hun-*

garica 55, 381 – 395.

[11] Kuznetsova, A., Brockhoff, P. B., Christensen, R. H. B. 2013. *lmerTest: Tests in linear mixed effect models*. R Package Version 2.0 – 20. http://CRAN.R-project.org/package=lmerTest

[12] Liu, Z., Chen, A., Van de Velde, H. 2014. Prosodic focus marking in Bai. D. (eds), *Proceedings of the 7th International Conference on Speech Prosody*, Dublin, 628 – 631.

[13] Liu, Z. 2017. *The Development of Prosodic Focus-Marking in Early Bilinguals' L2: A study of Bai-Mandarin Early Bilinguals' Mandarin*. PhD dissertation, Utrecht University.

[14] Magezi, D. A. 2015. Linear mixed-effects models for within-participant psychology experiments: An introductory tutorial and free, graphical user interface (LMMgui). *Frontiers in Psychology* 6, 1 – 7.

[15] Müller, A., Höhle, B., Schmitz, M., Weissenborn, J. 2006. Focus-to-stress alignment in 4-to 5-year-old German-learning children. *Proceedings of Generative Approaches to Language ACquistion 2005*, Siena, 393 – 407.

[16] R Core Team. 2014. *R: A language and environment for statistical computing*. R Foundation for Statistical Computing, Vienna, Austria. http://www.R-project.org/.

[17] Romøren, A. S. H. 2016. *Hunting Highs and Lows: The Acquisition of Prosodic Focus Marking in Swedish and Dutch*. PhD dissertation, Utrecht University.

[18] Turk, A., Nakai, S., Sugahara, M. 2006. Acoustic segment durations in prosodic research: A practical guide. In Sudhoff, S. (ed), *Methods in Empirical Prosody Research*. Berlin: Mouton de Gruyter, 1 – 28.

[19] Wonnacott, E., Watson, D. G. 2008. Acoustic emphasis in four year olds. *Cognition* 107, 1093 – 1101.

[20] Yang, A. 2017. *The Acquisition of Prosodic Focus-Marking in Mandarin Chinese and Seoul Korean-Speaking Children*. PhD dissertation, Utrecht University.

[21] Yang, A., Chen, A. 2017. The developmental path to adult-like prosodic focus-marking in Mandarin Chinese-speaking children. *First Language* 1., 26 – 46.

[22] 李嵬、祝华、Barbara Dodd、姜涛、彭聃龄、舒华:《说普通话儿童的语音习得》,《心理学报》2000年第2期,第170—176页。

[23] 李宇明:《儿童语言的发展》,华中师范大学出版社1995年版。

[24] 刘璐、王蓓、李雪巧:《白语焦点和边界的韵律编码方式》,《民族语文》2020年第6期,第71—79页。

[25] 刘兆吉、彭新鼎、陈志君:《三—六岁儿童语音发展水平调查研究》,《儿童心理与教育心理》1980年第2期,第161—170页。

[26] 司玉英:《普通话儿童语音习得的个案研究》,《当代语言学》2006年第1期,第1—16页。

[27] 许政援:《三岁前儿童语言发展的研究和有关的理论问题》,《心理发展与教育》1996年第3期,第1—11页。

[28] 张云秋:《汉语儿童早期语言的发展》,商务印书馆2014年版。

[29] 赵燕珍:《赵庄白语参考语法》,中央民族大学,2009年。

[30] 朱曼殊:《儿童语言发展研究》,华东师范大学出版社1986年版。

[31] 朱智贤主编:《中国儿童青少年心理发展与教育》,中国卓越出版公司1990年版。

刘增慧 云南大学文学院,博士,讲师,主要研究领域为言语韵律、L1 & L2 语音习得、儿童语言发展。
E-mail: zenghui_liu@ynu.edu.cn

梁淑芬 江西工程学院教育学院,硕士,研究领域包括言语韵律、L1 & L2 语音习得、儿童语言发展。
E-mail: liangshufen@mail.ynu.edu.cn

汉语词汇层面的轻重音研究

殷治纲

摘　要　汉语是否有音系学意义的词重音一直是个存在争议的问题。本文以该问题为研究目标，首先提出了判断词汇层面轻重音的两条音系学标准，然后通过感知实验和数据分析方法，列出了影响轻重音感知的主要声学因素和语言学因素。在语言学因素中，音节在韵律词中的位置和声调是最重要的两个影响因素。通过分析实验结果并比对两条音系学标准，研究发现：（1）在韵律位置方面，虽然韵律词体现出“左重”（或前重）趋势，但这只是一种语音学统计规律，不构成音系学规律；（2）在声调方面，声调和词重音有密切关系，并可构成轻重音的音系学规则——有声调音节形成韵律词的重音，而无声调（轻声或轻读）音节形成轻音。最后，文章在此基础上讨论了轻重音的作用，以及汉语和英语轻重音系统的联系和区别。

关键词　词重音，轻重，影响因素，音系学标准，有调，无调，轻声

A Study of Chinese Word Stress

YIN Zhigang

Abstract Whether there is phonological word stress in Chinese has been a controversial issue for a long time. This paper takes on this issue and proposes two phonological standards for judging the word stress. Based on perceptual experiments and data analysis, the order of acoustic factors and linguistic factors that affect the perception of stress levels is arranged. Among linguistic factors, *prosodic position* and *tones* are the two most important influencing factors. The experimental results show that (1) in term of *the prosodic position*, prosodic words showing the trend of the *left - heavy* (or *front - heavy*) pattern is only statistically relevant in phonetics, and it does not form a phonological rule; (2) *tones* are closely related to word stress, and they meet two phonological standards, which can form the phonological rules of the word stress: toned syllables form the heavy syllables, and atonal (neutral tone) syllables form the light syllables. Finally, the article discusses the role of stress, as well as the difference between Chinese word stress and English word stress.

Key words word stress (lexical stress), light & heavy (unstressed & stressed), influencing factors, phonological standards, tonal, atonal, neutral tone

1. 引言

1.1　轻重音的概念

轻重音是语音韵律研究的一个重要问题。以往很多研究认为，轻重是人们对语音单元凸显程度的一种主观感知，但与音高、时长等客观声学特征有密切关系[10，25，28，50]。

从研究对象看，重音可以分为词重音和句重音。前者主要研究词汇层面的轻重音问题，而后者则主要研究语句层面的轻重音问题。如果再细分的话，词重音层面又包括音步、词汇等低层韵律单元重音，而句重音层面则包括了短语、语句等高层韵律单元的重音。

从轻重的静态性与动态性看，可以分为静态的轻重音和动态的轻重读音节。在很多语言中，词汇的重音位置是固定的（或静态的），比如法语的词重音总是落在最后一个音节上，英语词重音位置也有相应音系规则。这些语言的词重音可称为固定的或者静态的。也有一些重音的位置是不固定的（或动态的），如语

义重音、语句重音等。这些重音是根据语义、语用表达需要，通过重读方式形成的临时重音。同样，对轻声和轻音而言，也存在固定的轻声（neutral tone）音节和轻读音节的差异［13］。在本研究中，我们将不区分“固定”轻重音和“临时”轻重读音节，而将它们统一纳入轻重音研究的范畴。

1.2 和轻重音相关的研究

以往语言学理论对轻重音问题研究颇多。结构主义音系学重视描写词汇的重音位置和等级关系。SPE（Sound Pattern of English）理论则重视探索重音位置规律，分析重音与音节结构间的关系。SPE认为，重音是元音固有属性，在分析重音时应该把句法结构作为规则运用的范围，将词重音问题和句重音问题统一考虑。从底层强弱二元对比出发，根据一定条件向上多次套用，从而得到语言表层的重音规则。但此后很多研究证明重音规则范围不限于句法成分。节律音系学认为，重音不是元音固有特征，也不是区别性特征，而是一种相对概念。它表现为音节间的相对强弱（relative prominence），而不是传统理论或SPE理论认为的可以施加于每个元音的绝对强弱的等级关系。节律是决定重音模式的主要特征，重音表现为等级形式［48］。

以往关于汉语轻重音的研究也很多，内容主要集中于以下方面。

1.2.1 汉语词重音有无的问题

现代语言学通常认为英语有词重音，并且词重音可以区别词义，具备音系学意义。英语至少可以分为三级词重音音位，即主重音（main stress）、次重音（secondary stress）、非重音（stresslessness），某些英语方言还可以分为四级重音（多了弱重音 weak stress）［3］。

不过，汉语是否存在音系学意义的词重音则存在争议。有的学者认为，汉语有词重音［15，16，30，46，52］。但是，也有学者认为，汉语除了轻声音节外，音系学层面的词重音并不存在或不明显［18，19，29，55］。

1.2.2 词重音的级别和位置

以往，词重音研究主要集中于音系学和语音学两个领域，前者关注音系学层面词重音有无、重音级别和位置关系等，后者则从语音学视角关注实际发音表现出来的重音级别和声学表现等。

徐世荣［45］认为，北京话两音节的重音格式有两个，一个是前重的“重轻式”，另一个是后重的“中重式”。陆致极［30］、殷作炎［52］则认为，应是重中式和中重式。端木三［15］认为，普通话不带轻音两字组重音模式是“前重”，而造成后重说的原因是把末音节的停顿前延长算成了音节时长所致。王志洁、冯胜利［43］认为，北京话词汇重音有三种类型，分别是左重、右重和不分（同重），但最后可以归纳为左重和右重。杨璐［49］则认为，词汇重音有四种类型，分别是重轻、重中、中重和不分（重重）。

很多学者从语音表现方面研究了重音模式。林茂灿、颜景助、孙国华［25］对普通话不带轻音的两字组考察发现，大多数是后重式，也有的前重，但并非必需。林焘、王理嘉［28］发现，汉语普通话双音节往往后重，而三音节词一般中间音节较轻，前后音节较重，且前后音节重的差别并不明显。王晶、王理嘉［38］认为，普通话两音节词的首音节比末音节时长更长，故其重音模式是前重。曹剑芬［14］认为，韵律词内虽然存在“重”“中”的相对差异，但是并不构成区别性对立。词重音“重中”和“中重”的差异只是其随机变体，而不是两种词重音类型。

1.2.3 轻音和轻声问题

轻音是汉语轻重音研究的重要问题。虽然学界对汉语有无词重音存在分歧，但是对于汉语存在轻音（轻声）则基本上没有异议。不过，对于轻音在汉语轻重音（或词重音）问题中的地位仍有不同观点。有的认为，它足以反映汉语有词重音［15，17］；有的则认为，它只是一种特殊现象，不足以构成汉语存在词重音的依据［55］。

1.2.4 汉语句重音问题

汉语句重音是不同于词重音的另一个领域。王洪君［37］认为，语句重音是指比词重音更高等级的重音，包括和句法相关的句法常规重音（短语重音、句重音），与语义相关的语义重音，与语用相关的焦点重音等。

汉语句重音研究中一些较重要的理论包括赵元任的“橡皮筋”理论［53］、沈炯的高低音双线理论和调域括敛说［32，33，34］，以及吴宗济音阶移调（音高移块）理论等［44］。Duanmu（端木三）［1］认为，在句法常规重音方面，短语重音遵循“辅重原则”，即句法辅助成分重于中心成分；在语义重音方面，语义关系和焦点会影响重音。

1.2.5 本研究的内容

相对于汉语句重音而言，汉语词重音存在的争议更大。例如，汉语到底有无词重音，轻重级别如何划分，词重音具有什么功能等。因此，本文将主要研究汉语词汇层面的轻重音问题。本研究的语言对象是汉语普通话，不涉及方言。此处的“词汇”不限于语法词，还包括更广泛意义上的韵律词。

在本研究中，我们将重新审视普通话词重音问题，分析其声学特征、影响要素，并尝试就汉语词汇轻重音的有无问题进行讨论。希望本研究的内容和相关结论对系统了解汉语韵律规律，以及深入探讨轻重音在英、汉等不同语言中的地位和特点有参考价值。

2. 研究数据与方法

2.1 实验材料

本研究使用的语音数据是由中国社会科学院语言研究所语音研究室制作的汉语普通话朗读语篇语料库 ASCCD（Annotated Speech Corpus of Chinese Discourse），其内容由语音数据、语音学标注和语篇文本等组成。语音数据采用16KHz、16位、WAV双声道格式在专业录音室录制。本数据库收集了语音和声门两种信号，所以左声道存储的为语音信号，右声道则是喉头仪信号。

该语料库的内容包括记叙、议论、通讯、散文等多种题材的18篇文章。18篇文章字数合计约9850字。语音数据由10位（男女各5人）普通话标准的北京地区发音人朗读。发音人年龄在30—50岁。在本研究中，我们重点选取了一男一女（M001，F001）两位发音人的数据进行了分析。

语音学标注信息采用人工标注方法完成，标注软件为Praat，标注符号采用C－ToBI标注系统［23］。标注内容包括拼音（PY）、声韵母（DE）、韵律层级（BI）、重音级别（ST）等信息。其中，韵律层级（BI）的1—4级标注分别表示韵律词（1）、韵律短语（2）、语调短语（3）和语句（4）边界。重音层（ST）标记了每个韵律单位内的相对重音（基于单位内各音节相互比较而感知到的重音），重音级别分为1、2、3级，分别表示韵律词、韵律短语和语调短语的重音，且每一个韵律单元只有唯一该级别重音（如一个语调词内只能有一个词重音“1”，其他级别类似）。若某一音节在多层韵律单元中都是重音时，只标注最高级别重音。例如某音节既是1级重音，又是2级重音时，只标2。其他情况类推。

由于语料库原来的重音层（ST）没有轻音标记，并且汉语很多韵律词中各音节轻重相当，难以标出唯一重音，所以我们对该数据库补充设计了第5层——绝对重音层（ST2）。

和原来C－ToBI重音层（ST）相比，绝对重音层（ST2）有以下特点。

（1）绝对重音层定义了0、1、2、3、4五级重音。和原来的重音层级相比，增加了轻音（或轻读）层级0，并将1定义为正常音节（其他重音级别向上类推），内容见表1。

表1 绝对重音标记

名称	标记	说明
轻化音节	0	轻声或轻读音节
正常音节	1	发音正常自然的音节
较重音节	2	发音响亮，比正常音节感觉稍重
很重音节	3	发音用力，有明显突现的音节
极重音节	4	带强烈情感或者特殊语用含义的强调重音

（2）绝对重音标记依赖标注人的轻重感知，不严格绑定韵律单元结构。但是它也没有完全抛弃韵律单元，而是以一个语句为参考范围来比较音节轻重。这是因为语句是交际中最重要的独立韵律单元，且其长度一般不会超过人们的短时记忆范围。

（3）每个韵律单元不限定唯一该级别重音。例如，一个两音节韵律词若两个音节轻重感知相似，可以都标为1级（或某级）重音。

（4）由于在朗读语篇中没有过于激烈的轻重变化，所以本语料实际只标了0、1、2、3四级重音，没有给出4级重音。4级重音在情绪强烈的口语语料中可能会出现。

需要说明的是，使用朗读篇章语料研究词重音问题可能存在以下优点和问题。

优点是真实语篇语料包括了全面的特征因素和语境信息，避免了以往孤立词实验可能出现的设计偏误和信息缺失（如缺乏短语、语句等大单元韵律位置信息），可以反映最全面真实的语言规律。

可能的问题包括：（1）语料库标注的不是严格的语法词，而是相对宽泛自由的韵律词。（2）传统词重音研究的是词汇层面的轻重音，而本语料重音标记除了词汇重音，实际还包含了语句重音等高层信息。这些都可能给研究带来数据“噪音”干扰问题。

不过，考虑到以上“噪音”在宏观词汇层面是随机分布的，虽然可能在个别词汇上带来偏误，但在宏观层面可以通过大规模数据统计方法消除整体性偏差，所以并不妨碍从中统计、抽象出一般性词汇轻重音规律。

图1是一个语音学标记的图例。

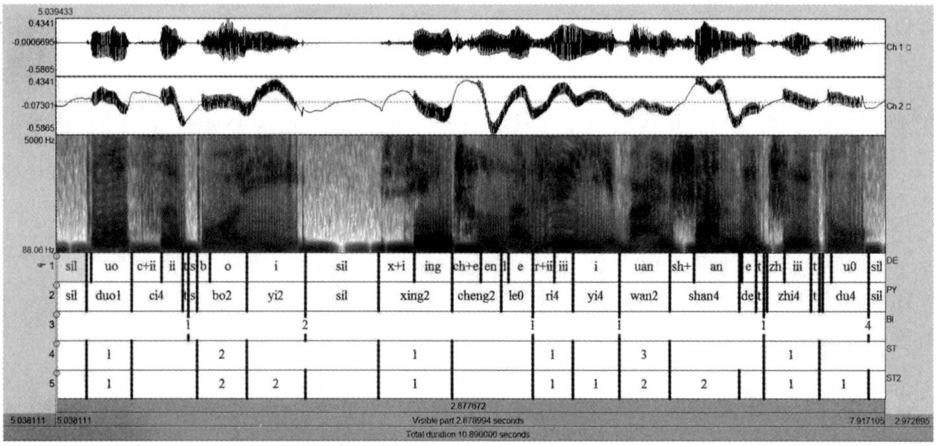

图1 语音学标注示意

2.2 研究方法与内容

本研究关注的主要问题是汉语有无音系学意义的词重音。为此，需要先确定有关轻重的音系学标准。基于前人研究基础，我们认为有音系学意义的轻重音至少应该符合“质”和“量”两方面的标准。

（1）轻重音在一定情况下具有区别词汇意义的作用。表达意义是语言系统最重要的功能。轻重音能够区别意义，一方面可以说明其重要性，另一方面也说明其不可违反性（否则会影响语义表达和理解）。这是关于轻重音的“质”的标准。

（2）普通听音人应该能够非常清晰地分辨出轻重区别，不易混淆。如果要达到这种区分标准，轻、重音的听辨差异率最好达到一个数量级（10倍）以上。这是关于轻重音的“量”的标准。

本研究的具体过程包括以下步骤。

（1）分析和轻重感知有关的语音特征

量，并按影响力大小排列出顺序，从中筛选出影响轻重音感知的主要语言学因素。虽然轻重音是一个主观感知量，但是以往研究指出，它们受诸多语音特征影响［10，28，31，51］。从这些特征中找出最重要的影响因素，是分析汉语词重音规律的首要任务。

（2）依次分析影响汉语词重音感知的主要影响因素，找出其规律，并按照两条音系学标准判断它们是否构成有音系学意义的词重音规律。

（3）分析汉语和英语词汇轻重音的异同，从语言类型学角度讨论轻重特征及其形成原因。

3. 汉语轻重音的关联因素

3.1 影响汉语轻重音感知的因素

人们对重音的感知来源于对多重因素的综合评价。这些因素既包括时长、音高等物理声学因素，也包括元辅音、声调等具有符号意义的语言学因素。

3.1.1　声学因素

影响轻重感知的声学因素主要包括音高、时长、音强等声学特征量。它们也是随着发音状态可以变化的“可变”因素。

以往研究认为音高和时长都是影响重音感知的重要因素。很多学者都强调了时长是重音感知的重要因素［10，25，28，50］。有的学者则提到音高对重音感知同样很重要——重音音节通常表现为音高上限抬高（上声为压低）、音域加宽、重音后音节调域压缩等现象［11，32，33，35，54］。

对于音高和时长对轻重音感知哪个更重要，目前尚存在争议。有的学者认为，时长比音高重要，可能是首要影响因素［56，58］。也有学者认为，音高对重音感知影响更大，且音高、时长作用力存在互补关系或交换关系［47，50，57］。还有研究发现，双音节韵律词重音差与高音点的差值相关性强于时长差值［42］。蔡莲红等［8］提出了一个拟合重音听感的线性公式 $L=1.5F$（音高）$+0.95$（时长）$+0.65R$（调域），从系数上暗示音高的重要性更大。

此外，在较早的语音研究中，音强也曾被认为是重要因素［31］，但后来研究认为，音强的作用相对较小［25，28，50］。并且语料音强容易受录音电平、录音距离等因素影响，不易准确测量分析，所以本研究没有考虑音强特征。

3.1.2　其他语言学因素

除了以上音高、时长和音强等声学因素外，很多研究关注到韵律位置、声调、音节音质，以及语法结构等因素对轻重音感知的影响。这些因素是具有语言学意义的“固定”性因素。

位置信息对轻重音感知有重要影响，以往绝大多数轻重音研究甚至都是和韵律位置信息绑定的。西方语音学研究认为，英语单词内部音素遵循轻重音交替模式，并形成了音步（feet）概念。在音步基础上，又形成了词重音及节律模式［2，5］。受英语影响，很多学者认为，汉语韵律词中也存在音步概念［7，16，36］。此外，很多学者关于汉语两音节词“左重”还是“右重”的讨论也是基于韵律位置进行的。但与此同时，也有很多学者认为，汉语韵律词内部不存在明显的轻重交替，也不存在词重音。

声调也被认为是影响轻重感知的一个因素。声调本身就包含前面提到过的音高和时长因素，但是，声调系统又在这些声学特征基础上形成了本身特有的调型和调值特征。贾媛［20］认为，汉语焦点对于音高的作用主要体现在“H”特征上。具有H特征多的声调容易承载重音，所以阴平调更容易被重读。殷治纲［51］认为，除了H特征外，高低对比特征（H–L）也容易形成重音感知，所以普通话阴平和去声比其他声调更容易被感知为重音。

音素的音质可能在一定程度上会影响轻重感知。曹剑芬［12］指出，重音凸显音段会有发音增强现象，其表现除了时长、音高等因素外，还在音质上有表现。音质响度顺序原则（SSP，Sonority Sequencing Principle）认为，在其他条件相同时，音节的响度顺序原则（Sonority Sequencing Principle）从大到小是：元音（低元音 > 中元音 > 高元音），半元音，流音，鼻音，擦音（浊>清），塞音（浊>清）［37］。殷治纲［51］从音素在不同频段的能量分布状况和人耳听觉灵敏度角度分析了音质响度顺序产生的生理学原因。不过，有的学者认为，虽然音质响度存在差异，但是对轻重感知影响力比较有限，通常不作为重音感知的变量［28，50］。

还有研究关注语法结构对词重音的影响，认为偏正式两字组倾向于左重，动宾式和主谓式两字组倾向于右重［41］。但是贾媛［21］利用同音异构两字组的实验研究发现，在非轻声的两字组中，句法结构无法对重音分布起决定作用，只有在其中一个音节为“轻声”或“轻读”时，二者才能区分开。

3.2 影响因素排序

受英语轻重音研究影响，以往关于汉语词重音有无的讨论基本都是围绕韵律位置信息开展的。但是，由于影响轻重音感知的因素有很多，我们认为，首先需要考虑的问题是——轻重音是否一定和韵律位置信息绑定？汉语轻重音有没有可能是由其他影响因素决定的？为了确定汉语轻重音的决定性影响因素，我们有必要先对所有影响因素进行一下梳理和排序。

我们首先用R语言混合线性模型对各因素对重音级别的影响力进行初步分析。这些因素既包括上面提到的音高（上限）、时长等声学因素，也包括声母、韵母、声调、韵律位置等语言学因素。

通过比较方差分析结果的F值大小，可以看出各因素对重音感知影响力从大到小分别为：音高上限或时长（两发音人次序不同）、声调、韵律词内位置、韵母类型、声母类型、韵律短语内位置或语调短语内位置、语句内位置。

表2a 各因素与重音的关系排序（F001）

因素（F001）	Sum Sq	Mean Sq	F值	显著性
音高上限	349. 72	349. 72	1235. 32	***
音节时长	498. 30	498. 30	1760. 12	***
声母	564. 15	25. 64	90. 58	***
韵母	1201. 82	33. 38	117. 92	***
声调	169. 65	169. 65	599. 24	***
韵律词内位置	458. 67	152. 89	540. 04	***
韵律短语内位置	8. 95	2. 98	10. 54	***
语调短语内位置	4. 85	1. 62	5. 71	***
语句内位置	2. 37	0. 79	2. 79	*
Residuals	2426. 48	0. 28		
显著性符号	0 ‘ *** ’ 0. 001 ‘ ** ’ 0. 01 ‘ * ’ 0. 05 ‘.’ 0. 1			

表2b 各因素与重音的关系排序（M001）

因素（M001）	Sum Sq	Mean Sq	F值	显著性
音高上限	989. 41	989. 41	3497. 64	***
音节时长	764. 86	764. 86	2703. 82	***
声母	556. 85	25. 31	89. 48	***
韵母	1034. 74	27. 97	98. 86	***
声调	140. 77	140. 77	497. 64	***
韵律词内位置	392. 59	130. 86	462. 61	***
韵律短语内位置	13. 32	4. 44	15. 70	***
语调短语内位置	37. 45	12. 48	44. 13	***
语句内位置	0. 80	0. 27	0. 94	
Residuals	2424	0. 28		
显著性符号	0 ‘ *** ’ 0. 001 ‘ ** ’ 0. 01 ‘ * ’ 0. 05 ‘.’ 0. 1			

上述结果显示，在声学因素中，时长和音高都对轻重感知显示出重要影响力。在语言学因素中，声调和（音节在）韵律词内位置对轻重音感知影响力最大。

在音系学层面上，我们更关注汉语词重音与哪些语言学因素有关。因此，接下来将主要从音节在韵律词内位置和声调两个方面分析汉语的词重音问题，看看哪个因素是影响汉语词汇轻重音的决定性因素。

4. 音节位置（在韵律词内）与轻重音的关系

我们将音节在韵律词内的位置分为L、M、R、W四种：L代表音节处在韵律词首位置，M代表词中位置，R代表词末位置，W代表音节为韵律词内唯一音节（独音节词）。这样，韵律词模式主要有以下几种。

表3　　韵律词组成模式

韵律词类型	音节组合模式
两音节韵律词	LR
三音节韵律词	LMR
四音节以上韵律词	L（M1，M2，…）R
单音节韵律词	W

音节的轻重级别如前文所述，共分为5级标注（本语料库实际使用了4级）。0代表轻读的音节，1代表词内自然音节，2代表比自然音节略重的音节，3代表很重的音节，4代表极重音节（本语料中没有）。

本研究对音节轻重级别与韵律位置关系的分析主要是从各位置音节重音均值和重音率（或重读率）两个方面来进行的。

4.1 各位置音节的重音均值

我们首先研究了音节重音级别和它在韵律词中位置的关系，统计数据见表4。

表4a　　韵律词内各位置音节重音均值（所有声调，F001）

音节位置	均值	N	标准差
L（开始）	2.10	3403	0.608
M（中间）	1.57	1438	0.740
R（末尾）	1.46	3403	0.888
W（唯一）	1.95	518	0.711
总计	1.75	8762	0.811

表4b　　韵律词内各位置音节重音均值（所有声调，M001）

音节位置	均值	N	标准差
L（开始）	2.15	3496	0.665
M（中间）	1.44	1259	0.777
R（末尾）	1.28	3496	0.833
W（唯一）	1.88	508	0.739
总计	1.69	8759	0.857

发音人数据显示，音节重音级别和它在韵律词中的位置显著相关（$p<0.001$）。在多音节韵律词中，词首音节的重音均值最高，其次是词中音节（如果有的话），最低的是词末音节。在单音节韵律词中，唯一音节的重音均值也较高。

不过，考虑到汉语轻声词缀多处于词末位置，而轻声相比于其他四个声调成为重音的概率明显偏低，对词末韵律词的重音统计可能产生影响，所以我们在排除轻声音节后又进行了一次统计，结果见表5a、表5b。

表5a　　韵律词内各位置音节重音均值（去除轻声，F001）

音节位置	重音均值	数量	标准差
L	2.10	3401	0.608
M	1.64	1349	0.689
R	1.78	2661	0.643
W	2.00	500	0.650
总计	1.91	7911	0.663

表5b　　韵律词内各位置音节重音均值（去除轻声，M001）

音节位置	重音均值	数量	标准差
L	2.16	3477	0.650
M	1.53	1167	0.731
R	1.55	2838	0.661
W	1.92	495	0.698
总计	1.84	7977	0.733

数据显示，去除轻声后，音节重音级别和它在韵律词中的位置仍显著相关（$p<0.001$），韵律词末音节的平均重音级别有所上升，并超过了中间音节（如果有的话）。因此，在排除轻声情况下，多音节韵律词词首音节最重，其次是词尾音节，中间音节（如果有的话）一般最轻。

由以上感知结果统计数据可知，在韵律词层面，韵律词呈现出“左重”（前重）的倾向。但是词首音节的重音优势相较于其他位置音节并不悬殊，并没有达到我们在本研究2.2部分给出的具有音系学意义的第二条标准。因此我们认为，此处轻重音表现出来的位置差异性仍然是语音学层面的（量的差异），而不是音系学层面的（质的差异）。

4.2 各位置音节的重音分布

表6统计了韵律词内不同位置处音节的轻重分布。由于重音级别2和3重于普通水平，所以被标记为2、3级重音的音节可以看作重音（或重读）音节。

表6a 韵律词内音节位置与重音级别（F001）

韵律位置	重音级别（F001）				重读比例	合计
	0	1	2	3		
L	22	410	2178	793	87%	3403
M	89	572	649	128	54%	1438
R	638	858	1625	282	56%	3403
W	12	109	291	106	77%	518
合计	761	1949	4743	1309		8762

表6b 韵律词内音节位置与重音级别（M001）

韵律位置	重音级别（M001）				重读比例	合计
	0	1	2	3		
L	46	409	2007	1034	87%	3496
M	130	534	501	94	47%	1259
R	710	1236	1401	149	44%	3496
W	12	138	259	99	70%	508
合计	898	2317	4168	1376		8759

我们把每个位置的重音音节（2级和3级重音）比例进行了分析，发现两位发音人词首音节的重读比例均为87%，明显高于他们词尾音节重读比例（56%和44%）。不过，本处词尾音节没有去除轻声的情况，否则重度比例会更高。

我们也统计了各位置音节的音高（上限）、时长数据与重音级别的情况，发现音节位置、音高、时长特征对于重音级别均有显著性影响（$p<0.001$）。词首音节的音高（上限）一般高于（或不低于）词尾音节，而词尾音节的时长值一般长于词首音节。可以认为，词首重音多表现为音高（上限）升高，而词尾重音多表现为时长延长［51］。

从以上结果看，多音节韵律词呈现出“左重”（或前重）的倾向。不过，按照本研究2.2部分提出的判断音系学轻重音的两条参考标准，韵律词这种前重优势仍然只是语音学统计意义上的，而非音系学意义上的。这是因为：

（1）和韵律位置相关的音节轻重差异一般不具有区别语义的功能。

（2）词首音节重读比例（87%）相对于词尾音节的重读比例（44%和56%，包含轻声）也难以形成听辨上的绝对优势（一般），没有形成数量级（10倍）优势。

因此，综合上述两方面分析结果，可以认为，汉语韵律词层面的“左重”（或前重），不具有音系学意义，只具有语音学统计意义。

5. 声调与轻重音的关系

5.1 声调与重音级别

除了音节在韵律词内的位置信息外，声调特征是我们要考察的另外一个重要因素。

我们分析了音节声调与重音级别的对应关系（具体数据见表7a、表7b），数据显示声调类型与轻重音存在显著相关性（$p<0.001$）。

表中0声表示轻声，1声表示阴平，2声表示阳平，3声表示上声，4声表示去声。

表7a　　声调与重音（F001）

韵律位置	重音级别（F001）				重读比例	合计
	0	1	2	3		
0声	656	133	57	5	7%	851
1声	8	211	1083	366	87%	1668
2声	25	530	1142	222	71%	1919
3声	42	453	826	168	67%	1489
4声	30	621	1635	548	77%	2834
合计	761	1949	4743	1309		8762

表7b　　声调与重音（M001）

韵律位置	重音级别（M001）				重读比例	合计
	0	1	2	3		
0声	673	101	8	0	1%	782
1声	27	298	985	361	81%	1671
2声	55	599	982	275	66%	1911
3声	45	521	707	218	62%	1491
4声	97	798	1486	522	69%	2903
合计	898	2317	4168	1376		8759

从上面数据可以看出，如果将2和3作为显著重读音节的话，F001发音中，1声重读率约87%，4声重读率约77%，2声重读率约71%，3声重读率约67%，而0声（轻声）重读率只有约7%。从M001声调发音数据看，1声重读率约81%，4声重读率约69%，2声重读率约66%，3声重读率约62%，而0声（轻声）重读率仅约1%。两人数据规律基本是一致的。

如果将各声调重读率（2级和3级重音比例）成柱状图，可以得到图2a、图2b。

从图2a、图2b可以发现，轻声音节和其他有声调音节分成了截然不同的两大类。其中，轻声音节被重读的概率很低（1%，7%），而其他有声调音节重读比例都高得多（60%以上）。两类声调之间的重度比例基本达到了数量级（10倍）的差异。

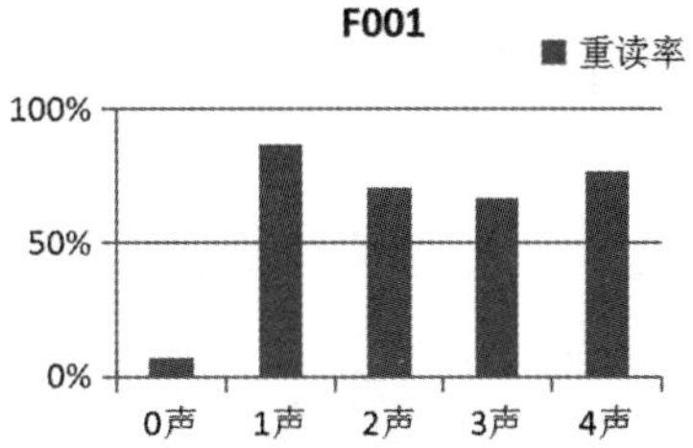

图2a　各声调重读比例（F001）

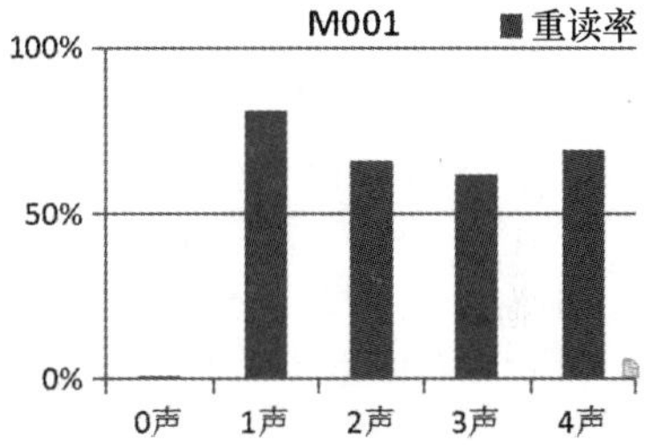

图2b　各声调重读比例（M001）

5.2　有无声调决定了词汇轻重音

那么声调信息是否是影响汉语轻重音感知（音系学层面）的决定性因素呢？下面我们对照前面2.2部分提出的判断音系学轻重音的两条标准进行分析。

（1）从区别语义的角度，阴平、阳平、上声、去声等声调都有区分意义的作用，而轻声（或轻读）音节对部分词汇而言也有区分意义的作用，例如“东西（dong1 xi1，表示方向）”和“东西（dong1 xi0，表示物品）”以及“买卖（mai3 mai4，表示买入和卖出）和买卖（mai3 mai0），表示交易项目”。因此，所有声调都符合本研究2.2部分给出的第一条标准。

（2）从各声调之间重音感知的差异性而言，阴平、阳平、上声、去声等声调之间虽然重读比例也有差异，但是这四个声调之间的差异性不大，并没有达到数量级（10倍）的差异。但是轻声音节重读比例（1%，7%）和其他四个声调之间的重度比例差异非常巨大，差异性达到了10倍以上，足以形成非常明确的辨别标准，符合本研究2.2部分给出的第二条标准。

综合以上分析，只有“轻声”（无调）和“非轻声”（有调）两类音节之间的对立可以满足上面两条音系学判定标准，因此可以认为，音节有无声调构成了汉语词汇轻重音的音系学判断标准。

凡是有声调的音节都是重音，而无声调的（或轻声）音节则是轻音。

因为普通话有声调类别又包括阴平、阳平、上声、去声四类，所以有音系学意义的汉语词汇轻重音和声调系统的对应规律可以用表8表示。

表8　汉语轻重音与声调的关系

轻重音类别（音系学层面）	相关因素	声调类别
重音	有调音节	阴平
		阳平
		上声
		去声
轻音	无调音节	轻声

5.3 对轻声地位的再思考

5.3.1 轻声的本质属性

从以上分析可以发现声调类别，尤其是轻声，对判断汉语词汇轻重音具有决定性作用。轻声的地位需要重新被思考。

以往一些研究具体分析了轻声的性质。曹剑芬［13］指出了轻音、轻读、轻声的联系与区别，并认为轻音分结构轻音和语调轻音——前者主要指韵律边界处的轻读音节，如“的、了、吗”等，后者则是语流中临时轻读的音节。叶军［50］分析了轻声和轻音问题，认为轻声是语流中读得又轻又短，且失去本调或不带声调的音节。

尽管目前学界大多把轻声和轻音看作是有关联但并不完全相同的概念。但是，我们希望从本质上来重新探讨轻声到底属于声调范畴还是轻重音范畴?

赵元任［54］把轻声和弱重音联系起来，认为轻声的本质来源是轻重音。我们也认为，从本质上，与其说轻声是一个声调，不如说它代表弱重音（或轻音）。因为正常声调都有自己确定的调型和调值，所以，轻声并没有自己固有的调型和调值——它的音高曲线往往是随着前后音节的声调特征而相应变化的。

另外，如表8所示，和轻声形成对立的并不是其他某个声调，而是其他所有声调的集合，即“有调”音节（包括其他四个声调），而轻声代表的则是另一类，即“无调”音节。

因此，对于轻声的地位可以如此概括：

（1）轻声与其说是个声调概念，不如说是个轻重音（或弱重音）概念。

（2）轻声的本质不是一个具体声调，而是一类声调的集合，即无（固定）调集合。

轻声包括的音节范围不限于词典上标注为轻声的那些音节（如“的、地、得，了、着、过、吧、呢、啊”等）。只要是一个有调音节失去了本调，都可以作为轻声，如“哥哥（ge1 ge0）”“兄弟（xiong1 di0）”“我们（wo3 men0）”的后音节，本来都是有调的，但是在词汇中失去本调后就变成了轻声音节，其本质是从重音节（heavy syllable）变成了轻音节（light syllable）。

5.3.2 轻声的声学特征

轻声（或轻音）作为和重音相对立概念，其声学特征主要表现在时长和音高（或声调特征）上。

在时长方面，一些研究发现轻声音节时长平均比相应非轻声音节的时长缩短一半或更多［24，26］。在音高方面，轻声音节失去本调，其音高由其前接音节的音高类型决定［22］。

在时长和音高哪个重要性更大的问题上，林焘［27］认为，声调特征在听辨轻音时的作用没有时长重要。曹剑芬［9］、王韫佳［39］认为，音高的作用比时长大。李爱军等人（Li & Fan）［4，22］发现单念时，音高作用大于时长；语流中，轻声相关量与所处的信息结构和轻声底层调有关（ 即轻声音节与其对立非轻声音节之间音高 F0 空间大小相关)。与非轻声词相比，词尾的轻声音节会使前字音域拉大，从而形成更强的轻重对比感。

5.4 汉语两类词汇轻重音：重重式和重轻式

从上面分析可知，有音系学意义的汉语词汇轻重音是由音节声调类别决定的，而与音节在词中的韵律位置没有必然关系。不过，考虑到汉语两音节词中，轻声音节基本只可能出现在词尾，而不会出现在词头，所以汉语两音节韵律词实际有两种重音模式——“重重式”（有声调音节+有声调音节）和“重轻式”（有声调音节+轻声音节）。具体模式如表9所示。

表9　汉语两音节词重音模式

两音节词重音模式	说明	例子
重重式	两个音节均为有调音节	利器，鸭头
重轻式	末尾音节为轻声音节	力气，丫头

这两种模式在数量上具有明显的不平衡性。由于在本研究使用的数据库中，轻声音节数量占总音节数不足10%，这也意味着在两音节韵律词中，“重轻式”比例很小，而“重重式”比例很大。

在以往研究中，“重轻式”是学界常用的概念，但“重重式”则较少被使用。曾经使用过该概念的有王志洁、冯胜利［43］和杨璐［49］等。前者曾提出三种重音类型（左重、右重和同重），但是，之后将“同重”并入“右重”［43］。后者则分为四种轻重音类型，分别是重中、中重、重轻和不分（重重）［49］。

在其他更多研究中，“重重式”则常被分成“重中”“中重”等模式［30，45，52］。

我们认为，从语音学角度，上述研究“重、中、轻”三级划分法可以理解，但是从音系学角度（参见本研究2.2两条音系学标准），实际构成对立的只有“重、轻”两级。以往三分法中的“中”级实际上可以并入“重”级中。因为“中”和“重”只是一种语音学层面“量”的区别，并不构成音系学层面“质”的区别，所以二者（即“中”和“重”）在本质上都属于“重”音。换句话说，所谓“重中”和“中重”，在音系学层面都应被描述为“重重”。这样，本研究提出的汉语两音节词轻重音模式，和前人研究中的轻重音模式的对照关系就形成了表10分类对应关系（例词选自研究［49］）。

表10　汉语两音节词重音模式的语音学变体

音系学类别	语音学变体	例子
重重式	重中	霸道，教养
	中重	补课，包扎
	不分（重重）	冬笋，版主
重轻式	重轻	称呼，冲突

本研究提出的两音节词轻重音模式中，“重轻式”一般没有异议，但是“重重式”（由两个带调音节构成的词）可能存在争议，因为两个音节之间并没有形成轻重对立。这不同于英语中一个词只有唯一词重音的模式，和以往各种汉语词重音理论分类法也不同。但是，这一模式却比较符合实际听感情况，例如以表10中“重中”“中重”例词来说，普通人通常很难分辨词中各音节的轻重差异。

和英语词重音规则相比，汉语词重音有以下特点：

（1）与英语的“唯一”词重音理念不同，汉语词汇中不一定有唯一词重音；

（2）汉语词重音不是词内位置对立，而是由声调形成的类别间对立。

综合来看，轻重特征在汉语中不像声调等特征那么显著而重要，但是这并不能否定汉语不存在词汇层面的轻重音。从汉语词重音和声调的关系，以及汉语和英语词重音的差异性中，我们会从更宏大的维度看到人类语言的一些规律。

6. 讨论和结语

6.1 以往各种理论的问题所在

本部分，我们将尝试讨论以往研究中可能存在的问题。

（1）以往有的研究认为汉语有词重音且认为模式有“重中”“中重”等观点的理论，其问题是混淆了音系学轻重音和语音学轻重音，或者说把轻重的“质”和“量”混在了一起进行讨论。这些理论中的“重”和“中”一般都是指有调音节。它们之间可能存在轻重感知上的差异，但是这种差异只是语音学层面“量”的对立，不足以构成音系学层面“质”的差异，因为这种“重”“中”差异既没有区分意义的作用，也没有很强的听感区分性。在音系学层面，真正形成“质”的对立的只有“重”（有调）和“轻”（无调）的对立，不存在“重”和“中”的对立。两类不同性质对立切记不可混在一起讨论。

（2）以往认为汉语没有词重音的研究理论，主要关注了由带调音节构成的两音节汉语词（即上文所说“重重”式）中没有明显的轻重对立，但是忽视了轻声（或轻读）的地位，或者把轻声当成了例外［55］。轻声音节虽然数量有限（通常只占所有音节的十分之一左右），却是汉语中不可或缺的重要类别。事实上，也正是由于轻声（或轻读）音节的存在，才使得汉语有了真正音系学意义上的词汇轻重音。

6.2 词汇轻重音的作用

本研究关心的另外一个问题是，词汇层面的轻重音（包括音步重音和词重音）在人类语言系统中的作用是什么？这关系到如何客观看待汉语词重音地位的问题。

我们认为，词重音主要有两大功能，首先是帮助区分语言符号及其语义信息，其次是韵律节奏功能。

（1）词汇轻重音的首要功能是区分语言符号，区别语义信息。

“区别语义，正确传信”是语言系统最重要的任务。词重音的首要功能也是这样。

对英语而言，由于大多数单词是多音节词，所以准确识别单词内音节构成非常重要。尽管音节的辅元结构在很大程度上可以帮助人们区分单词的音节结构，但是，由于在自然语流中音素很容易发生音变、缩减，甚至脱落，这就可能给听音人带来识别困扰。如果在单词的相邻音节上增加轻重交替的冗余特征（音步重音），那么就会使音节识别更加容易、准确，从而提高对单词的识别率。另外，英语单词除了音步重音外，每个单词通常还有一个更高级别的词重音。这种词重音可以使得听音人更容易识别相邻单词，起到帮助分词的作用。当然，英语词重音除了分词（或音节）功能，本身还有更重要的辨义功能，例如区分同音词/近音词（如 below—billow）、词性（如动词 record—名词 record），以及词和词组（如 overall—over all）等［17］。

对于汉语而言，词汇轻重音的作用明显比英语小了很多。例如，对于非轻声音节构成的多音节词（重重式），词内几乎感觉不到明显的轻重对立。之所以出现这种情况，可能有以下几个原因，一是汉语是单音节性语言，而非多音节性语言，不需要音步重音来区分音节等单元边界；二是汉语在重音基础上发展出了更加精细的声调系统。每个声调具有完善的调型和调值，可以起到更好地区分音节（汉字）意义的作用。正是由于有了更加精细的声调系统，所以，汉语的轻重音系统退后到了相对次要的功能。

（2）词汇轻重音具有韵律节奏功能。

词汇层面的轻重差异可以形成韵律节奏类型的差异。众所周知，英语属于重音计时型（stress - timed）语言，而汉语属于音节计时型（syllable - timed）语言［6］。英语这种重音计时型特点和其音节轻重音以及词汇重音的交替出现有重要关系。汉语由于大多数音节是带声调的，所以，其词汇轻重特征以“重重式”为主，这就形成了以音节为单元的音节计时型节奏特征。

6.3 从英汉对比中，看汉语词汇轻重音特点

汉语和英语两种语言都有轻重音系统，轻重音也都具有辨义功能。不过汉语和英语的轻重音特点也存在很大差异。这种差异性可以帮助我们更深刻地了解汉语轻重音的特点和地位。

首先，汉语轻重音不是组内位置对立（词内音节间对立），而是组间类别对立。英语的词汇层面轻重音是和音节位置密切相关，通常形成轻重交替的音步现象和固定的词重音。汉语词汇轻重音和位置关系不大，而是由声调构成的类别间对立（有调—无调）。所以汉语大部分带调音节构成的词汇上体现不出轻重对立，只有出现轻声音节时才会出现轻重对立现象。

其次，汉语轻重音和“音步”单位没有必然关联。英语的轻重音理论是和音步单位密切相关的，认为轻重交替是形成音步的基础。但是，很多学者认为，汉语不存在明显的音步，有的学者虽然认为汉语有音步，但是其主要特征也不是轻重［29，36］。

最后，汉语词重音作用较弱，地位不显赫，轻音数量也较少。与之相对，英语中词重音作用很大，和语义、语法、韵律都有关联。总的来看，汉语词汇轻重音地位远不如英语轻重音。在汉语中，真正显赫的语音特征是声调特征。

6.4 结语

本研究围绕汉语词重音问题，从“质”和“量”的角度提出了判断词汇层面轻重音的两条音系学标准。

（1）具有区别意义的作用。

（2）具有显著听觉区分性。

依此标准，研究发现汉语韵律词“左重”（或前重）趋势只是一种语音学统计规律，不构成音系规律，而声调类别（有调和无调）才构成轻重音的音系学规则。具体规则如下：

（1）有调音节（包括阴平、阳平、上声、去声）构成重音。

（2）无调音节（轻声或轻读）构成轻音。轻声在本质上可能是个轻重概念，而非一个声调。

根据以上规则，汉语普通话两音节韵律词可以分为两类：

（1）重重式（音节均为有调音节）。

（2）重轻式（词尾音节为轻声或轻读）。

上述分类认为，在音系学层面只存在“重、轻”二元对立，不存在“重、中、轻”多元对立。多元对立中的“中”在音系学层面可以归入“重”的类别。

最后，文章讨论了轻重音的作用，以及汉语词汇轻重音系统的特点。一方面，要承认汉语存在词汇层面的轻重音，而且这种轻重音是和声调系统存在密切关系的；另一方面，相对于英语等语言而言，汉语的轻重音系统是不发达的，不具有英语轻重音的很多特征和功能。

本研究也存在很多需要改进之处，以及有待继续研究的内容。（1）本研究采用的发音人语料数量比较有限，还需要补充更多语料数据；（2）基于语料库统计方法的研究是宏观的、粗线条的，未来还可以开展控制性更好的微观、细致的实验研究；（3）轻重音和声调系统之间的关系、音系学与语音学层面的关系，以及汉英等不同语言轻重音规律的异同，来源于语言系统更深层的规律与特性。这些内容未来还需要进行更深入的探查和思考。

参考文献

［1］Duanmu, S., 1990, *A formal study of syllable, tone, stress and domain in Chinese language*, PhD dissertation, MIT.

［2］Halliday, M. A. K., 1985, *An Introduction to Functional Grammar*, Edwrd Arnold.

［3］Hayes, B., 1995, *Metrical stress theory: pricnciple and case studies*, University of Chicago Press.

［4］Li, A. & Fan, S., 2015, Correlates of Chinese neutral tone perception in Different Contexts. *Proceedings of the 18th International Congress of Phonetic Sciences (ICPhS 2015)*, Glasgow, Scotland.

［5］liberman, M., Prince, A., 1977, On stress and Linguistic Rhythm, *linguistic inquiry 8*.

[6] Pike, K. N. , 1945, *The Intonation of American English*, *Ann Arbor*, *University of Michigan Press at* .
[7] Shih, C. (石基琳), 1986, *The Prosodic Domain of Tone Sandhi in Chinese*, PhD disserttation, University of Califonia at San Diego.
[8] 蔡莲红、吴宗济、蔡锐、陶建华:《汉语韵律特征的可计算性研究》,《新世纪的现代语音学》,清华大学出版社2001年版。
[9] 曹剑芬:《汉语普通话词重音问题再探》,《南大语言学》第三编,2008年。
[10] 曹剑芬:《普通话轻声音节特性分析》,《应用声学》1986年第4期。
[11] 曹剑芬:《现代语音基础知识》,人民教育出版社1990年版。
[12] 曹剑芬:《汉语声调与语调的关系》,《中国语文》2002年第3期。
[13] 曹剑芬:《发音增强与缩减》,《第七届全国语音学学术会议暨语音问题国际论坛论文集》,2006年。
[14] 曹剑芬:《加强汉语轻音的研究》,《燕园远去的笛声——林焘先生纪念文集》,商务印书馆2007年版。
[15] 端木三:《重音理论和汉语的词长选择》,《中国语文》1999年第4期。
[16] 冯胜利:《论汉语的"自然音步"》,《中国语文》1998年第1期。
[17] 何善芬:《英汉轻重音对比研究》,《外语与外语教学》1999年总第128期。
[18] 高名凯、石安石:《语言学概论》,中华书局1963年版。
[19] 黄伯荣、廖序东:《现代汉语》(增订三版),高等教育出版社1991年版。
[20] 贾媛、熊子瑜、李爱军:《普通话焦点重音对语句音高的作用》,《中国语音学报》第1辑,商务印书馆2008年版,第119—124页。
[21] 贾媛:《普通话同音异构两音组重音类型辨析》,《清华大学学报》(自然科学版)2011年第51卷第9期。
[22] 李爱军:《普通话不同信息结构中轻声的语音特性》,《当代语言学》2017年第19卷第3期。
[23] 李爱军:《汉语口语语篇库:建构与标注》,中国社会科学出版社2021年版。
[24] 林茂灿、颜景助:《北京话轻声的声学性质》,《方言》1980年第3期。
[25] 林茂灿、颜景助、孙国华:《北京话两字组重音的初步实验》,《方言》1984年第1期。
[26] 林焘:《探讨北京话轻声性质的初步实验》,《语言学论丛》第10辑,商务印书馆1983年版。
[27] 林焘:《探讨北京话轻音性质的初步实验》,《北京语音试验录》,北京大学出版社1985年版。
[28] 林焘、王理嘉:《语音学教程》,北京大学出版社1992年版。
[29] 刘现强:《现代汉语节奏研究》,北京语言大学出版社2007年版。
[30] 陆致极:《普通话双音词"重中式"和"中重式"声学性质初探》,《汉语学习》1984年第6期。
[31] 罗常培、王均:《普通话语音学纲要》,商务印书馆1981年版。
[32] 沈炯:《北京话声调的音域和调域》,《北京语音实验录》,北京大学出版社1985年版。
[33] 沈炯:《汉语语势重音的音理》,《语文研究》1994年第3期。
[34] 沈炯:《汉语音高载信系统模型》,《中国语言学的新拓展》,香港城市大学出版社1999年版。
[35] 王蓓:《汉语韵律知觉的研究》,博士学位论文,中国科学院心理所,2002年。
[36] 王洪君:《论汉语的节奏类型——松紧型》,《语言科学》2004年第3期。
[37] 王洪君:《汉语非线性音系学》(增订版),北京大学出版社2008年版。
[38] 王晶、王理嘉:《普通话多音节词音节时长分布模式》,《中国语文》1993年第2期。
[39] 王韫佳:《音高和时长在普通话轻声知觉中的作用》,《声学学报》2004年第5期。
[40] 王韫佳、初敏:《关于普通话词重音的若干问题》,《中国语音学报》第1辑,中国社会科学出版社2008年版。
[41] 王韫佳、初敏、贺琳:《普通话语句重音在双音节韵律词中的分布》,《语言科学》2004年第3卷第5期。
[42] 王韫佳、初敏、贺琳:《汉语焦点重音和语义重音分布的初步实验研究》,《世界汉语教学》2006年第2期。
[43] 王志洁、冯胜利:《声调对比法与北京话双音组的重音类型》,《语言科学》2006年第1期。
[44] 吴宗济:《普通话语调分析的一种新方法:语句中基本调群单元的移调处理》,英文稿载1993年《语音研究年报》(中国社会科学院语言研究所内部刊物),中文稿(曹文翻译)载2004年《吴宗济语言学论文集》,商务印书馆1993/2004年版。
[45] 徐世荣:《双音缀词的重音规律》,《中国

语文》1956年第2期。
[46] 徐世荣:《普通话语音常识》，语文出版社1999年版。
[47] 许洁萍、初敏、贺琳、吕士楠:《汉语语句重音对音高和时长的影响》,《声学学报》2000年第25卷第4期。
[48] 颜宁:《非线性音系学》，人民出版社2009年版。
[49] 杨璐:《北京话双音节词重音研究》，硕士研究生学位论文，北京大学，2011年。
[50] 叶军:《现代汉语节奏研究》，上海世纪出版集团2008年版。
[51] 殷治纲:《汉语普通话朗读语篇节奏研究》，博士学位论文，中国社会科学院大学，2011年。
[52] 殷作炎:《关于普通话双音常用词轻重音的初步考察》,《中国语文》1982年第3期。
[53] 赵元任:《中国言语字调的实验研究法》,《科学》1922年第8期。
[54] 赵元任:《汉语口语语法》，商务印书馆1968/1979年版。
[55] 张吉生:《也论汉语轻重音》,《中国语文》2021年第1期。
[56] 仲晓波、王蓓、杨玉芳、吕士楠:《普通话韵律词重音知觉》,《心理学报》2001年第6期。
[57] 仲晓波、杨玉芳:《国外关于韵律特征和重音的一些研究》,《心理学报》1999年第4期。
[58] 仲晓波、郑波、杨玉芳:《关于普通话韵律短语重音的实验研究》,《声学学报》2002年第2期。

殷治纲 中国社会科学院语言研究所语音室、语料库暨计算语言学研究中心，副研究员。主要研究领域为语音学、语料库语言学、法律语言学，以及语音和语法、语义、语用的接口研究。
E-mail：yinzhg@ cass. org. cn

山东方言对英语元音学习的影响及可视化教学设计

郑雅錤　雷丁一　徐若敖　汪高武

摘　要　本文通过对比单元音的声学特征研究山东方言（冀鲁官话，以济南话为例）对英语语音学习的正负迁移影响，并利用声学元音图设计可视化教学方法纠正英语发音。实验对象为 12 名大学生，分为实验组和对照组进行为期一个月的语音教学实验，并由 3 位英语专业评审对两组被试教学前后的发音进行评估打分。实验表明，济南话单元音/ɔ/和/ə/的舌位与英语单元音/ɔ：/和/ə/的舌位基本一致，对英语学习有明显的正迁移影响；济南话单元音/i/、/ɛ/、/A/、/ɔ/对与之发音位置接近的英语单元音/i：/、/e/、/æ/、/ɑ：/、/ʌ/、/ɒ/等存在较普遍的负迁移影响；经过一个月的可视化教学，实验组发音人的单元音发音有明显改善，学习效果优于对照组发音人，验证了声学元音图可视化语音教学的有效性。

关键词　英语教学，济南话，正负迁移影响，声学元音图，可视化教学

The Influence of the Shandong Dialect on Learning English Vowels and the Visualization in Teaching

ZHENG Yaqi　LEI Dingyi　XU Ruoao　WANG Gaowu

Abstract This paper studied the positive and negative transfers of Shandong dialect—using the Ji' nan dialect as an example—on English pronunciation learning by comparing the acoustic features of single vowels, and then discussed a visualization teaching method using vowel charts. Twelve college students, six in the experimental group and six in the control group, participated in the one-month pronunciation practice. The pronunciations of the two groups, before and after the practice, were evaluated and scored by three raters. The results showed that single vowels /ɔ/ and /ə/ in the Ji' nan dialect share the same tongue positions as /ɔ:/ and /ə/ in English, leading to a significant positive transfer effect on the English learning. However, /i/, /ɛ/, /A/ and /ɔ/ in the Ji' nan dialect have different tongue positions from /i:/, /e/, /æ/, /ɑ:/, /ʌ/ and /ɒ/ in English, and the differences have a negative transfer effect. After one-month's training, participants in the experimental group showed significant improvement in their pronunciation of single English vowels, and performed better than those in the control group, which showed the effectiveness of the visual teaching method using acoustic vowel charts.

Key words Shandong dialect, English learning, Transfer effect, Acoustic vowel charts, Visualization teaching

1. 引言

在中国，使用冀鲁官话的人口有 8942 万，人数排在官话区的第四位［17］。山东是冀鲁官话的使用大省。山东学生在学习英语语音的过程中不仅要面对英汉语音的差异，还要考虑到山东方言口音带来的迁移影响，包括正迁移（positive transfer）和负迁移（negative transfer）。Flege 提出的“语言学习模型”（Speech Learning Model）［1］认为，学习者因常以母语语音代替第二语言中的相似语音而难以习得地道的外语发音。同时，由于应试教育模式下教学者对英语口语能力的忽视及语音跟读训练教学方法的单一，山东学生的英语口语存在较多问题［23］。

围绕山东方言对英语语音习得的影响这一问题，目前学界在声学实验、理论分析等方面已取得了一定成果。在研究对象方面，有立足于超音段（如［5］、［18］）

和音段音位（如［19］、［22］）两方面的研究。在研究方法方面，纯理论分析较多，如［2］、［9］等，这些研究拓展了研究的理论基础，但需要声学实验的进一步检验。通过声学实验探讨方言迁移的研究相对较少，比较典型的有［7］、［8］和［21］。［7］比较了济南英语学习者所发英语元音和标准美式发音在整体趋势上的差异，并重点讨论了济南英语学习者顶点元音和松紧元音的习得情况；贾媛、王宇等人［8］利用声学实验的方法，指出了宁波方言区英语学习者与本族语者在单元音发音中存在的系统性差异，重点以/i/、/u/、/a/为例讨论了宁波方言和普通话对英语发音的负向迁移影响；钟欣、翟红华等［21］则以元音/i/、/ɪ/、/e/、/æ/为例，对比分析了泰安地区大中学生在英语学习过程中受方言影响的情况。在教学反馈和跟进实验设计方面，许多研究都有意识地为山东方言区的英语语音教学提供参考，注重研究的实用性，如［11］、［14］。但这些研究大部分侧重讨论负迁移影响，对正迁移的关注不足；且多将山东方言视为一个均质整体，针对某一地区方言的研究甚少。而且多数研究没有设计教学实验，教学效果有待检验。因此，本次实验拟以济南方言为例，研究其对英语学习的正负迁移影响，设计可视化教学方案。

目前学界关于可视化教学的研究大部分停留在理论层面，如［3］、［10］等，他们在理论阐释、量化语音分析和初步提出教学方案等方面做出了一定贡献，但其建议的可行性和有效性有待实验检验。有一部分研究在理论介绍的基础上进行了实践，利用相关软件绘制可视化图像或提取可视化数据，并提出相应的发音调整建议，如［12］、［16］等，这些研究对探索可视化教学方案有很强的借鉴意义，但具体的教学效果也需要进一步检验。此外，一些学者虽然提出了完整的可视化教学方案，绘制了相应的可视化图像，如［28］、［24］等，但这些图像专业性较强，对技术的要求较高，掌握起来比较困难，在实际教学中可能难以推进。

综上所述，本次研究将从声学实验的结果出发，在总结济南话对英语元音学习产生的正负迁移影响的基础上，借助Praat软件绘制用于标明元音位置的声学元音图（vowel chart），设计较为直观的、更有针对性的教学方案，并通过教学实验来检验其可行性和有效性，为一线的教学工作提供参考。

2. 实验方法

2.1 被试信息

本实验的被试为12名大学生（4男8女），均为山东省济南市人，从小在济南话环境中成长。被试人均非英语专业学生，其英语语音习得的主要途径为义务教育阶段学校开设的英语课程。所有被试人口齿清晰，无发音和听力障碍。被试人编号1—6号为实验组（2男4女），7—12号为对照组（2男4女）。虽然济南市大部分地区属冀鲁官话区，但其内部不同地区也存在语音上的细微差别。就实验中考察的相关音素而言，元音/ɔ/仅存在于东部济南方言中，3号被试人和10号被试人表现得较明显，因此以下涉及元音/ɔ/的论证或结论皆以此二位为例。

2.2 实验设备及数据收集

实验所使用的录音设备为内置麦克风的MacBook Pro（13-inch, 2017）笔记本电脑，录音和分析软件为Praat（Version 6.1.26）。录音保存为wav文件格式，单声道，采样率44.1kHz。录音在安静的环境中进行，发音人在录音时保持稳定速度，每个例词读两遍。在绘制声学元音图时使用Praat提取元音稳定段的第一、第二共振峰。

2.3 实验过程

（1）根据何善芬［6］和丹尼尔·琼斯［4］的英汉元音系统，比较济南话与英语的单元音，发现可能存在迁移影响的音素主要有9组（以下列举前者为济南话单元音，后者为英语单元音）：/i/和/iː/、/ɛ/和/e/、/ɛ/和/æ/、/A/和/ɑ/、/A/和/ʌ/、

/ɔ/和/ɔ/、/ɔ/和/ɒ/、/u/和/uː/、/ə/和/ə/。三个英语元音/ɪ/、/ʊ/、/ɜː/的舌位与济南话元音相对较远，因而本次研究暂未考虑。我们优先考虑济南话对更近英语元音的影响，待教学校正后再考虑较远元音的研究和校正。另外，考虑到在记音时，不同记录者记录的精度不同，因此音标一致的两个音在实际音值上可能出现偏差，所以实验结合元音四边形图进一步确定了重点考察的音素。

（2）设计普通话和济南话例词（表1），根据普通话例词确定每位发音人的元音发音范围，根据济南话例词确定济南话主要元音的发音位置，由此在普通话确定的发音范围基础上绘制12位发音人的济南话声学元音图。对发音人的发音数据进行归一化处理，并借助投影变换对归一后的图像进一步规整（具体操作见后文）。由此，以普通话为桥梁建构起济南话元音四边形图与英语元音四边形图（何善芬［6］绘制，如图1所示）之间相互比较的可能性，在比较中明确济南话中具有正迁移影响的单元音音素。

表1 汉语例词

单元音	普通话例词	济南话例词
/i/	闭	闭
/ɛ/	别扭	拜年
/A/	爸	爸
/ɔ/	—	报纸
/o/	簸箕	—
/u/	布	布
/ə/	—	薄荷

语音学界常采用的元音共振峰归一方法有 Bark Difference Metric、Watt & Fabricius Method、Lobanov Method（s）、Z值等［20］，本研究采用 Bark Difference Metric 对发音数据进行归一处理［15］，具体公式为：

$$Bark = 7\ln\{(f/650) + [(f/650)^2 + 1]^{1/2}\} \quad (1)$$

处理后的结果如图2所示。

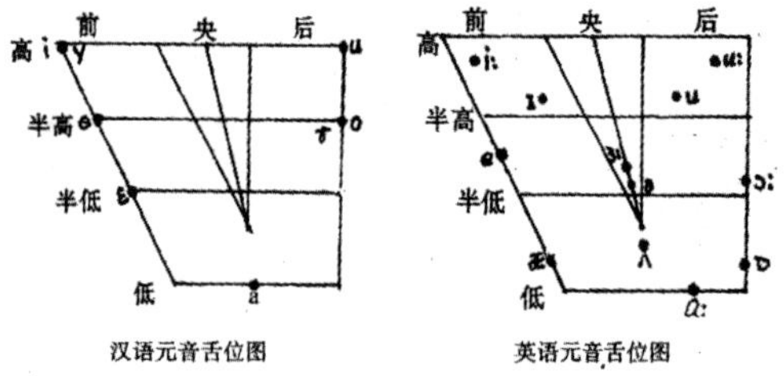

图1 何善芬（2002）英汉元音四边形图

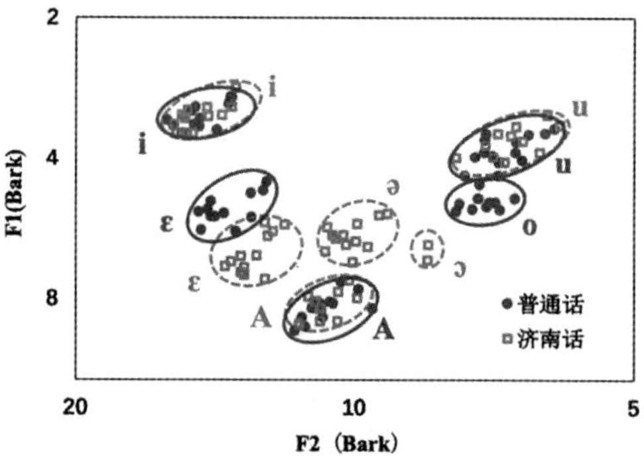

图2 归一后的元音散点图

对图2进一步规整，以每个元音聚合的中心点为代表点，分别连接普通话和济南话代表点可得图3。

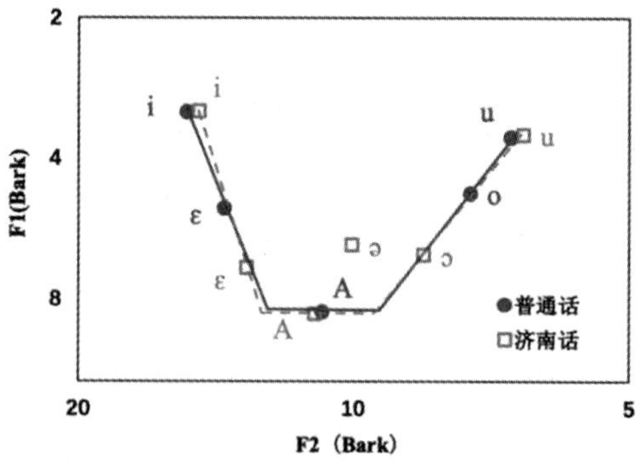

图3 济南话主要元音四边形图

图3中的普通话元音四边形与何善芬［6］所绘四边形并不一致，为方便二者比较，分别建立坐标，利用自编写的 Python 脚本对图3中的四边形进行投影变换，并将英语元音添至四边形图中，变换后的图

像如图4所示。

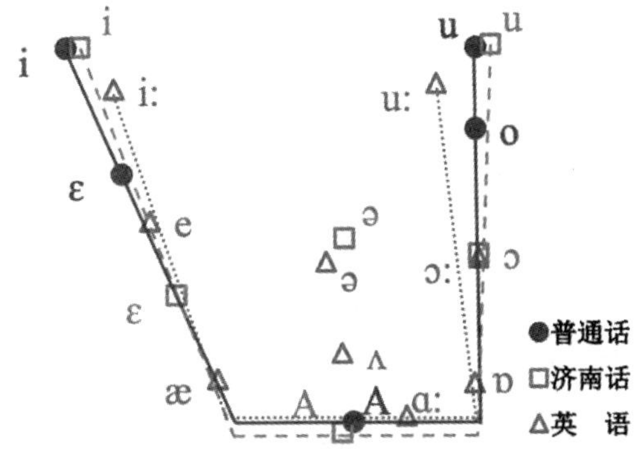

图4 投影变换后的元音四边形图

由图4可知，济南话单元音/ɔ/的舌位与英语单元音/ɔ：/的舌位基本一致，因此该元音对英语元音习得存在明显的正迁移影响。另外，济南话单元音/ə/虽然与英语元音/ə/有一点距离，但由于二者同为央元音，与其他元音距离较远，因此借助济南话元音/ə/可以帮助学习者初步确定英语元音/ə/的发音位置。再者，部分学习者在学习英语元音/ə/时往往受到普通话元音/ɤ/的影响，相较之下济南话元音/ə/与标准发音更接近，容易帮助学习者摆脱普通话元音/ɤ/的负迁移影响。所以，可认为济南话元音/ə/对英语元音/ə/的习得存在正迁移影响。不过，发音人在学习过程中是否注意到了/ɔ/和/ə/的正迁移影响，以及利用这种正迁移影响帮助济南英语学习者学习相关元音是否可行，仍有待实验检验，相关问题将于下文讨论。除去/ɔ/和/ə/，剩余的7组元音可能存在负迁移影响。

（3）结合以上结果，设计英语例词，检验发音人是否充分注意到济南话中/ɔ/和/ə/的正迁移影响，同时检验济南话可能出现负迁移影响的7组元音，根据检测结果进一步明确存在负迁移影响的单元音。考虑到被试的英语水平，本研究选择较为常见不容易发错音的例词，暂未用“h_d”来设计例词以考虑协同发音问题。英语例词如下：/i：/ key、/e/ set、/æ/ cap、/ɑ：/ sharp、/ʌ/ cup、/ɒ/ got、/ɔ：/ short、/u：/ shoot、/ə/ again。

根据拟定的例词对发音人进行语音采样，并绘制每人的声学元音图，将之与图4对比，我们发现虽然济南话中的/ɔ/和/ə/对英语的/ɔ：/和/ə/有正迁移影响，但是多数发音人并未注意到这种正迁移影响；济南话中的/i/、/ε/、/A/、/ɔ/对与之发音位置接近的英语元音/i：/、/e/、/æ/、/ɑ：/、/ʌ/、/ɒ/等存在普遍的负迁移影响，而上文中猜测的济南话单元音/u/与英语单元音/u：/之间实则不存在明显的影响关系。以下具体说明济南话对英语元音的负迁移影响。

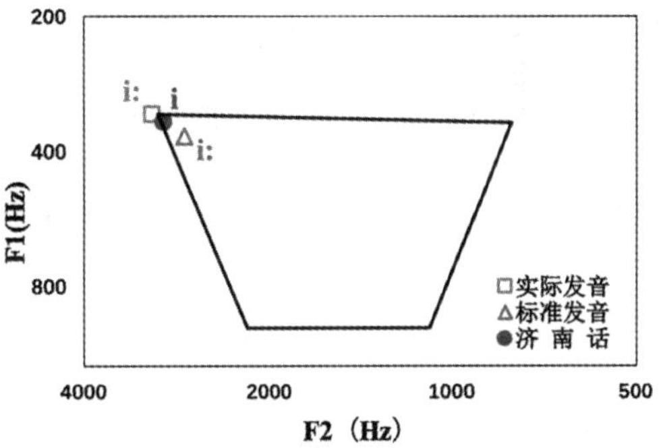

图5 1号发音人key中元音/i：/的发音位置

如图5所示，济南话单元音/i/相较英语单元音/i：/舌位更靠上靠前，济南地区的学习者在英语学习过程中不自觉地以济南话的/i/代替了英语的单元音/i：/，在英语发音过程中元音/i：/的舌位明显靠上靠前（图中标准发音位置坐标根据投影变换确定）。类似地，济南话的单元音/A/在英语习得过程中，主要对元音/ɑ：/和元音/ʌ/存在负迁移影响。发音人在发/ɑ：/时，发音的位置更靠前，而发音人在发/ʌ/时，发音位置较靠下。济南话中的单元音/ε/为舌面前半低不圆唇元音，该元音在英语习得过程中主要对与之接近的元音/e/和元音/æ/具有负迁移影响。大部分发音人在发单词cap和set时，主要元音与济南话中/ε/的位置大致相同。单元音/ɔ/在济南话中的位置与英语大致相同，所以对习得英语元音/ɔ/存在正迁移作用，但由于单元音/ɒ/与之在发音位置和语音听感上均较为接近，所以部分发音人在发单元音/ɒ/时，常代之以 /ɔ/，从而使济南话元音/ɔ/对英语元音/ɒ/的习得产生一定的负迁移影响。

（4）根据以上分析结果，对被试的实验组6人和对照组6人，分别进行语音教学。对照组采用传统的语音跟读教学方式，实验组采用可视化教学方式。具体的可视化教学方式为，利用 Praat 绘制每位发音人的声学元音图，对比个人声学元音图和英语标准四边形图，指出发音人的发音偏误，并为发音人提供语音改善建议，指导发音人根据四边形图的提示调整舌位。同时，在语音训练的不同阶段多次采录发音人的发音，根据录音材料及时、多次绘制个人声学元音图，不断向发音人反馈语音学习效果。在语音训练过程中，反复强调济南话的正迁移影响，同时不断提醒发音人注意负迁移作用，并将语音跟读与声学元音图结合起来，两者参照以更有效地改善发音人的英语发音。

（5）以上步骤完成后，对教学效果进行了评估。研究小组继续收集发音人经过语音训练后的录音材料，通过对比训练前后的发音数据和声学元音图，检验可视化教学效果。另外，为进一步检验教学效果，由三位英语专业的高年级大学生作为评审，以双盲测试的形式进行教学效果评估。将实验组、对照组中所有被试的初始录音和训练后的录音混在一起，打乱顺序，让评审对录音进行评分。

3. 结果分析

为了检验可视化语音教学的教学效果，这里利用 Praat 绘制的声学元音图对比训练前后的不同，并对专业评审给训练前后的英语发音的评分进行统计分析。

3.1 各单元音的可视化教学效果

在语音训练过程中，反复向实验组发音人强调济南话的正迁移影响，引导他们充分利用正迁移影响习得相应的英语单元音，实验证明该方法对改善英语发音有明显作用。以下为3号和6号发音人最终/ɔ：/和/ə/的发音位置。

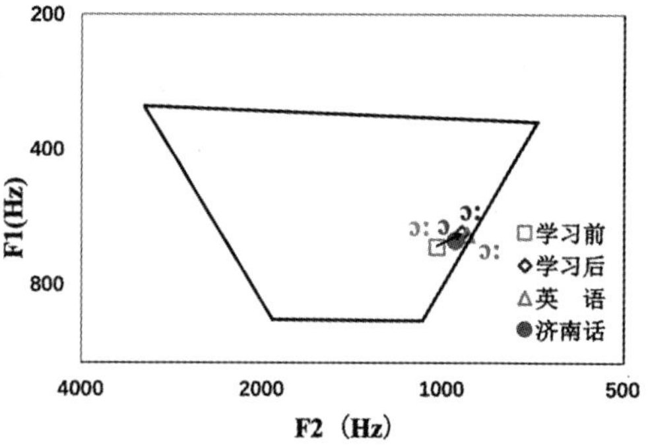

图6　3号发音人学习前后元音/ɔ：/发音位置

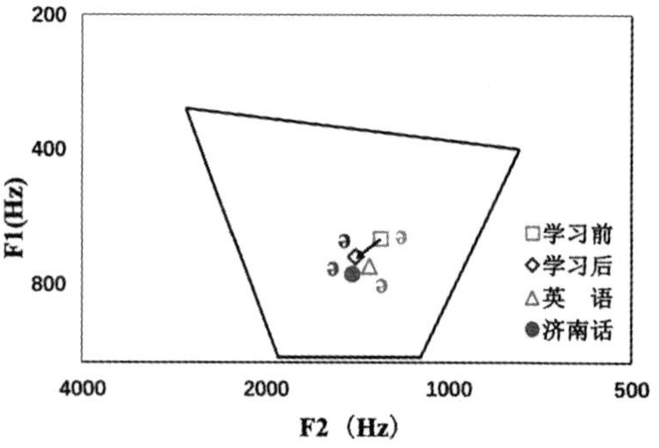

图7　6号发音人学习前后元音/ə/发音位置

由图6和图7可见，语音学习后两位发音人 /ɔ：/和/ə/的舌位已基本接近标准舌位，说明充分注意并利用济南话的正迁移影响对准确习得英语中的相应元音有积极作用。

而可视化教学手段对克服济南话的负迁移影响也同样有明显效果。以下列举了部分发音人在语音训练前后所发/iː/、/e/、/æ/、/ɑː/、/ʌ/、/ɒ/等的声学元音图，通过对比可以明显看到可视化教学手段的教学效果。

由图8可见，经过一段时间的语音训练，发音人对英语元音/iː/的掌握有了明显改善，舌位明显向后向下移动，与标准发音的舌位更接近，基本克服了济南话单

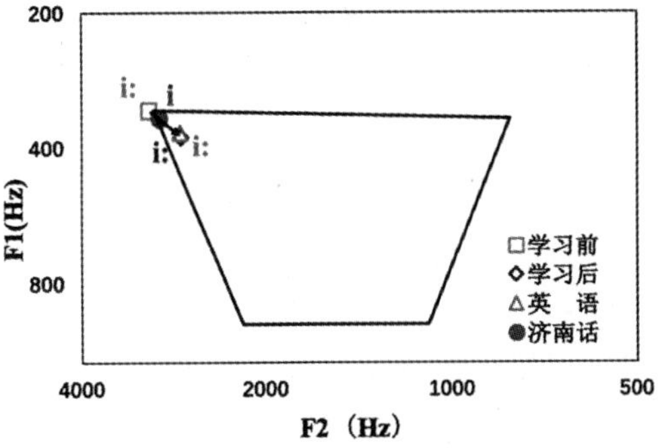

图8　1号发音人学习前后元音/i：/发音位置

元音/i/的负迁移影响。这一情况在其他5位实验组发音人中普遍存在。

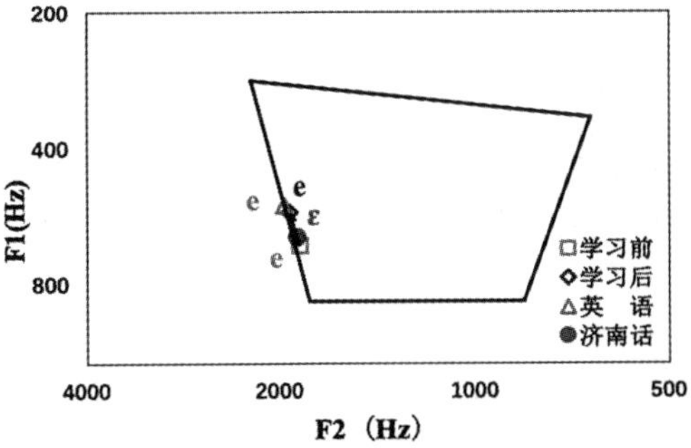

图9　2号发音人学习前后元音/e/发音位置

由图9可见，发音人最初在发单元音/e/时，舌位靠下靠后，开口度略大。经过一段时间的语音训练后，发音人在发音时舌位明显向上向前，与标准发音更接近。这一改善情况在其他5位实验组发音人中普遍存在。

由图10可见，发音人在最初发音时，英语单元音/æ/舌位靠前靠上，经过学习后，发音人在发/æ/时舌位明显向后向下调整，发音时的开口度更大，与标准发音更接近。这一改善情况在其他5位实验组发音人中普遍存在。

由图11可见，发音人最初在发单元音/ɑ：/时，舌位靠近中间位置，经过语音训练后，舌位明显向后靠拢，与标准英语舌位更接近。这一改善情况在其他5位实验组发音人中普遍存在。

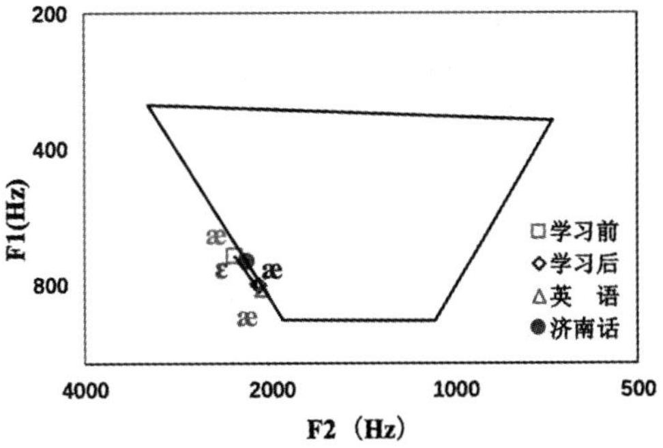

图10　3号发音人学习前后元音/æ/发音位置

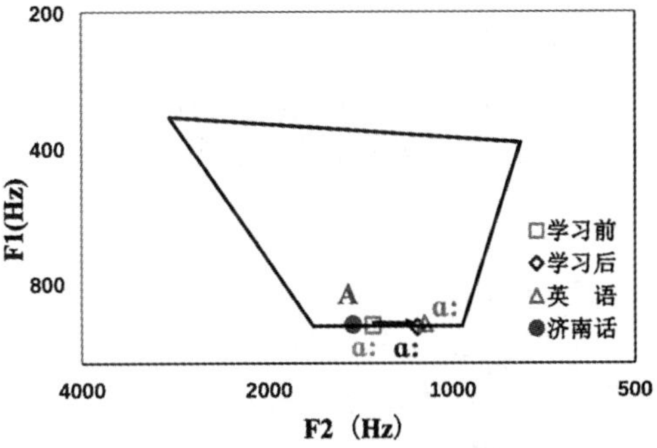

图11　4号发音人学习前后元音/ɑ：/发音位置

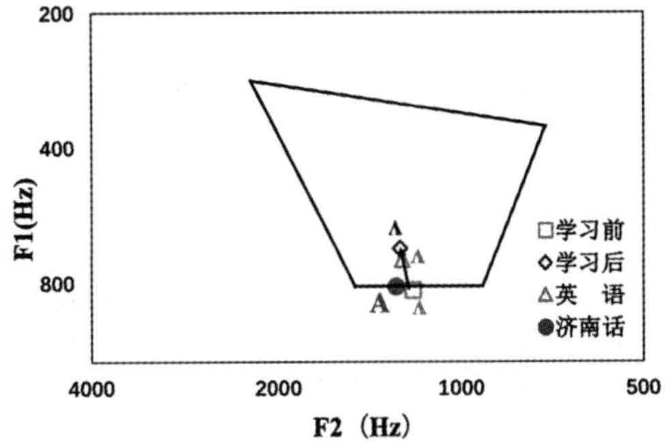

图12　5号发音人学习前后元音/ʌ/发音位置

由图 12 可见，发音人在发元音/ʌ/时，最初舌位较靠下，与济南话中单元音/ʌ/接近。经过一段时间的语音训练后，舌位明显抬高，与标准发音位置更接近。以上提到的改善情况在其他 5 位实验组发音人中普遍存在。

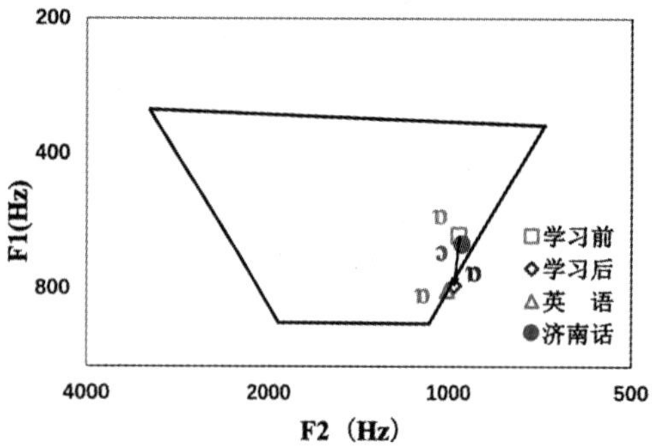

图 13　3 号发音人学习前后元音/ɒ/发音位置

由图 13 可见，发音人最初发单元音/ɒ/时，舌位较靠上，经过一段时间的语音训练后，单元音/ɒ/的发音位置明显向下调整，与标准发音更接近。

综上所述，对比实验组发音人学习前后的发音，可以明显看出，可视化教学手段存在较为显著的教学效果。另外，根据实验组发音人的反馈意见，借助元音四边形图这一可视图像进行语音学习，相比传统的跟读训练，更容易使他们明确发音偏误，帮助他们明确舌位调整目标，对找到准确的发音位置有很大帮助。

3.2　可视化教学效果的整体评估

三位英语专业评审人对被试学习前后的英语发音进行了打分（1—10 分），其结果如表 2 所示。

根据表 2 中数据，利用 SPSS 对语音学习前后实验组和对照组的平均分差异情况进行 t 检验。结果表明，训练前不同组别之间差异并不显著（$p = 0.961$）；训练之后，实验组前后平均分差异显著（$p < 0.05$），且不同组别的平均分也呈现出显著差异（$p < 0.05$）。由此可见，可视化教学手段具有显著的教学效果，实验结果很好地证明了可视化教学手段在英语语音教学中的有效性。

表 2　发音测评得分

发音人 \ 例词		key	set	cap	sharp	cup	got	short	again	平均分
1	学习前	5.33	5.67	5.33	5.00	4.33	5.00	4.67	5.00	5.04
	学习后	6.67	7.67	7.33	7.33	6.33	6.67	7.67	6.67	7.04
2	学习前	5.33	5.33	5.33	4.67	4.33	4.00	4.33	4.33	4.71
	学习后	7.33	7.67	7.67	7.33	6.67	6.67	7.33	6.67	7.17
3	学习前	5.67	5.33	6.00	5.00	5.00	5.00	5.33	5.33	5.33
	学习后	6.33	7.67	7.67	6.67	7.67	7.00	8.33	7.33	7.33
4	学习前	5.33	5.67	5.33	5.00	4.67	4.67	4.67	4.33	4.96
	学习后	6.67	6.33	7.00	7.00	6.67	6.67	6.67	6.33	6.67
5	学习前	6.33	5.67	5.33	5.67	4.67	4.67	5.33	4.67	5.29
	学习后	7.67	6.33	7.00	7.00	7.67	7.33	7.33	7.00	7.17

续表

发音人	例词	key	set	cap	sharp	cup	got	short	again	平均分
6	学习前	6.33	5.33	6.33	5.33	5.67	6.33	5.67	5.67	5.83
	学习后	7.33	7.33	8.00	7.33	7.67	7.67	7.67	7.67	7.58
7	学习前	5.33	4.67	5.33	4.67	4.67	5.00	4.67	5.67	5.00
	学习后	6.67	6.33	5.00	5.67	5.67	5.67	5.67	5.33	5.75
8	学习前	5.67	5.67	5.33	5.33	5.33	5.33	4.67	5.33	5.33
	学习后	6.33	6.00	6.00	5.00	5.67	6.33	5.33	6.67	5.92
9	学习前	5.33	5.67	5.33	4.67	4.67	4.67	4.33	5.00	4.96
	学习后	5.67	5.33	5.67	6.00	5.67	6.00	5.00	5.33	5.58
10	学习前	6.33	5.67	5.00	5.33	7.33	4.67	5.33	5.33	5.63
	学习后	6.33	5.67	5.67	6.67	6.33	5.67	5.67	6.00	6.00
11	学习前	5.33	5.33	4.33	5.33	4.67	4.33	4.67	5.00	4.88
	学习后	5.67	6.33	5.67	6.67	5.67	5.67	4.67	4.33	5.58
12	学习前	5.67	5.33	5.33	5.33	5.33	5.67	5.33	5.33	5.42
	学习后	6.67	7.00	5.33	6.33	5.67	6.33	6.00	5.00	6.04

4. 讨论与反思

本次研究通过语音分析明确了济南话在英语习得过程中的正负迁移影响，同时教学实验也证明了可视化教学手段的有效性，为一线的教学工作提供了参考。意见如下：

第一，合理利用母语迁移作用进行有效的英语教学。通过本研究可知，实验组发音人的英语语音在语音训练后有了明显提升，普遍关注了济南话在英语语音学习中的正迁移影响，克服了济南话的负迁移影响。因此，就一线教学而言，准确区分母语在二语习得过程中的迁移作用，并积极顺应正迁移，引导克服负迁移是展开语音教学的重要步骤。

第二，英语教学者可以积极尝试可视化的教学手段，帮助学习者直观地寻找发音位置，克服发音偏误。传统语音教学中的口耳相传模式以及单一的跟读模仿不利于学习者克服母语音系的影响，也不利于对语音学习效果进行客观评价。而可视化的教学手段将跟读与声学元音图结合起来，将听觉与视觉打通，有助于学习者直观地理解发音偏误、纠正发音位置、评价学习效果。

第三，科技工作者可开发操作简单、便于使用的语音学习软件，以帮助一线英语教学者改善教学手段、提高教学质量。英语教学者也可以积极了解各类专业软件(如Praat、Speech Analyzer、Wavesufer等)的功能和特点，借助软件更好地从事可视化语音教学，优化语音教学效果。

同时，本研究也存在一些不足和可以继续改进的地方：其一，受客观条件限制，12名被试样本容量偏小，语音训练也只进行了一个月。如果能够联系到一线教学单位，在整个英语教学过程中采用可视化教学方法，学习者的语音面貌或许也会有更大改善。其二，虽然在设计可视化教学方案时尽量采用声学元音图这一简单易懂的图像进行辅助性教学，但理解和绘制声学元音图依然需要英语教学者具备一定的专业能力，需要设计出更简洁的辅助方案。其三，为了尽可能降低可视化教学方案的复杂程度，在教学过程中并未对每位发音人的声学元音图进行投影变换，而是直接向发音人反馈个人的声学元音图和标准英语元音舌位图的差别。因此，发音人看到的声学元音图与标准元音舌位图并不具有相同的四边形，语音训练中反馈的舌位调整建议实则只是指明了舌位移动的大致方向。如果将来能够借助程序自动化对所有发音人的声学元音图都进行投影变换，则舌位调整的方向可能会更加具体、准确，语音学习效果也可能会更好。

5. 致谢

本研究得到国家自然科学基金项目“基于X光和MRI磁共振成像的汉语普通话发音生理模型研究”（11974054）和教育部社会科学青年基金项目“面向语音教学的汉语普通话发音生理研究”（16YJC740065）的资助。

参考文献

[1] Flege, J. E. 1987. The instrumental study of L2 speech production: Some methodological considerations. *Language Learning* 2, 285 – 296.

[2] 曹珊娜：《英汉语音差别对山东学生英语语音学习的影响》，《黑龙江教育学院学报》2011年第5期，第191—192页。

[3] 陈红：《可视化英语语音教学改革研究——Praat软件在英语语音教学中的应用》，《兰州教育学院学报》2013年第9期，第53—54页。

[4] 丹尼尔·琼斯：《英语语音学大纲》，郭作、周开颀译，四川教育出版社1987年版。

[5] 丁云霞：《中国英语学习者英语疑问句的语调特征研究》，硕士学位论文，山东农业大学，2017年。

[6] 何善芬：《英汉语言对比研究》，上海外语教育出版社2002年版。

[7] 贾媛：《中国方言区英语学习者元音习得类型研究》，中国社会科学出版社2019年版。

[8] 贾媛、王宇、李爱军、徐亮：《中国方言区英语学习者单元音声学特征分析——以宁波地区为例》，《中国语音学报》2017年第1期，第74—80页。

[9] 孔文：《山东方言在英语语音中的负迁移》，《东岳论丛》2005年第3期，第202—203页。

[10] 李晓丽：《舌位图与英语元音音素学习》，《语文学刊》（外语教育与教学）2011年第4期，第123—125页。

[11] 李玉华：《山东学生英语发音常误分析》，《聊城大学学报》（社会科学版）2009年第1期，第118—121页。

[12] 马照谦：《语音分析软件在英语语音教学中的辅助作用探悉》，《牡丹江大学学报》2007年第5期，第130—132页。

[13] 尚春雨：《英语语音课可视化研究——以Praat软件为例》，《无锡职业技术学院学报》2016年第2期，第35—37页。

[14] 王妃妃：《山东方言区英语学习者英语元音音段习得的实验语音研究》，硕士学位论文，山东农业大学，2016年。

[15] 吴宗济、林茂灿：《实验语音学概要》高等教育出版社1989年版。

[16] 谢萍：《Speech Analyzer在英语语音教学中的应用》，《外语电化教学》2007年第6期，第26—29页。

[17] 熊正辉、张振兴：《汉语方言的分区》，《方言》2008年第2期，第97—108页。

[18] 赵爱敏：《山东方言区英语学习者语调格局声学研究：以陈述句、一般疑问句和选择疑问句为例》，硕士学位论文，山东农业大学，2018年。

[19] 赵吉玲：《山东东莱区英语学习者音段习得的声学研究》，硕士学位论文，山东农业大学，2015年。

[20] 周学文：《元音归一化的对数商模型》，《第十二届全国人机语音通讯学术会议论文集》，2013年。

[21] 钟欣、翟红华、巩韦丽：《简析泰安方言对大中学生英语元音习得的影响》，《第十四届全国人机语音通讯学术会议论文集》，2017年。

[22] 朱方杰：《如何应对汶上方言对英语发音的负迁移》，《学周刊》2015年第31期，第233页。

[23] 朱珊珊：《任务型教学法在高中英语口语教学中的应用调查研究》，硕士学位论文，山

东师范大学，2014年。
[24] 庄木齐、卜友红:《语音教学可视化研究》,《电化教育研究》2011年第2期，第92—98页。

郑雅鎮 北京师范大学文学院，本科生，汉语言文学专业。
E-mail：2198629217@ qq. com

雷丁一 北京师范大学文学院，本科生，汉语言文学专业。
E-mail：529016260@ qq. com

徐若敖 北京师范大学文学院，本科生，汉语言文学专业。
E-mail：450713437@ qq. com

汪高武 北京师范大学文学院，副教授，研究方向为实验语音学。
E-mail：wgw@ bnu. edu. cn

日本、韩国、哈萨克、越南普通话学习者的轻声产出

张　驰　胡宁萱　张劲松

摘　要　普通话学习者习得轻声存在困难，因而本研究对比考察了四种韵律特征相异的学习者的轻声产出模式：日本、韩国、哈萨克、越南，试探究母语韵律特征对学习者轻声产出的影响问题。研究共由两个实验组成：实验一由3位母语者对来自4种母语背景的75位学习者产出的3519条轻声数据进行听辨判断，以获得偏误率信息；实验二以20位母语者的轻声产出作为基线数据，与各组学习者的数据进行对比分析，以获得其轻声产出的声学特性信息。实验结果发现：（1）母语为语调语言且主要靠时长区分重音与非重音的哈萨克学习者的轻声偏误问题相较于同为语调语言、但在短语层级有音高重音的韩国学习者及母语为音高重音语言的日本学习者和声调语言的越南学习者更为严重，各组学习者轻声偏误的共性主要是轻声的前接音节易出现偏误，这点在阳平和上声调境中尤为突出；（2）韵律特征相异的各组学习者轻声产出的音高偏误模式有差别：日韩学习者的音高偏离集中于阳轻和上轻组合，与越南学习者主要出现在阴轻组合，哈萨克学习者易出现在各调境下的轻声组合的高度、斜率和拱度的多个维度上形成差异。（3）各组学习者产出轻声的时长偏误模式有一定共性，均主要集中于去轻组合。

关键词　轻声，二语习得，母语迁移

Comparative Studies of the Production of Neutral Tone in Japanese, Korean, Kazakh and Vietnamese Learners of Mandarin

ZHANG Chi　HU Ningxuan　ZHANG Jinsong

Abstract L2 learners of Mandarin find it hard acquiring neutral tone in Mandarin Chinese. The present study investigates the non – native production of neutral tone by Japanese, Korean, Kazakh and Vietnamese learners of Mandarin, whose L1s' suprasegmental systems are distinct from Chinese. Two experiments were conducted in this study: a judgment paradigm by native speakers who were asked to evaluate 3519 syllables in neutral tone produced by a total of 75 learners, and an acoustic analysis was conducted to compare f0 and duration patterns found in groups of learners with a group of 20 native speakers. Results of the experiments showed: (1) Kazakh learners happened to yield more mispronunciations of neutral tone than other groups of learners while in general learners made erroneous productions mainly in the preceding tones in T2 + TN and T3 + TN combinations. (2) Groups of learners from divergent suprasegmental systems exhibited distinctive deviated f0 patterns, in which Japanese and Korean learners tended to flatten and decrease the curvature of f0 in T2 + TN and T3 + TN, Vietnamese learners solely produced T1 + TN by lowering the f0 height, and Kazakh learners produced a general distinctive f0 patterns from native speakers. (3) Groups of learners produced consistently longer duration of neutral tone in T4 + TN combination.

Key words Neutral Tone, Second Language Acquisition, Transfer

1. 引言

轻声是汉语普通话中的一种特殊现象，与轻重音关系密切。赵元任先生[44]把它归为轻重音中的弱重音，对应的声学特性描述为："调幅差不多拉平，时间相当短，音调不同于四声。"轻声在词汇上主要分布在语助词和一些词缀性成分上，一些重叠词和习惯性轻读的词的末

尾音节上也常负载轻声。轻声最主要的两个声学相关物在于音高和音长，而与音强关系不大［30，37，38，43］，不同前接声调下的轻声的声学特性有差异。在音高维度，四个声调后的轻声调值分别为2，2，3，1。阴平、阳平和去声后为降调，上声后为平调，同时伴有起点音高高度的差异性［4，43］。在时长维度，不同前接声调下轻声缩短的幅度不同，轻声相比于前接音节的时长比从50%到70%不等，去声后轻声缩短幅度最大［43］。

能否正确发出轻声是影响二语学习者普通话语音面貌的重要因素。朱川［45］较早发现了普通话学习者存在“轻声重读”的问题；在Hussein和Ding的研究中也发现了轻声产出偏误率较高的现象［6］。因而，一些研究者分析了不同国别学习者的轻声习得状况，汤平［41］分析了音高重音母语背景的日本学习者的轻声词产出；刘磊、顾文涛［39］分析了声调母语背景的粤语母语者的轻声产出；王功平、周小兵、李爱军［42］针对四种非声调母语国家学习者轻声产出的调型进行了聚类分析；邓丹、朱琳［32］考察了欧洲非声调语言母语者的轻声产出和感知情况。这些研究发现学习者轻声产出存在调域相比于母语者偏窄［41］、调型趋于平缓［41，42］、时长延长严重［39，41］等问题。但因为这些研究所针对的学习者的母语背景存在差异，实验中发现的问题是否会因母语韵律特征相异而彼此存在差异，在实验材料、实验方法不统一，未进行跨实验类比的情况下，难以得到相对确切的答案。

学习者母语的韵律特征有类型上的差异，根据Best［2］和Ladd［12］中韵律结构（Prosodic Structure）层级划分，可将普通话、粤语、越南语一类区别意义的音高变化发生在音节（Syllable）层级的语言归为声调语言（Tone Language），将日本语、瑞典语一类功能性音高变化发生在音节以下的音拍（Mora）层级的语言归为音高重音语言（Pitch Accent Language），而将音高变化发生在韵律短语（Prosodic Phrase）及以上层级的语言划归为语调语言（Intonational Language）。相关实证研究显示母语韵律特征不同的学习者在习得二语声调时常表现出差异：Chen［5］对比了母语背景为声调语言粤语的汉语学习者和母语背景为语调语言英语的汉语学习者产出连上组合时的声学特征，发现粤语背景学习者的产出模式异于英语背景学习者，在调型上更接近汉语母语者；Wayland等人［25，26］对比了母语背景为汉语的学习者与英语的学习者区分泰语中平调和低平调的能力，发现声调母语背景的学习者相比于语调母语背景的学习者，对细微的音高变化更加敏感，可以相对较好地区分这组声调的音高高度差异。So等［20］对比了母语为声调语言粤语、音高重音语言日本语和语调语言英语的汉语学习者区分汉语普通话声调时的表现，结果发现：在区分阴平和去声时，粤语背景的学习者的正确率低于日本语背景和英语背景的学习者。这些实验在产出和知觉维度对比了母语韵律特征存在差异的学习者习得二语声调时的模式差异。

基于上述讨论，在轻声习得的问题上，我们提出以下问题：（1）母语背景将如何影响学习者的轻声产出？（2）来自韵律特征相异母语背景的普通话学习者的轻声产出是否存在差异？（3）这些差异性在轻声最主要的两个声学相关物音高和时长维度将如何表征？

在实验问题的基础上，本研究基于现有语料库，选择了越南语、日本语、韩国语、哈萨克语4种母语背景普通话学习者的轻声产出数据进行对比分析。这几种语言涵盖了上述的三类韵律特征：越南语是声调语言［9］，且其声调系统相对于汉语普通话更加复杂，声调的区别性特征包含了音高高度、音高拱度、喉塞特征（Glottalization）等多个维度；日本语属于音高重音语言，其重音音节（Stressed Syllable）和非重音音节（Unstressed Syllable）在音高维度存在区分，重音音节上会出现音高峰值（F0 Peak），而非重音音节上则会出现音高骤降（F0 Fall）［8，10］；韩国语属于语调语言，但在其韵律系统内部，具有重音短语（Accentual Phrase）这一特殊韵律单元，有音高表征为升（LH）的特定重音模式［7］，一定程度上使用音高变化区别意义；哈萨克语也属于语调语言，不倾向于使用音高变化区别除语气之外的意义，而主要使用时长区分重音与非重音，带有重音重读（Stress - Accent）特色［16］。

2. 方法

2.1 语料及发音人

本研究基于语料库，所用的母语者和学习者语音数据均取自北京语言大学智能语音习得实验室中介语语音库。其中包含了越南、日本、韩国、哈萨克四种母语背景的学习者数据 3519 条，另外有汉语普通话母语者数据 766 条，共 4275 条，数据集剔除了音段存在偏误的音节。语音材料包含四种前接声调调境（阴平、阳平、上声和去声）和三种词汇类型的“重叠型”“词汇型”和带词缀的“语法型”双音节轻声词，共 45 个轻声词，具体词表如表 1 所示。

表 1　轻声产出语料

	阴平	阳平	上声	去声
重叠型	姑姑 /ku1ku/	娃娃 /ua2ua/	姐姐 /tɕie3tɕie/	爸爸 /pa4pa/
	妈妈 /ma1ma/	伯伯 /puo2puo/	姥姥 /laʊ3laʊ/	弟弟 /ti4ti/
	哥哥 /kɤ1kɤ/		奶奶 /nai3nai/	妹妹 /mei4mei/
			宝宝 /paʊ3paʊ/	谢谢 /ɕie4ɕie/
词汇型	啰唆 /luo1suo/	麻烦 /ma2fan/	喇叭 /la3ba/	力气 /li4tɕ^{h}i/
	唠叨 /laʊ1taʊ/	觉得 /tɕɥe2tə/	耳朵 /ɚ3tuo/	意思 /i4sɿ/
	衣服 /i1fu/	媳妇 /ɕi2fu/	我们 /uo3mən/	大方 /ta4faŋ/
	休息 /ɕiou1ɕi/	咳嗽 /kɤ2sou/	暖和 /nuan3xuo/	客人 /k^{h}ɤ4ʐən/
	兄弟 /ɕiʊŋ1ti/		怎么 /tsən3mə/	丈夫 /tʂaŋ4fu/
				下巴 /ɕia4 ba/
语法型	悠着 /iou1tʂə/	得了 /te2lə/	本着 /pen3tʂə/	袜子 /ua4tsɿ/
	锥子 /tʂuəi1tsɿ/	谁的 /ʂuəi2tə/	有的 /iou3tə/	这个 /tʂe4kə/
		橘子 /tɕy2tsɿ/		
		勺子 /ʂaʊ2tsɿ/		
		馒头 /man2t^{h}ou/		
		儿子 /ɚ2tsɿ/		

筛选学习者数据时，我们尽量保证选取的每个国别发音人数量相近，性别平衡，汉语学习时长相仿，汉语语言水平相近，均在 HSK 汉语水平中高级，涵盖所有发音人信息的统计汇总表如表 2 所示。

表 2　发音人信息统计汇总

母语背景	数量（人）（男 + 女）	年龄（岁）（标准差）	汉语学习时长（年）
日本语	20（10 + 10）	21.6（3.2）	2.6（0.8）
韩国语	20（10 + 10）	20.2（4.1）	1.7（1.3）
哈萨克语	15（8 + 7）	24.3（2.8）	3.6（2.4）
越南语	20（10 + 10）	19.4（1.2）	1.2（0.7）
普通话	20（10 + 10）	21.3（0.9）	母语者

2.2 实验流程

研究共有两个实验组成模块，实验一为母语者听辨判断实验，以母语者的听辨判断结果对比不同组别学习者在偏误分布特点上的差异。沿用强制选择的实验范式，该组实验邀请三位语音学专业同学作为听辨人，根据自写程序上的对应选项“正确（YY）”“轻声偏误（YN）”“非轻声偏误（NY）”“轻声和非轻声均存在偏误”（NN）的提示，对耳机中播放的刺激选择判断。因为本实验语料数目较多，听辨分多次进行，每次听辨时间约为两小时，播放刺激数约为500个。听辨完成后，实验人对听辨人判断不一样的语料予以重新判断，以完成最后分类，该步骤完成后，又对四种判断类型下的语料进行频次计量，统计各母语背景学习者的偏误情况。

实验二为声学分析实验，分析学习者轻声产出在音高和时长两个维度的声学特性。声学参数提取主要基于 Praat［3］。基频参数和时长参数的提取脚本使用的是 ProsodyPro［27］，提取过程中标记出了音节边界信息，以此获得基频段和时长段，每个音节等距离提取十个基频点，所有数据的基频段都经过了手工的周期修补，以确定基频曲线的完整，时长段的绝对时长由脚本直接获得。

我们对提取的频率域的基频值首先以每个发音人的基频最小值作为基准，进行了半音的转换（*st*），之后进一步进行 *z-score* 转换，以消除话者间差异，规整见公式（1）。其中，y_i 是每个基频的具体数值，m_y 是话者频域的均值，s_y 是话者频域的标准差，公式还原了每个基频值在话者频域中的相对位置。

$$z_i' = \frac{y_i - m_y}{s_y} \tag{1}$$

考虑到之前轻声习得的研究分析基频轮廓曲线多基于视觉观察，缺乏客观性，以及曹剑芬［35］指出的，轻声起点高度和音高形状都是轻声较为关键的线索，本研究使用增长曲线分析（Growth Curve Analysis）［17］的方法，拟合原基频曲线为一元二次，以时间为自变量的方程式，保留每个时间点上对应的频值信息，将每条轻声产出的基频数据转化为音高拱度（二次项系数）、音高斜率（一次项系数）和音高截距（零次项系数）三个参数信息［22］，并将这三个参数为输入，比较各组学习者相对于母语者在各调境下的差异。增长曲线分析基于公式（2）：

$$Yij = \beta_0 i + \beta_1 i \cdot Timej + \beta_2 i \cdot Time_2 j + \varepsilon ij \tag{2}$$

之后的统计调用 R 4.0［21］中的 lme4［1］、lmerTest［11］和 lsmmeans 包［14］进行进一步的统计分析。

时长方面，与［36］类似，我们计算了轻声音节相对于前接音节的时长比，具体见公式（3）。其中，D_1 为轻声音节的绝对时长，D_2 为前接声调音节的绝对时长。

$$R_i' = \frac{D_1}{D_2} \tag{3}$$

3　听辨实验结果

各学习者组轻声产出的偏误情况如图1所示。从调境角度来看，阴平和去声调境的产出情况要优于阳平和上声调境，两调境下都有三组（日本、韩国、越南）的YY比率高于60%，说明阴平和去声调境轻声产出的难度对于学习者来说相对低于阳平和上声调境；从学习者国别来看，四个国别的轻声产出正确率成梯度分布：越南学习者的正确率均高于60%，阴平和去声调境高于70%；在四调境下，日本和韩国学习者的正确率能保持在50%—60%，而哈萨克学习者的正确率仅能保持在20%—30%，偏误问题较为严重。从学习者出现的主要偏误类型来看，轻声前音节出现偏误是学习者易出现的主要问题，在各组学习者的数据结果中出现了NY+NN类的比率高于纯轻声YN类偏误的情况，在哈萨克学习者的数据中，NY+NN的比率可达YN类的5—7倍。

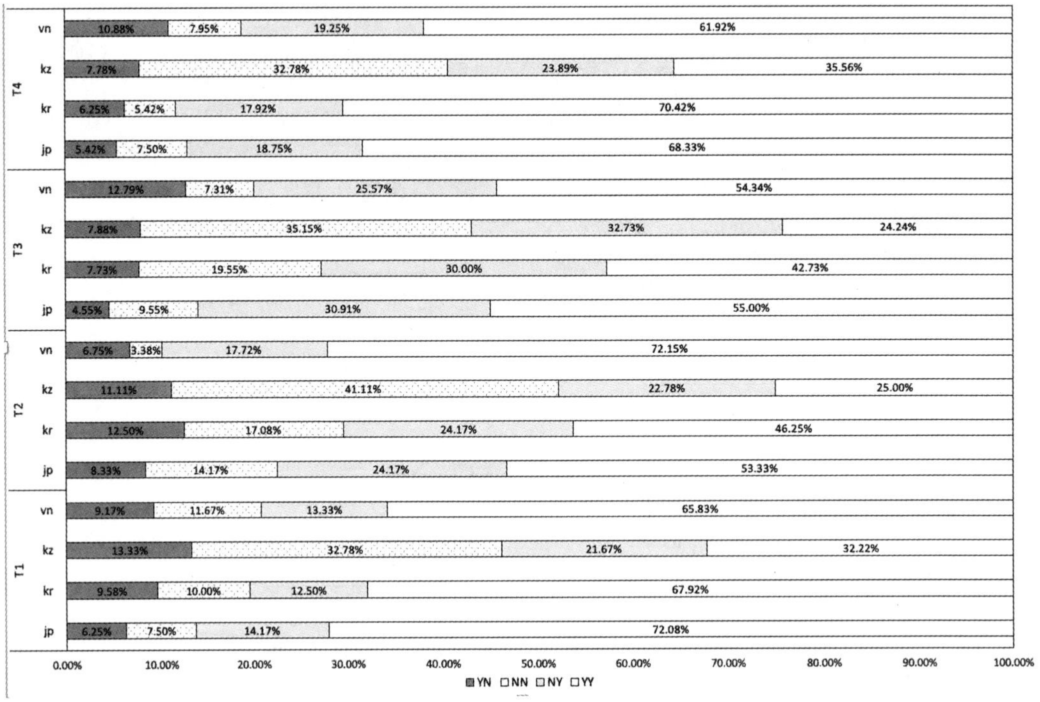

图1　不同学习者组轻声产出的各偏误类型的分布比率
(jp-日本；kr-韩国；kz-哈萨克；vn-越南)

4. 声学分析结果

4.1　基频特征

各学习者组的轻声产出的音高模式如图2所示，从左至右分别为母语者、日本学习者、韩国学习者、哈萨克学习者和越南学习者的产出。我们对轻声词的前接音节和轻声音节分别进行了统计分析，因为调境数量较多，我们分四次构建结构类似于lmer（f0 ~（poly1 + poly2） × Groups +（1 + poly1 + poly2 | syllables）+（1 + poly1 + poly2 | subjects））的线性混合效应模型，固定效应为组别（Groups）、混合效应为音节（syllables）和发音人（subjects），最终模型都经由多次调优过程，以保证最终模型可以最优拟合数据分布，每个模型都将母语者组设置为参考水平，各学习者组作为对照组。统计结果见表3，上面为前接音节的结果，下面为轻声音节的结果（<0.001、<0.01、<0.05为不同程度的显著性差异，n.s.表示不形成显著性差异）。

各组学习者轻声产出的前接音节和轻声音节显著性偏离于母语者的趋势有一定的同步性，其中，日本学习者组和韩国学习者组出现了一定的相似性，他们在阳平和上声调境下轻声产出都显著偏离于母语者，而在阴平和去声调境中可以产出相对较类似母语者的轻声音高模式。越南学习者组的轻声音高产出模式较类似普通话母语者，仅在阴平调境下的前接音节上的音高斜率和音高拱度维度和后接轻声音节上的音高截距维度及上声后轻声的斜率和拱度维度偏离于母语者。哈萨克学习者轻声音高的产出模式较为特殊，在四个调境下实现的轻声音高模式均显著差异于母语者。

4.2　时长特征

时长维度，我们使用线性混合模型（Linear Mixed Effect Model）[1]，以轻声时长比作为观测变量，将母语者的产出数据作为参考水平，分别考察不同调境下学习者轻声产出的时长情况。描述性统计结果如图3所示，母语者在四个调境下轻声时长占比在0.5到1，上声后轻声最长，几乎与前接音节等长，阴平、阳平、去声后轻声相对较短，这与之前研究结果相符[35]。统计分析各组别学习者与母语者的差异性结果显示：阴平调境下，哈萨克组的轻声时长占比显著区别于母语者组（$\beta=0.27$，$t=3.93$，$p<0.001$），轻声时长相对延长，其他学习者组未与母语者组出现显著性差异；阳平调境下，韩国组和哈萨克组与母语者出现显著差异（$\beta=0.17$，$t=3.10$，$p<0.01$；$\beta=0.28$，$t=4.66$，$p<0.001$），两组学习者都存在不同程度的轻声音节延长的问题，而日本组和越南组未与母语者出现显著差异；上声调境下，四组学习者均未见显著差异；去声调境下，各学习者组出现了一致性的轻声延长，四组别均与母语者组出现显著性差异，其中日本组（$\beta=0.13$，$t=2.25$，$p<0.05$）、韩国组（$\beta=0.18$，$t=2.25$，$p<0.01$）和越南组（$\beta=0.17$，$t=2.99$，$p<0.01$）轻声延长的程度较轻，而哈萨克组学习者的轻声延长问题最明显（$\beta=0.31$，$t=3.06$，$p<0.001$）。

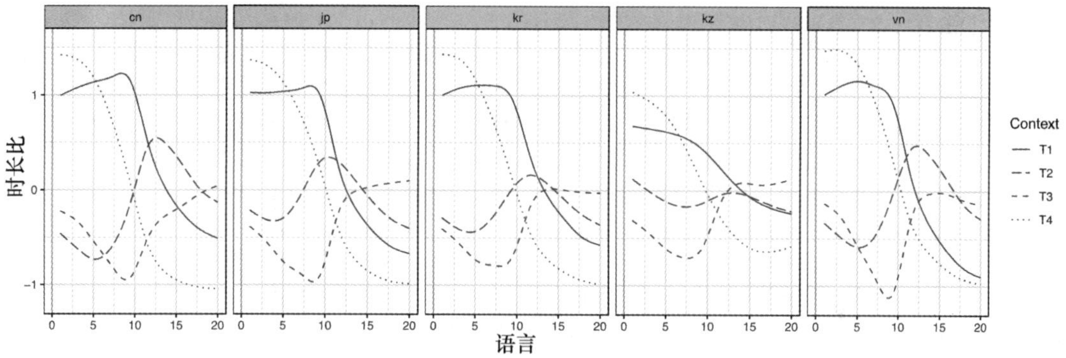

图2 不同组学习者轻声产出的调型轮廓

表3 各学习者组与母语者轻声产出音高数据的统计分析结果

母语背景	阴平			阳平			上声			去声		
	截距	斜率	拱度	截距	斜率	拱度	截距	斜率	拱度	截距	斜率	拱度
JP v.s. CN	n.s.	n.s.	n.s.	**<0.001**	**<0.050**	**<0.010**	n.s.	n.s.	**<0.010**	n.s.	n.s.	n.s.
KR v.s. CN	n.s.	n.s.	n.s.	**<0.010**	n.s.	**<0.001**	n.s.	**<0.001**	**<0.001**	n.s.	n.s.	n.s.
KZ v.s. CN	**<0.001**	**<0.010**	n.s.	**<0.001**	**<0.001**	**<0.001**	n.s.	**<0.010**	**<0.010**	**<0.001**	**<0.050**	**<0.010**
VN v.s. CN	n.s.	**<0.050**	**<0.001**	n.s.	n.s.	n.s.	n.s.	n.s.	n.s.	n.s.	n.s.	n.s.

	截距	斜率	拱度	截距	斜率	拱度	截距	斜率	拱度	截距	斜率	拱度
JP v.s. CN	n.s.	n.s.	n.s.	**<0.001**	**n.s.**	**<0.001**	**<0.050**	n.s.	n.s.	n.s.	n.s.	n.s.
KR v.s. CN	n.s.	n.s.	n.s.	**<0.001**	n.s.	**<0.050**	n.s.	**<0.001**	n.s.	n.s.	n.s.	n.s.
KZ v.s. CN	n.s.	**<0.001**	n.s.	**<0.010**	**<0.010**	**<0.050**	**<0.010**	**<0.010**	n.s.	**<0.010**	n.s.	n.s.
VN v.s. CN	**<0.001**	n.s.	n.s.	n.s.	n.s.	n.s.	n.s.	**<0.001**	**<0.001**	n.s.	n.s.	n.s.

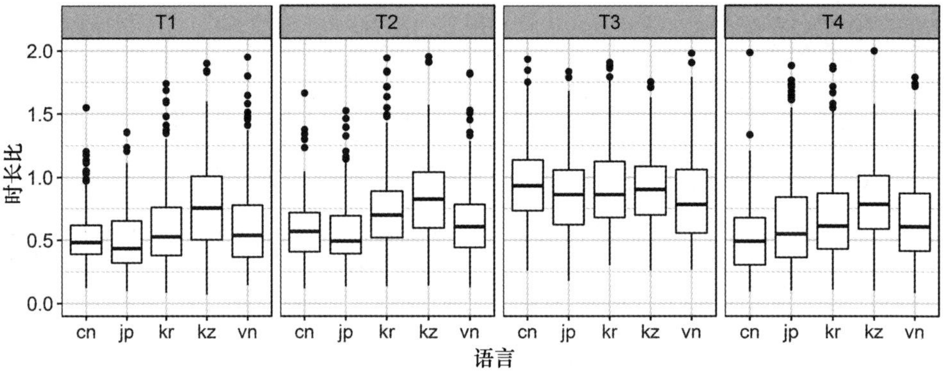

图3 不同组别轻声产出的轻声音节占比

5. 讨论和结论

在本研究中，我们共进行了两个实验，探究来自韵律特征存在差异的母语背景（日本、韩国、哈萨克、越南）的普通话学习者轻声产出在正确率和声学特征上的共性与差异。实验一的听辨实验结果显示，阳平和上声加轻声时，无论母语背景，各组学习者均出现了较多的偏误问题，表明“阳平+轻声”和“上声+轻声”组合对二语学习者普遍较难。另外，结果也显示出纯轻声出现偏误的情况，在四个国别学习者的产出数据中都远少于前音节出现偏误的情况，这表明学习者学习轻声的主要难点在于无法正确实现轻声的前接音节，类似的结果也在邓丹等人［37］的研究中出现过。同时，母语韵律特征对轻声实现的影响也可以从实验结果中得出，其中母语为语调语言且使用时长特征实现轻重凸显的哈萨克学习者的正确率相较于其他几组较低。

在实验二的声学分析实验中，通过在音高和时长两个维度进行的组间比较，我们发现了日本和韩国学习者在轻声产出音高模式上的相似性：他们都在“阳平+轻声”和“上声+轻声”组合中出现显著区别于母语者的倾向，而在“阴平+轻声”和“去声+轻声”的组合中产出较类似于母语者。普通话当中的阴平和去声调值分别为55和51，都具有高特征（H）［29］，而在日本语和韩国语当中，无论是日本语以音高峰值（F0 peak）来负载词汇重音，还是韩国语以抬高音高的方式实现重音短语（Accentual Phrase）都使得学习者对音高高特征（H）的实现有一定的把控性，因而他们在“阴平+轻声”和“去声+轻声”的组合中可以较好地实现前接声调，顺延至其后的轻声音节需要自然放松声带的降型音高，也能实现得相对较好。比之，在“阳平+轻声”和“上声+轻声”组合中，无论是阳平35调的升特征（R）和上声214调的低特征（L）都是两种母语背景的韵律系统中不具有的，因而可能对学习者造成学习难度。以及，“阳平+轻声”和“上声+轻声”后的轻声音高实现较为特殊，阳平后轻声上负载阳平的音高延迟（Peak Delay）［28］，上声后轻声的调型实现不是自然放松声带而形成的降调，而是平调，这些轻声组合本身的难点也都可能影响学习者对两种调境下轻声音高的正确产出。

哈萨克学习者在四个调境下轻声产出的音高特征都显著偏离于母语者，考虑到其母语中主要依靠时长对立凸显轻重，而不倾向于使用音高线索，这种音高特征的偏离可能是学习者受到母语韵律特征影响导致的词汇层级音高变化不敏感。与哈萨克学习者的产出状况形成对立的是，越南学习者在除了“阴平+轻声”和“上声+轻声”组合中的轻声音节的音高上出现了偏离于普通话母语者的情况，在其他调境下均产出较类似母语者。越南语的声调系统的跌声（ngã）与普通话上声调相似，锐声（sắc）与阳平调相似，问声（hỏi）与去声调相似，这些相似性可能使其学习普通话这些调境下的轻声产出时具有一定的优势，虽然越南语中也有和阴平调调型相似的横声（ngang）[9]，但调值高度远达不到阴平调的55，所以使学习者在学习“阴平＋轻声”组合时仍然面临困难，可见母语声调系统的影响。

时长方面，各组学习者出现了一定的共性偏离于母语者的模式：都在去声调境下延长了轻声的时长，考虑到“去声＋轻声”组合中，轻声音节缩短幅度最大，所以，可能对于学习者而言，控制音节间的时长比，尤其是这种重轻间存在较大差异的音节间时长比，可能仍然需要加强学习。

本研究仅为较初步的实验，在之后的研究中，我们将关注以下问题：(1) 不同组别学习者轻声音高调型偏误是否与听辨判断结果具有相关性，不同国别是否存在差异。(2) 不同组别个体层级的调型的变异情况是否有共性和差异性，以进一步探讨母语影响和二语声调系统的制约。(3) 学习者对轻声词的知觉加工模式，主要依靠音高线索还是时长线索。(4) 不同组别学习者产出不同词汇类别的轻声的声学特征是否会有差异性等。

6. 致谢

本研究得到语言资源高精尖创新中心项目“面向智能语音教学的汉语中介语语音多模态语料库研究”(KYR17005)、中央高校基本科研业务专项基金(21YJ040004)、北京语言大学梧桐创新平台（19PT04）的资助。本研究部分内容曾在第十四届中国语音学学术会议（2021年7月18日）上宣读，感谢诸位老师惠赐意见。

参考文献

[1] Bates, D., Sarkar, D., Bates, M. D., Matrix, L. 2007. The lme4 package. *R package version*, 2 (1), 74.

[2] Best, C. T. 2019. The diversity of tone languages and the roles of pitch variation in non-tone languages: considerations for tone perception research. *Frontiers in Psychology 10*, 364.

[3] Boersma, P., Van Heuven, V. 2001. Speak and unSpeak with PRAAT. *Glot International 5* (9/10), 341-347.

[4] Chen, Y., Xu, Y. 2006. Production of weak elements in speech - Evidence from Fo patterns of neutral tone in Standard Chinese. *Phonetica* 63 (1), 47-75.

[5] Chen, S., He, Y., Wayland, R., Yang, Y., Li, B., Yuen, C. W. 2019. Mechanisms of tone sandhi rule application by tonal and non-tonal non-native speakers. *Speech Communication* 115, 67-77.

[6] Hussein, H. ed. al. 2011. Mandarin tone perception and production by German learners. In *Speech and Language Technology in Education.*

[7] Jun, S. A. 1996. *The Phonetics and Phonology of Korean Prosody: Intonational Phonology and Prosodic Structure.* Taylor & Francis.

[8] Kawahara, S. 2015. The phonology of Japanese accent. In: Knbozono, H. (eds) *The handbook of Japanese Phonetics and Phonology*, 445-492.

[9] Kirby, J. P. 2011. Vietnamese (Hanoi Vietnamese). *Journal of the International Phonetic Association* 41 (3), 381-392.

[10] Kubozono, H. 2012. Varieties of pitch accent systems in Japanese. *Lingua* 122 (13), 1395-1414.

[11] Kuznetsova, A., Brockhoff, P. B., Christensen, R. H. 2017. lmerTest package: tests in linear mixed effects models. *Journal of statistical software* 82 (13), 1-26.

[12] Ladd, D. R. 2008. *Intonational Phonology.* Cambridge University Press.

[13] Lee, W. S., Zee, E. 2008. Prosodic characteristics of the neutral tone in Beijing Mandarin. *Journal of Chinese Linguistics* 36 (1), 1-29.

[14] Lenth, R., Lenth, M. R. 2018. Package ‘lsmeans’. *The American Statistician* 34 (4), 216-221.

[15] Li, A., Fan, S. 2015. Correlates of Chinese neutral tone perception in different contexts. In *ICPhS.*

[16] McCollum, A. G., Chen, S. 2019. Ka-

zakh. *Journal of the International Phonetic Association*, 1 – 23.

[17] Mirman, D. 2014. *Growth curve analysis and visualization using R*. CRC press.

[18] Pierrehumbert, J. 1988. Japanese tone structure. *Language Inquiry Monograph Series*.

[19] Shen, X. S. 1992. Mandarin Neutral Tone Revisited. *Acta Linguistica Hafniensia* 24 (1), 131 – 152.

[20] So, C. K., Best, C. T. 2010. Cross – language perception of non – native tonal contrasts: Effects of native phonological and phonetic influences. *Language and Speech* 53 (2), 273 – 293.

[21] Team, R. C. 2013. R: A Language and Environment for Statistical Computing.

[22] Tupper, P., Leung, K. K., Wang, Y., Jongman, A., Sereno, J. A. 2018. Identifying the distinctive acoustic cues of Mandarin tones. *The Journal of the Acoustical Society of America* 144 (3), 1725 – 1725.

[23] Wang, Y., Behne, D. M., Jongman, A., Sereno, J. A. 2004. The role of linguistic experience in the hemispheric processing of lexical tone. *Applied Psycholinguistics* 25, 449 – 466

[24] Wang, Y., Jongman, A., Sereno, J. A. 2003. Acoustic and perceptual evaluation of Mandarin tone productions before and after perceptual training. *The Journal of the Acoustical Society of America* 113 (2), 1033 – 1043

[25] Wayland, R. P., Guion, S. G. 2004. Training English and Chinese listeners to perceive Thai tones: A preliminary report. *Language Learning* 54 (4), 681 – 712.

[26] Wayland, R., Guion, S. 2003. Perceptual discrimination of Thai tones by naïve and experienced learners of Thai. *Applied Psycholinguistics* 24 (1), 113 – 129.

[27] Xu, Y. 2013. ProsodyPro—A tool for large – scale systematic prosody analysis. *Laboratoire Parole et Langage*, France.

[28] Xu, Y. 1997. Contextual tonal variations in Mandarin. *Journal of phonetics* 25 (1), 61 – 83.

[29] Yip, M. J. 1980. *The Tonal Phonology of Chinese* (Doctoral dissertation, Massachusetts Institute of Technology).

[30] 曹剑芬:《普通话轻声音节特性分析》,《应用声学》1986年第4期,第1—6页。

[31] 邓丹:《普通话轻声感知特性再分析》,《语言文字应用》2019年第1期,第66—75页。

[32] 邓丹、朱琳:《二语学习者汉语普通话轻声的感知与产出》,《语言教学与研究》2019年第5期,第13—24页。

[33] 冯胜利:《北京话的轻声及其韵律变量的语法功能》,《语言科学》2012年第6期,第586—595页。

[34] 冯胜利:《北京话是一个重音语言》,《语言科学》2016年第5期,第449—473页。

[35] 李爱军:《普通话不同信息结构中轻声的语音特性》,《当代语言学》2017年第3期,第348—378页。

[36] 李爱军、高军:《不同语境中音高和时长特征与普通话轻声的感知》,载《第十一届中国语音学学术会议(PCC2014)论文集》,2014年。

[37] 林茂灿、颜景助:《北京话轻声的声学性质》,《方言》1980年第3期,第166—178页。

[38] 林茂灿、颜景助:《普通话轻声与轻重音》,《语言教学与研究》1990年第3期,第88—104页。

[39] 刘磊、顾文涛:《香港粤语人群普通话轻声偏误的实验分析》,《南京师范大学文学院学报》2018年第4期,第116—123页。

[40] 路继伦、王嘉龄:《关于轻声的界定》,《当代语言学》2005年第2期,第107—112页。

[41] 汤平:《日本高级汉语学习者汉语轻声韵律习得偏误分析》,《华文教学与研究》2014年第4期,第39—47页。

[42] 王功平、周小兵、李爱军:《留学生普通话双音节轻声音高偏误实验》,《语言文字应用》2009年第4期,第113—121页。

[43] 王韫佳:《音高和时长在普通话轻声知觉中的作用》,《声学学报》2004年第5期,第453—461页。

[44] 赵元任:《中国话的文法》,河北教育出版社1968年版。

[45] 朱川:《汉日超音质特征对比实验》,《华东师范大学学报》(哲学社会科学版)1994年第1期,第84—87页。

张　驰　北京语言大学信息科学学院智能语音习得实验室,硕士,研究兴趣包括言语产出、言语知觉、语音习得。
E-mail: recanace@hotmail.com

胡宁萱　北京语言大学信息科学学院智能语音习得实验室,硕士,研究兴趣包括语音习得。
E-mail：1435519512@ qq. com

张劲松 通讯作者，北京语言大学信息科学学院智能语音习得实验室教授，博士，研究员，研究兴趣包括韵律建模、语音识别、实验语音学、语音习得、计算机辅助发音教学。
E-mail：jinsong. zhang@ blcu. edu. cn

越南留学生汉语四字组韵律偏误研究

陈雪嫚　曹　文

摘　要　本研究的语料来自教育部人文社会科学重点研究基地重大项目“不同国别学习者汉语语音语料库”。其中，完成相关标注的20位越南学生和6位中国学生的全部四字组语音语料是本文的研究对象。研究采用了听辨实验的方法。在听辨人对越南学生四字组的发音分别进行了时长、停顿、音高三方面的判断后，将出现偏误的四字组与母语者的数据进行对比与分析。研究结果表明，越南学生汉语四字组的发音中，音高方面最容易出现偏误，停顿次之，时长的偏误率最低。随着发音人汉语水平的提高，时长和停顿的偏误问题都有一定的好转，但音高的偏误问题仍比较明显。汉语声调音高模式的习得即使对具有声调母语背景的越南学生来说，也仍应是教学重点。

关键词　越南汉语学习者，四字组，时长，停顿，音高，韵律偏误

A Study on the Prosody Errors of Chinese Quadrisyllabic Words by Vietnamese Students

CHEN Xueman　CAO Wen

Abstract The data in this study were obtained from “the Acoustic Corpus of Chinese Spoken by Learners from Different Countries”, a project funded by the Key Research Program in Humanities and Social Sciences of the Ministry of Education of PRC. The annotated quadrisyllabic words produced by 20 Vietnamese learners of Chinese (L2) and 6 native Chinese students were used as the data for this study. In the experiment of listening evaluation, the listeners assessed pronunciations of Vietnamese students in terms of duration, pause, and pitch. Erroneous tokens were analyzed and compared with the production of native speakers. The results show that in the data of Chinese quadrisyllabic words spoken by the Vietnamese students, pitch errors are most likely to occur, followed by pauses and duration, which has the lowest error rate. As the Chinese proficiency of the learners improves, the errors in duration and pauses have decreased to a certain extent, but the errors in pitch still persist. The acquisition of Chinese tonal pitch patterns should still be emphasized even for Chinese learners whose L1 has tones, such like Vietnamese.

Key words Vietnamese Chinese (L2) learner, quadrisyllabic Chinese word, Duration, Pause, Pitch, Prosody Errors

1. 引言

本文所说“四字组”可以认为是“普通话常见、较固定四音节组合”的简称。与单字、二字组、三字组一样，四字组也是可用以连缀成句的汉语备用单位。但相比二字组、三字组而言，四字组的韵律变化规律更加复杂多样。吴宗济先生［10］指出“把四字组的韵律变量分析好，就为研究成句的语调、轻重、时长奠定了基础”。在后期的研究中吴先生又将四字组的语法结构分为双双、并列、单三、三单四种格式，分析四字的韵律变化［11］。

韵律是人类自然语言的一个典型特征，是语音研究的基本问题之一。关于韵律的定义和特征，Beckman 和 Edwards［1］提出：“音段是语段的内容，韵律表示它的组织结构。”《语音学和音系学词典》中词条“韵律特征”的第一个义项为：“超音段的”［9］。林焘先生［7］指

出："韵律特征又称超音质特征、超音质成分或超音段成分，指的是语音中音高、音长和音强的变化。"

从语言类型学的角度来说，越南语和汉语有一定的共同点。比如两种语言都属于声调语言，而且是拱度声调语言；汉、越语的音节都由声母、韵母、声调三部分构成；甚至越南语中也存在大量的四音节成语，其性质与汉语四字成语相似。[3]

但是越南语和汉语也存在很多不同之处，主要表现在声调方面。越南语有六个声调，分别是平声（横声）、玄声、问声、跌声、锐声和重声。越南语中虽然有类似于汉语去声的下降调，但是玄声的下降幅度平缓，重声是要先平行发展然后再迅速下降，这与汉语去声的音高特点是不同的。此外，汉语中的变调现象较为复杂，但是在越南标准语以及大部分的方言区都没有变调现象，也没有轻声现象。

关于越南学生汉语发音音高方面的偏误情况，以声调的偏误研究为多，关于更高层级韵律方面的研究，现有成果较少。韩明［4］、刘晓军［8］、黎翠云［5］、黎霞贞［6］等学者的研究均发现越南学习者难以区分阴平和去声。

本文以在华学习汉语的越南大学生为研究对象，分析其汉语四字组的读音，重在考察其在韵律层面容易出现偏误的地方，并据此向对越汉语教学的从业者给出相关提醒和建议，为国别化汉语教学及研究添一块砖或加一片瓦。

2. 分析过程

2.1 语料

本文所使用的语音材料全部来自教育部人文社会科学重点研究基地重大项目"不同国别学习者汉语语音语料库"中的"越南学生四音节语音语料（子）库"和中国发音人的"四音节标准语音语料（子）库"。作者选取了录音质量较好的20位越南学生的语音样本，发音人的具体情况如表1所示。为了对比，我们也选取了3男3女共6位中国大学生的语音样本，其普通话等级均为一级乙等。

表1　　越南发音人情况统计

汉语水平	性别	人数
初级	男	5
	女	2
中级	男	1
	女	6
高级	男	2
	女	4

语音材料2013—2014年录制于北京语言大学对外汉语研究中心语音实验室，采用Shure-SM 48话筒，台式电脑Dell 5150，外接声卡M-Audio和Yamaha调音台等设备。录音软件是中科院自动化所研制的Recorder，采样率16000Hz，单声道，量化精度16bit。

四音节库的词语（表）来源于教育部、国家语委2010年10月发布的《汉语国际教育用音节汉字词汇等级划分》白皮书中的一级词汇，具体包括常见成语（如：耳熟能详）、熟语（如：综上所述）、专有名词（如：伊斯兰教）和临时短语（如：有两下子）等在内的433个四字组。该词表除涵盖了256种不含轻声的四音节声调组合类型——尽管数量不等，还有一些含轻声和"一、不"等语素变调的组合。此外，按照词语内部的语法结构，这些四字组还可分为2+2组合（共422个，其中含轻声5个；不含轻声417个）、1+3组合（均含轻声，共3个）以及3+1组合（均不含轻声，共6个）三种形式。在本研究考察的语音样本中，越南人的有8660条（=433×20人），中国人的有2598条（=433×6人）。

2.2 分析步骤

首先通过Praat软件对越南及中国发音人的语音样本进行细致的标注。标注规范与原则参照曹文、张劲松［2］。标注一共有四层，分别为词语—汉字层（Word）、正则拼音层（TPY）、声韵音段层（SY）及声调层（Tone），后两层标注声母、韵母、声调的偏误情况。声调层的标注不计“弯头”“降/弯尾”，只针对调型段。对于听感上被感知为停顿的音节间空白段，按照出现位置，分别被标注为“1、2、3”（音节1和音节2之间的空白段标注为“1”，以此类推）。需要说明的是，塞音前的gap段，如果听感上未将其判断为停顿，则计入音节时长；如果听感上将其判断为停顿，则计入停顿时长。具体样式参见图1。

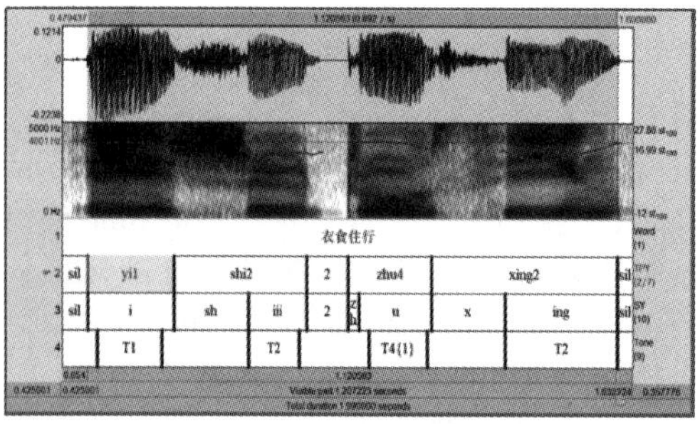

图1　标注样式示意

三名语音学背景的中文母语者对越南学生所朗读的四字组进行两轮听辨。第一轮先判断所听四字组韵律上是否存在偏误；第二轮对存在偏误的四字组进行判断——到底是时长、停顿还是音高存在偏误，抑或是兼而有之。最后将三名听辨人的判断结果进行汇总、整理，对有2人或3人意见相同的样本做进一步的考察与分析。

2.3　数据提取与整理

在这一环节，我们使用Praat（http://www.praat.org）并参考熊子瑜[12]编写的脚本来提取基频和时长。对所得数据进行手工校验后，分别对时长、停顿与音高进行处理与整理。具体方法，下文依次说明。

2.3.1 时长

每个人都有自己的发音习惯，有人说话语速快，有人说话语速慢，语速的快慢并不影响韵律的正确与否。但是对于二语学习者来说，语速的快慢在一定程度上可以反映出他们对所发音节的熟练程度。出于这两方面的考虑，本文将时长分为绝对时长和相对时长两个指标。

①绝对时长：单位为秒，反映的是发音的实际用时，本研究中主要用于计算四字组的音节总时长。需要注意的是，音节总时长包括停顿的时长在内。

②相对时长：单位为百分比，反映的是四字组内部各音节的时长占比/分布情况，这样的处理方式可去除发音人语速不同带来的差异。音节时长占比的计算公式如下：

各音节时长占比 = 各音节时长/四字组有声段总时长 × 100%　　(1)

四字组有声段总时长 = 四字组音节总时长 − 四字组停顿总时长　　(2)

2.3.2　停顿

同样，本文将停顿分为各停顿时长与各停顿占比两个评价指标。其中各停顿时长反映的是不同位置停顿的绝对时长，各停顿占比反映的是不同位置的停顿占音节总时长的比例。计算公式如下：

停顿占比 = 停顿时长/音节总时长　(3)

例如：

停顿1占比 = 停顿1时长/音节总时长。

2.3.3　音高

运行praat脚本，自动提取各音节调型段10等分后各点的基频值，并将其由赫兹值转换为半音（St）。转换公式为：

$Semitone(st) = 12 \times \log 2(f/fr)$　(4)

其中，f表示测量点的基频值，fr表示参考频率（经验值）。男生的参考频率为55Hz，女生的参考频率为100Hz。

3. 结果描写与分析[①]

本节主要对研究结果按照时长、停顿、音高的顺序依次进行描写和分析。在各小节内部，依据其偏误表现的实际情况，决定是否对其进行组别上的细分。

① 因为音强在韵律层面的作用争议较大，所以本文暂不作音强分析，只对音高和音长的相关数据进行研究。

3.1 时长

时长的偏误分为基于听感判断的“音节时长占比过大”和“音节时长占比过小”两种情况。

例如发音人 VJF2① 的“恍然大悟”，听辨人将其判断为音节 1 的发音时长过长，甚至有“头重脚轻”感。考察其时长数据可以发现，该四字组样本的发音总时长（含停顿）为 2.09 秒，有声段总时长（不含停顿）为 1.67 秒；而音节 1（“恍”）的发音时长为 0.78 秒，占发音总时长的比例为 37.32%，占有声段总时长的比例为 46.70%。VJF2 发音人该音节的发音语图如图 2 所示。

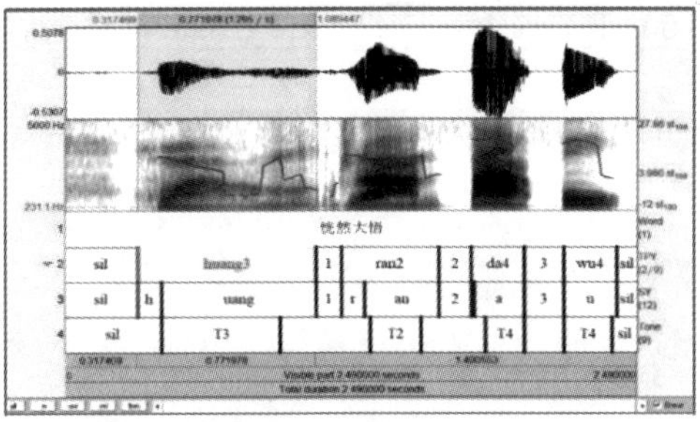

图2 时长偏误示意

越南汉语学习者四字组在时长方面总的偏误率为 7.20%。本小节按照他们的性别、汉语水平以及四字组的音节组合形式和是否含有轻声进行细分。

3.1.1 绝对时长

不同汉语水平越南留学生的四字组音节总时长如图 3 所示。

由图 3 可以看出，随着留学生汉语水平的提高，他们发四字组所用的总时长也越来越接近汉语母语发音人。

从母语者的数据中，我们还可以发现，不同组合的音节总时长有所不同：2+2组合 > 3+1 组合 > 1+3 组合。这主要是因为 1+3 组合下的四字组多为口语色彩浓重的“说老实话”“有两下子”等，发音时的语速相对较快。2+2 组合下多为成语，3+1 组合下多为专有名词，这两类组合书面语色彩较浓，发音时语速相对较慢。这也回证了本文对四字组按不同组合形式进行分类分析的必要性。

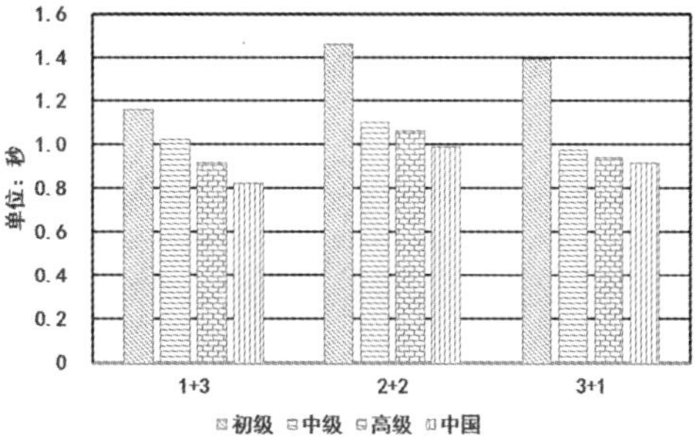

图3 音节总时长对比

3.1.2 相对时长

因为 1+3 组合、3+1 组合和 2+2 组合的四字组细分到不同等级、不同性别学习者的数量较少，出现偏误的数量不符合统计检测对样本量的要求，所以本部分只选取了不含轻声 2+2 组合的四字组进行分析和统计检验。学习者出现时长偏误的音节的相对时长占比及与汉语母语者之间的独立样本 T 检验的结果如表 2 所示。表中“中国”表示汉语母语者的相关数据，“越南”表示越南学习者的相关数据；“长”代表听感上判断为“音节时长占比过大”，“短”代表听感上判断为“音节时长占比过小”；“sig”代表显著性结果。

表 2 中标有阴影的部分，统计检验并未表现出显著性差异，但是听辨人在听感上将其判断为出现了时长占比偏误。究其原因，主要是因为听感上对音节时长的判断，不仅取决于该音节时长的长短，还会受到前后音节时长长短的影响。所以前后音节间时长占比的差值大小可能也会影响听感判断。

① 为保护发音人隐私以及更简洁地呈现发音人的国别、性别、汉语水平（中国人缺省）等信息，除了以阿拉伯数字编号外，本文采用相应的英文首字母进行标识，具体对应关系为：V（Vietnam）—越南；C（China）—中国；J（Junior）—初级；M（Middle）—中级；H（High）—高级；F（Female）—女发音人；M（Male）—男发音人。

表2　学习者偏误音节相对时长占比及与汉语母语者统计检验结果

偏误类型 \ 音节占比				音节1		音节2		音节3		音节4	
				音节占比	sig	音节占比	sig	音节占比	sig	音节占比	sig
女发音人	中国			23%		24%		22%		31%	
	越南	初级	长	31%	0.000	29%	0.000	27%	0.000	32%	**0.457**
			短	21%	**0.372**	19%	0.006	18%	0.044	20%	0.000
		中级	长	31%	0.000	34%	0.000	32%	0.000	42%	0.000
			短	16%	0.000	20%	0.009	17%	0.000	23%	0.000
		高级	长	30%	0.002	28%	0.000	28%	0.000	——	——
			短	19%	0.018	——	——	19%	0.015	20%	0.003
男发音人	中国			24%		23%		22%		31%	
	越南	初级	长	32%	0.000	35%	0.000	30%	0.000	35%	**0.436**
			短	16%	0.007	20%	**0.330**	16%	0.000	19%	0.000
		中级	长	30%	0.000	33%	0.000	31%	0.000	——	——
			短	12%	——	13%	——	16%	0.000	20%	0.000
		高级	长	29%	0.000	28%	0.000	27%	0.000	37%	0.007
			短	14%	——	18%	0.001	13%	——	23%	0.004

3.1.3　时长偏误率

首先，本文对不同组合的时长偏误率进行对比，结果参见图4。

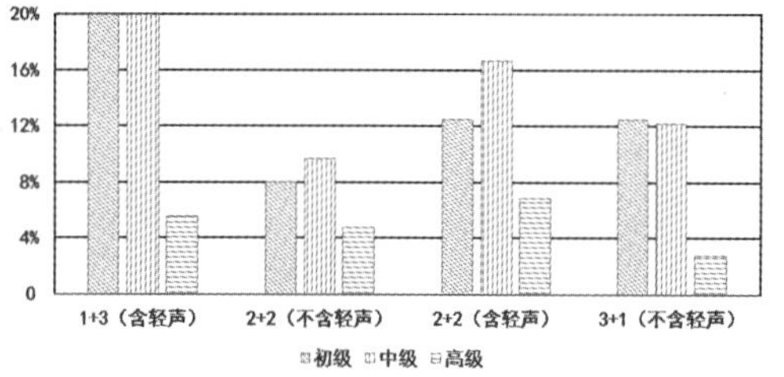

图4　不同组合时长偏误率对比

通过图4所示不同组合的对比我们可以发现，含轻声的两个组合，其偏误率明显高于不含轻声的两个组合。含轻声四字组的时长偏误主要表现为轻声音节发音时长过长。例如发音人VJM5的19号四字组“说老实话”的发音，听辨人将其判断为轻声音节“实”的发音时长过长。因为音节间未停顿，该四字组有声段时长与四字组音节总时长相等，为1.49秒；轻声音节“实”的发音时长为0.43秒，占有声段时长/音节总时长的比例为28.89%，远高于中国男发音人该四字组中“实”的时长占比（17.79%）。VJM5发音人19号四字组的发音语图如图5所示。

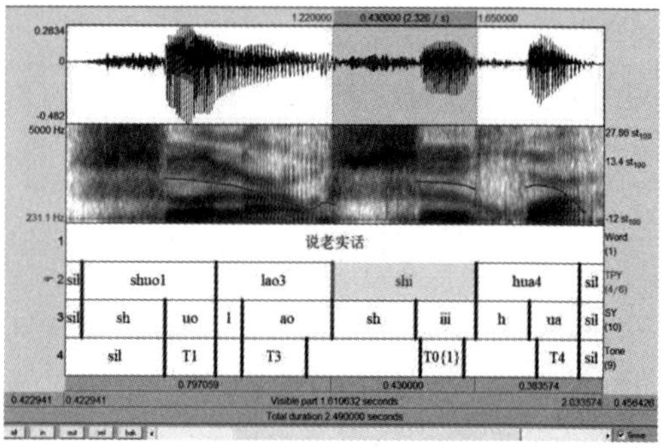

图5　含轻声四字组时长偏误示意

由图5我们还可以发现，与轻声音节的时长偏误伴随出现的是音高偏误，这应该是与越语音系中没有轻声现象有很大的关系。

然后，我们又对不同性别发音人的时长偏误率进行了考察，结果如图6所示。

由图6各组别的对比我们可以看出，越南女发音人在四字组发音时长占比分配方面的偏误率与她们的汉语水平成反比——换言之，水平越高，正确率也越高；而男发音人的情况并未体现出这种比例关系，初级和高级水平的学生差异不大，中级水平的偏误率最高。

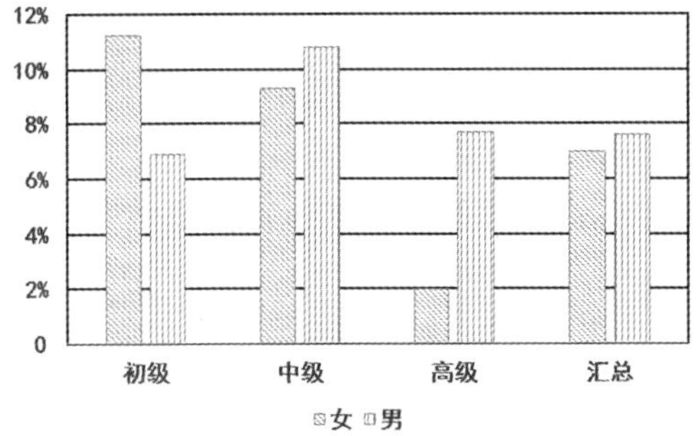

图6　不同性别发音人时长偏误率对比

3.1.4　各音节时长偏误表现

为了总结出哪些位置的音节容易发得过长，哪些位置的音节容易发得过短，本文按照时长偏误的种类，统计了偏误音节占音节总数的比率。例如，某个水平的汉语学习者音节1发音过长的发生率就等于其出现发音过长偏误的音节数量除以四字组音节总量。有关结果如图7所示。

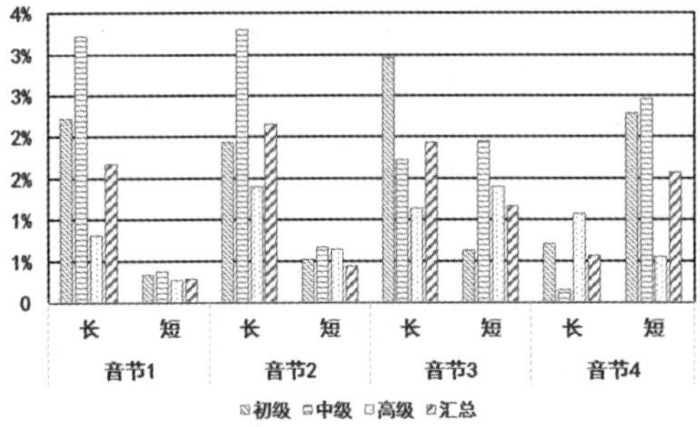

图7　各音节时长不同偏误表现的发生率

从图7我们可以看出，不同音节的时长偏误表现出一定的共性：音节1、音节2和音节3的时长容易发得过长，而音节4的时长容易发得过短。为了探究这种偏误表现是否与学习者的汉语水平有关，我们又对初级、中级、高级的学习者的数据进行了汇总分析（参见图7中“汇总”对应的柱状图）。分析结果表明，学习者不同音节的时长偏误表现并不受其汉语水平的影响。

3.2　停顿

停顿偏误是指四字组音节内部本来没有停顿但学习者停顿了，或者停顿时间较长。

例如编号VJM4的发音人在发206号四字组“想方设法”时，发音总时长（含停顿）为2.93秒，音节“设”和音节“法”之间的停顿时长为1.11秒，占发音总时长的比例为37.88%，在听感上就会感觉“法”字与整个776四字组音节割裂开了。这种情况听辨人会将其判断为停顿3的停顿时长过长。VJM4发音人该音节的发音语图如图8所示。

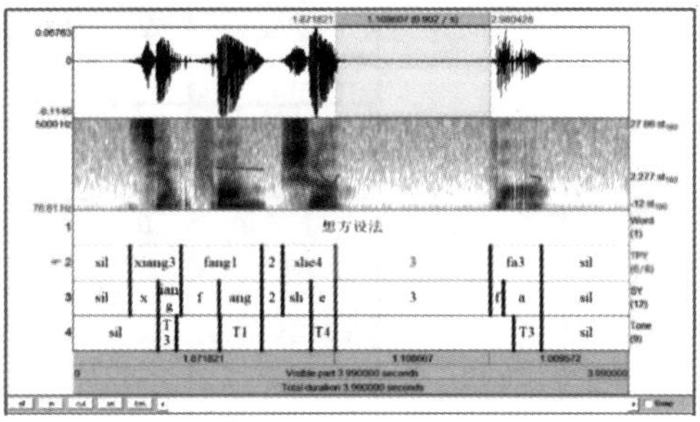

图8　停顿偏误示意

停顿的总偏误率为21.90%。四字组音节中是否含有轻声音节，对音节内部停顿的影响很小，所以本小节没有对各组合形式下是否含有轻声进行细分。不同水平的发音人在停顿偏误方面的差异体现在偏误率上，凡出现偏误的停顿，其停顿占比在表现上有一定的共性。为了避免论文重复描写，本小节将不同级别的发音人的结果汇总到一起进行展示与分析。

3.2.1　1+3组合

在该组合形式下，母语者的发音中均未出现停顿，所以本部分只展示各位置出现偏误的次数，以及偏误位置停顿占比的平均值。如表3所示。

表3　1+3组合停顿偏误统计

停顿位置	偏误次数	停顿占比
停顿1	5	22%
停顿2	3	12%
停顿3	1	10%

由表3我们可以看出，在1+3组合下，停顿1的位置更容易出现停顿偏误，且出现停顿占比的平均值也最大，达22.00%。

3.2.2 2+2组合

2+2组合下的四字组音节个数较多，为了更简洁有效地分析该组合下的偏误情况，我们绘制了该组合的偏误统计表。其中，偏误音节的“停顿占比”为平均值，“标准差”为停顿占比的标准差，“sig”代表学习者存在停顿偏误的停顿占比与对应性别的母语者该位置停顿占比的独立样本T检验的结果见表4。

表4　　2+2组合停顿偏误统计表

等级		初级女	初级男	中级女	中级男	高级女	高级男
停顿1	偏误个数	107	109	101	5	31	80
	偏误率	13.91%	5.36%	4.54%	1.20%	1.83%	9.49%
	停顿占比	9.55%	11.40%	10.38%	11.09%	6.29%	7.95%
	标准差	0.056	0.058	0.051	0.031	0.023	0.037
	sig	0.000	0.000	0.000	0.000	0.000	0.000
停顿2	偏误个数	161	632	202	17	21	46
	偏误率	20.94%	31.06%	9.08%	4.07%	1.24%	5.46%
	停顿占比	7.36%	17.72%	18.29%	12.92%	13.04%	10.77%
	标准差	0.074	0.077	0.11	0.048	0.067	0.042
	sig	0.000	0.000	0.000	0.000	0.000	0.000
停顿3	偏误个数	138	131	115	11	22	32
	偏误率	17.95%	6.44%	5.17%	2.63%	1.30%	3.80%
	停顿占比	8.67%	10.46%	10.13%	8.88%	6.17%	6.55%
	标准差	0.056	0.05	0.071	0.038	0.021	0.024
	sig	0.000	0.000	0.000	0.017	0.003	0.006
总偏误率		41.48%	38.87%	17.71%	7.18%	4.14%	17.20%

由表4可以看出，统计检验结果与听感上对停顿的偏误判断结果相一致。横向来看，随着越南发音人汉语水平的提高，停顿偏误率总体上呈现出下降趋势，但是高级水平男发音人的情况比较特殊；纵向来看，初级和中级发音人更容易在停顿2处出现偏误，高级水平的发音人更容易在停顿1处出现偏误。

表5　2+2组合母语者各位置停顿占比

性别	停顿1占比		停顿2占比		停顿3占比	
	平均数	标准差	平均数	标准差	平均数	标准差
女	3.84%	0.016	4.40%	0.02	4.75%	0.021
男	5.05%	0.016	5.41%	0.019	5.50%	0.017

表5为母语者的对照数据，对比表4和表5可以发现，母语者的停顿占比控制在5.00%左右，越南发音人出现停顿偏误的四字组音节间的停顿占比大部分在10%左右。由于停顿占比过大，停顿时长过长，在听感上就会觉得将四字组割裂开了。

3.2.3 3+1组合

在该组合下，母语者的发音中均未出现停顿，所以本部分只展示各位置出现偏误的次数，以及偏误位置停顿占比的平均值如表6所示。

表6　　3+1组合停顿偏误统计

停顿位置	偏误次数	停顿占比
停顿1	16	9.19%
停顿2	15	11.88%
停顿3	8	5.72%

由表6可知，在3+1组合下，停顿3的偏误率最低。

3.3 音高

在标注和听辨的过程中，我们发现，越南留学生声调的偏误情况比较顽固，从初级水平一直持续到高级水平。为了检验音高部分是否有必要依旧按照发音人的汉语水平进行细分，我们先对不同水平发音人的声调偏误率进行了统计。如表7所示。

表7　　　声调偏误率汇总

等级	偏误个数	总数	偏误率
初级	767	2938	26.11%
中级	1473	2614	56.35%
高级	723	2581	28.01%
汇总	2963	8133	36.43%

由表7可知，声调总偏误率为36.43%，随着越南留学生汉语水平的提高，声调的偏误率并没有下降。甚至在初级、中级、高级三个水平中，初级发音人的声调偏误率是最低的（26.11%），这可能与初级发音人发音时停顿最多有关。鉴于越南发音人的汉语水平对声调偏误率的影响并不明显，所以本部分不再按照发音人的汉语水平进行细分。

越南留学生的声调偏误主要集中在第一声（T1）和第四声（T4）的混淆，尤其是易将T4发成T1，这一偏误在T4与T4相连时表现得更为突出。两个及两个以上T4相连的四字组的偏误率为12%，是声调总偏误率36.43%的三分之一。图9显示了涉及T4的主要偏误类型，上面的语图中学习者VMF2将327号四字组“面面俱到”的“面面”和“到”发成了一声；下面的语图中学习者VHM1将290号四字组“风和日丽”中的“丽”发成了轻声。

解决了越南留学生去声相连情况下声调的发音问题，也就攻克了越南留学生声调学习过程中的老大难问题，所以本文按

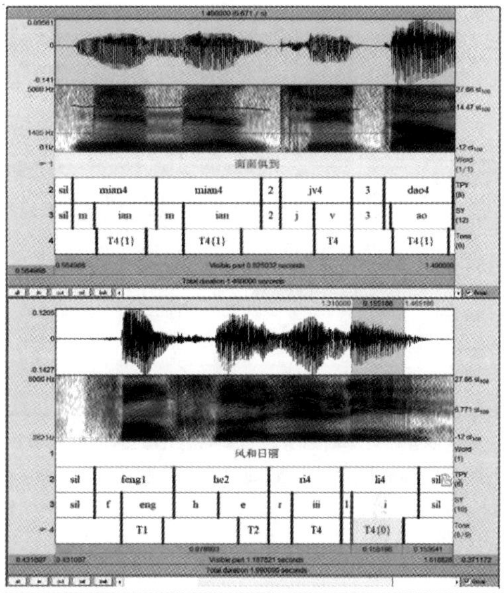

图9　涉去声的主要偏误类型（例）

照两个及两个以上T4相连时的情况进行分组，并对分组后的六种声调组合类型进行偏误率的统计，结果如图10所示。

由图10我们可以获取三个信息，一是在两个及两个以上T4相连的四字组中，越南男发音人的声调发音要好于越南女发音人；二是只有两个T4相连时，前一个T4出现声调偏误的概率高于后一个T4。当三个及四个T4相连时，声调偏误率的表现男女发音人并不完全相同；三是随着四字组中T4音节数量的增加，发生声调偏误的概率也逐渐增加。

因为三个及四个T4相连的四字组数量较少，所以本文选取了样本量较大的$T4T4T_XT_X$、T_XT_XT4T4与T_XT4T4T_X三种类型的四字组进行声调的描写与统计检验。为了考察T4与T1的混淆情况，本文选择四字组中各T4音节均与T1混淆的偏误情况进行分析。

在对具体声调偏误分析之前，本文对不同国别、不同性别发音人的音高调域进行了计算和统计。高音点、低音点和调域的认定、计算公式如下。

高音点：四字组首音节声调无偏误的阴平、去声起点的最高点；

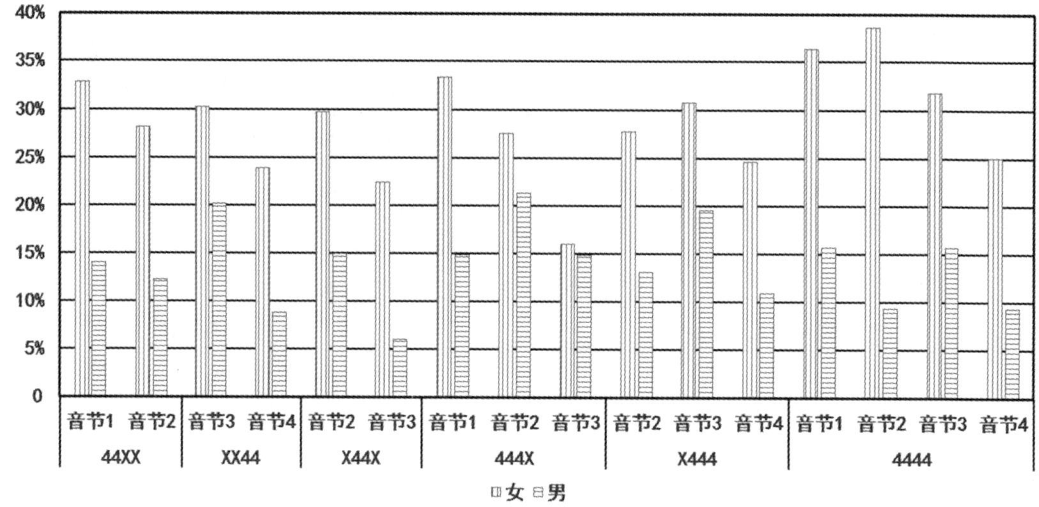

图 10　声调偏误率

低音点：四字组末音节声调无偏误的上声、去声末点的最低点。

调域 = 高音点值 - 低音点值　(5)

调域数据见表 8，单位为半音（st）。

表 8　调域

性别	国别	高音点	低音点	调域
女	中	21	1	20
	越	20	2	18
男	中	11	-3	14
	越	12	-2	14

由表 8 可知，在相同性别条件下，中国发音人的调域与越南发音人的调域差别不大。故而在接下来的声调偏误对比图（见图 11）中，纵坐标刻度的最小值选取中越发音人调域的最小值（女：1st，男：-3st），纵坐标刻度的最大值选取中越发音人调域的最大值（女：21st，男：12st）。

3.3.1　T4T4 组合声调偏误情况

由图 11 可知，对于 $T4T4T_XT_X$ 和 T_XT_XT4T4 组合，越南发音人的偏误表现具有一致性：第一个 T4 的偏误主要表现在 T4 起点音高不够高，第二个 T4 的偏误主要表现在 T4 的末点音高不够低。此外，越南男发音人第一个 T4 的偏误还表现在末点音高不够低；对于 T_XT4T4T_X 组合，越南女发音人的偏误主要表现为两个 T4 的起点音高不够高。

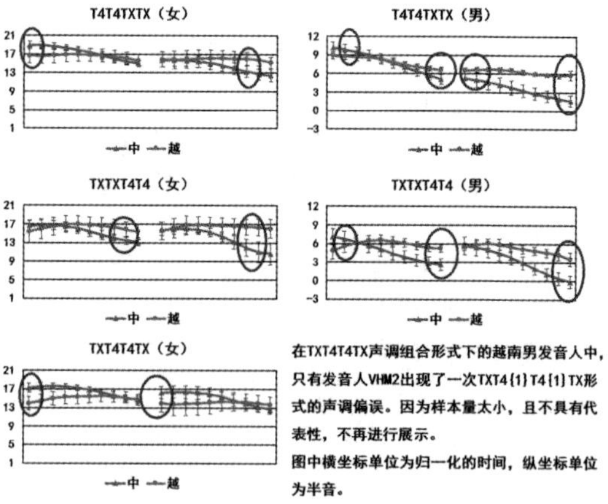

图 11　T4T4 组合声调偏误对比

3.3.2　性别与音节位置的影响

为了继续探究越南留学生四字组声调偏误的规律与特征，本文按照发音人的性别与音节位置对偏误率进行了统计，见表9。

表9 不同性别不同位置声调偏误率

音节	女	男	平均偏误率
音节1	17.24%	7.88%	13.37%
音节2	15.65%	8.26%	12.59%
音节3	18.79%	10.67%	15.43%
音节4	12.58%	6.15%	9.92%
总偏误率	43.92%	25.82%	36.43%

纵向来看，在越南学生所发的汉语四字组词语中，音节3较之其他音节最易发生声调偏误，而末音节的声调偏误率最低（音节3与音节4的声调分布情况不存在显著性差异，$p=0.996$）。横向来看，越南男发音人四字组的声调偏误率明显小于女发音人，这在一定程度上可以推出这样一种看法——对于综合评价汉语水平（如HSK）差不多的越南留学生来说，在汉语声调的习得和把握方面，男生好于女生。

4. 总结

总的来说，越南留学生汉语四字组的时长偏误率为7.20%，停顿偏误率为21.90%，音高偏误率为36.40%。由上述数据我们可以简单推断，对于越南留学生来说，在汉语四字组的发音过程中，音高的难度最大，停顿次之，时长最小。此外，随着发音人汉语水平的提高，时长和停顿的偏误问题都有一定的好转，音高的偏误即使在中高级水平的发音人中也仍比较明显。

4.1 韵律偏误归因

汉语母语者四字组的发音中，各音节的时长占比表现出一定的规律性：前三个音节的时长占比相对较小，在25.00%以下，末音节的时长占比相对较大，超过30.00%。很多母语者都没有意识到四字组内部的这种时长分配规律，更不用说越南留学生了。对四字组内部音节时长分配规律的认识不足，是导致时长出现偏误的主要原因。

对汉语四字组音节发音的不熟练以及受不同语法结构的影响，是停顿出现偏误的主要原因。汉语母语者在四字组的发音过程中很少会出现停顿，有些越南发音人为了强调不同的语法结构，会在动宾结构（如“说老实话”）的动词后停顿过长，或是在定中结构（如“伊斯兰教”）的定语后停顿过长，从而导致了停顿偏误的出现。

母语负迁移的影响是音高产生偏误的主要原因。越南声调系统中虽然有类似汉语去声的下降调“玄声”和“重声”，但是玄声的下降幅度平缓，重声要先平行然后迅速下降，二者都与去声差异显著。很多越南留学生并不能很好地区分汉语中的去声与越南语中的降调。

4.2 对面向越南学习者汉语四字组韵律教学的建议

对老师来说，应提高对汉语四字组韵律教学的重视程度，同时对不同水平、不同性别的学习者应该进行有针对性的训练。此外，汉语音高模式的习得即使对有声调母语背景的越南学生来说，也仍应是教学重点。对于越南留学生易出现的第一声与第四声的混淆，教师应点明并强化训练。比如教师可选取T1T1T1T1（忽高忽低、息息相关）与T4T4T4T4（变幻莫测、各式各样）这样的词语或声调组合对学生进行听辨与发音训练。

对学生来说，需要重视对汉语四字组韵律的学习。四字组发音的韵律正确，不仅包括声调发音正确，还包括正确的停顿及各音节时长的合理分配。此外，还要自觉将汉语声调和越南语声调进行对比，做到知异而求同，避免负迁移，努力正迁移。

5. 致谢

本研究得到教育部人文社会科学重点研究基地重大项目“不同国别学习者的汉语语音语料库”（11JJD740003）和北京语

言大学院级科研项目“语言资源的深度开发与利用”（20YJ140013）资助。

参考文献

［1］Beckman, Mary E, and Edwards, Jane, 1994. Articulatory evidence for differentiating stress categories. In: Keating, P., (eds), *Phonological Structure and Phonetic Form*. Cambridge: Cambridge University Press, 7－33.

［2］曹文、张劲松:《面向计算机辅助正音的汉语中介语语音语料库的创制与标注》,《语言文字应用》2009年第4期，第122—131页。

［3］陈氏映月:《汉越语四字格成语的对比研究》，博士学位论文，华中师范大学，2016年。

［4］韩明:《越南留学生声调偏误分析及教学对策》,《玉林师范学院学报》2005年第2期。

［5］黎翠云:《越南人学习汉语语音的偏误分析及教学策略》，硕士学位论文，天津大学社会科学与外国语学院，2007年。

［6］黎霞贞:《二语经验对声调感知的影响——以越南语与汉语为例》，硕士学位论文，上海外国语大学，2018年。

［7］林焘:《汉语韵律特征和语音教学》,《林焘语言学论文集》，商务印书馆2001年版，第208—218页。

［8］刘晓军:《越南留学生汉语声调偏误实验分析》，硕士学位论文，广西大学，2006年。

［9］［英］特拉斯克:《语音学和音系学词典》，语音学和音系学词典编译组译，语文出版社2000年版。

［10］吴宗济:《普通话语句中的声调变化》，1981年在中国语言学会第1届学术年会宣读，2004年收于《吴宗济语言学论文集》，商务印书馆1981/2004年版，第141—161页。

［11］吴宗济:《吴宗济语言学论文集》，商务印书馆2004年版，第190—213页。

［12］熊子瑜:《语音库建设与分析教程》，西安交通大学出版社2017年版。

陈雪嫚　北京语言大学语言科学院，硕士研究生，主要研究领域为二语语音习得、实验语音学。
E-mail: 18931217124@189.cn

曹　文　北京语言大学语言科学院研究员，博士生导师，主要研究领域及学术兴趣包括：对外汉语教学、语音学、汉语中介语语音语料库、计算机辅助汉语语音学习等。
E-mail: tsao@blcu.edu.cn

视听及听觉训练下的日本学生汉语焦点重音习得声学分析

王颖阳　彭文杰　张劲松

摘　要　为了帮助日本学生更好地习得汉语焦点重音，我们先前提出了一套视听训练方案。本文通过分析声学参数，包括焦点词高音点、调域、焦点词—焦点后词音高落差和焦点词相对时长，进一步对比视听和听觉两种不同训练方法对焦点重音的训练效果，并考察焦点词位置和焦点句长度的影响。实验结果表明：（1）对两种方法而言，焦点重音的音高落差特征训练效果均不太理想；（2）焦点词在句中所处位置对听觉训练的效果有一定影响，句首焦点句的训练效果优于句末焦点句；（3）焦点句长度对视听及听觉训练的效果均有影响，二、三音节句的训练效果优于五音节句。

关键词　汉语焦点重音，视听训练，听觉训练，声学分析，日本学生

Acquisition of Focal Accent by by Japanese Learners of Chinese Receiving Audiovisualand Auditory Training: An Acoustic Study

WANG Yingyang　PENG Wenjie　ZHANG Jinsong

Abstract In order to help Japanese students learn Chinese focal accent better, a targeted audiovisual training program was proposed in our previous work. The present study further investigated whether and how the focus position as well as the sentence length affect learners' acquisition after they received the audiovisual training and traditional auditory training based on the acoustic analysis of their speech. Maximum F0, F0 range, relative duration of focused words and dropped F0 values of post-focus words were measured. Results show the following. (1) The focal accent characterized by the dropping F0 values is most difficult to acquire in both trainings. (2) The focus position has an effect on the outcome of the auditory training, which is manifested as a better acquisition of the sentence-initial focus than the sentence-final focus. (3) Sentence length has an effect on both auditory and audiovisual trainings. Learners performed better after training in shorter sentences composed of two to three syllables than sentences of five syllables.

Key words Chinese focal accent, Audiovisual training, Auditory training, Acoustic analysis, Japanese student

1. 引言

焦点指在谈话中令人感兴趣的，具有交际价值的信息的中心［2］，重音是焦点在语音学层面的关键性标记。汉语焦点重音的声学表现已得到广泛的研究，其中音高是最主要的线索，具有“三区段”的特征：当焦点音节的声调为阴、阳、去三声时，其高音点抬升且调域扩张，焦点前成分音高无明显变化，焦点后成分高音点骤降，焦点成分与焦点后成分之间存在音高落差［1，6，10，13，15］。但上声焦点重音的音高表现尚存在争议：Xu［10］发现其低音点明显下降；王蓓［16］认为其相邻音节的音高上升更为凸显。此外，时长延长也是汉语焦点得以凸显的重要辅助手段［13］。

日语是音高重音语言，焦点韵律受词重音影响，并主要表现在音高上：当焦点成分为有重读词时，其高音点抬高，调域扩张，焦点后调域压缩；但当焦点成分为无重读词时，焦点后调域没有明显变化［4，5］。此外，日语焦点成分的能量和时长也有所凸显［5］。汉日焦点重音的声学标记有诸多相似之处，但日

本学生在学习汉语焦点重音时并未表现出正迁移的作用。裘珊珊［14］、肖瑶和刘艺［17］指出，日本学生运用韵律手段凸显焦点的能力较弱，这些韵律手段包括焦点词的高音点、低音点、调域、焦点词—焦点后词音高落差、焦点词时长和声调调型等，其中时长问题最为明显。此外，汉语焦点句的韵律特征随焦点词位置不同而有所改变，但日本学生在这方面存在困难。焦点成分大小对日本学生的习得也有影响，从 zhang［11］的实验数据可以看出，与单音节焦点相比，日本学生所产出的双音节焦点声调正确率低、习得难度大。

焦点在交际信息传递的过程中扮演着重要作用，二语者若无法准确运用声学线索标记焦点，就难以与母语者进行高效的沟通。因此，帮助二语者改善焦点重音产出是汉语语音教学的重要任务。传统课堂多采用听觉模仿的方式进行教学。张劲松等［19］提出一套有针对性的视听训练方案：以圆圈图案的圆心和直径表示与焦点重音相关的高音点、调域、音高落差及时长线索，并将母语者和二语者的发音所生成的可视化图形同时呈现于交互界面左右两边，如图1所示。在视听训练过程中，二语者不仅可以听到而且可以看到自己的发音与母语者的差异，更好地将注意力集中到焦点语调上，提高学习效率。

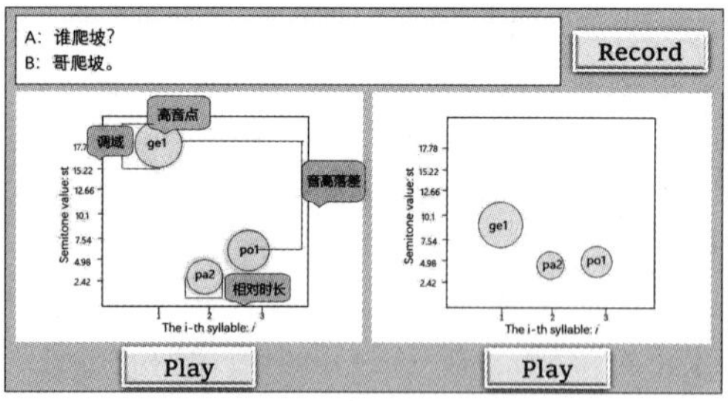

图1　视听训练交互界面

本文在张劲松等［19］的基础之上，进一步探索和传统的听觉训练相比，在视听训练方案的辅助下，日本留学生习得汉语焦点重音的特点和趋势。具体关注如下两个问题：（1）经过系统的发音训练，焦点词高音点、调域、焦点词—焦点后词音高落差、及焦点词相对时长等几项重要的声学参数，哪些容易习得？哪些习得难度大？其原因何在？（2）焦点重音在句中所处位置及焦点句长度对日本学生的习得有无影响？如有，其原因何在？

2. 方法

2.1　实验语料

实验语料为同文异焦句，即一组具有相同音段序列、词语构成、语法结构和语法关系，但焦点位置不同以凸显不同信息的句子［13］。语料选取 HSK5 级及以下的词汇，并排除日本学生发音困难的声韵母。语料设计考虑焦点位置和句子长度两个变量：焦点位置包括句首焦点和句末焦点；句子长度设计遵循由易到难的教学原则，分为二音节句、三音节句和五音节句，其中二、三音节句中的焦点成分为单音节词，五音节句中的焦点成分为双音节词。举例如下：

· 二音节句：他喝。/ 他喝。

· 三音节句：他回家。/ 他回家。

· 五音节句：包希飞苏州。/ 包希飞苏州。

需要注意的是，由于上声是二语者声调习得的难点，且上声作为焦点重音时的音高表现尚无定论，语料设计中避免上声音节，其余三声均匀分布。最终，实验语料共有54条句子（=9种声调组合×2种焦点位置×3种句子长度）。

2.2　实验被试

共选取29名被试的实验数据，包括21名日本留学生和8名汉语母语者。日本留学生平均年龄22岁，学习汉语1—3年，HSK水平为4—5级，均无听力障碍。为了对比不同发音训练的效果，21名被试随机分为三组：视听组8人（2男6女）、听觉组8人（2男6女）、对照组5人（1男4女）。8名汉语母语者（2男6女）平均年龄26岁，普通话水平二级甲等及以上。

2.3 实验流程

实验流程为“焦点重音基础知识讲解—前测—视听/听觉训练—中测—视听/听觉训练—后测”。两次训练均为期3天，每天45分钟，其间主试在旁监督，如有音段或声调错误则及时纠正。

视听组被试接受视听训练，在训练程序语音问句的引导下产出实验句，随后不仅可以听到而且可以通过视觉图形看到自己与母语者语调的差异。听觉组被试接受听觉训练，不提供视觉图形进行语调对比。对照组被试仅和另外两组被试一起在实验前接受简单的理论指导。

2.4 实验数据收集和整理

日本学生前、中、后测语料和汉语母语者语料均在安静的录音室中录制，录音软件为X-Recorder，采样率为16K。语料收集结束后，通过计算机程序自动提取焦点词的音高（高音点、调域、焦点词—焦点后词音高落差）及时长相关参数。数据具体处理方式如下：

（1）音高参数：实验句中的每个音节等距离提取十个点的基频，参考朱晓农［20］的方法，先根据公式①将全部基频值转化为对数值，再根据公式②将所得到的对数值按照发音人进行z-score规整，其中μ和σ分别表示该发音人对数音高值的平均值和标准差。

$$x = \log_2 x_i \quad ①$$

$$Z' = \frac{x - \mu}{\sigma} \quad ②$$

随后从对数z-score数据中提取焦点词的各项音高参数。在二、三音节实验句中，焦点词为单音节词，则提取这一单音节词的高音点（基频最大值）、调域（基频最大值减去基频最小值）、焦点词—焦点后词音高落差（焦点音节的基频最大值减去焦点后音节的基频最大值）。在五音节实验句中，焦点词为双音节词，则以这一双音节词为整体，提取其高音点、调域、焦点词—焦点后词音高落差。

（2）时长参数：为避免音段及发音人语速、不正常停顿等因素造成的影响，根据公式③计算焦点词的相对时长。其中d_i表示第i个音节的时长，μ表示句子中音节的平均时长。对于双音节焦点词而言，先分别计算每个音节的相对时长再取平均值。

$$Z'_i = \frac{d_i}{\mu} \quad ③$$

因前、中、后测语料为重复测量数据，且训练效果除与训练方案相关之外，也客观地受到发音人和实验句的影响，我们选择混合线性模型进行统计检验。具体步骤为：在R语言中进行先通过*lmerTest*包中的*lmer*函数建立以组别和测试为固定因素，以被试和实验句为随机因素的混合线性模型，随后使用*lmerTest*包中的*anova*函数来确定固定效应的显著性水平，最后使用*emmeans*包中的*emmeans*函数进行简单效应分析，详细对比各个训练阶段二语者与母语者之间的差异。

3. 结果

3.1 焦点词高音点习得情况

图2展示了三组日本学生焦点词高音点的习得趋势，整体而言，前测时三组日本被试彼此间差异不大，但与母语者差异明显。经过训练，视听组和听觉组明显进步，而对照组无明显改善。

方差分析的结果显示组别和测试在各种焦点位置及句子长度条件下均存在主效应，并且两者存在交互作用。由于篇幅所限，具体统计数据详见附录，其余三项参数同理。从表1所示的简单效应分析结果中可看出，视听组和听觉组在中测时已与母语者无显著差异（$p > 0.05$），但在五音节句中，听觉组在后测时出现退步的现象，与母语者存在显著差异（$p < 0.05$）。

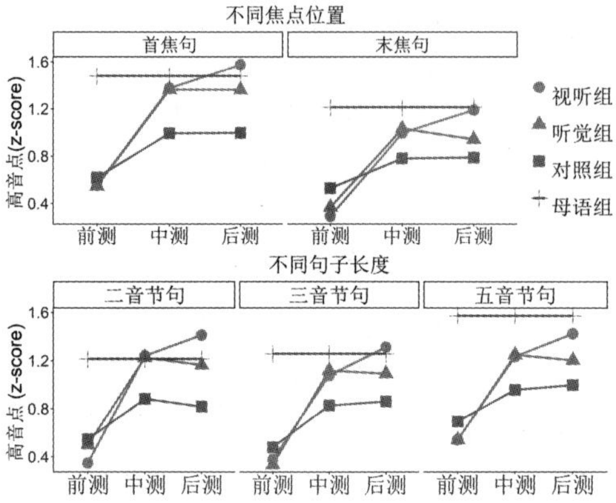

图2 焦点词高音点习得趋势①

表1 视听、听觉和母语组在中测及后测中焦点词高音点的简单效应检验统计值结果

	中测		后测	
	视听 vs 母语	听觉 vs 母语	视听 vs 母语	听觉 vs 母语
首焦句	$p=0.841$	$p=0.747$	$p=0.842$	$p=0.770$
末焦句	$p=0.147$	$p=0.257$	$p=0.997$	$p=0.051$
二音节句	$p=0.990$	$p=1.000$	$p=0.205$	$p=0.961$
三音节句	$p=0.457$	$p=0.641$	$p=0.936$	$p=0.511$
五音节句	$p=0.070$	$p=0.079$	$p=0.685$	$p=0.041$

3.2 焦点词调域习得情况

图3展示了日本学生焦点词调域的习得趋势。视听组和听觉组的习得效果明显优于对照组，但听觉组在焦点词位于句末或位于五音节句中时，后测表现出退步的趋势。

方差分析的结果显示组别和测试在各种焦点位置及句子长度条件下均存在主效应，并且两者存在交互作用。表2所示的简单效应结果显示，除五音节句外，其余焦点情况下视听组及听觉组在中测时焦点词调域已与母语者无显著差异，但听觉组在句末焦点情况下后测时与母语者存在显著差异。在五音节句中，仅有视听组在后测时与母语者无显著差异。

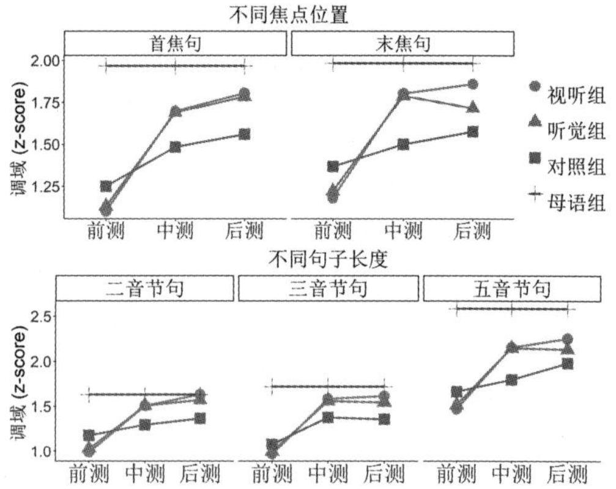

图3 焦点词调域习得趋势

表2 视听、听觉和母语组在中测及后测中焦点词调域的简单效应检验统计值结果

	中测		后测	
	视听 vs 母语	听觉 vs 母语	视听 vs 母语	听觉 vs 母语
首焦句	$p=0.190$	$p=0.174$	$p=0.606$	$p=0.473$
末焦句	$p=0.553$	$p=0.555$	$p=0.839$	$p=0.048$
二音节句	$p=0.698$	$p=0.822$	$p=0.999$	$p=0.891$
三音节句	$p=0.771$	$p=0.579$	$p=0.852$	$p=0.548$
五音节句	$p=0.041$	$p=0.044$	$p=0.069$	$p=0.040$

3.3 焦点词—焦点后词音高落差习得情况

图4展示了日本学生焦点词与焦点后词音高落差的习得趋势。由于句末焦点句不存在焦点后词，无法测量该参数，此处只分析句首焦点句。从图4中可看出这一

---

① 图2、图3、图5中，上图展示不同焦点位置对习得效果的影响，左右两幅小图分别为包含三种句子长度的首焦句和末焦句；下图展示不同句子长度对习得效果的影响，左中右三幅小图分别为包含两种焦点位置的二音节句、三音节句和五音节句。

参数对于日本学生而言并不容易掌握，句子长度对习得效果有重要影响。

方差分析的结果显示组别和测试在3种句子长度条件下均存在主效应，并且两者存在交互作用。表3的简单效应检验结果显示，在二音节句中，视听组和听觉组在中测时已取得不错的学习效果，但在三音节句中，仅有视听组在后测时与母语者无显著差异。而当句子长度为五音节时，视听组、听觉组和对照组一样，在后测时均与母语者有显著差异。但整体而言，视听组比另外两组进步更大，习得效果更好。

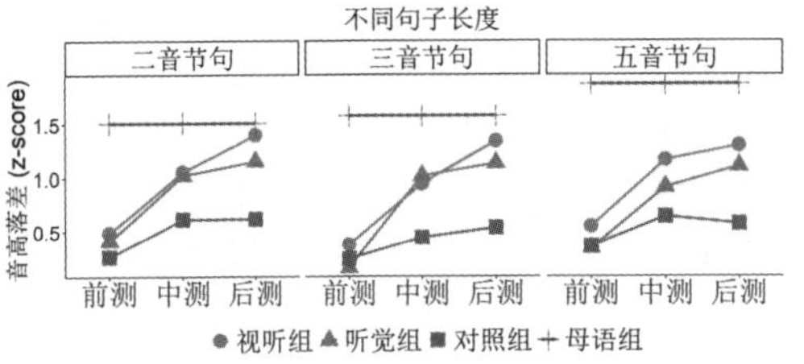

图4 焦点词—焦点后词音高落差习得趋势

表3 视听、听觉和母语组在中测及后测中焦点词—焦点后词音高落差的简单效应检验统计值结果

	中测		后测	
	视听 vs 母语	听觉 vs 母语	视听 vs 母语	听觉 vs 母语
二音节句	$p=0.093$	$p=0.063$	$p=0.941$	$p=0.242$
三音节句	$p=0.002$	$p=0.005$	$p=0.480$	$p=0.037$
五音节句	$p=0.000$	$p=0.000$	$p=0.001$	$p=0.000$

3.4 焦点词相对时长习得情况

图5展示了日本被试焦点词相对时长的习得趋势。当焦点词位于句末或位于三音节句中时，视听组较之听觉组和对照组，习得效果更好。

方差分析的结果显示组别和测试在各种焦点位置及句子长度条件下均存在主效应，并且两者存在交互作用。从表4的简单效应结果可看出，在各种焦点条件下，

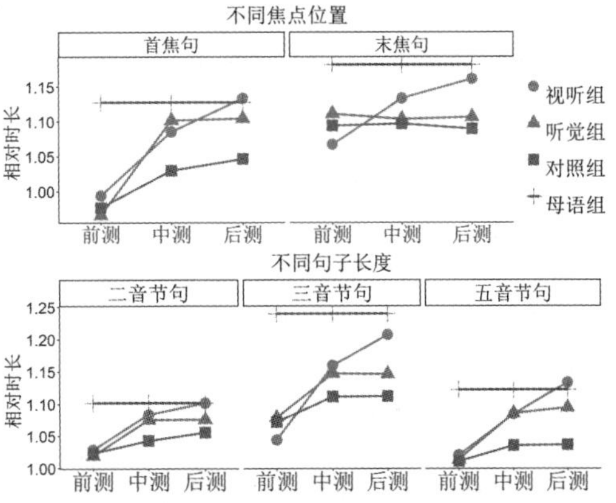

图5 焦点词相对时长习得趋势

视听组在后测时均与母语者无显著差异，但听觉组在焦点词位于句末及三音节句中时，始终与母语者有显著差异。

杨立明［18］认为，受到母语时长辨义功能的影响，日本学生不习惯使用时长手段来调整汉语节奏。但在本研究中，我们发现经过系统的视听训练，延长焦点词时长对于日本学生而言并非十分困难。

表4 视听、听觉和母语组在中测及后测中焦点词相对时长的简单效应检验统计值结果

	中测		后测	
	视听 vs 母语	听觉 vs 母语	视听 vs 母语	听觉 vs 母语
首焦句	$p=0.313$	$p=0.699$	$p=0.998$	$p=0.766$
末焦句	$p=0.136$	$p=0.004$	$p=0.761$	$p=0.006$
二音节句	$p=0.579$	$p=0.256$	$p=0.999$	$p=0.285$
三音节句	$p=0.043$	$p=0.014$	$p=0.676$	$p=0.014$
五音节句	$p=0.192$	$p=0.199$	$p=0.930$	$p=0.450$

4. 讨论

从以上分析可以看出：(1) 视听及听觉训练均能辅助日本学生习得汉语焦点重音，但视听训练的效果优于听觉训练。主要体现在视听组在前、中、后测中持续进步，而听觉组的进步常常止步于中测，甚

至在后测中有所退步（如高音点和调域两项参数）。（2）在四项声学参数中，焦点词—焦点后词音高落差的习得难度最大。主要体现在对视听组而言，其余参数大部分在中测，小部分在后测时与母语者无显著差异，但这一参数在三音节句条件下后测时才能与母语者无显著差异，在五音节句条件下始终与母语者有显著差异。（3）焦点位置对听觉训练的效果有一定影响，句首焦点句的训练效果优于句末焦点句。主要体现在句末焦点句中，听觉组的高音点及调域两项参数在后测时出现退步，时长参数始终与母语者有显著差异。（4）句子长度对视听及听觉训练的效果均有影响，二、三音节句的音高特征训练效果优于五音节句。主要体现在五音节句中，听觉组的三项音高参数后测时均与母语者有显著差异，视听组的音高落差在后测时与母语者有显著差异。

视听训练的优势得益于它通过视觉与听觉的双重编码［7］，帮助学习者将注意力集中到焦点成分上，提高学习效率。Schmidt［8］指出注意是二语习得的必需条件。二语习得效果与学习者在输入信息中所注意的内容及程度密切相关。在传统的听觉训练中，输入的语音包含多个维度的信息，学习者即使意识到焦点重音的交际功能，也难以准确地将注意力聚焦到音高和时长线索上，模仿发音时缺乏明确的目的和参照标准。从实验数据中可以发现，听觉组被试在中测时进步明显，但在后测时常常难以继续进步甚至出现退步。这或许是因为听觉组被试依据主观感受自我纠音，中测时已经达到自我标准，在后续学习中注意力分散，不再认真关注相关声学参数。而视听组被试在视觉图形的辅助下，注意力始终聚焦于声学参数的习得，并且在自己与母语者的语音图形对比当中，可以清楚地知道应该在哪个参数上、在多大程度上纠正自己的发音，从而在前、中、后测中取得持续进步。

但是，注意力资源是有限的并且是有选择性的，当学习者的工作记忆难以兼顾所有的任务要求时，难免要进行取舍［8］。这影响了学习者对焦点词—焦点后词音高落差这一声学特征的掌握。对于母语者而言，合理分配发音资源，在有限的时间内高效传达交际信息是不假思索的［12］，焦点成分的扩张和焦点后成分的压缩是不省力与省力发音方式的自然协调，无需刻意关注。但对于二语者而言，两者都是需要通过学习才能掌握的技能，并且一扩张一压缩，对声学参数的应用恰好相反，存在注意力资源的竞争。因为学习的对象是焦点重音，学习者可能更多地将注意力集中到焦点成分上。并且对于视听组而言，视觉图形的圆心和半径分别表示音节的高音点和时长，焦点圆圈大而高，焦点后圆圈小而低，引导学习者在更加关注焦点成分的同时难免会造成对焦点后成分的忽略。因此视听组被试在这一参数的习得上并没有表现出明显的优势。此外，课堂教学中教师常要求学习者将每个音节都发得饱满准确，这也可能会误导学习者将焦点后音节发得过重。

注意力资源的有限性和选择性也影响了五音节句的习得。语音产出任务包含音段、声调、语调等多要素，二、三音节句的焦点成分为单音节词，相对简单，学习者在进行足够的训练之后可以很好地协调各方面要素。但五音节句不仅长度增加，焦点成分也扩展成双音节词，产出任务量增大，认知负担加重。［3］与［9］认为，当任务难度增大时，学习者的注意力集中于语言产出的内容，而不是复杂度和准确度。因此，在五音节句的产出中，学习者将更多注意力集中于音段与声调，以保证产出的基本内容能让母语者听得懂，但难以同时顾及韵律运用的准确度。值得注意的是，尽管听觉组和对照组五音节句的习得效果不甚理想，但视听组在视觉图形的提示下，仍然可以注意到焦点的韵律信息，取得相对不错的习得效果。

5. 结论

本文从声学分析的角度考察日本学生汉语焦点重音的习得特点，主要关注焦点位置及句子长度对视听及听觉训练效果的影响。结果发现，焦点词—焦点后词音高落差是最难以习得的声学特征；随着句子长度的增加，习得难度增大。这与学习者注意力资源的有限性和选择性有关。根据学习者的习得特点，有针对性地选择合适的发音训练方法，将能有效帮助学习者高效利用注意力资源，习得汉语焦点重音。

6. 致谢

本研究得到语言资源高精尖创新中心项目“面向智能语音教学的汉语中介语语音多模态语料库研究”（KYR17005）、中央高校基本科研业务专项资金（21YJ040004）、北京语言大学梧桐创新平台（19PT04）、北京语言大学中外研究生创新基金（21YCX179）的资助。本文的通信作者是张劲松。

参考文献

[1] Chao，Y. 1968. *A Grammar of Spoken Chinese*. Berkeley：University of California Press.

[2] Crystal，D. 2008. *A Dictionary of Linguistics and Phonetics*（*6th Edition*）. Oxford：Blackwell Publishers.

[3] Foster，P.，Skehan，P. 1996. The influence of planning and task type on second language performance. *Studies in Second Language Acquisition* 18，299 – 323.

[4] Ishihara，S. 2011. Focus prosody in Tokyo Japanese Wh – Questions with lexically unaccented Wh – Phrases. *The 17th International Congress of Phonetic Sciences*（*ICPhS XVII*）Hong Kong，946 – 949.

[5] Lee，A.，Xu，Y. 2012. Revisiting focus prosody in Japanese. *Proceedings of the 6th International Conference on Speech Prosody* Shanghai，274 – 277.

[6] Liu，F.，Xu，Y. 2005. Parallel encoding of focus and interrogative meaning in mandarin intonation. *Phonetica* 62，70 – 87.

[7] Paivio，A. 1986. *Mental representations：a dual coding approach*. Oxford：Oxford University Press.

[8] Schmidt，R. 2001. Attention. In：Robinson，P.（eds），*Cognition and Second Language Instruction*. Cambridge：Cambridge University Press，2 – 32.

[9] Skehan，P. 1998. *A Cognitive Approach to Language Learning*. Oxford：Oxford University Press.

[10] Xu，Y. 1999. Effects of tone and focus on the formation and alignment of f0 contours. *Journal of Phonetics* 27，55 – 105.

[11] Zhang，H. 2016. Focal Prominence Marking in Second Language Chinese Tones. In：Tao，H.（eds），*Integrating Chinese Linguistics Research and Language Learning*. Amsterdam：John Benjamins，195 – 214.

[12] 曹剑芬：《韵律结构与语音的变化》，《南京师范大学文学院学报》2011 年第 3 期，第 12—22 页。

[13] 曹文：《汉语焦点重音的韵律实现》，北京语言大学出版社 2010 年版。

[14] 裘珊珊：《日本留学生汉语陈述句核心重音的韵律表现》，硕士学位论文，北京语言大学，2007 年。

[15] 沈炯：《汉语语调模型刍议》，《语文研究》1992 年第 4 期，第 16—24 页。

[16] 王蓓：《汉语韵律知觉的研究》，博士学位论文，中国科学院心理学研究所，2002 年。

[17] 肖瑶 、刘艺：《日本学生汉语焦点句语调的习得分析》，《汉语学习》2018 年第 3 期，第 83—93 页。

[18] 杨立明：《汉语自然音步的语音特征》，载《第六届国家汉语教学讨论会论文选》，北京大学出版社 1999 年版，第 565—573 页。

[19] 张劲松、吴静、王颖阳：《视听训练在日本学生汉语焦点重音产出中的作用》，《华文教学与研究》2020 年第 4 期，第 28—39 页。

[20] 朱晓农：《基频归一化——如何处理声调的随机差异?》，《 语言科学》2004 年第 2 期，第 3—19 页。

王颖阳 北京语言大学，硕士研究生，主要研究领域为语音习得、实验语音学。
E-mail：yingyangwx@ gmail. com

彭文杰 北京语言大学，硕士研究生，主要研究领域为语音切分、语音识别。
E-mail：yuebanyishenqiu@ gmail. com

张劲松 北京语言大学，博士，教授，主要研究领域为语音习得、韵律建模、语音识别、实验语音学、计算机辅助发音教学。
E-mail：jinsong. zhang@ blcu. edu. cn

附录

附表1　　混合线性模型中主效应及其交互作用的方差分析结果

统计模型		“组别”主效应	“测试”主效应	交互作用
焦点词高音点	首焦句	F [2, 2257] =381.96, p =0.00	F [3, 30] =12.04, p =0.00	F [6, 2257] =72.76, p =0.00
	末焦句	F [2, 2224] =222.30, p =0.00	F [3, 30] =12.58, p =0.00	F [6, 2224] =50.29, p =0.00
	二音节句	F [2, 1491] =213.35, p =0.00	F [3, 30] =8.72, p =0.00	F [6, 1491] =47.91, p =0.00
	三音节句	F [2, 1489] =190.97, p =0.00	F [3, 30] =10.62, p =0.00	F [6, 1489] =360.84, p =0.00
	五音节句	F [2, 1480] =200.95, p =0.00	F [3, 30] =13.18, p =0.00	F [6, 1480] =40.59, p =0.00
焦点词调域	首焦句	F [2, 2266] =133.03, p =0.00	F [3, 30] =6.78, p =0.00	F [6, 2266] =24.42, p =0.00
	末焦句	F [2, 2245] =70.73, p =0.00	F [3, 30] =5.05, p =0.01	F [6, 2245] =16.64, p =0.00
	二音节句	F [2, 1515] =51.87, p =0.00	F [3, 1515] =28.19, p =0.00	F [6, 1515] =11.85, p =0.00
	三音节句	F [2, 1512] =63.22, p =0.00	F [3, 30] =5.01, p =0.01	F [6, 1512] =11.55, p =0.00
	五音节句	F [2, 1503] =62.81, p =0.00	F [3, 1503] =122.06, p =0.00	F [6, 1503] =13.09, p =0.00
焦点词—焦点后词音高落差	二音节句	F [2, 737] =27.91, p =0.00	F [3, 31] =14.43, p =0.00	F [6, 737] =5.20, p =0.00
	三音节句	F [2, 743] =51.99, p =0.00	F [3, 31] =23.88, p =0.00	F [6, 743] =12.13, p =0.00
	五音节句	F [2, 740] =38.10, p =0.00	F [3, 33] =51.97, p =0.00	F [6, 740] =8.11, p =0.00
焦点词相对时长	首焦句	F [2, 2278] =197.88, p =0.00	F [3, 30] =8.92, p =0.00	F [2, 2278] =33.27, p =0.00
	末焦句	F [2, 2267] =7.72, p =0.00	F [3, 30] =8.86, p =0.00	F [2, 2267] =10.67, p =0.00
	二音节句	F [2, 1499] =23.16, p =0.00	F [3, 38] =10.22, p =0.00	F [6, 1499] =4.43, p =0.00
	三音节句	F [2, 1525] =43.15, p =0.00	F [3, 30] =11.17, p =0.00	F [2, 1525] =12.02, p =0.00
	五音节句	F [2, 1497] =55.03, p =0.00	F [3, 31] =12.29, p =0.00	F [6, 1497] =13.50, p =0.00

鼻音测量计应用指南

陈禹风

摘　要　近年来国内高校和研究所纷纷建立语音实验室，鼻音计等实验设备也得以推广并逐渐应用到语言学和病理研究当中。本文介绍了 Nasometer 的发展历史、设计原理、注意事项等内容。同时，本文也对其汉译名称进行讨论，避免译名问题引起的混淆与迷惑。最后提醒研究者们不宜直接比较不同测量系统得到的鼻化度值。

关键词　鼻音，鼻音计，鼻流计，实验语音

A Guide to Nasometry

CHEN Yufeng

Abstract In recent years, domestic universities and research institutes have established speech laboratories, and experimental equipment such as Nasometer has also been promoted and gradually applied to linguistic phonetics and pathological research. This article introduces Nasometer's development history, design principle, instructions of use, etc. At the same time, this article also discusses the Chinese translation of the name, and the potential confusion caused by the translation. Finally, researchers are reminded that it is not appropriate to directly compare the nasalization values obtained by different measurement systems.

Key words Nasal, Nasometry, Nasometer, Experimental Phonetics

1. 引言

鼻音和鼻化现象普遍存在于世界语音中，历时的音韵资料也表明鼻音是稳定的音类之一。[23] 同时，腭咽功能不全的人往往会出现鼻音过高或鼻音过低的语音错误，这往往使患者难以产生易于理解的目标音。因此，鼻音和鼻化是语言学之语音学和病理语音学共同关心的话题。

无论是声学分析还是生理技术，鼻音研究始终存在困难。尽管如此，仍然有很多优秀的学者致力于发展新的实验方法。本文将介绍一种基于声学能量测量的实验技术，这种设备在国内更广为人知的名称是“鼻音计/鼻流计”，得益于一些学者的努力，该设备在语言学领域的研究中逐渐被推广。但是，从目前的中文文献材料看，对于该设备的发展历史、原理设计、注意事项在以往文章中还未尽数澄清。为了帮助此类设备在今后研究中更好地应用，本文会分别进行梳理。同时，本文也对其汉译名称进行讨论，避免译名问题引起的混淆与迷惑。

2. 鼻音测量计（Nasometry）的种类

本文所指的鼻音测量计（Nasometry）是对不同的产品/种类的总称，是一个上位概念。限于篇幅，我们主要谈论的是国内常用的，由 KayPENTAX 公司（前身为 Kay Elemetrics）生产的 Nasometer，文献中常见的型号是 6200、6400 和 6450。同时本文作为技术指引，也将对其他系统略作介绍，这些设备之间的区别不止在于生产厂商的不同，在具体设计上也有差异。

另外，在我们讨论这些设备及相应参数的汉译名合理性问题之前，本文都将暂时保留相应的英文名称。

2.1 Nasometer

Nasometer 的汉语叫法最常见的是"鼻音计"［41，47］、"鼻（气）流计"［40，42，44］，还有不多见的"口鼻分流仪"的说法①。在讨论何种翻译更为适合之前，我们先回顾 Nasometer 的发展历史。

Nasometer 的前身是 Fletcher［11—15］开发的 TONAR，即 The Oral Nasal Acoustic Ratio 的缩写。顾名思义，这是一项比较语音口鼻通道声学信号能量比率的技术。长期以来，临床上评估语音的口鼻平衡（oral-nasal balance）一直缺少一种可靠稳定的工具。20 世纪中叶，Weatherley-White 等［35］提出一种可以根据声学信号自动测量过高鼻音的设想。之后 Fletcher 将之实现为 TONAR，其原理如图 1。通过分隔口鼻的装置，采集到来自口腔和鼻腔麦克风的信号，同时做了 300Hz 带宽的带通滤波，中心频率为 500 Hz，因为作者预计该频率最符合鼻音的感知。②带通滤波信号的强度测量值显示为示波器读数，平均在一秒间隔内。

Fletcher 和 Bishop［14］进而实验论证鼻腔信号与口腔信号声压级的比率与鼻音过高的听觉—感知评级非常吻合。因此，Fletcher［12］建议 TONAR 的读数可用于在言语治疗中提供生物反馈。同时 Fletcher 等人［15］引入了术语"nasalance"，由以下公式计算所得：

$$\%Nasalance = \frac{Nasal\ SPL}{Nasal\ SPL + Oral\ SPL} \times 100$$

SPL（Sound Pressure Level）为"声压级"，Nasal SPL 表示鼻腔信号的声压级，同理 Oral SPL 为口腔信号声压级。在 Weinberg、Noll 和 Donohue［36］指出 TONAR II 麦克风的频率响应不平衡的问题后，Fletcher［13］作了改进。TONAR II 的后继仪器被称为 Nasometer 6200。根据 Bressmann［8］，"Nasometer"一词首次出现在 1957 年的文献［27］中，描述的是一种评估鼻腔开放（nasal patency）的仪器，但是它似乎没有经受住时间的考验。商业化的 Nasometer 6200 在硬件方面使用带金属隔板的头戴装置③，该隔板放置在发音人的口前方（prolabium）上，垂直于面部。同时，该系统配套的软件提供了"鼻音图（nasogram）"功能，可以实时显示 nasalance 轨迹作为生物反馈（biofeedback）。之后，该设备又进行了几代更新。

2.2 其他商业化的鼻音测量技术

Baken［4］总结过侵入性较小的鼻音测量方法，大致分为以下四类。

（1）测量口鼻气流，同时测量口内压力。

（2）在鼻子上放置一个加速度计来检测通过鼻子的声音。

（3）通过隔板和麦克风分别测量从口鼻发出的声音（声压波形）。

（4）分析语音辐射的声学特性以检测与鼻化相关的声学特性。

以上设计都有相应的商业化产品。这里只简单介绍几套主流方案。④

美国 TigerDRS 公司推出的 NasalView［2］系统也是使用了与 Nasometer 类似的声音分离板和头戴支架。为了改善声音分离效果，苯乙烯材质的分离板顶部和底部被附上了载重橡胶层。⑤ 但是，有研究指出，该设计的声音分离效果不如金属隔板［7］。

美国 Glottal 公司的 Nasalance 系统（以前叫 OralNasal 系统）提供了两种方案：口鼻分隔的面罩和塑料隔板。Rothenberg 指出面罩的声音分离度比隔板好，并

---

① https：//mp. weixin. qq. com/s/hP1S7cR6P jijfqWvlC2qLQ.

② Nasometer II Model 6400 的使用手册中指出：两个通道（口腔和鼻腔）都通过硬件上的模拟滤波器，以限制正在处理的信号带宽进行 nasalance 分析。该滤波器的特性如下：带通滤波器，其中心频率为 500 Hz，低频（－3dB）截止频率为 300 Hz，上限截止频率为 750 Hz。

③ 金属隔板由于介质密度大能够更好地分隔声音，同时有防腐的优点。因此，尽管可能增加头戴装置重量，但是金属隔板在使用效果上要比塑料板或者其他复合材料版更理想。

④ 部分产品可通过 www. freeber. cn 了解。

⑤ TigerDRS，Inc 的中国大陆代理商为上海泰亿格康复医疗科技股份有限公司，相关产品叫作鼻音测量与训练仪。

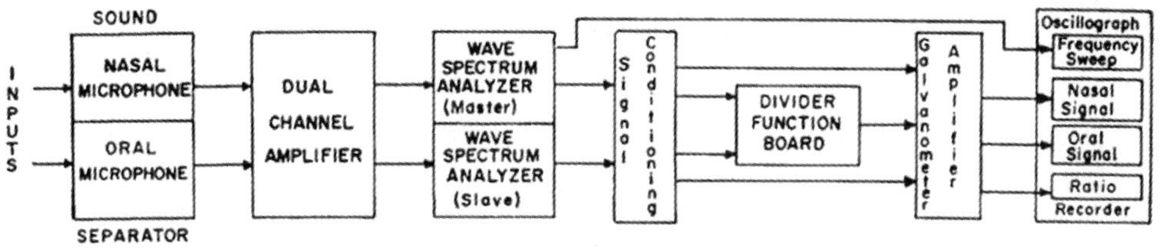

图 1　TONAR 系统示意（引自［11］）

通过相关研究进行了验证［27，38］。为了补偿口鼻通道之间的声音溢出，专有算法会计算校正后的 nasalance 分数。但是，需要强调的是，不同于 Nasometer 的滤波器设计，Glottal 的这套系统测量的是 F0-nasalance（开发者 Rothenberg 把 Nasometer 测得的结果叫作 F1-nasalance①）。另外，该软件还可以计算 oralance。Glottal 公司还有 Dualview 系统，其设计也是基于开发者对 F0 – nasalance 的认识，通过 50Hz 低通滤波之后的口鼻气流的直流信号计算，定义为：100 × Ndc /（Odc + Ndc）。作者将其计算结果称为“DC Nasalance/Flow Nasalance”，有别于基于声学信号的测量结果（为了区分，作者将该结果叫作“AC Nasalance”）。英国 ROSE 公司 SNORS 系统也具有相似功能。另外还有 Donald W. Warren 等人开发的气压—气流技术，主要用于腭咽功能评估。

利用加速度计的方法可参看 Horii［18］。作者通过连接到鼻子和喉部侧面的加速度计来计算鼻腔 SPL 与喉源信号的比率，该设计没有用到麦克风和分隔板。由此产生的测量被称为 Horii 口鼻耦合指数（Hori：Oral-Nasal Coupling Index，HONC）。

英国的 Laryngograph 公司在 D – 800 系统上提供了用于鼻振动测量的加速度传感器接口，而且可以实现鼻共振和鼻压的同步测量。利用固定在鼻侧的小型加速度计可以获得与鼻壁振动强度相应的信号，该信号作为与鼻音感知相关的简单物理测量。

还有 lingWAVES Nasality（由 WEVOSYS 经销）、Rivener［10］、NORAM（Nasal Oral Ratio Meter）［19］等类似设备/系统，感兴趣的读者可以参看 Bressmann［8］和维基百科“nasalance”词条对它们的引用②。

3. 关于几个汉译名的讨论

3.1　鼻音计还是鼻流计

有了上一节内容的铺垫，我们再回过头来讨论 Nasometer③ 的汉译名问题。根据笔者在知网和百度学术所能检索到的文献资料，马莲教授［45］早在 1985 年就采用了“鼻音计”这一说法介绍 TONAR 系统。时秀娟、向柠［48］2008 年将 Nasometer 应用于语言学领域的方言研究，并称之为“鼻音计”。而“鼻流计”这一说法较早见于杨宝琦等 1995 年的《鼻咽缩窄术治疗儿童开放性鼻音》一文［50］，文章作者将美国 Kay Elemetrics（KayPENTAX 前身）公司生产的 Nasometer Model 6200 称为“鼻流计/鼻气流计”。之后，周杨［51］在语言学背景下提及“鼻流计”，但并未指明是何种设备。

根据之前对 Nasometer 的介绍，我们

① Rothenberg 认为，与 F1-nasalance（通带带宽大概是元音 F1 的范围）相比，F0-nasalance（通带频率更低）受元音共振和基频的影响小。关于两者的比较讨论详见作者个人网页：http：//www. rothenberg. org/Nasalance/Nasalance. htm.

② https：//en. wikipedia. org/wiki/Nasalance.

③ “Nasometer”一词首次出现在文献中，描述了一种评估鼻腔开放（nasal patency）的仪器。［29］

将它归为 Nasometry 的一种类型，尤指 KayPENTAX 公司的一款产品，起源于 TONAR，测量的是口鼻信号的声学能量。所以它测量的不是口鼻气流信号，即 Nasometer 并不是一套气压气流测量系统。因此，我们认为，“鼻流计/鼻气流计/口鼻分流仪”不是对 Nasometer 这类设备合适的称呼，因为“流”容易引起读者误解，让人以为跟口鼻气流相关，容易引起不必要的理解困难。而“鼻音计”的说法则没有关于气流的暗示。同时我们也不必提出新的说法，该译名出现较早［41］，也一直得到沿用（如时秀娟教授研究团队的一系列文章）。所以，从术语传统、表达准确性、可接受度等方面考虑，“鼻音计”或许是对 Nasometer 合适的翻译。而作为上位概念的 Nasometry 可以考虑用“鼻音测量计”来指称，或许由于 Kay 公司在仪器制造上的影响力，Nasometry 这个说法在国内远不如 Nasometer 使用广泛。另外，我们也不反对将“鼻流计”这一说法用来称呼基于气流技术的鼻音测量计，这样可以对不同技术原理的设备进行区分。①

3.2 鼻化度还是鼻音度

这里主要讨论 Nasalance 的译名问题，目前天津师范大学的研究团队［47］以及其他一些学者将之称为“鼻化度”，西北民族大学、暨南大学、上海师范大学的一些研究者称为“鼻音度”［42，44，46］。

我们先回顾 Nasalance 作为术语的提出。在谷歌学术中检索 Nasalance，我们查到 Fletcher 等在［15］中最早引入了该术语，Fletcher 将 Tonar II 的测量结果称为“nasalance”，而在此之前［12，14］，他用的是“nasality”这一说法。对此，作者在注释中进行了说明，术语“nasality”用于识别人类对鼻音质量的感知判断。按照作者的说法，引入术语“nasalance”是特别用于描述鼻腔与口腔共振的声学对比，即是 TONAR（The Oral Nasal Acoustic Ratio）的本义，“Nasalance”排除了人类感知中的错误。换句话说，nasalance 是用鼻音计方法对 nasality 主观判断的客观量化结果，并且可以用以评估发带音时的腭咽闭合状况。

“nasality”一词是语言学研究者相对熟悉的术语，R. L. Trask 编的《语音学和音系学词典》［49］收录了该术语，编译组（鲍怀翘、曹剑芬、林茂灿、吕士楠、沈炯、王嘉龄、周流溪、周同春）将它译为“鼻音性”。在方言学和音位学讨论中鼻音通常都是一种音类，在生成音系学中作为一种特征。从某种意义上说，语言学领域对鼻音是一种定性判断。实验语音学将鼻音共振的程度进行量化，如果沿用“鼻音度”一说容易把定性问题和定量问题混为一谈。我们前面已经看到，相关研究（设备）已经引入“oralance”这一概念，我们是否又要称之为“口音度”。由于口鼻腔的生理耦合，口鼻声学共振是一个“一体两面”的关系，但“口/鼻音度”隐喻了两个分离的事件而不是互补的事件。同时，当单独使用“口音度”的说法时，“口音”一词也可能引起新的误解。因此，笔者更支持用“鼻化度”作为“nasalance”的汉译名，“nasality”仍可使用“鼻音性”这一翻译。下文也将直接采用鼻音计和鼻化度的说法。

4. 鼻化度相关问题

4.1 为什么测不到 0 或 100 的鼻化度

Rothenberg 在 Glottal 公司开发的 Dualview 程序手册中也指出“由于声学交叉（crossover）现象的存在，以及声音会通过声道闭合点（腭咽闭合时的软腭）肌肉组织的影响，其他基于音频信号计算出的鼻化度只能显示一个不到100%的数值”。这段文字直白地说明了基于声学信号的鼻化度计算无法回避的一个问题，即口鼻隔板无法完全分离振动产生的声学信号，就其结果来说，基于麦克风信号的鼻音计达不到理论上的两个极端值，同时也无法测量到不带音的鼻化情况。

---

① 分辨声学/气流鼻音计类型的一个简单方法：气流测量设备通常需要预热以及使用空气注射器对特定压力传感器灵敏度校准，声学测量设备是用声学信号对麦克风进行校准。

Kummer［18］在其编著的书中指出，鼻化度达不到100的原因一个是分隔板不能完全阻挡从板的一侧到另一侧的信号接收（即存在声学交叉）。因此，在产生带音，特别是元音时，麦克风之间可能会存在溢出（spillover）效应。另一个原因是，在带音（尤其是元音）的产生过程中似乎存在声音的跨腭（transpalatal）传输。［1，17，24］可以假设硬腭就像一堵砖墙，几乎不允许声音通过。而软腭更像是一层厚重的帘子（heavy curtain）——让一些声音进入鼻腔。关于后一原因，Blanton、Watterson和Lewis［6］的实验结论是，大部分声音能在软腭转移，但这种影响对前高元音更明显。高元音比低元音具有更多的鼻腔共振，因为舌位高导致口腔通道变小，因此对口腔的阻抗增加。同时，对软腭软组织的声压增加。相比之下，低元音会导致更大的口腔尺寸和更低的阻抗。因此，口腔共鸣在低元音上更为明显。［20］除此之外，Blanton等［6］认为，元音共振峰的位置和鼻音计滤波器的特性也有影响。但这仍然是未来需要研究的问题。［26］

值得注意的是，Benson［5］利用头颅测量X线照相术（Cephalometric roentgenography）发现健康人在发不同元音的时候存在不同程度的腭咽间隙（residual palatopharyngeal lumen）。相关的结论甚至在更早时候就被William［37］和Moll［25］报道过，之后也得到了新的研究的证实。中国学者刘晖等人［43］在《应用鼻咽镜对健康人腭咽闭合功能的观察研究》中发现，相当数量的健康人在念韵母时存在不同程度的腭咽闭合不全。从这方面说，鼻化度达不到极值本身也可能存在生理构音的影响。

尽管基于麦克风/声学信号的鼻音计可能存在设计缺陷，但是，目前大量研究仍然在验证它的实践价值。由于其本身的技术难度不大，常有新的、成本更低的产品/系统被开发出来。考虑到语言学研究中声学鼻音计的推广，本文认为，同一项研究中的实验数据是比较可信的，但是，如果涉及不同设备的研究应当审慎对待得到的鼻化度（nasalance）数值，下一小节也将讨论鼻化度信度的问题。另外，建议对每个人的鼻化度数据进行归一化处理，根据Rothenberg［27］，通常被试内的鼻化度是稳定的，归一化数据更利于不同发音人、不同方言、不同研究（设备）之间的比较。

4.2 鼻音计测量的信度问题

信度（Reliability）是指测验结果的一致性、稳定性及可靠性。Watterson和Lewis［31］评估了鼻音过高说话人鼻化度分数的重复测量变异性，发现大多数重复结果误差在5%的范围内。然而，他们也指出，改变头戴装置会增加测量之间的可变性。Nasometer以及the NasalView或the OralNasal System等类似设备通常将麦克风置于离鼻子和嘴约5厘米的地方。Švec和Granqvist［30］解释了麦克风近距离测量声强时，其位置的微小变化会产生很大的差异。可能会导致在鼻子和嘴附近或上面放置加速计或麦克风的记录有相当大的可变性，还可能会影响根据这些测量结果计算出的鼻化度评分。对于声音研究的强度测量，Švec和Granqvist［30］建议在声源和测量麦克风之间设置30厘米的距离，以获得可重复的分贝读数。但是对于目前的商业化方案来说，并没有做到这一点，30厘米的距离将需要一个相当大的隔板。

对于上述问题，Rothenberg［27］企图通过在软硬件上的调整来改善这一问题。它提供了带有筛网环的口鼻分隔面罩（如图2）配合录音软件上的补偿功能来减少声学交叉的影响。面罩相对隔板来说，限制了置于手柄中的麦克风的可调整角度。配套软件上的补偿功能如果打开，则在计算鼻化度之前，会从测量的口能量值中减去一小部分测量的鼻能量，并从鼻能量中减去相同百分比的测量口能量。

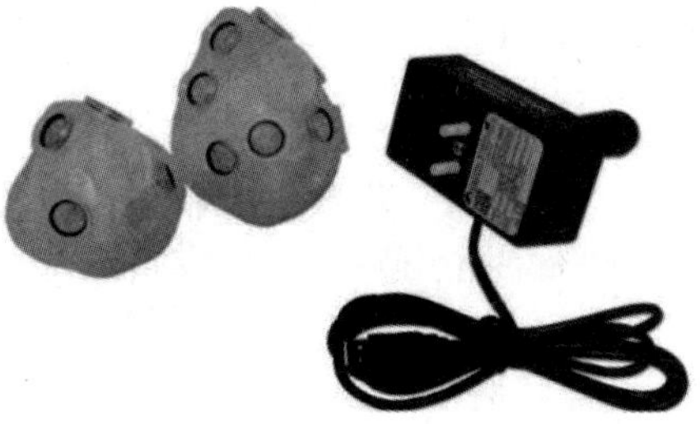

图2 Glottal公司的鼻化度系统
(图片来源于Linglab网站①)

除头戴位置之外，Zajac、Lutz 和 Mayo［39］甚至认为不同麦克风灵敏度（不同的频响特性）产生了鼻化度分数的微小差异。这种硬件差异可能会影响来自不同研究中心的鼻化度分数的比较。

还有一些研究比较了前后代产品的差异。Watterson、Lewis 和 Brancamp［32］发现使用 Nasometers 6200 和 6400 获得的分数之间存在显著差异。作者将差异主要归因于被试内部的变异性和头戴装置变化，而较少归因于机器之间的实际差异。同时认为，在戴或不戴头盔的机器内重复得分没有显著差异。之后 Awan 和 Virani［3］报告说 Nasometers 6200 和 6400 之间的非鼻音刺激存在 7% 的显著差异。而相比之下，De Boer 和 Bressmann［9］发现使用 Nasometers 6200 和 6450 获得的鼻化度得分只有 1%—2% 的微小差异。

还有跨设备的比较，Lewis 和 Watterson［21］比较了 Nasometer 6200 和 NasalView 的鼻化度评分，得出的结论是，由于信号处理的不同，它们在质量和数量上都有所不同。Bressmann［7］比较了 Nasometer 6200、NasalView 和 OroNasal System 获得的鼻化度值。作者认为三种系统以不同的方式测量鼻化度，得到的结果不可直接比较（not interchangeable）。Nasometer 和 NasalView 的重复测量变异性可能高于以前的报道。Awan 等［1］也使用 Nasometer 6200、Nasometer II 6400 和 NasalView 获得 Nasalance 评分测量了含有包含各种元音的句子。结果是用 NasalView 测得的鼻化度值显著高于用 Nasometer 6200 测得的值。而 6200 测得的值显著高于 Nasometer II 6400。虽然使用不同系统计算的鼻化度数据不容易比较，但三个系统的评估结果都表现出相同的趋势。这个趋势提示我们，要避免对不同设备/型号的原始测量数值进行直接比较，但是，对于相对粗略的趋势判断是有价值的。

一些非硬件因素也可能存在影响，根据 Bressmann［8］的整理，说话的音量［34］、辅音气压［33］、语速［16］和基频［24］都可能对鼻化度分数有一定影响。关于鼻化度分数是否因说话人性别而异，文献中有不同的报道。此外，鼻化度分数在多大程度上可以直接对应于生理上的腭咽闭合/开口程度，仍然需要依靠成像技术作进一步研究。

上述文献尽管提出了这些问题，但是有些因素并未得到重复实验的证实。对于那些硬件设备之外的因素，或许为社会语音学研究更提供了思路。尽管有观点认为 Nasometer 软件只显示鼻化度轨迹，不能提供相应的语音波形图，因此不适合对语音段进行更精细的研究。［8］不过，Kummer［20］描述了如何在鼻化度轨迹中观察到一些语音细节的见解。感兴趣的读者可以自行了解。此外，笔者认为，使用额外的麦克风进行录音也是一种方案，只要能够实现信号同步，那么额外的声学录音有助于我们精确地确定音段边界②。还可以使用 Praat 等软件打开 Nasometer 的双通道 .wav 文件，再跟 KayPENTAX 的主程序中的图形对应也有助于定位音段起止。

总之，为了尽可能确保研究结果的可靠性，比较不同设备实验结果时，研究者应当谨慎讨论，尽可能回避基于具体数值的论断。

5. 余论

近年来，国内高校和研究所纷纷建立语音实验室，但仍有许多刚涉足相关研究

① https://linglab.cn/tools.

② 这一信号仍不宜用来作频域分析，因为我们无法排除鼻音计装置的声学干扰。

的学者对仪器实验的技术原理和参数指标不甚了解，本文对 nasometer 等有关鼻音研究设备以及 nasalance 等相关概念进行了梳理，并且探讨了相关术语汉译名等其他问题，希望能帮助后续研究者理解相关的实验设计和实验结果。尽管从实际应用到理论讨论的过程中仍显示出这类设备可能存在的不足，但一个无法回避的事实就是：不存在完美的实验设备，任何研究手段都会有其本身的限制。本文引出的几个问题是想留给后续研究者有更深入的思考和讨论。

总之，我们希望有更多人将这些设备应用到语言学领域的工作中，在实践中探索如何去改进技术以得到更加符合真实情况的数据。当然，本文也提醒研究者们，在比较使用不同型号的实验设备的研究时，一定要考虑所用设备默认技术处理的潜在影响，哪怕这些设备报告的最终参数都被称为如“nasalance”这样的术语，仍不宜直接进行比较甚至过分推导结论！因为它们使用的麦克风或滤波器都可能存在差异，甚至信号都是不同性质的。我们还需要更广泛的研究来明确这些设备测量结果之间的一致性和可比性。

参考文献

[1] Awan, S. N., Omlor, K., Watts, C. R. 2011. Effects of computer system and vowel loading on measures of nasalance. *Journal of Speech, Language, and Hearing Research* 54 (5), 1284 – 1294.

[2] Awan, S. N. 1997. Analysis of nasalance: Nasalview. In: Ziegler, W., Deger, K. (eds), *Clinical Phonetics and Linguistics*. London: Whurr Publishers, 518 – 525.

[3] Awan, S. N., Virani, A. 2013. Nasometer 6200 versus Nasometer II 6400: Effect on measures of nasalance. *Cleft Palat Craniofacial Journal* 50 (3), 268 – 274.

[4] Baken, R. 1987. *Clinical Measurement of Speech and Voice*. Boston: College Hill Press.

[5] Benson, D. 1972. Roentgenographic cephalometric study of palatopharyngeal closure of normal adults during vowel phonation. *The Cleft Palate Journal* 9 (1), 43 – 50.

[6] Blanton, A., Watterson, T., Lewis, K. 2015. The differential influence of vowels and palatal covering on nasalance scores. *Cleft Palate Craniofacial Journal* 52 (1), 82 – 87.

[7] Bressmann, T. 2005. Comparison of nasalance scores obtained with the Nasometer, the NasalView, and the OroNasal System. *Cleft Palate Craniofacial Journal* 42 (4), 423 – 433.

[8] Bressmann T. 2021. Nasometry. In Ball, M. J. (ed) *Manual of Clinical Phonetics*. Routledge, 322 – 338.

[9] De Boer, G., Bressmann, T. 2014. Comparison of nasalance scores obtained with the nasometers 6200 and 6450. *Cleft Palate Craniofacial Journal* 51 (1), 90 – 97.

[10] Derrick, D., Duerr, J., Kerr, R. G. 2019. Mask less oral and nasal audio recording and air flow estimation for speech analysis. *Electronics Letters* 55 (1), 12 – 14.

[11] Fletcher S. G. 1969. Theory and instrumentation for quantitative measurement for nasality. *The Cleft Palate Journal* 7 (2): 601 – 609.

[12] Fletcher, S. G. 1972. Contingencies for bioelectronic modification of nasality. *Journal of Speech and Hearing Disorders* 37 (3), 329 – 346.

[13] Fletcher, S. G. 1979. Response to article on TONAR calibration (Weinberg, Noll and Donohue). *Cleft Palate Journal* 16 (2), 162 – 163.

[14] Fletcher, S. G., Bishop, M. E. 1970. Measurement of nasality with TONAR. *Cleft Palate Journal* 7, 610 – 621.

[15] Fletcher, S. G., Sooudi, I., Frost, S. D. 1974. Quantitative and graphic analysis of prosthetic treatment for "nasalance" in speech. *Journal of Prosthetic Dentistry* 32 (3), 284 – 291.

[16] Gauster, A., Yunusova, Y., Zajac, D. 2010. The effect of speaking rate on velopharyngeal function in healthy speakers. *Clinical Linguistics and Phonetics* 24 (7), 576 – 588.

[17] Gildersleeve-Neumann, C. E., Dalston, R. M. 2001. Nasalance scores in noncleft individuals: Why not zero? *Cleft Palate-Craniofacial Journal* 38 (2), 106 – 111.

[18] Horii Y. 1980. An accelerometric approach to nasality measurement: A preliminary report. *The Cleft Palate Journal* 17 (3), 254 – 261.

[19] Karling J., Lohmander A., de Serpa-Leitão A., et al. 1985. NORAM: Calibration and op-

erational advice for measuring nasality in cleft palate patients. *Scandinavian Journal of Plastic and Reconstructive Surgery* 19 (3), 261–267.

[20] Kummer A. W. 2013. *Cleft Palate and Craniofacial Anomalies: The Effects on Speech and Resonance*. Cengage Learning.

[21] Lewis, K. E., Watterson, T. 2003. Comparison of nasalance scores obtained from the Nasometer and the NasalView. *Cleft Palate-Craniofacial Journal* 40 (1), 40–45.

[22] Litzaw, L. L., Dalston, R. M. 1992. The effect of gender upon nasalance scores among normal adult speakers. *Journal of Communication Disorders* 25 (1), 55–64.

[23] Maddieson, I. 1984. *Patterns of Sounds*. Combridgc: Cambridge University Press.

[24] Mandulak K. C., Zajac D. J., 2009. Effects of altered fundamental frequency on nasalance during vowel production by adult speakers at targeted sound pressure levels. *Cleft Palate Craniofac Journal* 46, 39–46

[25] Moll K. L. 1962. Velopharyngeal closure on vowels. *Journal of Speech and Hearing Research* 5 (1), 30–37.

[26] Rothenberg M. 1977. *Measurement of airflow in speech. Journal of Speech and Hearing Research* 20 (1), 155.

[27] Rothenberg, M. 2014. *Rethinking nasalance and nasal emission*. http://www.rothenberg.org/Rethinking–Nasalance–Nasal–Emission/Rethinking_Nasal_Emission_and_Nasalance.pdf

[28] Seaver, E. J., Dalston, R. M., Leeper, H. A., Adams, L. E. 1991. A study of nasometric values for normal nasal resonance. *Journal of Speech and Hearing Research* 34 (4), 715–721.

[29] Seltzer, A. P. 1957. The Seltzer nasometer for measuring nasal patency. *Transactions: American Academy of Ophthalmology and Otolaryngology* 61 (3), 413–415.

[30] Švec, J. G., Granqvist, S. 2018. Tutorial and guidelines on measurement of sound pressure level in voice and speech. *Journal of Speech, Language, and Hearing Research* 61 (3), 441–461.

[31] Watterson, T., Lewis, K. E. 2006. Test-retest nasalance score variability in hypernasal speakers. *Cleft Palate-Craniofacial Journal* 43 (4), 415–419.

[32] Watterson, T., Lewis, K., Brancamp, T. 2005. Comparison of nasalance scores obtained with the Nasometer 6200 and the Nasometer II 6400. *Cleft Palate-Craniofacial Journal* 42 (5), 574–579.

[33] Watterson, T., Lewis, K. E., Deutsch, C. 1998. Nasalance and nasality in low pressure and high pressure speech. *Cleft Palate-Craniofacial Journal* 35 (4), 293–298.

[34] Watterson, T., York, S. L., McFarlane, S. C. 1994. Effects of vocal loudness on nasalance measures. *Journal of Communication Disorders* 27 (3), 257–262.

[35] Weatherley–White, R. C., Dersch, W. C., Anderson, R. M. 1964. Objective measurement of nasality in cleft palate patients: A preliminary report. *Cleft Palate Journal* 16, 120–124.

[36] Weinberg, B., Noll, J. D., Donohue, M. 1979. TONAR calibration: A brief note. *Cleft Palate Journal* 16 (2), 158–161.

[37] Williams R. L. 1952. A serial radiographic study of velopharyngeal closure and tongue position in certain vowel sounds. *Northwestern University Bulletin* 52: 9–12.

[38] Woo, S. T., Park, Y. B., Oh, D. H., Ha, J.-W. 2019. Influence of the nasometric instrument structure on nasalance score. *Applied Sciences* 9 (15), Article Number 3040.

[39] Zajac, D. J., Lutz, R., Mayo, R. 1996. Microphone sensitivity as a source of variation in nasalance scores. *Journal of Speech, Language, and Hearing Research* 39 (6), 1228–1231.

[40] 丹静静、陶树东、黄永望:《功能性鼻内镜鼻窦手术对慢性鼻窦炎男性患者鼻音的影响》,《听力学及言语疾病杂志》2021年第3期,第3页。

[41] 高涛、马莲、罗奕等:《声门塞音对鼻音计评价腭咽闭合状态的影响》,《中华口腔医学杂志》2020年第12期,第958—962页。

[42] 郭蕾、李永宏、于洪志:《普通话单音节鼻化元音的实验分析》,载《第九届中国语音学学术会议论文集》,2010年。

[43] 刘晖、刘善学:《应用鼻咽镜对健康人腭咽闭合功能的观察研究》,《中华口腔医学杂志》1989年第3期,第134—137页。

[44] 刘新中:《粤语台山台城话音系中的鼻音与后塞鼻音》,《中国语文》2019年第5期,第80—91、129—130页。

[45] 马莲:《评价腭咽闭合的方法》,《国际口

腔医学杂志》1985年第3期，第90页。
[46] 苗佳丽：《鼾症儿童普通话鼻音度研究》，硕士学位论文，上海师范大学，2020年。
[47] 时秀娟：《鼻音研究》，中国社会科学出版社2017年版。
[48] 时秀娟、向柠：《武汉话语音的鼻化度考察》，载《中国语音学学术会议暨庆贺吴宗济先生百岁华诞语音科学前沿问题国际研讨会》，2008年。
[49] [英] 特拉斯克（Trask，R. L.）：《语音学和音系学词典》，语音学和音系学词典编译组译，语文出版社2000年版。
[50] 杨宝琦、张玉庚、黄永旺等：《鼻咽缩窄术治疗儿童开放性鼻音》，《中华耳鼻咽喉头颈外科杂志》1995年第5期，第273—275页。
[51] 周杨：《计算机技术与汉语方言研究》，《现代语文》（语言研究版）2007年第2期，第17页。

陈禹风 硕士，毕业于天津师范大学文学院，主要研究领域为实验语音学，现为北京华睿宝科技有限公司语音实验仪器技术人员。
E-mail：yufeng_chen0575@foxmail.com

《元音研究》述评

叶俊廷　陈　滢

摘　要　元音是语音研究的重要对象，但在相当长的一段时间里，国内学界对于元音的认识有所偏差。中国社会科学院语言研究所胡方研究员撰写的《元音研究》一书结合国内外最新成果及其本人的研究，在以实验证据为导向的新描写主义视野下，厘清了传统上对元音的错误认识，并基于对复合元音在音系中地位的探讨，提出了“元音的动态理论”，对元音的概念、特征及其发音、声学和感知进行了较为系统和全面的阐述。
关键词　元音，元音的动态理论，新描写主义，述评

Review of *The Vowel: A General Introduction with Reference to Chinese Data*

YE Junting　CHEN Ying

Abstract The vowel is an important object of phonetic research. However, for a long period of time, the domestic academic circle has some deviations in the understanding of vowels. *The Vowel: A General Introduction with Reference on Chinese Data* written by HU Fang, a senior research fellow from the Institute of Linguistics of the Chinese Academy of Social Sciences, combines latest results, both home and abroad, in the study of vowels and his own research. In the framework of experimental descriptivism, it clarifies misunderstandings of vowels, and puts forward the "Dynamic Theory of Vowels" based on discussion of the status of compound vowels in phonology. The book offers a systematic and comprehensive account of the concept and features of vowels as well as their articulation, acoustics and perception.
Key words Vowels, Dynamic theory of vowels, Neo-descriptivism, Review

1. 引言

长久以来，在国内外语音学研究中，元音、辅音和声调一直都是核心话题。2018年，由外语教学与研究出版社出版的“外语学科核心话题前沿研究文库”问世，对于语音学这一学科，“文库”亦将其关注点放在上述三者之上。其中，由中国社会科学院语言研究所胡方研究员撰写的《元音研究》一书，吸收了国内外的最新研究成果，并结合了作者的大量研究，结合多种语言和多地汉语方言的数据，不仅澄清了关于元音的许多重要观念，介绍了元音研究的主要方法，而且以具有前瞻性的视角探讨了复合元音在元音中的地位，提出了“元音动态理论”及相关研究方法，是国内语音学界的又一力作。下文首先对全书各章进行简要介绍，其后对本书新颖之处进行评价。

2. 内容简介

《元音研究》一书分为六章，首先，从传统、科学两个视角出发，介绍元音及与之相关的一系列基础概念；其后，本书阐述了元音的感知和发音、元音的类型和特征等元音的声学特点和结构特点，以及作者本人提出的动态元音理论；最后，作者基于新描写主义视角，展望未来的元音研究及语音研究，并提出相关建议。

第一章为元音概论。由于学界在过去一个世纪中对元音的认识产生了根本性改变，因此，作者在阐述元音相关概念时，

分别采用了基于舌位概念的“传统视角”和目前学界更认同的、基于声学的“科学视角”。在“传统视角”一节中，本书首先在音段内厘清元音和辅音两个基本概念，提出元音和辅音的区分有声腔收窄程度、响度高低差异和音系考量三种依据，然后简要地介绍了国际音标元音图和正则元音（cardinal vowels）两个概念以及练习正则元音发音的方法。在“科学视角”一节中，基于声学物理学对语音的新认识和证据导向的（evidence - based）研究旨趣，文中锁定了三大问题：以“声源—滤波理论”为主要依据介绍元音如何产出；以共振峰模式、归一机制和元音的范畴感知为主要概念介绍元音在感知上的特点；从类型学视角出发，以Stevens［1，2］的“量子理论”（quantal theory）解释元音中的语音经济原则和最大对立，进而探讨如何分析语言中的元音。

第二章将关注点放在元音的声学与感知上。为了给后文的元音研究提供理论铺垫，首两节言简意赅地阐述了语音学研究中语音产出和语音感知的一系列声学现象、概念和参数。其后，介绍了共振峰结构分析这一获取元音声学参数的方法，并利用作者本人的一系列研究数据，分析不同元音在声波图和语图上的特点，并进而展示了利用共振峰数据绘制元音椭圆图的方法。由于个体之间发音存在差异，本章还讨论了元音的变异性问题，以及剔除变异因素的两种归一操作。另外，本章通过介绍元音内在音高和时长的理论模式，讨论了元音与韵律交互时的声学分析方法。

第三章从发音的角度探讨元音。首先提出了“语音的发音目标”这一核心问题，通过介绍发音音系学、语音感知的运动神经理论、DIVA模型等学界中不同的观点和理论，对这一问题展开讨论。后两节介绍了元音发音研究中的常用设备和研究方法，并重点介绍了20世纪末以来在学界受到欢迎的电磁发音仪（EMA）以及其设备选择、使用方法和数据处理流程的关键点。由于前文提及了元音图与感知声学间的关联，本章最后一节重点讨论了元音高低、前后等舌位概念与发音生理间的关系，主要采用了Harshman［3］发展的平行因子分析法（PARAFAC）处理数据，以舌位数据构造舌发音点因子，并绘制因子荷载的元音发音图。基于此，书中认为，“运动神经控制通过发音器官来实现感知声学”可以解释元音发音与声学感知间的关系。

第四章是全书最具新意之处，主要论述了作者提出的“实验证据导向的动态元音理论”。在探究元音结构时，前人文献多将元音分为单元音和复合元音。但事实上，学界对复合元音的定义存在分歧，在复合元音的性质及其与单元音的界定原则之上亦多有讨论。在对双元音的各种分类和称谓中，本章采用了前人提出的“降峰”和“升峰”等元音声学术语，利用共振峰客观地将复合元音分为降峰双元音和升峰双元音等。作者梳理前人研究后发现，降峰双元音和升峰双元音在语音和音系上呈现出不同表征，前者往往可以与相应的单元音产生交替，只有一个动态目标，应被视为单个发音事件；后者则是由两个发音目标构成的两个发音事件。由于研究复合元音对理解和分析汉语音系起关键作用，而发音目标的多寡和动态性的有无决定了复合元音的具体性质，在其后几节中，作者将分析的着眼点放在复合元音（尤其是双元音）的动态的共振峰结构上，抓住第二共振峰变化幅度与速度这一参数，从频谱特性、时间结构、动态特性和发音运动学四个角度对系属和类型各异的几种汉语方言的双元音的声学特征展开研究，论证了降峰双元音和升峰双元音在发音目标和动态特性上的差异，认为语言中的一些元音应当在动态性上存在对立，不同语言的双元音在共振峰模式、共振峰变化模式、首尾成分发音位置和发音器官运动策略等方面则各有异同。此外，元音内部的动态性对立使元音不宜再被简单地二分为单元音和复合元音，而应被视为一个连续统，其中便包括双元音化这一现象。本章专辟一节，利用安徽黟县、祁门、歙县和休宁等地的元音数据，讨论徽语中梯度渐变（gradient）的双元音化现象，展现了单元音在双元音化过程中从不具有音系对立，到具有完全音系对立，最终演变为普通双元音的连续统。基于动态元音理论的视角，本章最终认为，实验证据导向的语音与音系分析揭示了被传统元音分类所掩盖的语音事实，传统上定义的不同类型的元音应依照其是否包含相对动态或相对静态的频谱目标等内部结构差异，划归为单个发音事件或发音事件序列。

第五章探讨元音的特征。首先介绍了高低、前后、唇型这三项元音的基本特征，其中，根据瑞典语、吴语宁波方言等跨语言数据和前人研究，对唇形这一项特征做了较为详细的讨论，提出了两组四分的元音唇形区别特征。还从声学元音图出发，根据不同语言的元音在声学元音图中所处的相对位置，认为元音存在周边性这一基本特征。简单梳理了基本特征后，本章广泛讨论了元音的其他特征，如元音的长短与松紧、擦化元音与舌尖元音、元音咽化、会厌化、软腭化与小舌化、鼻化元音、r音化、发声态以及作为发音序列的复合元音等。讨论注重通过多样的研究数据获取分析证据，综合了粤语广州方言的长短元音对立等来自汉语方言的例子，以及非洲语言的ATR对立等来自外语的例子，必要时还加入了对实验仪器的讲解(如口鼻气流气压采集设备等)，对元音的总体特征做了较好的阐述。

第六章为全书作结。作者强调，实验语音学所秉持的是新描写主义的新范式，并围绕元音研究，回顾了元音的基本单位、语音单位的抽象性以及汉语和英语中的r音化这三个问题。另外，作者在讨论语言学发展历程中的多种方法的同时，多次强调当代语音描写应以实验证据为导向的研究范式，并就未来的元音和语音研究提出了方向性的建议。

3. 简评

作为国内元音研究领域的一部最新力作，《元音研究》一书的特色和优异之处可以概括为以下几点。

第一，本书基于实验描写主义新范式，厘清了传统上对元音的错误认识，突出科学视角下的元音声学与感知。一直以来，中国语言学界的描写主义传统土壤深厚，实验语音学的发展为语言学与语音学研究提供了新兴范式，研究者得以以语音证据为导向，利用与时俱进的研究工具和手段对语音现象进行描写，这便是“实验描写主义”，或称“新描写主义”，这为该书作者客观地、深入地探讨元音现象提供了新的方法论上的可能性。《元音研究》一方面梳理了传统视角下的元音理论，强调从舌位认识元音图的做法已然落后于最新研究成果；另一方面则从科学视角出发，利用各种实验仪器获取丰富的元音发音、声学和感知数据，并以此为证据，详尽地介绍了元音的声学和感知基础以及发音生理方面的实际特点，充分体现了新描写主义。值得一提的是，由于力求通俗性和前沿性相结合，本书在引用前人观点，多次强调传统视角下以舌位定义元音、描画元音图的不可靠的同时，仍在科学视角下论及元音图和正则元音概念与元音感知的关联，并富有创新性地教授学习者在练习元音发音时，利用录音画出声学元音图，借此让学习者调整其发音位置、矫正发音，以求利用科技手段，令学习者能够自主地习得较为准确的元音发音。

第二，书中以“元音的动态理论”领衔理论创新，利用多类型语音数据开展实验证据导向的元音研究，探究复合元音在语音体系中的地位。早先，在关于复合元音性质的讨论中，国内学者们通常认为复合元音是由两个及两个以上的音素直接组合而成。随着语音声学技术的发展，更多学者提出复合元音并不是单纯地通过两个音段的组合形成的。吴宗济［4］就曾通过声学的方式画出普通话复合元音的动态曲线，并提出复合元音可依据响度分真假性复合元音。此后，杨顺安［5］、曹剑芬［6］等研究也从声学、感知等各种角度探讨了复合元音的动态性质。作者重新审视了复合元音的性质问题，从实验的角度出发，引用作者本人的大量声学和发音材料，提出应该放弃传统上对于单、复元音机械的分类方法，而采用实验证据导向的动态元音理论。《元音研究》第四章从声学的频谱特性、时间结构、共振峰频率变化的幅度和速度、发音特点等角度重新考察了部分方言的复合元音，揭示了复合元音的多种特性。

第三，全书行文兼顾学术性与通俗性，多语种的数据用例凸显出元音理论的跨语言共性。首先，《元音研究》一书在语言表达上兼顾了学术性和通俗性，在使用学术用语之外，尽量避免使用过于艰深的表达，力求将问题从最基础处讲起，如正则元音的发音练习、元音的声学基础、电磁发音仪的使用方法等，旨在扩大该书的受众面，降低读者了解元音的知识门槛，使读者获得全面而清晰的认识。其次，虽然本书的英文副标题表明，与汉语相关的数据是书中的关键材料，但实际上作者并未将其视野囿于国内研究或西方研究，而是将汉语、英语、德语、瑞典语等丰富而崭新的多语用例和数据穿插于理论与介绍之中。即便是基于汉语数据、以厘清汉语复合元音性质为目的之一的“元音的动态理论”一章，作者也综合了吴语宁波方言、西南官话隆昌方言、晋语太原方言等多地汉语方言阐述其动态理论。多语言、多方言的例证不仅能够便于读者理解，还避免了孤证不立的情况，突出了书中理论的跨语言、跨方言共性。

与近年来国内外同类作品相比，《元音研究》内容全面、清晰、深刻、新颖，引用文献和资料全面、丰富。对于国内语音和相关领域研究者、爱好者而言，本书已然是一本不可多得的参考书。

参考文献

[1] Stevens, K. N. 1972. The quantal nature of speech: Evidence from articulatory - acoustic data. In: David Jr, E. E., Denes, P. B. (eds.), *Human Communication: A Unified View*. New York: McGraw - Hill, 51 - 66.

[2] Stevens, K. N. 1989. On the quantal nature of speech. *Journal of Phonetics*, 17, 3 - 45.

[3] Harshman, R. A. 1970. Foundations of the Parafac procedure: Model and conditions for an "explanatory" multi - modal factor analysis. *UCLA Working Papers in Phonetics*, 16, 1 - 84.

[4] 吴宗济、林茂灿：《实验语音学概要》，高等教育出版社1989年版。

[5] 杨顺安、曹剑芬：《普通话二合元音的动态特征》，《中国语文》1984年第1期，第15—22页。

[6] 曹剑芬：《普通话韵母/ao/与/ou/的时频协变对比分析》，《应用声学》1994年第2期，第21—27页。

叶俊廷 上海外国语大学语言研究院，硕士研究生，主要研究方向为实验语音学。
E-mail: jt. ye98@ qq. com

陈　滢 上海外国语大学语言研究院，硕士研究生，主要研究方向为实验语音学。
E-mail: ing_cy6@ 163. com